HANDBOOK FOR TEACHERS

2ND EDITION

Celebration SERIES

BY

Cathy Albergo   Reid Alexander   Marvin Blickenstaff

D1316825

COMPLIMENTARY

FREDERICK
HARRIS
MUSIC

The authors wish to acknowledge permission to reprint the following copyright material:

An excerpt from *Church Scene* by Violet Archer.
© Copyright 1946 Mercury Music Corp. Copyright assigned 1982 to
Berandol Music Limited. Used by permission.

An excerpt from *March* by David Duke.
© Copyright 1977 Waterloo Music Company Limited. Used by permission.

An excerpt from *Dorian Invention* by Pierre Gallant.
© Copyright 1987 Éditions Gallants Frères. Used by permission.

Canadian Cataloguing in Publication Data

Albergo, Cathy, 1951-
Celebration series : handbook for teachers

Includes index.
ISBN 0-88797-546-1

1. Piano - Instruction and study.
I. Alexander, Reid, 1949-
II. Blickenstaff, Marvin.
III. Title.

MT245.A5S 1996   786.2'07   C96-930074-3

Preface

Since its inception in 1988 and renewal in a second edition in 1994, the *Celebration Series* has established itself as an internationally acclaimed collection of piano teaching materials. The authors of the *Celebration Series Handbook for Teachers* were among a growing number of teachers who saw the need for an additional pedagogical resource to round out the *Series*. Their dedication and perseverance in bringing the *Handbook for Teachers* into being have been an inspiration to all of us involved with them in this project. In writing this book, the authors have affirmed a basic commitment to *why* it is that teachers teach – to impart to their students not only knowledge, but also a joy in learning that will last a lifetime.

With the completion of the *Handbook for Teachers*, the *Celebration Series* now includes materials that encompass both teachers' and students' perceptions. Together, the *Student Guides* and the *Handbook for Teachers* will yield new insights and pleasures as teachers and students explore the repertoire, studies, and recordings in this wide-ranging *Series*.

On behalf of The Frederick Harris Music Company, it is my pleasure and privilege to acknowledge here the tireless efforts of the authors as they refined the *Handbook for Teachers* over the course of many months. We wish to thank our editor, Ruth Pincoe, who contributed invaluable advice and attention to detail at every stage of the process and who was instrumental in shaping the final manuscript. Professor Rebecca Shockley of the University of Minnesota and Aasta Levene of The Royal Conservatory of Music provided timely comments at an early stage. Finally, as we welcome you, the readers, to explore the *Celebration Series Handbook for Teachers*, we invite you to share with us your impressions and suggestions and to become participants in our never-ending quest to improve and extend our publications.

Dr. Trish Sauerbrei
Publishing Manager

Table of Contents

Foreword

INTRODUCTION TO THE *CELEBRATION SERIES*

The *Celebration Series* is a comprehensive compilation of materials for piano teachers and students as well as pianists who play solely for their own enjoyment. The *Celebration Series*, however, is not a piano method in the traditional sense. Instead, this *Series* encompasses a carefully graded selection of piano literature with supporting teaching materials.

The *Celebration Series* comprises eleven *Piano Repertoire Albums*, five *Piano Studies Albums* (each album contains two levels of studies), eight *Student Guides*, eleven recordings, and the *Handbook for Teachers*. This material is organized into eleven Levels, as listed in the chart below. Collectively, these publications support the musical training of the eye, ear, mind, and body. To omit any segment diminishes the depth of the student's musical experience.

A major strength of the *Celebration Series* is its vast amount of repertoire. The 439 pieces contained in the *Repertoire* and *Studies Albums* present an extensive sampling of styles and composers covering a broad spectrum of piano music from four centuries. In addition, the *Series* includes

compositions by contemporary Canadian composers whose works are not regularly found in other collections.

Together, the editing, footnotes, and identification of sources provide students with helpful guidance as their awareness of musical styles matures.

- The editing in the *Celebration Series* is uncluttered and is limited to those compositions from the Baroque and Classical periods in which articulations and dynamics were not marked by the composer.
- Editorial fingerings help students achieve efficient movement. However, such fingerings are suggestions only. Teachers and students are encouraged to try alternate fingerings to suit individual cases. Similarly, metronome markings suggest an upper and lower setting within an appropriate tempo.
- Footnotes below the music include brief suggestions for articulation and examples for the realization of ornaments.
- Teachers and students alike will appreciate the scholarship evidenced through clear references to original sources for individual pieces.

Piano Repertoire Albums	Piano Studies Albums	Student Guides	Recordings
Introductory Level			Introductory Level
Level 1	Levels 1 & 2	Level 1	Level 1
Level 2		Level 2	Level 2
Level 3	Levels 3 & 4	Level 3	Level 3
Level 4		Level 4	Level 4
Level 5	Levels 5 & 6	Level 5	Level 5
Level 6		Level 6	Level 6
Level 7	Levels 7 & 8	Level 7	Level 7
Level 8		Level 8	Level 8
Level 9	Levels 9 & 10		Level 9
Level 10			Level 10

The Piano Repertoire Albums

There are eleven *Piano Repertoire Albums*:
- *Introductory Album:* appropriate for students who have completed one year of study
- *Repertoire Albums 1, 2,* and *3:* late elementary through early intermediate
- *Repertoire Albums 4, 5,* and *6:* intermediate through late intermediate
- *Repertoire Albums 7* and *8:* late intermediate to early advanced
- *Repertoire Albums 9* and *10:* advanced recital repertoire appropriate for highly skilled high school pianists or college piano majors

The pieces in *Repertoire Albums 1* to *10* are organized into Lists (A, B, C, D, E), according to style period or genre. Although these lists were developed for the purpose of Royal Conservatory of Music Examinations, they also provide a useful chronological and style reference. The contents of these lists are briefly explained in the introduction to each section of the *Handbook.*

The Piano Studies Albums

The five *Piano Studies Albums* contain works from the standard piano repertoire as well as etudes. Each Level includes works which can be used effectively as technique builders, recital or competition pieces, and pieces for enjoyment. Composers range from Bach and Handel to Burgmüller, Heller, Kabalevsky, Shostakovich, and Finney.

This graded series is designed to help students gradually master a variety of technical demands. Each piece has a technical focus. While the *Studies Albums* complement the *Repertoire Albums,* the studies do not necessarily correlate directly with specific repertoire pieces. However, in many instances, a study can be used as preparation for a similar composition in a *Repertoire Album.*

The Student Guides

The eight *Student Guides* in the *Celebration Series* are companion volumes to the *Piano Repertoire Albums* for Levels 1 through 8. As the name implies, the *Student Guides* are written for the student, using language and musical terminology appropriate for students at each Level. Each *Guide* contains an introduction, a detailed discussion of each piece in the *Repertoire Album,* and a glossary of terms.

The three- to five-page introduction covers general topics such as:

- how to practice
- dynamics
- articulation and tone
- accompaniment styles
- pedaling
- Baroque performance practices
- dances and other forms

The one-page discussions devoted to each piece in the *Piano Repertoire Albums* cover a remarkably wide range of topics. They provide the student with accessible information on the composer, explanations of style and form, and efficient practice procedures for the piece. Although the overall format is consistent, each discussion is unique. The topics include:
- biography and style
- form and analysis
- harmony and texture
- practice suggestions and exercises
- rhythmic preparation
- tone, touch, dynamics, and articulation
- ornamentation

The accumulated wealth of information in the *Student Guides* is striking. It would be a disservice to any student's musical education if the *Guides* were not incorporated into a plan of study with the *Repertoire* and *Studies Albums.*

The Celebration Series Recordings

It is reported that Bach performed newly assigned pieces for his students. He felt that hearing a work performed well was an effective bridge to learning. The *Celebration Series Recordings* of all the pieces in the *Repertoire* and the *Studies Albums* are a valuable resource for both teacher and student. The pianists on these recordings are members of The Royal Conservatory of Music faculty. These recordings enable students to hear professional performances of each work using tempos and interpretations which are realistic models for students.

The Handbook for Teachers

The *Handbook for Teachers* is a comprehensive teaching aid that draws together the *Repertoire* and *Studies Albums,* the *Student Guides,* and the *Recordings* and organizes this material for optimum use in the teaching studio. In addition to a detailed discussion of each piece in the *Repertoire* and *Studies Albums,* the *Handbook for Teachers* also includes suggestions for presenting and teaching the *Celebration Series* from start to finish, and a complete composer index for the *Series.*

ORGANIZATION OF THE *HANDBOOK FOR TEACHERS*

The Study Modules

The eleven sections of this *Handbook for Teachers* correspond to the eleven Levels of the *Celebration Series.*

In the sections covering the first nine Levels (Introductory through Level 8), the authors have divided each Level into a number of Study Modules. The Study Modules provide logical points of entry for teacher and student. The purpose of these Modules is to integrate the *Repertoire Albums* with the *Studies Albums* and to organize these compositions into units of study.

In general, the Study Modules represent a gradual increase in difficulty, both within each Module and from one Module to the next. Almost all the Modules include pieces from each List in the *Repertoire Album.*

The sections covering Levels 9 and 10 are not organized into Modules, but rather according to the order of the *Repertoire and Studies Albums.* A suggested order of difficulty is given for each List (A, B, C, D, E).

The Module Chart

Each Module is presented initially in a chart listing the pieces in the order in which they appear in the *Repertoire* and *Studies Albums.* The sample chart shown below is taken from Level 3.

The information in the two right-hand columns provides teachers with a detailed overview of the compositions contained in the Module. In the Page column, "R" indicates a page number from the *Piano Repertoire Album,* "S" a page number from the *Piano Studies Album,* and "SG" a page number from the *Student Guide.*

SAMPLE MODULE

Page	List	Composer	Title	Meter and Tempo	Musical and Stylistic Concepts
R5 SG10	A	German Folk Melody, Johann Philipp Kirnberger (arr.)	Lullaby	6/8 Andantino	✔ two independent voices ✔ broken-chord inversions ✔ four-measure phrases ✔ sequence
R14 SG18	B	Ludwig van Beethoven	Sonatina in G Major, Anh. 5 (Second Movement: Romanze)	6/8 Andante	✔ melody with broken-chord accompaniment ✔ scales ✔ *portato* touch
R22 SG23	B	Ignaz Pleyel	Rondo in G Major	2/4 Allegro	✔ two independent LH voices ✔ grace notes and slurs ✔ *staccato* articulation ✔ scale passages
R30 SG30	C	Linda Niamath	Turtle	3/2 Slowly and steadily	✔ slow half notes ✔ four-voice texture ✔ *legato* articulation ✔ 4ths, 5ths, 6ths ✔ ABA₁
R40 SG37	C	Otto Joachim	Plastic Soldier	4/4 Fast march	✔ changing rhythmic patterns ✔ LH octaves against melody ✔ twelve-tone technique
S8		Carl Czerny	Study No. 5: Op. 139, No. 7	3/4 Allegretto	✔ RH blocked 6ths and 3rds ✔ wrist *staccato* exercise
S11		Johann Nepomuk Hummel	Study No. 8	2/4 Andante con moto	✔ RH *staccato* articulation ✔ LH blocked intervals

Assign first:
Lullaby . . . .
Sonatina in G Major, Anh. 5
　(Second Movement: Romanze)
Plastic Soldier . . . .
Study No. 5: Op. 139, No. 7 . . . .

Assign next when ready:
Rondo in G Major

Turtle

Study No. 8

Order of Assignment

The two lists below the chart – "Assign first" and "Assign next when ready" – give a suggested order in which the pieces in the Module can be assigned.

The authors suggest assigning pieces in the first column (either as a group or individually) before pieces in the second column. Often, pieces listed opposite each other (for example, *Lullaby* and *Rondo in G Major*) have features in common (such as texture, articulation, or style period). In these cases, the piece in the "Assign first" column helps prepare the student for the piece in the "Assign next when ready" column. Thus, in the sample Module, *Rondo in G Major* can be assigned after the student has completed *Lullaby, Turtle* after *Plastic Soldier,* and *Study No. 8* after *Study No. 5.*

Pieces without a corresponding follow-up assignment (in this example, the *Sonatina in G Major: Romanze*) are usually lengthier, more difficult, and will take longer for the student to learn.

In developing these chronologies, the authors have made an effort to determine how the pieces might best be assigned to an average student. Points taken into consideration include:
- balance of style periods
- technical difficulties
- common features or stylistic traits between pieces
- sequence from easier to more difficult
- length of time required for a student to complete each piece

The organization of the Study Modules is not meant to be dogmatic. The authors encourage teachers to adjust the order of pieces within the Modules or create their own chronology for assigning the materials in a way which best meets the needs of the individual student. Teachers should also consider whether or not the student will play all pieces in the Study Module and how many pieces the student is accustomed to studying simultaneously.

Discussion of the Study Module

The discussion of each Study Module begins with a short introduction, often covering suggested approaches to the music in the Module. The discussions of individual compositions, presented in Module order, are divided into several categories:
- **Exploring the Score**
  Ideas for the introduction of pieces; observations and questions which may facilitate discussion between teacher and student.
- **Practice Suggestions**
  A variety of suggestions for practicing, usually addressed directly to the student in language a teacher might use in a lesson.
- **Creative Activities**
  Projects for the student's own compositions, based on concepts and elements discovered in the pieces (Levels Introductory through 8 only).
- **Background Information**
  Historical or stylistic points which may serve as a springboard for further discussion in the lesson or class (beginning in Level 5).
- **Teaching Suggestions**
  Specific suggestions directed to the teacher on developing the student's technique or mastering technical demands within a piece (Levels 9 and 10 only).

Much of the discussion of individual pieces, especially in the lower Levels, takes the form of questions a teacher might ask a student as they examine a piece of music together. Often, the answer is given in square brackets following the question.

The brief summary or conclusion at the end of each Level is intended to allow the student and teacher to reflect upon the experience gained through the study of the pieces in the Level and to review common musical characteristics found in those pieces.

In addition, some Levels involve specific learning activities – a Dance Chart is introduced in Level 2, and Musical Tips in Level 3. These activities encourage students to build their musical knowledge as they learn new pieces. Although these ideas only appear in one Level, teachers are encouraged to apply these concepts in higher Levels as appropriate.

Terminology used in the *Handbook*

Blocking is the action of grouping two or more notes into a chord whose tones are sounded simultaneously. Blocked intervals or chords are also known as solid intervals or chords.

Drop and lift describes a wrist motion which facilitates the grouping of two or more notes into one movement or gesture. In executing a two-note slur, for example, the wrist drops to play the first note and lifts to play the second note.

Double 3rds (*double 6ths,* etc.) refers to a succession of solid or blocked parallel intervals played in one hand.

Harmonic analysis is an extremely useful exercise for students. Chords can be labeled in a number of ways, according to the students' experience and knowledge of harmony. Here are some suggestions:
- harmony names (tonic, dominant)
- chord symbols (I, V, i, v)
- chord names (C major, G minor)
- chord abbreviations (C, G, c, g)

Accuracy often improves when students understand the harmonic progression of a passage. Have students name the harmonies aloud while they play.

Out of four, go for three: in a four-measure phrase, the focus of the phrase is often in the third measure. This simple rule of thumb is helpful for students who are learning to feel the shape of a musical phrase.

Throw and lift describes a continuous gesture which groups two or more notes and produces a *staccato* or accented sound. The throwing motion starts with the hand lifted off the key. As you play the first tone or chord, lift the wrist to play succeeding tones. Think of "shaking out" the successive notes, gradually lifting the wrist as you complete the passage. Keep the fingers close to the keys.

The *una corda* pedal (often called the soft pedal) is the left pedal on the piano. *Una corda* means one string. On older instruments, this pedal moved the hammers slightly to the right so that they struck only one string. On modern instruments, this pedal shifts the hammers so that they strike two strings instead of three. The term *tre corde* (or, less frequently, *tutte le corde*) indicates cancellation of the soft pedal.

One of the most important challenges of piano teaching is that the student, at whatever level of advancement, have access to materials which stimulate and educate. The *Celebration Series* provides a body of materials which furnishes the student with an outstanding selection of the highest quality teaching literature (the *Piano Repertoire* and *Piano Studies Albums*), guidance and instruction (the *Student Guides*), and inspiring sound models (the cassette and compact disc recordings).

We trust that this *Handbook for Teachers* will be helpful to you and your students as you explore the wealth of musical material in the *Celebration Series*. We anticipate that your journey through the *Celebration Series* will be exciting and musically rewarding.

Cathy Albergo, Professor of Music
Department of Music, William Rainey Harper College
Palatine, Illinois

Reid Alexander, Professor of Music
School of Music, University of Illinois at Urbana-Champaign
Urbana, Illinois

Marvin Blickenstaff, Professor of Music
Department of Music, Goshen College
Goshen, Indiana

Introductory Level

The Repertoire

What piano pieces will appeal to elementary students? The answers to that question will vary. Students enroll in piano lessons for diverse reasons and bring with them varying backgrounds and interests, and different physical and intellectual skills.

Most children are drawn to pieces which evoke images of scenes, activities, and events from their daily lives or from their fantasy world. What child could resist exploring *Balloons*, *Bear Dance*, *March of the Robots*, or *Little Monster*?

The *Introductory Album* also contains folk songs. Familiar words and melodies such as *Old MacDonald Had a Farm* and *Un canadien errant (Once a Canadian Lad)* have an immediate appeal. Use these folk songs to introduce younger students to rhythm and singing through the use of words and melody.

The *Introductory Album* is the only repertoire album in the *Celebration Series* that is not divided into lists by style period. The 18th and 19th centuries are represented with pieces by Cornelius Gurlitt, Daniel Gottlob Türk, Franz Joseph Haydn, and Giovanni B. Martini. In addition to traditional sounds and colors, students have the opportunity to play impressive sounding contemporary pieces which introduce expressive dissonance and unusual notation. The *Introductory Album* contains pieces written by both Canadian and American educational composers including Boris Berlin, Stephen Chatman, Linda Niamath, Walter and Carol Noona, Lynn Freeman Olson, and Nancy Telfer.

Encourage your students to listen to the Introductory Level recording of all the repertoire in the *Introductory Album*.

Development of Skills

The teacher is the best judge of when a student is ready to start the *Introductory Album*. For most students, a year of instruction is sufficient preparation for the reading and rhythmic challenges presented in the easier pieces in the *Introductory Album*. Some pieces use only quarter-note and half-note values. Other pieces include eighth notes and dotted rhythms. There are no sixteenth notes.

Major and minor five-finger patterns occur frequently throughout the *Introductory Album*. Although key signatures are limited to one sharp and one flat (most pieces are in C major, F major, or G major), a wide variety of sounds including major, minor, modal, whole tone, and pentatonic are created by the use of accidentals.

The *Introductory Album* provides literature through which students can develop:

- a *legato* touch
- the ability to balance an accompaniment with melody
- command over a variety of dynamics, tempos, and articulations
- technical fluency with position shifts and finger crossings
- command of dotted rhythms
- ensemble playing (duets)

The Range of Difficulty

The range of difficulty found in the *Introductory Album* is illustrated by these two pieces:

- *The Peacock's Fan* by Walter and Carol Noona is an example of an easier composition in Study Module 1.
- *Israeli Dance* by Terry Winter Owens is an example of a more difficult composition in Study Module 5.

The Study Modules

The five Study Module discussions in the Introductory Level are organized into the following categories:

- *Exploring the Score*
- *Practice Suggestions*
- *Creative Activities*

Exploring the Score is designed as an interactive voyage of discovery between teacher and student. *Practice Suggestions* deal with more specific areas for technical study. These suggestions are worded as if you were addressing your student directly. The *Creative Activities* act as reinforcement for your students' understanding of a musical concept and can provide a springboard for their creativity and imagination.

Please refer to the Foreword for an explanation of how to use the suggested order of assignment within each Module.

The chart on the opposite page lists the pieces in the *Introductory Album* with their assigned Study Module numbers.

Page	Composer	Title	Study Module
Introductory Album			
R4	John Milligan	Rowing Round	1
R5	Walter and Carol Noona	The Peacock's Fan	1
R6	David Duke	Bear Dance (Phrygian Mode)	3
R7	Dmitri Kabalevsky	Song, Op. 39, No. 8	2
R7	Dmitri Kabalevsky	March-Like, Op. 39, No. 3	2
R8	Mélanie Bonis	Prière (Prayer)	2
R9	Cornelius Gurlitt	Little Waltz, Op. 117	1
R10	Margaret Parsons (arr.)	Hush-A-Bye	2
R11	John Milligan	Tippi-Toes	3
R12	Daniel Gottlob Türk	Sonatina	4
R13	Gordon A. McKinnon	Leapfrog	3
R14	Nancy Telfer (arr.)	Un canadien errant (Once a Canadian Lad)	3
R15	Lynn Freeman Olson	Lady Moon	4
R16	Boris Berlin (arr.)	Old MacDonald Had a Farm	4
R17	Linda Niamath	Balloons	1
R18	Billie Ferrell	Little Monster	3
R20	Franz Joseph Haydn, Boris Berlin (arr.)	Surprise Symphony	5
R21	Daniel Gottlob Türk	A Carefree Fellow	2
R21	Giovanni B. Martini, Edward Janus (arr.)	Plaisir d'amour (Joy of Love)	4
R22	Stephen Chatman	Monkey Business	2
R23	Terry Winter Owens	Israeli Dance	5
R24	Pierre Gallant (arr.)	Sakura	5
R25	Brian Crone	March of the Robots	5
R26	Alexander Gedike	A Song, Op. 36, No. 3	2
R27	Jean Coulthard	The Jackhammer (for Christopher and Geoffrey)	4
R28	Cornelius Gurlitt	Waltz (duet)	3
R30	Edward Janus (arr.)	Polish Folk Song (duet)	1
R32	Stephen Chatman	Freak-Out	5

STUDY MODULE 1

Page	Composer	Title	Meter and Tempo	Musical and Stylistic Concepts
R4	John Milligan	Rowing Round	4/4 Brightly	✔ uses tune *Row, Row, Row Your Boat* ✔ G sharp in RH ✔ passing under of thumb
R5	Walter and Carol Noona	The Peacock's Fan	4/4 With a haughty air	✔ *legato* melody passes between hands ✔ black key *glissando*
R9	Cornelius Gurlitt	Little Waltz, Op. 117	3/4 Allegretto	✔ consistent rhythmic pattern ✔ simple texture: RH plays blocked intervals, LH plays single-note accompaniment ✔ one accidental (F sharp)
R17	Linda Niamath	Balloons	3/4 Smoothly	✔ LH plays four-note *ostinato* ✔ RH outlines triad inversions
R30	Edward Janus (arr.)	Polish Folk Song	4/4 Allegretto	✔ *staccato* articulation in Primo part ✔ C major five-finger pattern and triad outline; RH position shift in B section ✔ *forte-piano* dynamic contrast

Assign first:
The Peacock's Fan . . . .
Balloons . . . .
Polish Folk Song

Assign next when ready:
Rowing Round
Little Waltz, Op. 117

The easier pieces in Study Module 1 can be used as transition material from an elementary method into the *Celebration Series*. The pieces in Study Module 1 all have a quarter-note pulse. There are no eighth notes. The hand orientation is frequently a five-finger pattern. Finger crossings and shifts of hand position are limited.

Ask students to find the single black keys in *The Peacock's Fan* and *Rowing Round*. Use this opportunity to review the names of all sharps and flats (including the white keys: E sharp, F flat, B sharp, C flat).

At this level, rhythmic activities are helpful and important. Invent rhythmic activities or drills that can be shared between teacher and student. Here are some suggestions:
- Encourage students to count aloud while playing.
- Make a series of flash cards with rhythms from the pieces. Put the rhythm of a piece together, card by card.
- Move the lesson off the piano bench. Clap the RH rhythm and walk or stamp the LH rhythm.
- Use echo clapping for problem measures or phrases – the teacher claps the rhythm and the student repeats it.
- Tap the rhythm on the piano keyboard cover while counting aloud.
- Tap the rhythm on a tambourine or drum.

J. Milligan: *Rowing Round* (R4)
Exploring the Score
Each line of this piece is different. Find the lines that fit the following descriptions:
– hands move in contrary motion [line 4]
– LH imitates RH melody of previous line [line 2]
– RH solo [line 1]
– downbeats form stepwise motion [line 3]
– music gets softer *(diminuendo)* [line 3]
– music gets louder *(crescendo)* [lines 2, 4]

Practice Suggestions
- Circle finger number **1** in mm. 13-16 and practice hands separately until the fingering is secure.
- To find a comfortable speed, have students sing *Row, Row, Row Your Boat*, swinging their arms once per measure.

W. and C. Noona: *The Peacock's Fan* (R5)
Exploring the Score
This piano composition includes words. Have students say the words as they tap the rhythm.
- What dynamic level will you choose for a piece marked "With a haughty air"?
- The *glissando* is a special effect. What is the peacock doing?

C. Gurlitt: *Little Waltz, Op. 117* (R9)
Exploring the Score
Compare this waltz with Gurlitt's duet *Waltz* (pp. 28-29). How are they similar? Play other examples of waltzes for your student.

Use this waltz to review intervals.
- Look for melodic 2nds, 3rds, and 4ths in the LH.
- Look for blocked 3rds, 4ths, and 6ths in the RH.

Practice Suggestions
Think of the LH as the leader and the RH as the follower. Play the RH notes more softly than the LH notes.
- Practice the RH interval changes across the bar lines. Say the intervals as you play; for example, from mm. 1-2, say "3rd to 4th."

L. Niamath: *Balloons* (R17)
Exploring the Score
- In what way is the RH the same throughout? [repetition of rhythm and broken chord figure]
- In what way is the LH the same throughout? [repetition of C-B-A-G figure]
- An *ostinato* is a repeating musical figure. Which hand plays an *ostinato* in *Balloons*?
- How many notes are in the *ostinato*? What are they?

- This piece is a musical picture of balloons. What happens to the balloons before they float away in mm. 14-17?

Practice Suggestions
Use the following steps to help students learn the notes and fingering of the RH broken chords:
1. Block the triads. Say the finger number for the middle note of each chord as you play.
2. Play the broken chords. Lift the wrist gently at the end of each chord to emphasize the phrasing. Listen for the breath between phrases.
3. Label each chord major or minor. Include the note name of the root (for example, C major, D minor) if you wish.
4. Look for a chord that is neither major nor minor. [diminished triad on B, RH, m. 12]

E. Janus (arr.): *Polish Folk Song* (Primo, R31)
Exploring the Score
There are three lines of music:
- Which two lines are exactly the same?
- Label each line with A or B. [AABA: first line is repeated]
- Make a chart showing the form and the dynamics of each section. Can you see (and hear) an echo?

A mm. 1-4 *forte*
A mm. 1-4 *piano*
B mm. 5-8 *forte, piano*
A mm. 9-12 *forte, decrescendo*

CREATIVE ACTIVITIES
♪ The *glissando* in m. 9 of *The Peacock's Fan* is sustained by the damper pedal. Allow students to experiment with the damper pedal by improvising on the black keys while you play this accompaniment:

♪ Ask the student to make up a piece about another bird, using quiet, floating sounds on the black keys, sustained by the damper pedal.

♪ Create a variation on *Balloons* by composing a new LH *ostinato* pattern, or by playing Linda Niamath's *ostinato* in a different register of the keyboard.

STUDY MODULE 2

Page	Composer	Title	Meter and Tempo	Musical and Stylistic Concepts
R7	Dmitri Kabalevsky	Song, Op. 39, No. 8	4/4 Andante	✔ unison texture ✔ key signature and accidental ✔ Dorian mode in B section ✔ flowing eighth notes
R7	Dmitri Kabalevsky	March-Like, Op. 39, No. 3	4/4 Moderato	✔ RH melody mostly *staccato* ✔ LH plays blocked 3rds on downbeats
R8	Mélanie Bonis	Prière (Prayer)	3/4 Calmly	✔ both hands play minor and diminished triads ✔ RH imitates LH melody ✔ several accidentals ✔ position shifts ✔ extensions beyond five-finger position ✔ ends with four-note chords
R10	Folk song, Margaret Parsons (arr.)	Hush-A-Bye	3/4 Gently rocking	✔ dotted rhythm exchanged between the hands ✔ G major five-finger pattern throughout
R21	Daniel Gottlob Türk	A Carefree Fellow	4/4 Allegro moderato	✔ RH in G five-finger position ✔ melody in quarters and eighths ✔ simple LH accompaniment
R22	Stephen Chatman	Monkey Business	4/4 With fun	✔ accented notes and percussive unpitched sounds (indicated by X on staff) ✔ accidentals throughout ✔ RH motive grows by chromatic steps
R26	Alexander Gedike	A Song, Op. 36, No. 3	4/4 Allegro moderato	✔ hands together in unison ✔ repetition of tune with LH open 5th accompaniment

Assign first:
March-Like, Op. 39, No. 3 . . . .
A Song, Op. 36, No. 3 . . . .
Song, Op. 39, No. 8 . . . .
Monkey Business

Assign next when ready:
A Carefree Fellow
Hush-A-Bye
Prière (Prayer)

Study Module 2 includes a variety of styles and moods: a march, a prayer, two songs, a lullaby, and a contemporary-sounding composition *(Monkey Business)*.

This Module introduces eighth notes and key signatures. These pieces also present a new challenge – lifting the hands at the proper time. Explore these pieces, looking for different ways composers indicate a release of sound.
• Which markings indicate a sharp, quick release?
• Which markings indicate a gentle release, like taking a breath between phrases?

Buildings have architectural plans. Similarly, each piece of music has a form or shape, made up of sections. Encourage students to determine the form of each piece they study, labeling the sections and naming the form.

D. Kabalevsky: *Song, Op. 39, No. 8* (R7)
Exploring the Score
Both hands play the melody. There is no accompaniment. Compare mm. 1-4 with 5-8.
- Which measures are identical? [mm. 1 and 5]
- Which measures are almost identical? [mm. 2 and 6]
- Which measures outline a D minor five-finger pattern? [mm. 1 and 5]
- Which measure outlines a C major five-finger pattern? [m. 3]

D. Kabalevsky: *March-Like, Op. 39, No. 3* (R7)
Exploring the Score
Compare these two sections:
    A   mm. 1-4
    A₁   mm. 5-8
Which measures are different? [4 and 8]

The title *March-Like* is a clue to the character of this piece.
- What instrument does the RH imitate? [perhaps trumpet]
- What sound qualities suggest a trumpet? [dynamics, degree of *staccato*]
- Imagine that the LH is a drum. Play with a strong beat.

M. Bonis: *Prière (Prayer)* (R8)
Practice Suggestions
To create an atmosphere of prayer, play with a beautiful *legato* sound and follow the dynamics carefully. Exaggerate the hand lifts at rests and at the ends of phrases. Students with smaller hands can use this fingering for the LH, mm. 3-4:

M. Parsons (arr.): *Hush-A-Bye* (R10)
Practice Suggestions
Rhythms can be reinforced by verbalization. Counting aloud is effective, but making up words to match the rhythms often helps students play more accurately. Reinforce the dotted-quarter rhythm by chanting "hush-a-bye" or "mer-ri-ly."

hush - a - bye
mer   - ri - ly

To feel the larger pulse, make a rocking motion or draw large circles in the air (one motion per measure).

D.G. Türk: *A Carefree Fellow* (R21)
Exploring the Score
Rhythm is often related to dynamics.
- Clap this rhythm, with a *crescendo*:

- Play the slurred groups in the music, making a *crescendo* through the eighth notes to the quarter note. Notice the extra slurred group in m. 7. Why did Türk add this extra rhythmic energy at the end of the piece? [to intensify movement at the end of the piece]

S. Chatman: *Monkey Business* (R22)
Exploring the Score
This music is capricious and unpredictable. Are there any repeating patterns?
1. When the RH motive ends on a downbeat, the LH knocks twice.
2. When the RH motive ends on the second beat, the LH knocks once.

Practice Suggestions
Devise rhythmic activities before having the student play the piece: tap and count on the closed keyboard cover; play a teacher-student tambourine "duet"; tap with the RH and knock on wood with the LH, etc.

A. Gedike: *A Song, Op. 36, No. 3* (R26)
Practice Suggestions
Introduce the G major and E minor five-finger patterns before you assign this piece. Devise technical drills using these positions.

Encourage students to listen for a *legato* sound with gentle lifts between phrases. Draw attention to the finger change in both hands at the beginning of mm. 6 and 8. Playing these measures with the middle fingers helps produce a *legato* sound. Ask students what fingering they will use for the RH in m. 14.

CREATIVE ACTIVITIES
Monkey Business provides an opportunity to explore new sounds. Improvise short LH chromatic figures accompanied by RH percussive sounds.

Make up a piece using sounds created in some way other than playing on the piano keys. (You might borrow rhythms from *Monkey Business*.)

The G major and E minor five-finger positions found in Gedike's *A Song* use some of the same notes yet the two positions sound quite different. Create a new piece using these two positions. Make a strong contrast between the G major and the E minor sections. Use dynamics to exaggerate the moods.

STUDY MODULE 3

Page	Composer	Title	Meter and Tempo	Musical and Stylistic Concepts
R6	David Duke	Bear Dance	2/4 Slow	✔ unison texture ✔ white-key Phrygian mode ✔ low growl ✔ wide reading range ✔ *fortissimo* to *piano* dynamics
R11	John Milligan	Tippi-Toes	4/4 Mysteriously	✔ melody outlines diminished 7th ✔ use of accidentals ✔ *staccato* suggests tiptoe ✔ RH triads ✔ *crescendo, diminuendo,* and *ritenuto*
R13	Gordon A. McKinnon	Leapfrog	4/4 Scherzando	✔ both hands in G major five-finger pattern ✔ position shift at end ✔ *staccato* quarter notes ✔ imitative texture
R14	Canadian folk song, Nancy Telfer (arr.)	Un canadien errant (Once a Canadian Lad)	3/4 Gently	✔ tune shared between hands ✔ RH in bass clef in B section
R18	Billie Ferrell	Little Monster	4/4 Medium speed	✔ one rhythmic pattern ✔ accidentals create C minor, F minor, G minor ✔ LH *staccato* opens 5ths
R28	Cornelius Gurlitt	Waltz	3/4 Moderato	Primo part: ✔ in unison at the octave ✔ grace note and accidental ✔ requires phrase shaping and subtle dynamic contrast

Assign first:	Assign next when ready:
Little Monster	*Un canadien errant (Once a Canadian Lad)*
Waltz	*Bear Dance*
Leapfrog	*Tippi-Toes*

In Study Module 3, the student experiences various ways in which composers manipulate melodies. In *Un canadien errant* and *Tippi-Toes*, the melody is divided between the hands. In *Leapfrog*, the melody appears in both hands, in imitation. *Un canadien errant* combines two textures – melody divided between the hands and melody with accompaniment. The Primo part of Gurlitt's duet *Waltz* has the melody played by both hands in unison. *Little Monster* has a traditional RH melody with LH accompaniment.

In most piano music, the RH is written in the treble clef and the LH is written in the bass clef. Have your student find places in the pieces from this Study Module where both hands are written in the same clef.

D. Duke: *Bear Dance* (R6)
Exploring the Score
Have students discuss the sounds they would use in music about dancing bears:
- fast or slow rhythms
- *forte* or *piano* dynamics
- low or high pitches
- short or long phrases
- one position or several shifting positions
- quiet or loud ending

Look for these elements in *Bear Dance.*

This piece has two-measure phrases and one-measure slurred groups.
- How many two-measure phrases are there? [6]
- Do they all have the same rhythm? [no] Tap the rhythms, counting aloud.
- Find the one-measure slurred groups. Do they have the same dynamic level?
- Why does this piece end quietly?

Practice Suggestions
Have students practice shifting to each new position by playing the first note of each phrase (with the correct finger).

- Find the LH tied notes in mm. 7-11.
- Teacher plays the RH part; student plays the LH part.
- Listen for the growls here (the minor 2nd) and the mini-growl in mm. 13-14.

J. Milligan: *Tippi-Toes* (R11)
Exploring the Score
Have students clap the rhythm as they walk on tiptoe, changing direction with the music.
- How many beats do you tiptoe in one direction?
- In mm. 9-10 you march on tiptoe. Step the LH and clap the RH.

Use this piece as a basis for discussing major and minor 3rds and chord construction.

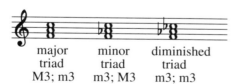

major triad	minor triad	diminished triad
M3; m3	m3; M3	m3; m3

Relate this discussion to pieces from Study Module 2. *Balloons* (R17) and *Prayer* (R8) both use major, minor, and diminished chords.

G.A. McKinnon: *Leapfrog* (R13)
Practice Suggestions
Discuss the relationship of the title to the imitation between the hands. Use words (for example, "leap-

frog **lands** rest") to reinforce the articulation of the opening *staccato-tenuto* motive. Practice the entire piece slowly, listening for this rhythm.

Both hands use a G major five-finger pattern in mm. 1-5. Isolate mm. 6-8 for spot practice.

N. Telfer (arr.): *Un canadien errant (Once a Canadian Lad)* (R14)
Exploring the Score
This Canadian folk song tells of a man who is sad because he is exiled from his homeland. Here is the tune:

Help your student trace the melody in Telfer's arrangement.

Practice Suggestions
Locate and circle the RH position shifts. Practice these shifts by playing the last note of the previous position and the first note only of the new position (for example, RH m. 13, LH m. 14). Listen for a *legato* sound as the melody passes from hand to hand.

B. Ferrell: *Little Monster* (R18)
Exploring the Score
- Tap the rhythm of mm. 1-8.
- Find other measures which have a short-short-long rhythm.
- This music has a minor sound. Find and name the minor chords Ferrell uses.

Practice Suggestions
As preparation for *Little Monster* (and also for *Israeli Dance* in Study Module 5), play an open 5th exercise hands separately, then hands together. For example:

C. Gurlitt: *Waltz* (Primo, R29)
Practice Suggestions

Primo part:
Practice the LH alone, then add the RH an octave higher.
- What five-finger pattern is used? [C major]
- Where do the hands extend outside this pattern? [B in m. 7] Circle the fingerings in m. 5 which create this position shift.
- Swing your arms as you chant the rhythm. Swing once per measure.

CREATIVE ACTIVITIES

♪ *Tippi-Toes* uses major and minor 3rds to make major, minor, and diminished 7th chords. Compose a short piece using major and minor 3rds.

♪ Create a new piece using the short-short-long rhythm from *Little Monster*. Title your piece *The Little Elf* and adjust the dynamics to suit this title.

♪ Make up your own *Bear Dance*, using low sounds on the keyboard, single notes, 5ths, and a *forte* dynamic level.

STUDY MODULE 4

Page	Composer	Title	Meter and Tempo	Musical and Stylistic Concepts
R12	Daniel Gottlob Türk	Sonatina (I, II, III)	2/8 Allegretto 3/4 Largo molto 2/4 Allegro	✔ three-movement miniature sonatina ✔ middle movement in E minor ✔ two-voice texture ✔ challenging crossings and shifts
R15	Lynn Freeman Olson	Lady Moon	4/4 Gently	✔ F sharp major tonality ✔ position shifts cover wide range ✔ long pedals create impressionistic effect
R16	Traditional, B. Berlin (arr.)	Old MacDonald Had a Farm	4/4 Brightly	✔ tune shared between hands ✔ *legato* and *staccato* articulation
R16	Giovanni Martini, E. Janus (arr.)	Plaisir d'amour (Joy of Love)	6/8 Gently	✔ lyrical melody ✔ eighth-note broken-chord accompaniment ✔ early Classical style
R27	Jean Coulthard	The Jackhammer (for Christopher and Geoffrey)	2/4 Hammer it out quickly	✔ articulation study for both hands ✔ repeated *staccato* eighth notes with vigorous accents ✔ accidentals throughout ✔ contemporary sound

Assign first:
Lady Moon . . . . *Plaisir d'amour (Joy of Love)*
Sonatina (I, II, III)
Old MacDonald Had a Farm . . . . *The Jackhammer (for Christopher and Geoffrey)*

Assign next when ready:

Study Module 4 presents challenges associated with two- and three-voice textures including melody and accompaniment (sometimes with the melody in the LH), parallel motion between the hands, and melodies passing between the hands.

Students should practice two-voice pieces hands separately to establish comfort and security. During lessons, create student-teacher duets, each playing one hand of a piece. This way, students can experience the complete sound of the piece.

D.G. Türk: *Sonatina* (R12)
Exploring the Score
This miniature sonatina exhibits formal elements of traditional sonatina structure. Balance between unity and contrast is central to sonatina form.

When studying all three movements, point out the following elements which contribute to a contrast of musical mood and expression:
- contrasting meters [2/8, 3/4, 2/4]
- contrasting keys [G major, E minor, G major]
- contrasting tempos [*Allegretto, Largo molto, Allegro*]
- contrasting form (notice the repeat marks)

Practice Suggestions
Movement I
- Find the places where the hands move in parallel motion, e.g., mm. 2-4, 9-12. Circle any finger crossings and practice those measures slowly.
- Give special practice to the notes moving in contrary motion, e.g., mm. 5-8. Practice hands separately, then hands together. Use the correct fingering.

Movement II
- Give the two-note slurs the sound of a sigh (play the second note quieter). Play the LH accompanying notes especially quietly and delicately.
- Make a musical breath (lift off the key) between each slurred group.

Movement III
- Play mm. 1-2 and 5-6 with joyful energy. Answer those measures with a *legato* touch and a *diminuendo*. Make this movement sound like a conversation between two people.

L.F. Olson: *Lady Moon* (R15)
Practice Suggestions
The wide keyboard range presents challenges for accurate reading and position shifts.
- Play and name the first note of each LH position change.
- Block and name the RH intervals.
- Play hands together in blocked position.
- While one hand is playing, move the other to its new position.
- Practice this piece on the closed keyboard cover, matching the hand crossings and shifts to the actual keyboard location.

The score includes pedal markings. Use this opportunity to explain the technique of catching the sound on a fresh pedal.

Traditional, B. Berlin (arr.): *Old MacDonald Had a Farm* (R16)
Practice Suggestions
- Trace the tune as it moves between the hands.
- Listen for the *legato* and *staccato* touches.
- Practice the RH 2nds in mm. 3, 4, 7, and 16 alone.
- How are these 2nds alike and different?
- Which 2nds repeat in a different octave?

G. Martini, E. Janus (arr.): *Plaisir d'amour (Joy of Love)* (R21)
Exploring the Score
Be a musical detective! Look for three-note groups:
- F-G-A (mm. 1-2)
- B flat-A-G (mm. 3-4)
- D-E-F (mm. 5-6)
- A-G-F (mm. 7-8)
These three-note groups are the musical skeleton of this piece.

Practice Suggestions
Think of this piece as a duet for RH and LH.
- Play the RH melody alone.
- Play the LH beat notes (bass line: F-E-F-G-F-C etc.).
- Play the complete LH part first in blocked chords, then as written.
- Name the LH harmonies. [F or I; C^7 or V^7]

J. Coulthard: *The Jackhammer (for Christopher and Geoffrey)* (R27)
Exploring the Score
- How do the accents contribute to the sound image of a jackhammer?
- Are all downbeats accented?
- Why does the last measure not have an accent?

CREATIVE ACTIVITIES

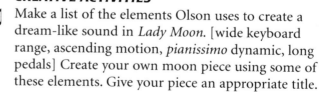

Make a list of the elements Olson uses to create a dream-like sound in *Lady Moon*. [wide keyboard range, ascending motion, *pianissimo* dynamic, long pedals] Create your own moon piece using some of these elements. Give your piece an appropriate title.

Now create a different piece with these same notes. Change the mood by using a *staccato* touch and no pedal. You might title this piece *Martians Walk on the Moon*.

STUDY MODULE 5

Page	Composer	Title	Meter and Tempo	Musical and Stylistic Concepts
R20	Franz Joseph Haydn, Boris Berlin (arr.)	Surprise Symphony	4/4 Moderately	✔ two-voice texture ✔ contrast of *staccato* and *legato*
R23	Terry Winter Owens	Israeli Dance	4/4 With energy	✔ altered scale creates modal, Middle Eastern sound ✔ RH eighth-note melody over LH *staccato* open 5ths ✔ octave shifts between sections ✔ full chord at end ✔ wide dynamic range
R24	Traditional Japanese, Pierre Gallant (arr.)	Sakura	4/4 Moderato	✔ RH white-key pentatonic melody ✔ LH two-voice accompaniment requires finger independence ✔ position shifts
R25	Brian Crone	March of the Robots	4/4 Tempo di marcia	✔ *forte* clusters on black keys ✔ pentatonic and whole-tone melodies
R32	Stephen Chatman	Freak-Out	3/4 Moderate	✔ contemporary notation for forearm clusters and random pitches ✔ use of entire keyboard ✔ extreme dynamic contrasts ✔ quick *crescendo* from *piano* to *fortissimo*

Assign first: **Assign next when ready:**
Israeli Dance . . . . *Surprise Symphony*
Sakura
March of the Robots . . . . *Freak-Out*

Study Module 5 could be subtitled "The International and Futuristic Module." The titles carry us around the globe and into the world of robots and wild experimentation. From a reading and technical perspective, this module contains the most challenging music in the *Introductory Album*.

F. J. Haydn, B. Berlin (arr.): *Surprise Symphony* (R20)
Exploring the Score
- This music was originally written for orchestra. Which instruments might Haydn have used?
- What gives mm. 9-12 a contrasting sound? [*legato* touch]
- Where is the big surprise? [m. 8] Play the notes before the *forte* quietly and give the surprise chord a full, rich sound.

Practice Suggestions
Ask the student to find the measures where the hands play together. Practice mm. 9-12 hands separately. Isolate mm. 7-8 and 15-16 for spot practice.

Practice the *staccato* measures with a *legato* touch to develop control and security.

T.W. Owens: *Israeli Dance* (R23)
Exploring the Score
The tonic is E, but this music is not in E major or E minor. Look through the music to pick out the notes of the altered scale. Point out the interval F-G sharp which gives the music a modal, Middle Eastern sound. Practice the five-finger position of m. 13 in both hands.

The accents in mm. 5-7 and 9-11 produce a syncopated rhythm.
- What movement would the dancers make on those accents?
- Chart the dynamic plan. Where is the loudest moment?

P. Gallant (arr.): *Sakura* (R24)
Practice Suggestions

1. Play the melody with both hands, an octave apart. Use a *legato* touch and lift at the end of each slur.
2. Practice the two-voice LH accompaniment, mm. 1-4. Lift both voices at the end of each measure.
3. Look for the places where both hands lift together.
4. Find the places where one hand lifts alone.
5. Practice hands together on the closed keyboard cover, exaggerating the hand lifts.
6. Play different combinations of two voices, one in each hand (RH soprano and LH bass, RH soprano and LH tenor, RH tenor and LH bass). Be careful not to tie the repeating whole notes on A in the LH.

B. Crone: *March of the Robots* (R25)
Exploring the Score
The key of this piece is neither major nor minor. It uses pentatonic and whole-tone melodies.

- What keys does Crone use in mm. 1-4? [all black keys]
- Are there other black-key passages? [mm. 9-12, 17-20]

Play the melody in mm. 5-8 and 13-16, then play each group of notes as a solid cluster. Each note is a whole step away from its neighbor. Discuss the whole-tone scale and perhaps play another piece based on a whole-tone scale for your student.

S. Chatman: *Freak-Out* (R32)
Practice Suggestions

- Which elements of the notation must be played exactly as written? [rhythm, dynamics, articulation]
- Which elements of the notation are not precise? [the pitches]

Have students practice first on the closed keyboard cover. Pick a slow tempo, keep the rhythm precise, and think about the dynamics and articulation.

CREATIVE ACTIVITIES

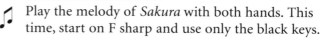 Play the melody of *Sakura* with both hands. This time, start on F sharp and use only the black keys.

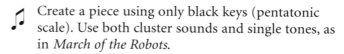 Create a piece using only black keys (pentatonic scale). Use both cluster sounds and single tones, as in *March of the Robots*.

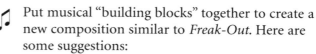 Put musical "building blocks" together to create a new composition similar to *Freak-Out*. Here are some suggestions:
  - single pitches picked at random
  - cluster sounds
  - *glissandi*
  - predetermined lengths of silence (rests)

Identify each building block with a number. Try changing the order of the blocks.

INTRODUCTORY LEVEL SUMMARY
- Which pieces in this album were your favorites? What did you like about them? Make a list of these pieces and continue playing them as you begin work in the next album.
- Which pieces contained the loudest and softest sounds? What physical motion did you use to obtain these dynamic levels?
- Which pieces indicate use of the damper pedal? Compare the use of the damper pedal in *The Peacock's Fan, Lady Moon, Plaisir d'amour,* and *Freak-Out*.

Level 1

The Publications
Level 1 of the *Celebration Series* includes the following publications:
Piano Repertoire Album 1
Piano Studies Album 1 & 2 (level 1 only)
Student Guide 1
Recording of *Repertoire & Studies 1*

The Repertoire
Piano Repertoire Album 1 is divided into three sections or lists.
- List A includes a selection of pieces composed during the Baroque period (*ca* 1600 to *ca* 1750) and the Classical period (*ca* 1750 to *ca* 1820).
- List B includes a selection of pieces composed during the Romantic era (*ca* 1820 to *ca* 1910) and the 20th century.
- List C consists of short pieces called Inventions. They are written for two voices in an imitative style.

Musical Development
The repertoire and studies in Level 1 present musical and technical challenges for late elementary students as they develop control over:
- balance between melody and accompaniment
- shaping a musical phrase
- articulation of two- and three-note phrases
- hand and finger independence
- two- and three-part forms
- chords in root position and inversions
- a variety of *legato* and *staccato* articulations

The seven Inventions are intended to develop hand independence and an awareness of imitative style. They provide valuable preparation for Baroque and Classical dances and contrapuntal textures. The *Student Guide* (p. 36) explains the musical characteristics of the Inventions, and gives several practice suggestions.

The Range of Difficulty
The range of difficulty within Level 1 is illustrated by the following two compositions:
- *Polly-Wolly-Doodle* arranged by Canadian composer Udo Kasemets is an example of an easier composition in Study Module 1.
- *Air in D Minor* by Henry Purcell is an example of a more difficult composition in Study Module 6.

The Study Modules
The six Study Module discussions in Level 1 are organized into the following categories:
- *Exploring the Score*
- *Practice Suggestions*
- *Creative Activities*

Exploring the Score is designed as an interactive exercise between teacher and student. Questions are addressed to the student, as you might ask them during the lesson. *Practice Suggestions* are also directed to the student. The *Creative Activities* act as reinforcement for your students' understanding of a musical concept and can provide a springboard for their creativity and imagination.

Please refer to the Foreword for an explanation of how to use the suggested order of assignment within each Module.

The chart below lists the repertoire and studies from Level 1. Page numbers for works in the *Piano Repertoire Album 1* and the *Piano Studies Album 1* are found in the first column. Study Module numbers for each composition are found in the fourth column.

Page	Composer	Title	Study Module
Piano Repertoire Album 1			
List A R4	Leopold Mozart	Minuet in F Major	5
R5	Johann Christoph Friedrich Bach	Schwäbisch	3
R6	Carl Philipp Emanuel Bach	Minuet in C Major	4
R7	Johann Heinrich Buttstedt	Air in F Major	3
R8	Johann Sebastian Bach	Minuet in G Major	6
R9	Henry Purcell	Air in D Minor	6
R10	Jean-François Dandrieu	The Fifes	2
R11	Ludwig van Beethoven (arr.)	German Dance	4

Page	Composer	Title	Study Module
R12	Franz Joseph Haydn, Clifford Poole (arr.)	Allegretto in G Major	5
R13	George Frideric Handel	Minuet in F Major	5
R14	Johann Wilhelm Hässler	Suite in C Major (First Movement)	2
R15	Johann Wilhelm Hässler	Suite in C Major (Second Movement)	1
R16	Johann Wilhelm Hässler	Suite in C Major (Third Movement)	4
R17	Leopold Mozart	Minuet in D Minor	2

List B

Page	Composer	Title	Study Module
R18	Cornelius Gurlitt	The Hunt	2
R19	Frederick Silvester (arr.)	Early One Morning	4
R20	Mélanie Bonis	The Sewing Machine	1
R22	Alexander Gedike	Rigaudon	2
R23	Pierre Gallant (arr.)	This Old Man	5
R24	Soulima Stravinsky	The New Dress	4
R25	Dmitri Kabalevsky	Battle Song, Op. 89, No. 30	6
R26	Udo Kasemets (arr.)	Polly-Wolly-Doodle	1
R28	Alexander Gedike	A Happy Tale, Op. 36, No. 31	3
R29	Linda Niamath	Bears	6
R30	Ernest Marsden	The Itchy Ant	6
R31	Boris Berlin (arr.)	Three Fine Ducks	5
R32	Dmitri Shostakovich	Soldier's March	5
R34	Nancy Telfer (arr.)	Monté sur un éléphant (Climb Up on an Elephant)	3
R35	David Duke	March (Lydian Mode)	1

List C

Page	Composer	Title	Study Module
R36	David Duke (arr.)	Invention No. 1: She's Like the Swallow	3
R37	Konrad Max Kunz	Invention No. 2: Canon on the Black Keys, Op. 14, No. 184	5
R38	Pierre Gallant (arr.)	Invention No. 3: Sur le pont d'Avignon	4
R38	Erasmus Sartorius	Invention No. 4: Canon	4
R39	Gordon A. McKinnon	Invention No. 5: Swirling Leaves	2
R40	Pierre Gallant	Invention No. 6: Dorian Invention	1
R40	Annibale Zoilo	Invention No. 7: Bicinium	3

Piano Studies Album 1

Page	Composer	Title	Study Module
S4	Carl Czerny	Study No. 1	1
S4	Dmitri Kabalevsky	Study No. 2: A Porcupine Dance, Op. 89, No. 8	1
S5	Carl Czerny	Study No. 3: Op. 777, No. 3	3
S6	Linda Niamath	Study No. 4: Sleepy Little Kitten	4
S6	Cornelius Gurlitt	Study No. 5	6
S7	Clifford Poole	Study No. 6	3
S8	Theodor Oesten	Study No. 7: Hunting Horns	5
S9	Ukrainian Folk Song	Study No. 8	2
S10	Linda Niamath	Study No. 9: On the Trampoline	2
S11	Dmitri Kabalevsky	Study No. 10: Playing, Op. 39, No. 5	6
S12	Clifford Poole	Study No. 11: Chords on Parade	6
S13	Boris Berlin	Study No. 12: Snowflakes	3
S14	Lajos Papp	Study No. 13: Martellato and Forte-piano	1
S15	Linda Niamath	Study No. 14: Robots	4
S16	Leon Aubry	Study No. 15: Woodland Scene	5

STUDY MODULE 1

Page	List	Composer	Title	Meter and Tempo	Musical and Stylistic Concepts
R15 SG18	A	Johann Wilhelm Hässler	Suite in C Major (Second Movement)	3/4 Andante	✔ parallel 10ths between hands ✔ sequences ✔ short *legato* phrases
R20 SG23	B	Mélanie Bonis	The Sewing Machine	Alla breve Allegro vivo	✔ LH quarter-note *ostinato* ✔ hand crossing ✔ RH dotted rhythms ✔ *staccato* and *legato* articulation
R26 SG28	B	Udo Kasemets (arr.)	Polly-Wolly-Doodle	4/4 Allegro	✔ melody repeated with variations in accompaniment ✔ detached and *legato* articulation
R35 SG35	B	David Duke	March (Lydian Mode)	4/8 Fast	✔ LH single-note *ostinato* ✔ RH broken and blocked chords
R40 SG39	C	Pierre Gallant	Invention No. 6: Dorian Invention	2/2	✔ D minor five-finger position ✔ overlapping phrases between hands ✔ *legato* articulation ✔ Dorian mode
S4		Carl Czerny	Study No. 1	4/4 Allegro	✔ dynamic contrast ✔ *staccato* articulation ✔ double 3rds
S4		Dmitri Kabalevsky	Study No. 2: A Porcupine Dance, Op. 89, No. 8	2/4 Allegretto staccatissimo	✔ *staccato* broken triads in contrary motion
S14		Lajos Papp	Study No. 13: Martellato and Forte-piano	2/4 Allegretto and Allegro	✔ overtones created through silently depressing keys ✔ RH plays melody and abrupt open 5ths

Assign first:
Suite in C Major (Second Movement) . . . .
Polly-Wolly-Doodle . . . .
Study No. 2: A Porcupine Dance, Op. 89, No. 8 . .
March (Lydian Mode) . . . .

Assign next when ready:
Study No. 13: Martellato and Forte-piano
Invention 6: Dorian Invention
Study No. 1
The Sewing Machine

Study Module 1 includes some of the easiest music in Album 1. These pieces involve single-line melodies, quarter- and eighth-note rhythms, and a few blocked chords. However, the variety of textures includes unison writing, parallel motion, contrary motion and mirror image, imitative phrases, and *ostinato* accompaniments. Discuss these elements as you explore this Study Module with your students. Comparison of the pieces in this Study Module can provide students with insights about the relationship between melody and accompaniment.

J.W. Hässler: *Suite in C Major (Second Movement)* (R15, SG18)
Exploring the Score
Circle the half notes in mm. 2, 4, 10, and 12. These longer notes are the musical goals of the phrase. Build toward the half note and play the third beat of these measures quietly.

Through most of this piece, the hands move in parallel motion.
- Find places where the hands are not in parallel motion.
- Are these places at the beginning or end of sections? Why? [change of motion signals the approaching cadence]

M. Bonis: *The Sewing Machine* (R20, SG23)
Exploring the Score
How does the LH *ostinato* pattern imitate a mechanical sewing machine? Discuss the importance of a steady beat to keep the sewing machine running evenly.

Practice Suggestions
To practice dotted rhythms, count and clap the following:

The *Student Guide* outlines the form.
• Mark the A and B sections in the music.
• Tap the rhythm of each section, counting aloud.
• In mm. 11-16 and 20-30, hold the RH high and the LH low to provide space for both hands.

U. Kasemets (arr.): *Polly-Wolly-Doodle*
(R26, SG28)
Exploring the Score
• Which hand repeats the tune? How many times?
• How does the LH change with each repetition of the tune?
• The third variation uses contrary motion and mirror fingering. Say the finger numbers as you play.
• Make a chart showing the dynamic plan of the piece.

D. Duke: *March (Lydian Mode)* (R35, SG35)
Practice Suggestions
Set a slow beat and tap the rhythm. Which measures have exactly the same rhythm?

Label the chords. Practice mm. 3-4, 7-8, etc. in blocked chords:

Can you find a broken major chord in the LH? [m. 10]

P. Gallant: *Invention No. 6: Dorian Invention*
(R40, SG39)
Practice Suggestions
These practice steps will help students hear the canon:

1. Practice hands separately at a slow tempo. Lift slightly at the end of each phrase.
2. Play the Invention as a duet (teacher-student or two students).
3. Play each RH two-measure phrase followed by the LH answer.

4. Play each two-measure unit as written.
5. Practice the entire piece hands together.

C. Czerny: *Study No. 1* (S4)
Practice Suggestions
• Notice the RH fingerings in mm. 9-11 and 15.
• Make up an exercise for double 3rds.
• Chart the dynamic plan of this study. Can you find a repeated dynamic pattern?
• Find the measures with tonic and dominant harmonies.

D. Kabalevsky: *Study No. 2: A Porcupine Dance, Op. 89, No. 8* (S4)
Practice Suggestions
This is a study in contrary motion with mirror fingering. There are three different hand positions (see mm. 1-3). To help students learn the notes and fingering, have them block the hand positions in each measure.
• How does Kabalevsky create interest? [variety of phrase length, dynamic contrast in mm. 9-12]

L. Papp: *Study No. 13: Martellato* and *Forte-piano* (S14)
Exploring the Score
Listen for the overtones created when the keys are silently depressed. Discuss the role of silence and the contrasting phrase lengths and dynamics.

CREATIVE ACTIVITIES
Use the following methods to create variations of Duke's *March:*
• Change the LH rhythm.
• Change the RH melody.
• Play steps instead of broken chords.
• Make a new dynamic plan.
• Play the piece in a different register.

Create new variations for Kasemets's *Polly-Wolly-Doodle* by changing the LH accompaniment style.

STUDY MODULE 2

Page	List	Composer	Title	Meter and Tempo	Musical and Stylistic Concepts
R10 SG13	A	Jean-François Dandrieu	The Fifes	2/4 Vivace	✔ quick tempo with eighth and sixteenth notes ✔ shifts to different five-finger positions ✔ *staccato* and *legato* articulation
R14 SG17	A	Johann Wilhelm Hässler	Suite in C Major (First Movement)	3/4 Andantino	✔ both hands *legato* ✔ 2 + 2 + 4 phrase structure ✔ double 3rds at cadence
R17 SG20	A	Leopold Mozart (attr.)	Minuet in D Minor	3/4 Moderato	✔ single-note texture in each hand ✔ melody and accompaniment ✔ ABA form
R18 SG21	B	Cornelius Gurlitt	The Hunt	3/4 Allegro	✔ quick tempo, one beat per measure ✔ two-note slurs (gallop rhythm) ✔ harmonies limited to I and V
R22 SG24	B	Alexander Gedike	Rigaudon	4/4 Allegro ma non troppo	✔ LH drone bass ✔ RH plays *legato* while LH lifts for repeated notes
R39 SG39	C	Gordon A. McKinnon	Invention No. 5: Swirling Leaves	3/4 Andante espressivo	✔ rhythm of quarter and half notes ✔ long *legato* lines ✔ imitative texture ✔ scale crossings and contractions
S9		Ukrainian Folk Song	Study No. 8	3/8 Moderato	✔ phrase study ✔ LH broken triads and RH step motion ✔ melody passes between hands
S10		Linda Niamath	Study No. 9: On the Trampoline	3/4 With a strong bounce	✔ accented chords create a bouncing effect

Assign first:
The Fifes . . . .
Minuet in D Minor . . . .
Invention No. 5: Swirling Leaves . . . .
Study No. 8 . . . .

Assign next when ready:
Suite in C Major (First Movement)
The Hunt
Rigaudon
Study No. 9: On the Trampoline

Study Module 2 includes pieces in two- and three-part forms (AB and ABA).

The three pieces in minor keys provide an opportunity to discuss the sound and color of the minor mode.
- Find the pieces which are in a minor key. [*Minuet, Swirling Leaves, Study No. 8*]
- Name the keys of these pieces. [D minor, D minor, A minor]

Several pieces in this Study Module use only tonic, subdominant, and dominant chords. Help your student find and label the chords in *The Hunt* [I and V] and *The Fifes* [I, IV, and V].

Composers create variety by using chords in different positions. Play I, IV, and V chords in root position, first inversion, and second inversion so that the student can hear the difference. Help your student find and label the chord inversions in *The Hunt* and *Suite in C Major (First Movement)*.

J.-F. Dandrieu: *The Fifes* (R10, SG13)
Exploring the Score
See the *Student Guide* discussion on form.
- Label the A and B sections in the music.
- Does the RH change in the B section?
- Does the LH change in the B section? [added notes create a more intense rhythm]
- How is the LH the same in both sections? [LH notes of mm. 1-8 can be found in mm. 9-16]

Practice Suggestions
This piece uses several five-finger positions.
- Identify the name and location of each pattern.
- Changes in fingering help you shift position. Circle the "fingering clues" in mm. 1-8. [RH **2** in m. 3, RH **2** in m. 5, RH **3** in m. 7, etc.]
- Tap the rhythm, counting aloud.
- Find words to fit the RH rhythm:

We're march-ing to the cap-i-tol of France

J.W. Hässler: *Suite in C Major (First Movement)* (R14, SG17)
Exploring the Score
Notice the short-short-long phrase structure in mm. 1-8 (2 + 2 + 4 measures).
- Is this structure repeated in the B section?
- Look for this same short-short-long phrase structure in other pieces.

Practice Suggestions
The *Student Guide* gives a practice procedure for playing blocked chords. Label these chords.

L. Mozart (attr.): *Minuet in D Minor* (R17, SG20)
Exploring the Score
How does Mozart provide contrast in the B section? [starts in major key, LH is more active]

The repeated LH notes in mm. 5, 7, and 9 add surprise and humor. The terraced dynamics reinforce the dialogue between the hands.
- How does Mozart surprise us in m. 10?
- What did you expect to hear in the RH?

Practice Suggestions
Review the D harmonic minor scale.
- What are the tonic, subdominant, and dominant chords in this key? [D minor, G minor, A major]
- Find examples of these harmonies in the music.

A. Gedike: *Rigaudon* (R22, SG24)
Practice Suggestions
Gedike uses a rhythmic motive to move the music forward. Use words to reinforce this movement.

to the 1   to the 3   to the 1   2   3

Create an exercise in C major using a drop-roll-lift wrist action with this motive.

drop roll lift   drop roll lift   drop roll lift *etc.*

The LH must lift slightly to repeat the drone 5ths, while the RH plays *legato*. Practice this by exaggerating the lift.

G.A. McKinnon: *Invention No. 5: Swirling Leaves* (R39, SG39)
Exploring the Score
See the *Student Guide* discussion of this piece. Discuss the musical portrayal of wind and leaves. Point out the role of free imitation. [McKinnon alters notes to create a cadence or avoid harmonic clashes.]

Ukrainian Folk Song: *Study No. 8* (S9)
Practice Suggestions
Focus on fingering and position shifts. To practice the position shifts, play the first note of each three-note group (with the prescribed finger) in a steady, rocking rhythm.

L. Niamath: *Study No. 9: On the Trampoline* (S10)
Practice Suggestions
- Notice the accents on the LH chords.
- Can you find four accented RH notes?
- Why are these RH notes accented? [help create the sensation of jumping higher and higher on the trampoline]

CREATIVE ACTIVITIES
Make up a story based on *The Hunt*.
- Which notes might represent the galloping horses and the hunting horns?
- What are they hunting or chasing?
- Where does the action change?
- Do the hunters find their prey?

Create your own version of *The Hunt* using the same rhythm.

♪ *Rigaudon* has an open-5th drone accompaniment. Improvise a new dance over this same drone.

♪ Compose or improvise pieces using only tonic and dominant chords.

♪ In *The Fifes*, the RH is basically the same in both the A and B sections. Create a new LH variation to accompany this melody.

STUDY MODULE 3

Page	List	Composer	Title	Meter and Tempo	Musical and Stylistic Concepts
R5 SG8	A	Johann Christoph Friedrich Bach	Schwäbisch	3/8 Moderato	✔ dance style ✔ *legato* and detached articulation ✔ two-voice texture ✔ scale crossings
R7 SG10	A	Johann Heinrich Buttstedt	Air in F Major	4/4 Andante cantabile	✔ two-voice texture: melody and bass ✔ ABA form, B modulates to dominant
R28 SG29	B	Alexander Gedike	A Happy Tale, Op. 36, No. 31	4/4 Allegro	✔ stress on beat two implies misplaced barline ✔ requires clear articulation of sixteenth notes ✔ LH blocked-interval accompaniment
R34 SG34	B	Nancy Telfer (arr.)	Monté sur un éléphant (Climb Up on an Elephant)	6/8 Awkwardly	✔ humorous use of lower range, LH melody, and 6/8 rhythm ✔ melody stated first in LH, then RH
R36 SG37	C	David Duke	Invention No. 1: She's Like the Swallow	6/8 Wistfully, moderate	✔ melody in Dorian mode ✔ canonic writing with overlapping phrases ✔ both hands shift positions
R40 SG40	C	Annibale Zoilo	Invention No. 7: Bicinium	4/4	✔ imitative duet between hands ✔ *legato* articulation ✔ feeling of E minor, but ends on A
S5		Carl Czerny	Study No. 3: Op. 777, No. 3	3/4 Allegro	✔ melody with waltz bass ✔ RH in C five-finger position ✔ LH tonic and dominant harmony
S7		Clifford Poole	Study No. 6	4/4 Allegro	✔ C and G major scales divided between hands into tetrachords ✔ I-V^7-I cadences
S13		Boris Berlin	Study No. 12: Snowflakes	2/4 Allegretto	✔ delicately detached articulation ✔ subtle dynamic contrasts ✔ variety of phrase lengths

Assign first :
Schwäbisch . . . .
A Happy Tale, Op. 36, No. 1 . . . .
Invention No. 1: She's Like the Swallow . . . .
Study No. 6. . . . .
Study No. 3: Op. 777, No. 3

Assign next when ready:
Air in F Major
Monté sur un éléphant (Climb Up on an Elephant)
Invention No. 7: Bicinium
Study No. 12: Snowflakes

Study Module 3 includes a variety of touches and textures. *Schwäbisch, A Happy Tale, Study No. 3*, and *Study No. 12* have light, *staccato*, dance-like articulation. *Air, Monté sur un éléphant*, and *Inventions Nos. 1* and *7* are *legato* and song-like. Textures range from contrapuntal two-voice compositions to melody with a waltz bass.

J.C.F. Bach: *Schwäbisch* (R5, SG8)
Exploring the Score
See the comments on slurs and detached notes in the *Student Guide.*

There are four four-measure phrases. Name the harmony of the last measure of each phrase.
- m. 4: A major, dominant
- m. 8: D major, tonic
- m. 12: A major, dominant
- m. 16: D major, tonic

Practice Suggestions
In music where there is independent movement between the hands, practice hands separately. This will help students develop secure fingering and position shifts.
- Circle the important fingerings.
- Compare the LH fingering in mm. 1-2 and 5-6.
- Choose the most comfortable fingering.

J.H. Buttstedt: *Air in F Major* (R7, SG10)
Exploring the Score
The title *(Air)* and the tempo *(Andante cantabile)* indicate a tuneful, singing style.
- Which notes of the phrase need to be played with special delicacy? [the final notes, to taper the sound after the high point of the phrase]
- Label the sections (ABA_1) in the music. (See the discussion of form in the *Student Guide.*)
- What is the key of each section?

A. Gedike: *A Happy Tale, Op. 36, No. 31* (R28, SG29)
Exploring the Score
The rhythm of this piece is predictable because it is dominated by this rhythmic motive:

- Circle each occurrence of this motive. Where does it come in the phrases?
- Find sixteenth-note groups which start on an up-beat.
- Find sixteenth-note groups which start on a down-beat.
- Experiment with contrasting dynamics for these different groups.
- Find two groups of measures which are exactly alike.

N. Telfer (arr.): *Monté sur un éléphant (Climb Up on an Elephant)* (R34, SG34)
Exploring the Score
Which sounds best suit a piece about an elephant ride?
- low sounds or high sounds?
- slow or fast speed?
- a wobbly rhythm or a marching rhythm?

Does Nancy Telfer use these sounds?

Practice Suggestions
See the *Student Guide* for suggestions about practicing rests and slurs. In addition, practice the RH chords for accuracy of notes and fingering. Have students swing their arms to a slow dotted-quarter-note pulse to feel the lilt of the melody.

D. Duke: *Invention No. 1: She's Like the Swallow* (R36, SG37)
A. Zoilo: *Invention No. 7: Bicinium* (R40, SG40)
Exploring the Score
These pieces are both canons – one voice is the leader and the other voice the follower. (See the *Student Guide* discussion of imitative styles.)
- In *Invention No. 1*, find the first place where the LH does not imitate the RH exactly. [m. 15]
- Compare the imitation in these two Inventions. Which piece has the more exact imitation?

C. Czerny: *Study No. 3: Op 777, No. 3* (S5)
Exploring the Score
Find and label the following musical elements:
- C major broken chords [mostly in LH, one in RH]
- G and G^7 broken chords
- descending C major five-finger pattern

Mark the measures that are exactly like m. 1 with an "*x*". Find the measures which are most unlike mm. 1-4. Label them "B section."

C. Poole: *Study No. 6* (S7)
Exploring the Score
In a major scale, each tetrachord has the same sequence: two whole steps followed by a half step (for example, C-D-E-F; G-A-B-C). The upper tetrachord of one major scale is the same as the lower tetrachord of the major scale a 5th higher (for example, G-A-B-C in C major and G major). This principle is illustrated in *Study No. 6.* Explore the possibility of continuing the C and G major scales of mm. 1-4 into scales and cadences of D and A major.

B. Berlin: *Study No. 12: Snowflakes* (S13)
Practice Suggestions
Look for repeated measures:
- Compare mm. 5-6 with mm. 13-14, 15-16, and 17-18.
- Compare mm. 1-2 with mm. 5-6.

To learn the piece quickly, play the hands in blocked position.

- What touch will you use to imitate lightly falling snow? (Why is a sharp *staccato* inappropriate for this study?)

CREATIVE ACTIVITIES

♫ Play Buttstedt's *Air in F Major.* Now make up your own ABA piece, with the A sections in F major and the B section in C major.

♫ Create a new RH part to go with the LH of *Study No. 3.* You can use Czerny's RH notes, but change the order and the direction.

♫ Play Berlin's *Snowflakes.* Improvise a piece about snow. It could be about snowflakes, a snow storm, or some other aspect of a snowy day. What is the title of your piece?

STUDY MODULE 4

Page	List	Composer	Title	Meter and Tempo	Musical and Stylistic Concepts
R6 SG9	A	Carl Philipp Emanuel Bach	Minuet in C Major	3/4 Moderato	✔ variety of beat subdivisions: eighths, triplets, dotted rhythms ✔ dynamic contrasts with echo motive ✔ frequent position shifts
R11 SG14	A	Ludwig van Beethoven (arr.)	German Dance	3/4 Allegretto	✔ LH waltz bass ✔ RH scale passages ✔ only tonic and dominant harmonies
R16 SG19	A	Johann Wilhelm Hässler	Suite in C Major (Third Movement)	3/4 Menuetto	✔ RH double 3rds and 6ths ✔ contrary motion between hands ✔ two- and three-note slurs
R19 SG22	B	Frederick Silvester (arr.)	Early One Morning	2/4 Moderato	✔ *legato* melody with scale and arpeggio figures ✔ LH double 3rds ✔ RH stretches and finger crossings
R24 SG26	B	Soulima Stravinsky	The New Dress	3/4 Tempo di valse	✔ single-note waltz bass ✔ repeated motive in RH melody ✔ contemporary sound
R38 SG38	C	Pierre Gallant	Invention No. 3: Sur le pont d'Avignon	2/2 Andante	✔ folk tune arranged in canon ✔ dotted quarter rhythm ✔ shifting hand positions
R38 SG38	C	Erasmus Sartorius	Invention No. 4: Canon	4/4	✔ canon with exact reversal of hands ✔ dotted quarter rhythm
S6		Linda Niamath	Study No. 4: Sleepy Little Kitten	4/4 Slowly and gently	✔ pedal study ✔ broken-chord pattern between hands ✔ control of quiet dynamic level
S15		Linda Niamath	Study No. 14: Robots	4/4 Very mechanically	✔ blocked 2nds ✔ dynamic contrasts ✔ parallel and contrary motion ✔ contemporary sound

STUDY MODULE 4 (cont'd)

Assign first:	Assign next when ready:
Minuet in C Major	*German Dance*
Suite in C Major (Third Movement)	*Early One Morning*
The New Dress	*Invention No. 4: Canon*
Invention No. 3: Sur le pont d'Avignon	*Study No. 4: Sleepy Little Kitten*
Study No. 14: Robots	

There are five dances in this Study Module: two minuets, a German dance, a waltz, and a French *ronde*. Challenges include double 3rds and 6ths and coordination of dotted rhythms.

The *Student Guide* discusses the form of most pieces. Have students study the form of each piece they play. When they have completed this Study Module, ask them to match the following forms with the pieces listed below: AABB, ABA₁, AABA₁.

> *Minuet in C Major* [AB]
> *German Dance* [AB]
> *Suite in C Major, Third Movement* [ABA₁]
> *Early One Morning* [AABA₁]

C.P.E. Bach: *Minuet in C Major* (R6, SG9)
Exploring the Score
See the discussions of form and key changes in the *Student Guide*.
- Label the A and B sections.
- Compare mm. 1-2 with mm. 9-10. What has changed? [theme moves to G major]
- Find the echo motive in mm. 2, 4, 10, and 14.

Discuss the effect of the echo. If the piece were played by an instrumental ensemble, what instrument should play the echo? Listen for the dynamic contrast of the echo on the *Celebration Series* recording.

Practice Suggestions
Bach uses triplets and a dotted figure to enhance the characteristic minuet rhythms. Just as dancers must perform a minuet with grace, balance, and control, pianists require rhythmic control to convey the delight of this charming piece. See the exercises for the triplet and dotted rhythms in the *Student Guide*.

Tap the rhythms, counting aloud. Invent words to match the rhythms of the echo pattern.

L. van Beethoven (arr.): *German Dance* (R11, SG14)
Exploring the Score
- How many different rhythmic patterns can you find?
- Which pattern emphasizes the first beat?
- Which pattern emphasizes the second beat?
- The *staccato* notes give this dance a lively quality. How short should they be?
- Find and label the tonic and dominant chords.

J.W. Hässler: *Suite in C Major (Third Movement)* (R16, SG19)
Practice Suggestions
See the practice suggestions for double 3rds and 6ths in the *Student Guide*. The **5-1** RH fingerings in mm. 1 and 3 seem unusual, but they will help students produce a *legato* sound and natural phrase release. In this style period, the first note of short groups is emphasized. The **5-1** fingering helps to focus weight on the half notes.

F. Silvester (arr.): *Early One Morning* (R19, SG22)
Practice Suggestions
As suggested in the *Student Guide*, singing the melody will help the student achieve a natural phrase flow.
- Try to sing each phrase in one breath.
- Does your voice naturally follow the dynamic markings in the music?

S. Stravinsky: *The New Dress* (R24, SG26)
Exploring the Score
This piece has an unusual phrase structure.
- Find the first two phrases. [mm. 1-5, 6-10] How long are they? [5 measures]
- Why might Stravinsky have added these extra measures?
- Make up a story to go with this piece. What happens in the measures of rest?

P. Gallant: *Invention No. 3: Sur le pont d'Avignon* (R38, SG38)
E. Sartorius: *Invention No. 4: Canon* (R38, SG38)

Practice Suggestions

Both Inventions have a dotted rhythm in one hand and steady quarters in the other. Use physical motion to help students resolve difficulties with rhythmic coordination. Work with a short excerpt (for example, m. 3 of *Invention No. 3*):

1. Tap the rhythm hands separately and hands together.
2. Tap the rhythm and chant:

both   left right both   right

3. Walk the LH rhythm while clapping the RH rhythm.

L. Niamath: *Study No. 4: Sleepy Little Kitten* (S6)

Exploring the Score

Involve the student in the quiet mood of this piece.
- What movements would a sleepy kitten make? [stretch, roll over, yawn, and meow]
- Where is the meow in the music?
- When does the kitten finally fall asleep? How does Linda Niamath portray this in the music?

Practice Suggestions

Blocking the intervals will help the student feel the difference between the LH 5ths and the RH 6ths. Isolate mm. 7 and 9-10 for special practice.

To work on pedal coordination, practice the LH alone. Lift the pedal on the first eighth note of the measure and depress it on the second.

L. Niamath: *Study No. 14: Robots* (S15)

Exploring the Score

- What interval is used throughout this piece? [2nd]
- Where do the hands move in parallel motion? [mm. 5-8]
- Where do the hands move in contrary motion? [mm. 9-12]
- In mm. 1-12, which finger does not play?

Practice Suggestions

Use this study to reinforce arm rotation. Have the student play only the outer note of each 2nd (thumb and fifth finger) using a rocking hand motion.

CREATIVE ACTIVITIES

Compose a short march using the LH of *German Dance*, mm. 1-8. You will have to change the meter to 4/4. How will you alter the LH to accommodate this?

The melody of *The New Dress* has a tonal center of B flat. Write a more traditional accompaniment for Stravinsky's melody using tonic, subdominant, and dominant chords. Play Stravinsky's melody with your accompaniment. Now compose a new melody for your waltz bass.

Compose a piece about robots. Decide what your robots are doing, then choose intervals and rhythms. Give your piece a title.

Compose your own accompaniment for the folk song *Sur le pont d'Avignon*.

STUDY MODULE 5

Page	List	Composer	Title	Meter and Tempo	Musical and Stylistic Concepts
R4 SG7	A	Leopold Mozart	Minuet in F Major	3/4 Allegretto	✔ RH eighths against LH quarters ✔ two-measure phrases ✔ new rhythms in final measures
R12 SG15	A	Franz Joseph Haydn, Clifford Poole (arr.)	Allegretto in G Major	3/4 Grazioso	✔ keyboard version of instrumental work ✔ short, predictable phrases
R13 SG16	A	George Frideric Handel	Minuet in F Major	3/4	✔ unusual form held together with repeated motives and sequences ✔ detailed articulation ✔ shift to parallel minor in *coda*
R23 SG25	B	Pierre Gallant (arr.)	This Old Man	2/2 Scherzando	✔ melody shared between hands ✔ meter change ✔ hands interlocking in treble clef
R31 SG32	B	Boris Berlin (arr.)	Three Fine Ducks	4/4 Allegretto	✔ LH pattern imitates waddling ✔ melody in RH
R32 SG33	B	Dmitri Shostakovich	Soldier's March	4/4 Allegro	✔ strong march tune ✔ two-voice texture ✔ difficult shifts to black keys ✔ many accidentals
R37 SG37	C	Konrad Max Kunz	Invention No. 2: Canon on the Black Keys, Op. 14, No. 184	2/4 Allegro	✔ all black keys ✔ G flat five-finger position ✔ *staccato* and *legato* articulation ✔ octave shifts
S8		Theodor Oesten	Study No. 7: Hunting Horns	6/8 Allegretto	✔ broken chords and inversions ✔ dynamic contrast ✔ two-note slurs ✔ rounded binary form
S16		Leon Aubry	Study No. 15: Woodland Scene	2/4 Moderato	✔ LH two-note slurs imitate cuckoo

Assign first:
Minuet in F Major (Mozart) . . . .
. . . .
This Old Man . . . .
Invention No. 2: Canon on the Black Keys, Op. 14, No. 184 . .
Study No. 15: Woodland Scene. . . . .

Assign next when ready:
Minuet in F Major (Handel)
Allegretto in G Major
Three Fine Ducks
Soldier's March
Study No. 7: Hunting Horns

This Study Module includes three dances: *Minuet in F Major* by Handel, *Minuet in F Major* by Leopold Mozart, and *Allegretto in G Major* by Haydn. All three dances require detailed articulation and phrasing. Discuss the similarities and differences in these three works.

- What features do these dances share? [meter, two-voice texture]
- How do they differ? [form, keys]
- Which dance has a *coda* and a shift to a minor key? [Handel's *Minuet*]
- Which dance features an upbeat? [Haydn's *Allegretto*]

Three Fine Ducks, This Old Man, Soldier's March, Study No. 7, and *Study No. 15* are all descriptive works. Some tell a story through the words of a song. Others create a musical picture through title and sound. Students can use their imagination to portray the picture or mood expressed in the music.

L. Mozart: *Minuet in F Major* (R4, SG7)
Exploring the Score
See the *Student Guide* discussion of the rhythmic structure. Explore Mozart's use of eighth notes to move the music forward. The eighth notes provide the energy, and the quarter notes provide relaxation.

F. J. Haydn, C. Poole (arr.): *Allegretto in G Major* (R12, SG15)
Exploring the Score
Compare this piece with Mozart's *Minuet in F Major*. Notice the use of eighth notes and repeated quarter notes for forward motion.

Divide the eight-measure phrases into smaller units: 2 measures + 2 measures + 4 measures. Mark these smaller units in the music.

G.F. Handel: *Minuet in F Major* (R13, SG16)
Exploring the Score
Label the sections of the piece (see *Student Guide*). The *coda* (mm. 20-25) includes a shift to F minor. Play the piece as if it ended at m. 19, then add the *coda* so that students can hear its surprising effect.

Practice Suggestions
See the *Student Guide* for suggestions on articulation and listen to the *Celebration Series* recording. Use articulation patterns consistently. For example, the falling 4ths in mm. 2, 4, 12, and 16 should have the same articulation.

P. Gallant (arr.): *This Old Man* (R23, SG25)
Exploring the Score
The words of this traditional children's song are printed in the *Student Guide*. Students can write the words in the music and sing the song as they play.

Discuss the different reasons composers might have for changing a time signature.
- Does the time signature change in this piece disrupt the tune?
- Why do you think Gallant made this change?

Practice Suggestions
See the suggested thumb position in the *Student Guide*.

Play the *Celebration Series* recording and listen for details of dynamics and articulations. Help students hear the difference between *mezzo piano*, *piano*, and *pianissimo* as they play.

B. Berlin (arr.): *Three Fine Ducks* (R31, SG32)
Exploring the Score
- The A section has a short-short-long phrase structure. How does this structure change in the B section?
- Compare the melody of this piece with the folk-song melody in the *Student Guide*. Where does the LH play melody notes?
- How does Berlin use the LH accompaniment to portray ducks?

D. Shostakovich: *Soldier's March* (R32, SG33)
Practice Suggestions
The *Student Guide* (p. 33) provides suggestions for interpretation and sets the scene of soldiers marching. Listen to the *Celebration Series* recording to reinforce the spirit of the piece.

- Choose a dynamic plan for the repeated notes. They should either "move forward" (*crescendo*) or "pull back" (*diminuendo*).
- Experiment with touch as well as dynamics to create a feeling of movement through the repeated notes.

The black-key phrases need special practice.
- For mm. 9-12: Practice the RH separately. Notice the fingering (**321 321 311**). Block the G major chord in m. 12 hands together.
- For mm. 13-16: The mirror-image fingering for the quarter notes is helpful. Say the finger numbers aloud as you play.
- For mm. 22-24: Practice hands separately. Draw brackets over small sections, as follows:
  - upbeat to m. 22 through beat three of m. 22
  - m. 22, beat four through m. 23, beat two
  - m. 23, beat three through m. 24

Practice each section several times hands together. Once you are confident of each section, play them in sequence.

K.M. Kunz: *Invention No. 2: Canon on the Black Keys, Op. 14, No. 184* (R37, SG37)
Exploring the Score
This Invention is based on one idea.
- Play the RH theme, mm. 1-3. How many times does this melody repeat? [six times]
- How many times do the hands shift position to a new octave? [five times]
- Where does the canon end and the melody change? [m. 12]

T. Oesten: *Study No. 7: Hunting Horns* (S8)
Exploring the Score

This music bounces back and forth between *piano* and *forte*.
- Which dynamic represents the galloping horses?
- Which dynamic represents the horn calls?

The galloping figure in m. 1 is a broken chord.
- What is the name of this chord?
- How many position shifts do you need to play this figure?

L. Aubry: *Study No. 15: Woodland Scene* (S16)
Exploring the Score
- What is the form of this piece? [ABA]
- How is the B section different? [change of key and rhythm]
- Count the two-note slurs. [32]
- Which hand plays only two-note slurs? [LH]

CREATIVE ACTIVITIES

Play the tune of the old French folk song *Three Fine Ducks* (see the *Student Guide*) and improvise an accompaniment to the tune.

Using Kunz's theme from *Canon on the Black Keys*, create a new piece by moving to different octaves in a different order. Make a surprise ending.

In *Study No. 15,* Aubry paints a musical picture of a woodland scene. Compose your own piece about animals in a forest and give it a title. Use a G major five-finger pattern and two-note slurs. The music could portray rabbits, deer, or an owl on a moonlit night.

STUDY MODULE 6

Page	List	Composer	Title	Meter and Tempo	Musical and Stylistic Concepts
R8 SG11	A	Johann Sebastian Bach	Minuet in G Major	3/4	✔ intricate articulation ✔ varied five-finger patterns ✔ finger crossings ✔ coordination challenges
R9 SG12	A	Henry Purcell	Air in D Minor	3/4 Grazioso	✔ RH repeating rhythm ✔ LH chromaticism imitates melodic minor scale ✔ shifts and crossings in LH
R25 SG27	B	Dmitri Kabalevsky	Battle Song, Op. 89, No. 30	2/4 Energico	✔ RH dotted rhythms ✔ easy LH allows concentration on RH ✔ quick tempo
R29 SG30	B	Linda Niamath	Bears	6/8 Plodding	✔ LH two-note *ostinato* ✔ RH blocked chords ✔ inversions
R30 SG31	B	Ernest Marsden	The Itchy Ant	4/4 Giocoso	✔ *staccato* articulations; quick shifts ✔ contrasting dynamics ✔ LH uses only third finger, covers three-octave range
S6		Cornelius Gurlitt	Study No. 5	3/8 Allegretto	✔ C major, five-note patterns ✔ two-note slurs, single notes and blocked intervals ✔ AA$_1$ form
S11		Dmitri Kabalevsky	Study No. 10: Playing, Op. 39, No. 5	3/4 Allegretto	✔ *staccato* articulation ✔ frequent direction changes
S12		Clifford Poole	Study No. 11: Chords on Parade	4/4 Allegro deciso	✔ five-finger patterns and scales with dynamic swell ✔ blocked 3rds and chords

Assign first:
Minuet in G Major. . . . .
Bears . . . .
Study No. 5. . . . .
Study No. 10: Playing, Op. 39, No. 5 . . . .

Assign next when ready:
The Itchy Ant
Air in D Minor
Battle Song, Op. 89, No. 30
Study No. 11: Chords on Parade

The pieces in Study Module 6 are some of the most difficult from Level 1. They present a variety of technical and musical challenges. *Minuet in G Major* and *Air in D Minor* are two-voice contrapuntal pieces in AB form with interesting rhythmic patterns. In *Bears* and *The Itchy Ant*, the student must interpret a musical picture while dealing with a variety of articulations and musical elements. The three studies include *staccatos*, chords, slurs, and five-note patterns.

J.S. Bach: *Minuet in G Major* (R8, SG11)
H. Purcell: *Air in D Minor* (R9, SG12)
Exploring the Score
Compare these two-voice Baroque pieces:
- What rhythmic values are used in both pieces?

- Is there any combination of eighths and quarters which is not used?
- Both pieces use the following rhythm. Which piece uses it in almost every measure?

- Do both pieces have the same form? (See the *Student Guide.*)
- Most of the time, the hands play different rhythms. Look for measures where both hands have the same rhythm.
- In Bach's *Minuet,* the opening theme returns at m. 17. Are mm. 17-20 a variation of mm. 1-4?

D. Kabalevsky: *Battle Song, Op. 89, No. 30* (R25, SG27)
Practice Suggestions

The RH *tenuto* markings indicate the focus of the phrases. First, practice each RH phrase *legato*, giving each note the same value, to establish the fingering and sequence of notes. Then add the dotted rhythm and articulation.

L. Niamath: *Bears* (R29, SG30)
E. Marsden: *The Itchy Ant* (R30, SG31)
Exploring the Score

- From their titles, how do you expect these pieces to sound?
- Which piece would have low notes?
- Which piece would move to many different places?
- Which piece would be slow and plodding?
- Which piece would be loud and powerful?
- Which piece would be fast and busy?

Did Linda Niamath and Ernest Marsden fulfill your expectations?

Practice Suggestions

Play the *Celebration Series* recording of *Bears* and listen to the majestic, rich chords. Point out the logic of the chord construction. See the suggestions for practicing chords in the *Student Guide.* Notice the all-white-key, all-black-key formula in mm. 5-8.

The LH of *The Itchy Ant* may require special attention. See the *Student Guide* for practice suggestions.

C. Gurlitt: *Study No. 5* (S6)
Practice Suggestions

Play the LH 3rds *legato*. Give each pair a stress-release dynamic shape. The LH dynamic shape will influence the RH sixteenth notes:

D. Kabalevsky: *Study No. 10: Playing, Op. 39, No. 5* (S11)
Exploring the Score

This piece looks deceptively easy – all *staccato* quarter notes – but students may find the changing patterns difficult. Discuss the different patterns and assign a letter to each one. Look for variations in:
- the direction of notes
- the number of notes in each hand
- the number of notes in the pattern

Most of the patterns have three notes. In mm. 9-14, there is a six-note pattern.

Practice Suggestions

Divide the piece into sections according to direction and figure. Practice each section until it is secure.

C. Poole: *Study No. 11: Chords on Parade* (S12)
Exploring the Score

Most students find the practice of scales and chords boring. Here's a chance to enjoy them! Shape the scales and five-finger patterns by following the dynamic markings in the score.
- What is the key of this piece? [D minor]
- How many different five-finger scale patterns can you find? [D minor, A major]
- Are there full octave scales? [mm. 7 and 15]
- How many different chords can you find? Are they all in root position?

CREATIVE ACTIVITIES

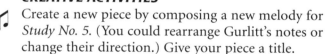
- Create a new piece by composing a new melody for *Study No. 5.* (You could rearrange Gurlitt's notes or change their direction.) Give your piece a title.

- Make up a story to go with Niamath's *Bears.* What is the bear doing? What happens when the dynamics change? Now write your own piece about a bear. Use RH chords and a lumbering LH figure. Experiment with all-white-key and all-black-key chords.

LEVEL 1 SUMMARY
- Which composers did you discover for the first time? Which composers in *Repertoire Album 1* are your favorites?
- Which pieces were most challenging technically? What practice techniques did you use to master these technical challenges? Did you use warm-up exercises for any of the pieces?
- Which pieces posed rhythmic difficulties? How did you practice the rhythm? Did you count aloud or tap to learn new rhythmic patterns?

Level 2

The Publications
Level 2 of the *Celebration Series* includes the following publications:
Piano Repertoire Album 2
Piano Studies Album 1 & 2 (level 2 only)
Student Guide 2
Recording of *Repertoire & Studies 2*

The Repertoire
The pieces in *Repertoire Album 2* have been divided into three sections or lists.
- List A includes a selection of pieces composed during the Baroque period (*ca* 1600 to *ca* 1750) and the Classical Period (*ca* 1750 to *ca* 1820).
- List B includes a selection of pieces composed during the Romantic era (*ca* 1820 to *ca* 1910) and the 20th century.
- List C consists of Inventions, short two-voice compositions written in an imitative style.

Musical Development
Level 2 offers the student a wide range of styles from the late elementary and early intermediate teaching literature. Many of the pieces emphasize two-voice textures in binary or rounded binary form. It is important for students to practice hands separately and hands together. Vary the length of practice units and increase the number of repetitions.

The repertoire and studies in Level 2 concentrate on:
- balance between melody and accompaniment
- independence of voices
- *legato* and *staccato* articulations
- two- and three-voice textures, both imitative and homophonic
- expressive nuances through subtle phrasing
- increased use of the damper pedal
- dance forms from various style periods
- traditional, impressionistic, and contemporary sounds

This level also includes thicker textures using various types of chord figurations. Practicing chords presents opportunities for teaching related skills and musical concepts such as:
- playing triads in inversions
- playing basic chord cadence patterns
- identifying and labeling each chord

The practice suggestions found in the *Student Guide* and in the following Study Module discussions will help the student to gain control over the various challenges.

As you work through Level 2, practice five-finger patterns in conjunction with the key of each piece.

Dance Chart
Many of the pieces in Album 2 are dances. Encourage students to keep a Dance Chart, adding each new dance they learn. For each dance, list the title, the meter, and the rhythmic characteristics. Here is a list of the dances in Level 2:
> *bourrée*
> *écossaise*
> German dance
> jig
> *Ländler*
> mazurka
> minuet
> polka
> quadrille
> waltz

The Range of Difficulty
The range of difficulty within Level 2 is illustrated by the following two compositions:
- *Study No. 11* by Pál Kadosa is an example of an easier piece from Study Module 1.
- *Penguins* by Linda Niamath is an example of a challenging piece from Study Module 6.

The Study Modules
The six Study Module discussions in Level 2 are organized into the following categories:
- *Exploring the Score*
- *Practice Suggestions*
- *Creative Activities*

Exploring the Score is designed as an interactive exercise between teacher and student. Questions are addressed to the student, as you might ask them during the lesson. *Practice Suggestions* are also directed to the student. The *Creative Activities* act as reinforcement for your students' understanding of a musical concept and can provide a springboard for their creativity and imagination.

Please refer to the Foreword for an explanation of how to use the suggested order of assignment within each Module.

The following chart lists the repertoire and studies from Level 2. Page numbers for works in the *Piano Repertoire Album 2* and the *Piano Studies Album 2* are found in the first column. Study Module numbers for each composition are found in the fourth column.

	Page	Composer	Title	Study Module
Piano Repertoire Album 2				
List A	R4	Georg Philipp Telemann	Fantasia in D Major	2
	R5	Wilhelm Friedemann Bach	Minuet in G Major	5
	R6	Sperontes (pseud.)	Minuet in D Major	3
	R7	Johann Sebastian Bach (attr.)	Bourrée in D Minor	1
	R8	Franz Joseph Haydn	Quadrille	4
	R10	Daniel Steibelt	Aria in A Minor	3
	R11	Franz Schubert	Ländler	5
	R12	Muzio Clementi	Waltz	5
	R14	Franz Schubert	Écossaise	4
	R15	Alessandro Scarlatti	Aria in D Minor	1
	R16	Ludwig van Beethoven	German Dance	6
List B	R18	Robert Schumann	Melody, Op. 68, No. 1	1
	R19	Cornelius Gurlitt	Theme and Variation	2
	R20	Mikhail Ivanovich Glinka	Russian Polka	3
	R21	Linda Niamath	Penguins	6
	R22	Clifford Poole	Fleas	4
	R23	Isak Berkovich	Mazurka	4
	R24	Nancy Telfer (arr.)	Land of the Silver Birch	5
	R25	Eddie Harris	Bulgarian Shepherd's Tune	1
	R26	Aram Khachaturian	An Evening Tale	4
	R28	Jean Coulthard	The Whale's Sad Story	5
	R29	Alexander Gedike	Military Trumpets, Op. 36, No. 53	5
	R30	István Szelényi	Faraway Regions	6
	R31	Barbara Pentland	Slow Song	3
	R32	Alexander Gedike	The Shepherd's Pipe, Op. 36, No. 55	3
	R34	Jean Coulthard	First Little Dance (Lavender's Blue)	2
List C	R35	Alexander Gedike	Invention No. 1: Fugato, Op. 36, No. 40	3
	R36	Gordon A. McKinnon	Invention No. 2: The Argument	6
	R36	Cornelius Gurlitt	Invention No. 3: Canon	1
	R37	Ludwig van Beethoven	Invention No. 4: Little Piece, WoO 61a	6
	R38	Pierre Gallant	Invention No. 5: In the Dorian Mode	5
	R39	Pierre Gallant	Invention No. 6: Jazz Invention	5
	R39	Carleton Elliott	Invention No. 7: Canon	4
	R40	Alexander Gedike	Invention No. 8: Fugato, Op. 36, No. 46	
Piano Studies Album 2				
	S17	Alexander Gedike	Study No. 1	3
	S18	Carl Czerny	Study No. 2: Op. 777, No. 8	2
	S19	Linda Niamath	Study No. 3: Kangaroos	2
	S20	Soulima Stravinsky	Study No. 4: Cross Hands	4
	S21	Carl Czerny	Study No. 5: Op. 777, No. 22	4
	S22	Henri Bertini	Study No. 6: Op. 166, No. 6	3
	S23	Joan Hansen	Study No. 7: Irish Jig	1
	S24	Aram Khachaturian	Study No. 8: Skipping Rope	6
	S25	Isak Berkovich	Study No. 9	2
	S26	Jean-Baptiste Duvernoy	Study No. 10: Op. 176, No. 17	3
	S27	Pál Kadosa	Study No. 11	1
	S28	Linda Niamath	Study No. 12: Butterflies	6
	S29	Alexander Gedike	Study No. 13	5
	S30	Carl Czerny	Study No. 14	2
	S31	Hermann Berens	Study No. 15	1
	S32	Dmitri Kabalevsky	Study No. 16: The Little Juggler, Op. 89, No. 21	6

STUDY MODULE 1

Page	List	Composer	Title	Meter and Tempo	Musical and Stylistic Concepts
R7 SG10	A	Johann Sebastian Bach (attr.)	Bourrée in D Minor	4/4 Allegro	✔ short, articulated RH groups ✔ LH quarter- and half-note accompaniment ✔ ABA₁ structure
R15 SG16	A	Alessandro Scarlatti	Aria in D Minor	3/2 Grave	✔ LH rhythm in 3/2 and 6/4 ✔ *legato* fingering, thumb crossing
R18 SG18	B	Robert Schumann	Melody, Op. 68, No. 1	4/4 Moderato	✔ outer voices in parallel motion ✔ RH quarter-note phrases ✔ eighth-note accompaniment ✔ *legato* fingering important
R25 SG25	B	Eddie Harris	Bulgarian Shepherd's Tune	5/8 Larghetto	✔ LH *ostinato*, tied notes ✔ RH stepwise melodic figure ✔ three-voice texture ✔ *legato* phrasing ✔ Phrygian mode
R36 SG35	C	Cornelius Gurlitt	Invention No. 3: Canon	4/4 Allegretto	✔ strict imitation ✔ two-voice texture ✔ five-finger patterns
S23		Joan Hansen	Study No. 7: Irish Jig	6/8 With spirit	✔ eighth-note melody ✔ single-note accompaniment
S27		Pál Kadosa	Study No. 11	5/8 Allegretto leggiero	✔ coordination exercise ✔ A minor five-finger pattern ✔ *staccato* articulation ✔ variable meter
S31		Hermann Berens	Study No. 15	2/4 Allegretto	✔ coordination study ✔ LH *legato*, *ostinato* patterns ✔ articulated RH ✔ both hands in C major five-finger pattern

Assign first:
Aria in D Minor . . . . *Bourrée in D Minor*
Study No. 7: Irish Jig . . . . *Invention No. 3: Canon*
Melody, Op. 68, No. 1 . . . . *Study No. 15*
Study No. 11 . . . . *Bulgarian Shepherd's Tune*

Assign next when ready:

Approach Study Module 1 with the idea that music can sing or dance. List *bourrée* and jig on the Dance Chart. Discuss these questions:
- Which pieces emphasize the melody (the singing aspect)? Are they played mostly *legato* or *staccato*?
- Which pieces have a dance quality? How do the rhythm and the articulation contribute to this?
- Which pieces start with an upbeat? (A clue: *bourrées* and jigs begin with an upbeat.)

Now look at the different styles of accompaniments.
- Which pieces have accompaniments that are actually independent melodies?
- In which piece does the LH imitate exactly what the RH has played?
- Which pieces have LH harmonic accompaniments?

Compare Robert Schumann's *Melody* and Alessandro Scarlatti's *Aria*. Both pieces have duet-like textures, but *Melody* has a more lyrical, Romantic style with the melody supported by the accompaniment.

J.S. Bach (attr.): *Bourrée in D Minor* (R7, SG10)
Exploring the Score
The *Student Guide* discusses the form. Circle each repetition of rhythm "*x*" in the A section, and rhythm "*y*" in the B section.

Practice Suggestions
Have students read the section "A Repeated Motive" in the *Student Guide*. Divide the piece into short practice units (one or two measures).

- Find places where the hands lift together.
- Find places where one hand plays *legato* and the other plays detached. Emphasize the hand lifts as you practice these measures.

A. Scarlatti: *Aria in D Minor* (R15, SG16)
Exploring the Score
When composers write in 3/2 or 6/4, they often group the quarter notes to show two different possibilities:

- Find measures in which Scarlatti writes in 3/2 (**1** 2 **3** 4 **5** 6). [LH mm. 1-3]
- Find other measures in which he writes in 6/4 (**1** 2 3 **4** 5 6). [LH mm. 4-6]
- Does the melody in the RH correspond to this grouping of the beats?

Practice Suggestion
As in the Bach *Bourrée in D Minor,* emphasize the hand lifts.

R. Schumann: *Melody, Op. 68, No. 1* (R18, SG18)
Exploring the Score
Point out the LH hidden duet (see the *Student Guide*).

Discuss the function of the short phrases in mm. 5-7 and 13-15. (The rising sequence creates musical tension in anticipation of the return of C major, the tonic key.)

Practice Suggestions
Concentrate on the contrast between melody and accompaniment.

- Play the RH-LH duet without the LH thumb notes.

- Practice the LH part keeping the thumb notes quietly in the background.
- Practice the RH of mm. 8 and 16 playing one part with each hand.

E. Harris: *Bulgarian Shepherd's Tune* (R25, SG25)
P. Kadosa: *Study No. 11* (S27)
Exploring the Score
Compare the rhythms of these two pieces.

- Both pieces are in 5/8. Are the five-beat measures created by combining 2 + 3 or 3 + 2?
- How do these two pieces differ? [tempo, articulation]
- Can you find a minor five-finger pattern in Kadosa's *Study?* [A minor]

C. Gurlitt: *Invention No. 3: Canon* (R36, SG35)
Practice Suggestions
Canon uses two five-finger positions: A minor (mm. 1-4) and E major (mm. 5-7). Practice each pattern, hands together, in parallel and contrary motion. Play this Invention as a duet (two students or student and teacher), with one person playing each part.

J. Hansen: *Study No. 7: Irish Jig* (S23)
Practice Suggestions
Accents can be played with an arm drop or with a high lifted finger. Try playing the accents in mm. 1-4 both ways and decide which method is easier and sounds best.

H. Berens: *Study No. 15* (S31)
Practice Suggestions
Use a rocking motion of the hand for the LH part. Have students play m. 1 using only the first and fifth fingers. Rotate the hand naturally and easily. Then add the inner notes, but keep the rocking motion.

CREATIVE ACTIVITY
This Study Module includes two pieces in 5/8: *Bulgarian Shepherd's Tune* and Kadosa's *Study No. 11.* Have your student choose a minor five-finger pattern, and improvise a melody in 5/8. Organize the notes in 3 + 2 or 2 + 3 groupings. Add a blocked-5th accompaniment to the melody and play hands together. Give your piece a title.

STUDY MODULE 2

Page	List	Composer	Title	Meter and Tempo	Musical and Stylistic Concepts
R4 SG7	A	Georg Philipp Telemann	Fantasia in D Major	3/4 Vivace	✔ short RH motives ✔ moving LH quarter-note line ✔ AABA form
R19 SG19	B	Cornelius Gurlitt	Theme and Variation	2/4 Moderato	✔ chordal theme ✔ variation with RH triplets ✔ short-short-long phrasing
R34 SG32	B	Jean Coulthard	First Little Dance (Lavender's Blue)	3/4 Freely	✔ hands remain close to F major five-finger position ✔ two-note slurs
R40 SG37	C	Alexander Gedike	Invention No. 8: Fugato, Op. 36, No. 46	4/4 Allegro, ma non troppo	✔ simple rhythmic structure ✔ *legato* phrasing ✔ two-voice texture ✔ hand independence
S18		Carl Czerny	Study No. 2: Op. 777, No. 8	6/8 Allegretto	✔ broken-triad accompaniment ✔ lyrical RH melody ✔ *legato* and *staccato* articulation
S19		Linda Niamath	Study No. 3: Kangaroos	3/4 Energetically	✔ octave-shift exercise in unison quarter notes ✔ two-note slurs
S25		Isak Berkovich	Study No. 9	2/4 Vivo	✔ consistent rhythm ✔ melody moves to LH ✔ both hands in treble clef
S30		Carl Czerny	Study No. 14	6/8 Allegretto	✔ flowing eighth notes alternating between the hands ✔ outlines triads and inversions

Assign first :

Study No. 9 . . . .
Theme and Variation . . . .
Study No. 3: Kangaroos . . . .
Invention No. 8: Fugato, Op. 36, No. 46 . . . .

Assign next when ready:

Fantasia in D Major
Study No. 14
First Little Dance (Lavender's Blue)
Study No. 2: Op. 777, No. 8

The pieces in Study Module 2 provide opportunities to discuss note groups and phrasing. For example, *Fantasia in D Major* is made up of short, articulated motives. *Invention No. 8* has longer *legato* lines. *Fantasia in D Major, First Little Dance, Study No. 3*, and *Study No. 9* have two- or three-note slurs. Use exercises (such as the one shown below) to practice these slurs. Have students play these exercises with different fingerings. Experiment with a drop and lift movement of the wrist.

First Little Dance, Invention No. 8, and *Study No. 2* are all tuneful pieces. Draw the student's attention to melodic organization and phrase grouping.

Theme and Variation and *Study No. 14* involve broken chords. Use this opportunity to discuss triads, chord inversions, and harmonic relationships.

G. P. Telemann: *Fantasia in D Major* (R4, SG7)
I. Berkovich: *Study No. 9* (S25)
Exploring the Score
Fantasia in D Major and *Study No. 9* use the same rhythmic figure:

- How are the rhythms in the two pieces different?
- What makes Telemann's piece more difficult? [key, fingering, LH movement]
- Both pieces have the same form. [AABA] Mark the beginning of each A section in your music.

Discuss the mood and style of these two pieces. Does the music dance or does it sing?

C. Gurlitt: *Theme and Variation* (R19, SG19)
Exploring the Score
- How does Gurlitt change the theme in the variation?
- Can you find a colorful harmonic progression? [cadence on III, m. 8]

Compare this piece with *Study No. 14.*
- What parts of these two pieces look alike?
- How do the eighth-note patterns differ?
- Find the tonic chords. Do these chords feel final and restful?

J. Coulthard: *First Little Dance (Lavender's Blue)* (R34, SG32)
Exploring the Score
See the original English folk song in the *Student Guide.* Have students sing the words and compare phrase construction and phrase lengths with Jean Coulthard's piece.

**A. Gedike: *Invention No. 8: Fugato,*
*Op. 36, No. 46*** (R40, SG37)
Exploring the Score
The phrasing in this Invention is irregular. As the student plays the piece, mark the phrases in the score.
- Where does the LH play the melody? [mm. 3-6; 10-12]

Practice Suggestions
Use the exercises on p. 33 of the *Student Guide* to practice this piece. Practice difficult spots slowly. (Rule: There is a slow tempo at which you can play the music perfectly.)

C. Czerny: *Study No. 2: Op. 777, No. 8* (S18)
Exploring the Score
Examine the length of each phrase. [two measures] The phrases come in pairs: one asks a musical question, and the next one gives a musical answer (see mm. 1-4).

Practice Suggestions
- Block the rolling LH broken chords for efficient practice.
- Take time to identify the chords and analyze the harmony.

L. Niamath: *Study No. 3: Kangaroos* (S19)
Exploring the Score
Play the *Celebration Series* recording of this piece.
- How does Niamath create a musical picture of kangaroos?
- What rhythmic figure suggests hopping?

Find the three different chords in this piece. (Notice that the note F appears in all three chords.) Each chord appears in several different positions. Explore the chord inversions.

Practice Suggestions
Practice the position shifts with blocked chords at a slow, steady tempo. Have students hold their fingers over the keys in each new position before they play the notes.

C. Czerny: *Study No. 14* (S30)
Exploring the Score
Explore the harmonic progressions with your student, and identify as many chords as possible.

Practice Suggestions
Practice the chords in blocked form.
- Circle the first LH note in each measure. What clue can you find? [notes form descending G major scale]

CREATIVE ACTIVITIES

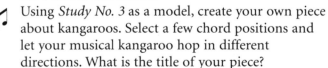

Using *Study No. 3* as a model, create your own piece about kangaroos. Select a few chord positions and let your musical kangaroo hop in different directions. What is the title of your piece?

Create a variation for the LH of Czerny's *Study No. 14.* Try changing the rhythm or using blocked chords. Now add your own RH part. Try an ascending melody based on a G major scale or a melody based on broken triads.

STUDY MODULE 3

Page	List	Composer	Title	Meter and Tempo	Musical and Stylistic Concepts
R6 SG9	A	Sperontes (pseud.)	Minuet in D Major	3/4	✔ parallel quarter notes ✔ challenging skips ✔ ABA₁ form
R10 SG12	A	Daniel Steibelt	Aria in A Minor	2/4 Andante	✔ three-voice texture (LH two-voice accompaniment) ✔ accidentals ✔ short-short-long phrasing
R20 SG20	B	Mikhail Ivanovich Glinka	Russian Polka	2/4 Allegretto	✔ *staccato* LH broken chords ✔ RH sixteenth-note phrases
R31 SG30	B	Barbara Pentland	Slow Song	4/4 Andante	✔ both hands in treble clef ✔ bitonal (C major, A flat minor) ✔ mirror intervals between hands
R32 SG31	B	Alexander Gedike	The Shepherd's Pipe, Op. 36, No. 55	3/4 Moderato con moto	✔ lyrical RH eighth notes ✔ long LH note values ✔ varied articulation ✔ two-voice accompaniment
R35 SG34	C	Alexander Gedike	Invention No. 1: Fugato, Op. 36, No. 40	4/4 Allegro energico	✔ hand independence ✔ *legato* and *staccato* articulation ✔ ties and suspensions ✔ requires careful voice leading
S17		Alexander Gedike	Study No. 1	2/4 Moderato	✔ tag-like imitation ✔ *staccato* articulation ✔ hands in octave unison ✔ both hands in treble clef
S22		Henri Bertini	Study No. 6: Op. 166, No. 6	4/4 Andante	✔ exercise in two-note slurs ✔ damper pedal
S26		Jean-Baptiste Duvernoy	Study No. 10: Op. 176, No. 17	3/4 Allegretto	✔ LH plays waltz bass ✔ RH eighth-note rhythmic motive

Assign first:
Aria in A Minor
Study No. 10: Op. 176, No. 17
Study No. 6: Op. 166, No. 6
Slow Song
The Shepherd's Pipe, Op. 36, No. 55

Assign next when ready:
Minuet in D Major
Russian Polka
Study No. 1
Invention No. 1: Fugato, Op. 36, No. 40

Subtle phrasing and interesting intervallic patterns highlight the music in Study Module 3. Both the *Aria in A Minor* and the *Minuet in D Major* contain short-short-long phrase structures. The shorter phrases create musical intensity in anticipation of the longer four-measure phrase. Other pieces are dominated by short slurred groups. *Study No. 6* is made up of two-note slurs. *Study No. 10* has five- and seven-note groups. In *Study No. 1*, the hands toss short groups back and forth. Use these groups to establish short practice units (always an efficient way to learn).

Study No. 6, *Study No. 10*, and *Aria in A Minor* are built on traditional harmonic patterns. Discuss harmonic progressions and help students label the tonic, subdominant, and dominant chords.

Discuss the form of each piece (see the *Student Guide*). Make a list of the pieces and a list of the different forms. Have the student match the letters to the titles. Add minuet and polka to the Dance Chart.

Sperontes (pseud.): *Minuet in D Major*
(R6, SG9)

Practice Suggestions

Pay particular attention to fingering and position shifts in this *minuet*. Have students circle fingerings which they find most helpful.

1. Practice hands separately in two-measure units.
2. Practice hands together in one-measure units (to learn the notes).
3. Practice in units of one measure plus one note (to practice the position shifts).

D. Steibelt: *Aria in A Minor* (R10, SG12)
Practice Suggestions

The *Student Guide* provides suggestions for practicing the LH. Although the LH looks easier than the RH, it may require more practice. Use a *legato* touch, especially for the double 3rds (mm. 21-24) and the moving quarter notes.

M.I. Glinka: *Russian Polka* (R20, SG20)
Exploring the Score

Notice the dynamic plan: *forte – mezzo piano – forte – piano*.

- What is the relationship between the loud measures and the soft measures?
- Can you find another piece in Level 2 with this same dynamic pattern?
- This polka is in binary form (A: mm. 1-8, B: mm. 9-16). What changes does Glinka make to create the contrasting B section? [shift to F major, more sixteenth notes]
- What is the effect of the additional sixteenth-note figures in mm. 11-12? [faster movement increases intensity and rhythmic momentum]

Practice Suggestions

See the description of a polka in the *Student Guide*. What markings in the music suggest a polka? [accents on second beat] Play the piece exaggerating the accents, then play it with no accents. Does the music still sound like a polka?

B. Pentland: *Slow Song* (R31, SG30)
Exploring the Score

Look at the RH and LH positions in the box above the music. The RH plays flats and sharps, and the LH plays white keys. The RH sounds like A flat minor, and the LH sounds like C major. Discuss the similarity between these two groups of notes:

- Place your hands over the positions shown in the box.
- Play the first two notes in both hands (first and second fingers). What is the interval?
- Play the second and third notes in both hands and name the interval.
- Are all the intervals in the two patterns the same? [yes]

A. Gedike: *The Shepherd's Pipe, Op. 36, No. 55* (R32, SG31)
Exploring the Score

See the *Student Guide* for discussions of form and phrasing. As you practice, imagine a shepherd in the open country. How do the changes or contrasts in the B section affect this musical picture?

A. Gedike: *Invention No. 1: Fugato, Op. 36, No. 40* (R35, SG34)
Exploring the Score

Explain the term *fugato* and discuss its relation to this piece. Find the themes presented in mm. 1-4. Where do the hands reverse parts?

Practice Suggestion

Each hand plays an independent melody. Why is it helpful to practice contrapuntal pieces hands separately?

A. Gedike: *Study No. 1* (S17)
Exploring the Score

- What is the form? [ABA$_1$ or AB *coda*]
- Find the contrasts in the B section. [key change, inverted intervals, reversed phrases]
- What is the dynamic plan?
- Can you find references to C major and C minor? [mm. 20-21]

Practice Suggestion

Have students practice *staccato* pieces, such as this study, with a *legato* touch. This helps establish accurate fingering.

H. Bertini: *Study No. 6: Op. 166, No. 6* (S22)

Exploring the Score

There are no phrase markings and the music does not have an obvious melody. Explore ways to determine the length of phrases.

- Block the chords and listen for a harmonic resolution.
- Look for other clues such as *crescendo* and *diminuendo* marks.

Practice Suggestions

The music is marked *con pedale*.

- When will you depress the pedal and when will you lift it? [change the pedal on beats 1 and 3]
- Compare mm. 1-4 and 9-12. Which hands play on which beats? Keep the pedaling pattern consistent, even though the hands exchange the lead.

J.-B. Duvernoy: *Study No. 10: Op. 176, No. 17* (S26)

Exploring the Score

This piece is in F major. Find and label the tonic, subdominant, and dominant chords.

Practice Suggestions

Block the LH harmonies, then play the RH melody with the LH blocked chords. Have students practice the following chord pattern in different keys:

CREATIVE ACTIVITIES

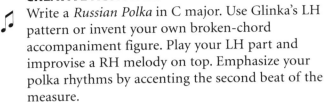
Write a *Russian Polka* in C major. Use Glinka's LH pattern or invent your own broken-chord accompaniment figure. Play your LH part and improvise a RH melody on top. Emphasize your polka rhythms by accenting the second beat of the measure.

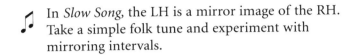
In *Slow Song*, the LH is a mirror image of the RH. Take a simple folk tune and experiment with mirroring intervals.

STUDY MODULE 4

Page	List	Composer	Title	Meter and Tempo	Musical and Stylistic Concepts
R8 SG11	A	Franz Joseph Haydn	Quadrille	3/8 Con spirito	✔ triads and 3rds in homophonic texture
R14 SG15	A	Franz Schubert	Écossaise	2/4 Allegretto	✔ melody with blocked chord accompaniment ✔ shifts in both hands ✔ contrasting dynamics in B section
R22 SG22	B	Clifford Poole	Fleas	6/8 Allegretto	✔ rests and *staccato* eighth notes ✔ requires careful counting
R23 SG23	B	Isak Berkovich	Mazurka	3/4 Allegro non troppo	✔ RH dotted rhythms ✔ *ostinato*-like LH pattern ✔ both hands in treble clef
R26 SG26	B	Aram Khachaturian	An Evening Tale	3/4 Andante cantabile	✔ waltz-style LH ✔ simple rhythmic patterns ✔ contrasting B section, RH accents ✔ numerous accidentals
R39 SG37	C	Carleton Elliott	Invention No. 7: Canon	4/4 Moderato	✔ moving eighth notes ✔ intricate coordination ✔ dovetail phrasing
S20		Soulima Stravinsky	Study No. 4: Cross Hands	3/4 Allegretto	✔ simple rhythms ✔ LH crosses over ✔ both hands in treble clef
S21		Carl Czerny	Study No. 5: Op. 777, No. 22	3/4 Allegro	✔ LH waltz bass ✔ RH grace notes and *staccato* ✔ rounded binary form

Assign first :

Study No. 5: Op. 777, No. 22	**Assign next when ready:** *Quadrille*
Écossaise.	*Mazurka*
Study No. 4: Cross Hands.	*An Evening Tale*
Invention No. 7: Canon	*Fleas*

Add quadrille, *écossaise*, mazurka, and waltz (*Study No. 5*) to the Dance Chart.

The style of accompaniment contributes to the mood and the contrasts of a composition. Use the repertoire in Study Module 4 as a basis for a discussion of accompaniment styles. Have students find examples of the following:
- accompaniments built of blocked or broken chords
- accompaniments consisting of single notes
- accompaniments where the LH crosses over the RH
- accompaniments which change to provide a contrast of sections

Also ask your students to find compositions that are made of two equal voices, rather than a single voice and an accompaniment.

F.J. Haydn: *Quadrille* (R8, SG11)

Exploring the Score

- How does Haydn create contrast in the B section? [change of key, change of register, new rhythmic figure with grace note]
- Name the two harmonies Haydn uses. [tonic and dominant]

Practice Suggestions

Articulate the RH two-note slurs by playing the second note *staccato*.

Grace notes give an additional sparkle to the notes they precede. This piece and *Study No. 5* by Czerny both include grace notes. Crush the grace note against the following note, and give it a *staccato* release.

F. Schubert: *Écossaise* (R14, SG15)

Exploring the Score

- How many two-measure phrases are there? [six]
- Can you find four measures that form a phrase? [mm. 5-8]
- Which group of four measures does not end in a C major cadence? [mm. 9-12, A minor cadence]

Discuss the relationship of the bass line to the harmony. Draw students' attention to the stepwise descent from tonic to dominant in mm. 1-4. Find the tonic and dominant harmonies in the B section.

C. Poole: *Fleas* (R22, SG22)

Exploring the Score

How does Poole suggest the movements of the fleas? Encourage students to use their imagination.

- Where do the fleas rest for a short time?
- Where do the fleas almost fall asleep?
- What happens to the fleas in mm. 14-17?

I. Berkovich: *Mazurka* (R23, SG23)

Exploring the Score

This piece is made up of four-measure phrases.

- Which two RH phrases are the same? [mm. 1-4, 17-21]
- Which two RH phrases are almost the same? [mm. 9-12, 13-16]

Practice Suggestions

Practice each four-measure phrase, first hands separately, then hands together.

Be sure to release the LH at the ends of slurs.

A. Khachaturian: *An Evening Tale* (R26, SG26)

Exploring the Score

The first four measures seem to say "Once upon a time…" and invite the listener in. Imagine a scene with someone dancing. What happens with the abrupt change in m. 20? Are there trumpets announcing the arrival of someone important? Is this a signal of something ominous or threatening?

C. Elliott: *Invention No. 7: Canon* (R39, SG37)

Practice Suggestions

See the exercise on p. 33 of the *Student Guide*. Concentrate on hand lifts at the end of slurs. Notice that in mm. 5-8 the slurs overlap.

S. Stravinsky: *Study No. 4: Cross Hands* (S20)

Exploring the Score

Compare this piece with *An Evening Tale* by Aram Khachaturian. Although the two pieces differ in sound, there are textural similarities. For example, both pieces rely heavily on 3rds.

Practice Suggestions

Read the LH in the treble clef (not the bass clef). Name other pieces where the LH part is written in the treble clef. [*Écossaise, Mazurka, An Evening Tale*]

C. Czerny: *Study No. 5: Op. 777, No. 22* (S21)

Exploring the Score

- This piece sounds like a dance. Name other dances that use triple meter.
- Block and label the LH chords.
- This piece is in F major. Can you find a group of measures in C major? [mm. 17-24]

Practice Suggestions

Play the RH melody and the LH in blocked chords. Listen carefully for RH dynamics and articulations. How does the term *scherzando* affect your interpretation?

CREATIVE ACTIVITIES

♪ Choose a familiar tune or folk song (such as *London Bridge, Row, Row, Row Your Boat*, or *Lavender's Blue*), and compose a short invention using this tune. (Review *Inventions Nos. 1, 3, 7*, and *8* for compositional ideas.) Write out your new *Invention* for a friend to play.

♪ Ask your students to suggest what sounds could be used in music about fleas, and have them play a short improvisation using these sounds.

STUDY MODULE 5

Page	List	Composer	Title	Meter and Tempo	Musical and Stylistic Concepts
R5 SG8	A	Wilhelm Friedemann Bach	Minuet in G Major	3/4 Grazioso	✔ RH eighth-note phrases ✔ LH quarter-note bass line ✔ dotted rhythms
R11 SG13	A	Franz Schubert	Ländler	3/4 Allegretto	✔ tonic and dominant harmonies outlined ✔ LH quarter-note waltz bass ✔ lyrical RH eighth-note phrases
R12 SG14	A	Muzio Clementi	Waltz	3/8 Allegro	✔ *sempre staccato* ✔ repeating LH 3rds and triads ✔ short RH phrases
R24 SG24	B	Nancy Telfer (arr.)	Land of the Silver Birch	4/4 With a steady pulse	✔ folk tune accompanied by descending scale pattern or triads ✔ clef changes in both hands ✔ wide reading range
R28 SG27	B	Jean Coulthard	The Whale's Sad Story	6/8 Not fast, moderately	✔ expressive ✔ RH occasionally in bass clef ✔ chromatic RH motive ✔ numerous accidentals
R29 SG28	B	Alexander Gedike	Military Trumpets, Op. 36, No. 53	6/8 Allegro vigoroso	✔ articulated rhythms imitate trumpet ✔ both hands in treble clef ✔ cadence patterns
R39 SG37	C	Pierre Gallant	Invention No. 6: Jazz Invention	4/4 Andante	✔ jazz sound from lowered 3rds and 7ths ✔ five-finger patterns outlined
S29		Alexander Gedike	Study No. 13	2/4 Allegro moderato	✔ contrary motion ✔ tetrachord patterns in each hand ✔ RH in bass clef

Assign first:
Invention No. 6: Jazz Invention . . . .
Study No. 13. . . . .
Waltz . . . .
Land of the Silver Birch . . . .

Assign next when ready:
Minuet in G Major
Military Trumpets, Op. 36, No. 53
Ländler
The Whale's Sad Story

Most of the pieces in this Module are in triple meter. This provides an excellent opportunity to review dance forms which use triple meter. Discuss the characteristics of the mazurka, the minuet, the waltz, and the *Ländler*. Compare Berkovich's *Mazurka* (R23) to the *Waltz* by Clementi and the *Ländler* by Schubert. The *Mazurka* has a natural stress on the second beat and often uses dotted rhythms. Both the *Waltz* and *Ländler* have a stress on the downbeat.

W. F. Bach: *Minuet in G Major* (R5, SG8)
Practice Suggestions

The LH part is challenging. Have students sight-read the piece hands separately, then divide the piece into short practice sections. Target a minimum number of repetitions for each section during practice. Increasing the number of repetitions is often a good way to learn a piece quickly.

Circle all the appearances of the RH rhythm found in m. 1.
- How many different versions can you find?
- Practice these measures, and add the first note of the following measure.

F. Schubert: *Ländler* (R11, SG13)
M. Clementi: *Waltz* (R12, SG14)
Exploring the Score

Although composers use many different chords to create contrast and variety, it is also possible to compose interesting music using only limited harmonic resources. In his *Ländler,* Schubert uses only tonic (I) and dominant (V) chords.
- Identify the I and V chords in the LH.
- Find the hidden I and V chords in the RH, mm. 1 and 3.
- Look for tonic and dominant chords (in both hands) in the A section of Clementi's *Waltz.*

Practice Suggestions

Both these dances are in E flat major. Review the E flat major scale.
Follow the pedal markings in Schubert's *Ländler:* down on the first beat, up on the second.

N. Telfer (arr.): *Land of the Silver Birch*
(R24, SG24)
Exploring the Score

The words to this camp song are printed in the *Student Guide.* How does the tune illustrate the words? Encourage students to imagine the sound of drums as this song is sung around a campfire.

J. Coulthard: *The Whale's Sad Story* (R28, SG27)
Exploring the Score

Making up a story to go with the music may help a student's musical interpretation of this piece.
- Why would a whale be sad?
- What kinds of sounds do whales make? How do we know?
- Why did Coulthard choose an accompaniment of broken intervals? What might the intervals represent?
- What happens to the whale when the RH moves down into the bass clef?

A. Gedike: *Military Trumpets, Op. 36, No. 53*
(R29, SG28)
Exploring the Score

Imagine the scene that Gedike is painting.
- What do you see? What is happening?
- How does the scene change in the B section?
- What is the mood of this piece? Is it calm or energetic?

P. Gallant: *Invention No. 6: Jazz Invention*
(R39, SG37)
Exploring the Score

Discuss the musical elements that contribute to the jazz flavor of this Invention. Draw the student's attention to the many D sharps and B flats. Play the piece without the accidentals so students can hear how essential the lowered 3rds and 7ths are to a jazz vocabulary.

A. Gedike: *Study No. 13* (S29)
Exploring the Score

The part that looks the hardest (the sixteenth notes) might actually be the easiest to play!
- What makes the sixteenth-note patterns easy?
- How many different sixteenth-note patterns are there?
- How many different eighth-note patterns are there?
- How are the last sixteenth note of each measure and the first eighth note of the next measure related?

CREATIVE ACTIVITIES

In *Land of the Silver Birch,* Telfer uses three different types of accompaniment: descending scale lines, blocked 5ths, and blocked triads. Create your own arrangement of a folk tune using three different accompaniment figures. Use *Land of the Silver Birch* or another song you know.

Having played the *Jazz Invention,* create your own jazz duet based on the following melodic fragment and chords.

STUDY MODULE 6

Page	List	Composer	Title	Meter and Tempo	Musical and Stylistic Concepts
R16 SG17	A	Ludwig van Beethoven	German Dance	3/4 Allegretto	✔ octave skips in both hands ✔ B section outlines G scale ✔ LH chord accompaniment ✔ minuet-trio structure
R21 SG21	B	Linda Niamath	Penguins	4/4 Waddling	✔ LH *staccato ostinato* ✔ lyrical RH melody ✔ challenging chromatic passages ✔ many accidentals
R30 SG29	B	István Szelényi	Faraway Regions	4/4 Lento armonioso	✔ unusual key signature ✔ whole-tone scale ✔ expressive, contemporary colors ✔ *p, pp, ppp,* and *pppp* dynamics
R36 SG35	C	Gordon A. McKinnon	Invention No. 2: The Argument	4/4 Moderato	✔ wide range, difficult skips ✔ dovetailing phrases ✔ syncopated entries ✔ several accidentals
R37 SG36	C	Ludwig van Beethoven	Invention No. 4: Little Piece, WoO 61a	2/4 Allegretto quasi andante	✔ several accidentals ✔ intricate coordination
R38 SG36	C	Pierre Gallant	Invention No. 5: In the Dorian Mode	2/4 Moderato	✔ ABA₁ form ✔ E minor five-finger pattern ✔ position shift for B section ✔ ends with LH E major triad
S24		Aram Khachaturian	Study No 8: Skipping Rope	4/4 Allegro	✔ both hands in treble clef ✔ numerous accidentals ✔ *staccato* texture
S28		Linda Niamath	Study No. 12: Butterflies	2/4 Delicately	✔ pentatonic scales ✔ use of pedal
S32		Dmitri Kabalevsky	Study No. 16: The Little Juggler, Op. 89, No. 21	3/8 Scherzando leggiero	✔ scherzo-like octave *staccato* study

Assign first:

Invention No. 2: The Argument . . . .
Penguins . . . .
Study No. 12: Butterflies . . . .
Study No. 8: Skipping Rope . . . .
Invention No. 5: In the Dorian Mode

Assign next when ready:

German Dance
Invention No. 4: Little Piece, WoO 61a
Faraway Regions
Study No. 16: The Little Juggler, Op. 89, No. 21

Study Module 6 could be subtitled "The Sound Study Module." Have students look for examples of whole-tone scales, pentatonic scales, and chromatic scales. In *Butterflies,* Linda Niamath uses the pedal to enhance the colors.

This Module contains the most challenging repertoire in Level 2. These pieces will require careful practice.

Add Beethoven's *German Dance* to the Dance Chart.

L. van Beethoven: *German Dance* (R16, SG17)
Exploring the Score
Discuss Beethoven's use of two- and three-note slurs in both sections. Remind students to stress the first note of each slur, even if it is an upbeat.

Practice Suggestions
Review the fingering of the G major scale and look for the complete scale in the Trio section. Block the scale in finger groups to promote fluency.

The LH accompaniment consists of blocked and broken chords.
- Label in the score the G major chords (tonic–I).
- In mm. 10 and 12, label the E minor and D major chords.
- Practice the harmonic progression I-V-I in G major, E minor, and D major.
- Find the ways in which Beethoven writes this harmonic progression using these chords.

L. Niamath: *Penguins* (R21, SG21)
Exploring the Score
Explain the tritone as an interval resulting from the combination of three whole steps (two whole steps makes a major 3rd). Help your student discover Linda Niamath's use of the tritone as the interval between the hands in the chromatic scale passages.

Practice Suggestions
Isolate the chromatic figures for technical practice. Practice hands separately, saying finger numbers aloud; then play hands together slowly. Give special attention to the RH second finger.

I. Szelényi: *Faraway Regions* (R30, SG29)
Exploring the Score
Szelényi created a special key signature for a whole-tone scale based on three black keys (F sharp, G sharp, A sharp) and three white keys (C, D, E). Circle the notes representing black keys. Explore whole-tone scales with your student:
1. Play whole-tone scales in different registers. Play black keys with the LH and white keys with the RH, then reverse the pattern.
2. Build another whole-tone scale. [F, G, A, B, C sharp, D sharp]

Faraway Regions is a gold mine of expressive sound. Play the *Celebration Series* recording of the piece. Discuss the markings in the score (dynamics, pedal indications, Italian terms).

- Can you imagine the sound of the piece just by looking at the music?
- Where should you use the pedal? Mark the pedal changes in the music.

G.A. McKinnon: *Invention No. 2: The Argument* (R36, SG35)
Exploring the Score
The *Student Guide* describes this musical argument.
- What two triads are outlined in mm. 1-2? [E minor, B major]

L. van Beethoven: *Invention No. 4: Little Piece, WoO 61a* (R37, SG35)
Exploring the Score
Look for these two melodic fragments, and label them in the music:

Discuss the relationship of "*y*" to the other voice (see mm. 4, 10, and 11).

P. Gallant: *Invention No. 5: In the Dorian Mode* (R38, SG36)
Exploring the Score
- What five-finger pattern is used in mm. 1-8? [E minor]
- Where do the hands change position? [m. 9]
- Where does the main theme return? [RH m. 14, LH m. 15; notice the D major scale, mm. 13-14]

A. Khachaturian: *Study No. 8: Skipping Rope* (S24)
Exploring the Score
- What is the form of this piece? [ABA]
- Examine the *legato* and *staccato* notes in the A sections. Do both hands have the same *legato-staccato* patterns in the B section (mm. 9-16)?

L. Niamath: *Study No. 12: Butterflies* (S28)
Exploring the Score
Another shocking key signature! Your student will be relieved to discover that in fact every note is played on the black keys. Discuss pentatonic scales in relation to this study.

Practice Suggestions
Play the *Celebration Series* recording and ask students to imagine a scene with butterflies. Use the recording as an example of the light, delicate touch this piece requires. Have students block the various hand positions for accuracy.

D. Kabalevsky: *Study No. 16: The Little Juggler,*
Op. 89, No. 21 (S32)
Exploring the Score
What goes up must come down.
- How do the laws of gravity affect our juggler?
- Can music defy these laws? [see ending]

Practice Suggestions
The many jumps and accidentals make this piece difficult to read. To discover Kabalevsky's note plan, transpose all the notes into one octave, centered on middle C.

- Choose one finger for the RH and one for the LH.
- Play the first two notes (B, C)–B with the LH, C with the RH.
- Stay in this keyboard position as you add the next pitches (C, D flat, C, C, C sharp, D, D, E flat, etc.). Play the D flat, C sharp, and E flat with your LH, the repeated Cs and Ds with your RH.
- Play through the piece using this condensed version of the notes. This type of exercise will help you learn whether the chromatic notes move up or down.

As you practice the actual pitches, first play *legato* to gain security on the leaps.

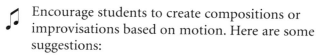

CREATIVE ACTIVITIES

Discuss the musical portrayal of physical movement in *German Dance* (dancing), *Penguins* (waddling), *Study No. 12: Butterflies* (fluttering), and *Study No. 16: The Little Juggler* (tossing and falling).

Encourage students to create compositions or improvisations based on motion. Here are some suggestions:
- Compose a piece called *The Flower Garden*. Include a butterfly and a bumblebee. Use the damper pedal and play only on the black keys.
- Improvise a musical picture of clouds on a summer afternoon. Use a whole-tone position (play three keys with the LH and three keys with the RH), and sustain the sounds with the damper pedal.
- Compose a new LH *ostinato* to go with the RH melody of *Penguins*.

LEVEL 2 SUMMARY
- How many different dances are on your **Dance Chart?** Add to this list as you continue study in the next album.
- What new pieces did you compose for Level 2? What are the titles of your compositions? With your teacher's help, notate some of the pieces.
- What studies were easiest for you? Which were the most difficult? Why? How did you solve those technical problems?

Level 3

The Publications
Level 3 of the *Celebration Series* includes the following publications:
Piano Repertoire Album 3
Piano Studies Album 3 & 4 (level 3 only)
Student Guide 3
Recording of *Repertoire & Studies 3*

The Repertoire
The *Piano Repertoire Album 3* is divided into three lists:
- List A includes a selection of pieces composed during the Baroque period (*ca* 1600 to *ca* 1750).
- List B includes a selection of pieces composed during the Classical period (*ca* 1750 to *ca* 1820) as well as pieces in the Classical style written during the 19th and 20th centuries.
- List C includes a selection of pieces composed during the Romantic era (*ca* 1820 to *ca* 1910) and the 20th century.

Musical Development
Level 3 provides a transition from the early intermediate level of piano study to the mid-range of the intermediate repertoire. With these pieces, the student will become further acquainted with Baroque dances and two- and three-part forms. The List B pieces introduce the Classical sonatina with its characteristic figures: scale passages, cadence patterns, and accompaniment styles. List C pieces feature three- and four-voice textures, independent hand and finger technique, and Romantic and contemporary forms and sounds.

Musical Tips
As students work through this Level, they will accumulate knowledge about musical style that they can apply to other pieces they study. Your student can use the blank page at the end of the *Student Guide* to write down these points, which are identified as musical tips (**TIP:**). Encourage your students to keep track of these points, and to add to their list as they progress from Level to Level.

The Range of Difficulty
The range of difficulty in Level 3 is represented by the following pieces:
- *Lullaby* by Johann Philipp Kirnberger is an example of an easier piece from Study Module 1.
- *Musette in D Major* by J.S. Bach and *Sonatina in G Major, Op. 151, No. 1* by Anton Diabelli are examples of the most difficult pieces from Study Module 6.

The Study Modules
The six Study Module discussions in the Level 3 are organized into the following categories:
- *Exploring the Score*
- *Practice Suggestions*
- *Creative Activities*

Exploring the Score is designed as an interactive exercise between teacher and student. Questions are addressed to the student, as you might ask them during the lesson. *Practice Suggestions* are also directed to the student. The *Creative Activities* act as reinforcement for your students' understanding of a musical concept and can provide a springboard for their creativity and imagination.

Please refer to the Foreword for an explanation of how to use the suggested order of assignment within each Module.

The chart on the opposite page lists all the repertoire and studies from Level 3. Page numbers for works in the *Piano Repertoire Album 3* and the *Piano Studies Album 3* are found in the first column. Study Module numbers for each composition are found in the fourth column.

	Page	Composer	Title	Study Module
Piano Repertoire Album 3				
List A	R4	George Frideric Handel	Gavotte in G Major, HWV 491	4
	R5	German Folk Melody, J. P. Kirnberger (arr.)	Lullaby	1
	R6	Christian Petzold, J. S. Bach (attr.)	Minuet in G Minor, BWV Anh. 115	5
	R8	Johann Adam Hiller	Andante in A Major	3
	R9	Johann Friedrich Graeff	Air in A Minor, Op. 7, No. 4	2
	R10	Henry Purcell	Hornpipe in B Flat	4
	R11	Johann Krieger	Sarabanda in D Minor	6
	R12	Anon.	Anglaise in D Minor	2
	R13	Anon., J. S. Bach (attr.)	Musette in D Major, BWV Anh. 126	6
List B	R14	Ludwig van Beethoven	Sonatina in G Major, Anh. 5 (Second Movement: Romanze)	1
	R16	Franz Joseph Haydn	Vivace in D Major, Hob. XVII: Anh.	4
	R18	Anton Diabelli	Sonatina in G Major, Op. 151, No. 1 (First Movement)	6
	R20	Wolfgang Amadeus Mozart	Viennese Sonatina No. 4 in B Flat	5
	R21	Alexander Gedike	Sonatina in C Major, Op. 36, No. 20	3
	R22	Ignaz Pleyel	Rondo in G Major	1
	R24	Carl Reinecke	Sonatina in G Major, Op. 136, No. 2 (First Movement)	2
	R25	Carl Reinecke	Sonatina in G Major, Op. 136, No. 2 (Second Movement)	2
List C	R26	Pyotr Il'yich Tchaikovsky	Morning Prayer, Op. 39, No. 1	6
	R27	Alexandr T. Grechaninov	A Frightening Story, Op. 98, No. 11	3
	R28	Béla Bartók	Bagatelle, Op. 6, No. 6	6
	R29	William Lea	Snoopy	2
	R30	Linda Niamath	Turtle	1
	R31	Boris Berlin	The Haunted Castle	3
	R32	Béla Bartók	Slovak Peasant's Dance	4
	R34	Jean Coulthard	A Little Joke	2
	R36	Alexandr T. Grechaninov	Mazurka, Op. 98, No. 13	4
	R37	Lajos Papp	Variations	5
	R38	Samuil Maikapar	Ballad, Op. 28	5
	R40	Otto Joachim	Plastic Soldier	1
Piano Studies Album 3				
	S4	Cornelius Gurlitt	Study No. 1	5
	S5	Carl Czerny	Study No. 2	2
	S6	Ludwig Schytte	Study No. 3	5
	S7	Henri Bertini	Study No. 4	4
	S8	Carl Czerny	Study No. 5: Op. 139, No. 7	1
	S9	Antoine Henry Lemoine	Study No. 6: Op. 37, No. 17	2
	S10	Ludwig Schytte	Study No. 7	3
	S11	Johann Nepomuk Hummel	Study No. 8	1
	S12	Cornelius Gurlitt	Study No. 9	3
	S13	Alexander Gedike	Study No. 10: Op. 32, No. 12	6
	S14	Carl Czerny	Study No. 11: Op. 139, No. 24	4
	S15	Johann Friedrich Burgmüller	Study No. 12: Op. 100, No. 2 (L'Arabesque)	3
	S16	Daniel Gottlob Türk	Study No. 13: Having Fun	5
	S17	Hermann Berens	Study No. 14	6

STUDY MODULE 1

Page	List	Composer	Title	Meter and Tempo	Musical and Stylistic Concepts
R5 SG10	A	German Folk Melody, Johann Philipp Kirnberger (arr.)	Lullaby	6/8 Andantino	✔ two independent voices ✔ broken-chord inversions ✔ four-measure phrases ✔ sequence
R14 SG18	B	Ludwig van Beethoven	Sonatina in G Major, Anh. 5 (Second Movement: Romanze)	6/8 Andante	✔ melody with broken-chord accompaniment ✔ scales ✔ *portato* touch
R22 SG23	B	Ignaz Pleyel	Rondo in G Major	2/4 Allegro	✔ two independent LH voices ✔ grace notes and slurs ✔ *staccato* articulation ✔ scale passages
R30 SG30	C	Linda Niamath	Turtle	3/2 Slowly and steadily	✔ slow half notes ✔ four-voice texture ✔ *legato* articulation ✔ 4ths, 5ths, 6ths ✔ ABA_1
R40 SG37	C	Otto Joachim	Plastic Soldier	4/4 Fast march	✔ changing rhythmic patterns ✔ LH octaves against melody ✔ twelve-tone technique
S8		Carl Czerny	Study No. 5: Op. 139, No. 7	3/4 Allegretto	✔ RH blocked 6ths and 3rds ✔ wrist *staccato* exercise
S11		Johann Nepomuk Hummel	Study No. 8	2/4 Andante con moto	✔ RH *staccato* articulation ✔ LH blocked intervals

Assign first:

Lullaby. . . . . *Rondo in G Major*

Sonatina in G Major, Anh. 5
   (Second Movement: Romanze)

Plastic Soldier. . . . . *Turtle*

Study No. 5: Op. 139, No. 7 . . . . *Study No. 8*

Assign next when ready:

The music in this Study Module features contrast and variety. For example, *Lullaby, Turtle,* and the Beethoven *Romanze* have long melodic lines that require *legato* fingering. *Study No. 5* and *Study No. 6* require a light *staccato* touch. In Pleyel's *Rondo in G Major,* the articulation is varied and the LH plays two independent voices.

Draw the student's attention to the relationship between tonic and dominant harmonies.

TIP: When harmony alternates between tonic and dominant, the stress is usually on the dominant.

- Find a six-measure emphasis on the dominant in the Beethoven *Sonatina.* [mm. 16-21]
- Find a twelve-measure emphasis on the dominant in Pleyel's *Rondo.* [mm. 16-27]

German Folk Melody, J. P. Kirnberger (arr.):
Lullaby (R5, SG10)
Exploring the Score
Have students play only the first note of each strong beat to discover the melodic line. This will make students aware of the dynamic shape of the melody and will aid in memorization. (See the section on "Dynamic Shaping" in the *Student Guide* article.)
- Find the sequence. [mm. 9 - 11]
- Find and label the chords in m. 1. [I_4^6, I_3^5]

Practice Suggestions
Clap the rhythm, counting aloud, to emphasize the rocking motion of two beats per measure.

TIP: To practice figures which change direction, group the notes which flow in one direction. Use words to reinforce the rocking motion.

L. van Beethoven: *Sonatina in G Major, Anh. 5 (Second Movement: Romanze)* (R14, SG18)
Exploring the Score
Look for contrasting themes, keys, and textures. The *Student Guide* stresses the importance of the *coda*.
- Where was the thematic material of the *coda* first presented?
- Find examples of short-short-long phrase structures (2 + 2 + 4 measures).
  TIP: This phrase structure is an important characteristic of music from the Classical era.
- Name and label the chords in this piece. [primarily I, IV, and V^7]

I. Pleyel: *Rondo in G Major* (R22, SG23)
Exploring the Score
TIP: Composers frequently approach a cadence with an increase of harmonic and rhythmic intensity.

How does Pleyel build the intensity in mm. 13-16? [faster notes, more frequent stresses]

Pleyel uses grace notes and chords to imitate the bells, triangles, and drums of a Turkish march.

Play the *Celebration Series* recording and listen for the exciting variety of sounds. The lower LH notes give the clue to the rhythmic stress.

L. Niamath: *Turtle* (R30, SG30)
Exploring the Score
Ask your student to think of musical elements a composer might use to write music about turtles. Look for these elements in the score. [*legato* touch, slow tempo, tenor register]

Practice Suggestion
Legato fingering is an important aspect of this piece. Hold the dotted whole notes for their full value and pay attention to the release of the shorter notes.

O. Joachim: *Plastic Soldier* (R40, SG37)
Exploring the Score
Use the *Student Guide* to help find and label the twelve-tone row in mm. 1-8 and 9-13.

Which instruments are represented in this piece?

C. Czerny: *Study No. 5: Op. 139, No. 7* (S8)
Practice Suggestions
Use this study to develop a comfortable hand *staccato*. Here are two preparatory drills. Maintain a rounded hand position. Practice hands separately.

J.N. Hummel: *Study No. 8* (S11)
Exploring the Score
Label the tonic, subdominant, and dominant chords. Circle the measures that include two harmonies.
TIP: A composer can increase musical tension by increasing the frequency of harmonic changes.

Practice Suggestions
To learn the notes and fingering:
1. Practice the RH melody with a *legato* touch.
2. Add the LH chords only on the first beat of the measure and on chord changes.

CREATIVE ACTIVITIES
♪ Listen to the *Celebration Series* recording of *Turtle* or *Plastic Soldier,* and make up a story to go with the music. Illustrate your story with a drawing.

♪ Create another piece using the same twelve-tone row that Otto Joachim used in *Plastic Soldier.* The pitches must be used in order. Give your piece a title.

STUDY MODULE 2

Page	List	Composer	Title	Meter and Tempo	Musical and Stylistic Concepts
R9 SG13	A	Johann Friedrich Graeff	Air in A Minor, Op. 7, No. 4	4/4 Andante con espressione	✔ *cantabile* melody ✔ *legato* RH, detached LH ✔ question and answer pattern
R12 SG16	A	Anon.	Anglaise in D Minor	4/4 Allegro	✔ early Classical style ✔ Alberti bass ✔ ABA form
R24 SG24	B	Carl Reinecke	Sonatina in G Major, Op. 136, No. 2 (First Movement)	4/4 Allegro moderato	✔ *cantabile* melody ✔ Alberti bass
R25 SG25	B	Carl Reinecke	Sonatina in G Major, Op. 136, No. 2 (Second Movement)	3/4 Tempo di menuetto	✔ minuet style ✔ upbeat figure ✔ three-voice texture
R29 SG29	C	William Lea	Snoopy	4/4 Very lively	humorous elements: ✔ frequent dynamic changes ✔ crushed four-note groups ✔ off-beat accents
R34 SG33	C	Jean Coulthard	A Little Joke	3/4 Quite fast and merrily	surprise elements: ✔ clapping ✔ missing downbeats
S5		Carl Czerny	Study No. 2	4/4 Allegretto	✔ RH broken-chord triplets ✔ melody indicated by double-stemmed notes
S9		Antoine Henry Lemoine	Study No. 6: Op. 37, No. 17	2/4 Allegretto	✔ RH zig-zag sixteenth-note patterns

Assign first:
Air in A Minor, Op. 7, No. 4 . . . .
Sonatina in G Major, Op. 136, No. 2 . . . .
   (First Movement)
Snoopy . . . .
Study No. 2 . . . .

Assign next when ready:
Anglaise in D Minor
Sonatina in G Major, Op. 136, No. 2
   (Second Movement)
A Little Joke
Study No. 6: Op. 37, No. 17

The pieces in Study Module 2 present an opportunity to discuss a variety of LH styles. LH accompaniments are written as countermelodies, melodic duets, and contrapuntal voices. What type of LH accompaniment or melody is used in each of these pieces?

   Air in A Minor [contrapuntal]
   Anglaise in D Minor [Alberti bass, countermelody]
   Sonatina in G Major, First Movement [Alberti bass]
   Sonatina in G Major, Second Movement [chordal]
   Snoopy [contrary motion]
   A Little Joke [part of melody]
   Study No. 2 [melody]
   Study No. 6 [countermelody, chords]

J.F. Graeff: *Air in A Minor, Op. 7, No. 4* (R9, SG13)
Exploring the Score
TIP: Composers often write phrases in balanced pairs. The first phrase – a question – usually ends on a note other than the keynote. The second phrase – the answer – usually ends on the keynote. A parallel answer starts the same as the question. A contrasting answer starts differently from the question.
- Find a pair of question-and-answer phrases in this piece. [mm. 1-4 and mm. 5-8]
- Is the answer parallel or contrasting?
- Does the question end on the keynote?
- Does the answer end on the keynote?

Practice Suggestion
Divide the piece into short practice units and plan the articulation. Decide where the LH should be *legato* and where it should be detached.

Anon: *Anglaise in D Minor* (R12, SG16)
Exploring the Score
Block the chords and analyze the LH harmony.
- What is the key of the B section? [F major]
- What is the relationship of this key to D minor? [relative major]

Practice Suggestions
Students may find it easier to hear and learn the correct articulation one hand at a time. For the first week, have students concentrate on RH articulation and dynamic shaping. Play the LH part in blocked chords so they can hear the accompanying harmonies. During the second week, practice the LH part as written, then add the RH.

C. Reinecke: *Sonatina in G Major, Op. 136, No. 2 (Second Movement)* (R25, SG25)
Exploring the Score
Use the *Student Guide* as a basis for examining the music. Downbeats can be interpreted in different ways, according to their time value and their position in a phrase or slur.
- Think of longer note values as musical goals. Find downbeats which are longer than a quarter note.
- Normally, you taper the last notes of a phrase. Look for downbeats which end a phrase.
- Give a slight emphasis to the first note of a slur. Find downbeats which are part of a two-note slur.

TIP: A musical "sigh" has its emphasis on the first note.

Practice Suggestions
Two suggestions for hands-together practice:
1. For mm. 1-4 and 7-10, play the RH as written. Play only the LH notes which sound exactly with RH notes. Listen to the duet between the hands.

2. For mm. 4-7 and 12-16, play the RH as written, and block the LH notes (use mostly half-note values). Check the accuracy of the dotted rhythm by counting sixteenth notes aloud.

W. Lea: *Snoopy* (R29, SG29)
Exploring the Score
Listen to the *Celebration Series* recording and have students make up a story to go with the music. Use this story to help emphasize dynamic contrasts, position shifts, and articulation. How do these elements create humor?

J. Coulthard: *A Little Joke* (R34, SG33)
Exploring the Score
Composers can create musical humor by doing the unexpected. Have your student think of ways to create musical surprises. Look for these musical jokes in the score:
- five-measure phrases (instead of four)
- a single two-measure phrase
- clapping (instead of playing)
- inconsistent endings for a familiar motive [mm. 1, 11, 26]
- imitation of laughter
- interruption of a long *crescendo* with a rest

C. Czerny: *Study No. 2* (S5)
Exploring the Score
Ask students to identify which hand plays the melody by looking for the following:
- melody in the LH [mm. 1-4, notice the *forte* marking]
- duet between the hands [mm. 5-8, notice the double stems in the RH]
- melody in the RH [mm. 9-12]

Practice Suggestions
- For mm. 1-4, play the LH melody as written and play the RH in blocked chords.
- Circle the RH quarter notes in mm. 5-8. Practice these notes using a drop-lift motion for the slurs. Then play the RH as written. Keep the eighth notes light, and remember to articulate the two-note slurs.

A.H. Lemoine: *Study No. 6: Op. 37, No. 17* (S9)
Exploring the Score
Sometimes composers create complicated figures from simple motives. This piece is constructed on a motive of three descending eighth notes.
- Can you see this motive in the LH?
- An expert musical sleuth will soon discover this motive hidden in the RH sixteenth notes.

- Can you find this motive anywhere else? Give it a try!

Practice Suggestion

Circle the notes of the melodic skeleton:

Have students play only these notes (so they can follow the melodic line), then play the RH as written.

CREATIVE ACTIVITIES

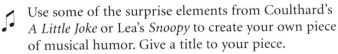 Improvise a new answer to the musical question in Graeff's *Air in A Minor*. Your answer can be either parallel or contrasting.

Use some of the surprise elements from Coulthard's *A Little Joke* or Lea's *Snoopy* to create your own piece of musical humor. Give a title to your piece.

Using the melody of Reinecke's *Sonatina in G Major, (First Movement)*, make your own arrangement trying different accompaniment styles, such as LH blocked chords in half notes, and LH duet countermelody in quarter notes. Remember to add dynamics and rests.

STUDY MODULE 3

Page	List	Composer	Title	Meter and Tempo	Musical and Stylistic Concepts
R8 SG12	A	Johann Adam Hiller	Andante in A Major	3/8 Andante	✔ predictable phrasing ✔ lilting dance
R21 SG22	B	Alexander Gedike	Sonatina in C Major, Op. 36, No. 20	4/4 Allegro moderato	✔ sonatina form ✔ contrasting themes, dynamics, textures
R27 SG27	C	Alexandr T. Grechaninov	A Frightening Story, Op. 98, No. 11	4/4 Moderato	✔ second inversion chords ✔ programmatic elements: strong accents, tempo changes, and chromaticism
R31 SG31	C	Boris Berlin	The Haunted Castle	4/4 Andantino	✔ double 3rds ✔ use of pedal ✔ whole-tone harmonies
S10		Ludwig Schytte	Study No. 7	3/8 Agitato	✔ blocked chords ✔ repeated notes
S12		Cornelius Gurlitt	Study No. 9	3/4 Allegretto	✔ undulating eighth notes ✔ broken-chord accompaniment
S15		Johann Friedrich Burgmüller	Study No. 12: Op. 100, No. 2 (L'Arabesque)	2/4 Allegro scherzando	✔ five-finger pattern ✔ *legato* and *staccato* articulation ✔ blocked chords

Assign first:
Andante in A Major
Sonatina in C Major, Op. 36, No. 20 . . . .
A Frightening Story, Op. 98, No. 11 . . . .
Study No. 9. . . . .

Assign next when ready:

Study No. 7
The Haunted Castle
Study No. 12: Op. 100, No. 2 (L'Arabesque)

The pieces in this Study Module vary widely in mood. Encourage your students to describe the pieces they study. Discuss the story or picture of the piece, the colors, or feelings. There are no wrong answers. Students will have their own individual perceptions. The goal is to develop musical imagination and sensitivity to the expressive quality of sound.

In the Baroque and early Classical periods, articulation was a primary means of defining meter and mood. The LH lines of many keyboard dances imitate the bowing of a cello or the tonguing of a bassoon. See the article "Playing Baroque Music" on p. 7 of the *Student Guide*. Explore the variety of possibilities for articulation with your student.

J.A. Hiller: *Andante in A Major* (R8, SG12)
Exploring the Score
There are two options for LH articulation:
1. Detach all the eighth notes.
2. Slur the eighth notes from the first beat to the second.

Compare the RH slurs in the A and B sections.
- Which section has ascending slurred notes?
- Which section has descending slurred notes?
- How does the direction of the notes affect the dynamics?

A. Gedike: *Sonatina in C Major, Op. 36, No. 20* (R21, SG22)
Exploring the Score
Explore the contrasting textures in this sonatina:
- *forte* chords
- sixteenth-note runs
- Alberti bass
- slurred eighth notes

A. T. Grechaninov: *A Frightening Story, Op. 98, No. 11* (R27, SG27)
Exploring the Score
- What effects does Grechaninov create with his use of the bass register, half steps (chromaticism), and changes of tempo?
- Can you hear and feel the tension in the music?

B. Berlin: *The Haunted Castle* (R31, SG31)
Exploring the Score
Have students listen to the *Celebration Series* recording with their eyes closed, imagining the scene this music evokes. Discuss the musical elements Berlin uses to create a mysterious, other-worldly effect:
- keyboard range
- damper pedal
- *staccato* articulation with pedal
- chords other than major and minor

Practice Suggestions
Touch and tone are of primary importance. Each sound contributes to a convincing interpretation. Use the performance on the *Celebration Series* recording as a model. Experiment with different *staccato* touches to create a similar sound on your piano.

L. Schytte: *Study No. 7* (S10)
Practice Suggestions
This study highlights quick repeated notes in both hands. **TIP:** There are two approaches to playing repeated notes. One method is to pull the fingers in toward the palm of the hand. The other is to extend the fingers as they play. As an exercise, have students play a C major scale, hands separately, repeating each note three times. Use a **3-2-1** fingering and try both of these approaches to repeated notes.

C. Gurlitt: *Study No. 9* (S12)
Practice Suggestions
This piece is primarily an exercise in dynamic contrast. Every note is part of the dynamic plan.
- How many dynamic markings can you find?
- What is the dynamic plan for two-note slurs?
- How can you make your practice focus on dynamics?

J.F. Burgmüller: *Study No. 12: Op. 100, No. 2 (L'Arabesque)* (S15)
Exploring the Score
- What is the form of this piece? Is the A section repeated exactly in mm. 19-26?
- Circle the chord tones in the RH slurred groups in mm. 3-6.
- Where does Burgmüller use syncopation? [mm. 8 and 24]
- Everyone loves *Arabesque*. What makes this piece such a student favorite?
  - sixteenths sound difficult, but are easy to play (no crossing)
  - rhythm is predictable and strong
  - LH chords feel comfortable
  - hands are rhythmically coordinated

Practice Suggestions
Use words such as *Mis-sis-sip-pi mud* to reinforce the even rhythm of the sixteenth-note patterns.

CREATIVE ACTIVITIES
Gedike's *Sonatina in C Major* is like a dance. Play the *Celebration Series* recording. What images come to mind with the contrasts in dynamics, rhythm, and texture? Choreograph the piece. Use different dance steps for the opening *forte* chords, the delicate *piano* answer, and the new motive in m. 5.

The *Student Guide* suggests a plot for *A Frightening Story*. Add more details to this adventure.

Berlin's *Haunted Castle* paints a vivid musical picture. Using chords other than major and minor, create a piece that tells a story about another haunted place. Give your piece a title.

STUDY MODULE 4

Page	List	Composer	Title	Meter and Tempo	Musical and Stylistic Concepts
R4 SG9	A	George Frideric Handel	Gavotte in G Major, HWV 491	4/4 Allegretto	✔ slurred groups in RH melody ✔ balanced phrases ✔ LH quarter-note accompaniment
R10 SG14	A	Henry Purcell	Hornpipe in B Flat	3/4 Allegretto	✔ characteristic hornpipe rhythm ✔ two-voice texture
R16 SG19	B	Franz Joseph Haydn	Vivace in D Major, Hob. XVII: Anh.	2/4 Vivace	✔ fast two-note slurs and *staccato* notes ✔ position changes ✔ LH double 3rds
R32 SG32	C	Béla Bartók	Slovak Peasant's Dance	2/4 Allegro	✔ rhythmic patterns of quarters and eighths ✔ *staccato* with syncopated accents
R36 SG34	C	Alexandr T. Grechaninov	Mazurka, Op. 98, No. 13	3/4 Tempo di mazurka	✔ three-voice texture ✔ typical mazurka dotted rhythms
S7		Henri Bertini	Study No. 4	3/4 Allegretto	✔ octave shifts ✔ scales ✔ written-out trill ✔ 7th chords
S14		Carl Czerny	Study No. 11: Op. 139, No. 24	3/8 Allegro	✔ short *staccato* motives ✔ written-out turn figures ✔ broken-chord waltz bass

Assign first:
Hornpipe in B Flat . . . .
Vivace in D Major, Hob. XVII: Anh.
Mazurka, Op. 98, No. 13 . . . .
Study No. 11: Op. 139, No. 24 . . . .

Assign next when ready:
Gavotte in G Major, HWV 491

Slovak Peasant's Dance

Study No. 4

Most of the pieces in this Study Module are dances or have a dance-like quality. Read through the list of dances on p. 7 of the *Student Guide*. Upbeats, downbeats, and rhythmic units have special significance in dance music. Composers vary the length of rhythmic units to provide interest and variety. These differing lengths create patterns of rhythmic intensity and relaxation.

An investigation of rhythmic units provides the student with insight into the composer's intent and clues for interpretation. Here are the rhythmic units for four dances in this Study Module. Compare these with the shape of the melody in each case:

STUDY MODULE 4 (cont'd)

Discuss the characteristics of each dance. If possible, show videos of Baroque dances or demonstrate the steps.

Encourage students to compare the different dances, and to add to this list as their dance repertoire expands. (If your students began a Dance Chart in Level 2, they can add these dances.)
- Which dances originated in a particular country? [*Gavotte* is French, *Hornpipe* is British, *Mazurka* is Polish]
- Which dances are in duple meter? [*Gavotte, Slovak Peasant's Dance*] in triple meter? [*Hornpipe, Mazurka*]
- Which dance has an upbeat? [*Gavotte*]
- Which dances use dotted rhythms? [*Hornpipe, Mazurka*]

G.F. Handel: *Gavotte in G Major, HWV 491* (R4, SG9)
Exploring the Score
Most *gavottes* have a duple meter and four-measure phrases that begin and end in the middle of the measure. However, since *Gavotte* has a quadruple meter and the phrases begin on the last beat of the measure, it has a different rhythmic emphasis. Find all the occurrences of this rhythm:

The quarter note is the goal of this pattern.
- How is the quarter note harmonized in mm. 1-2? [G major, the tonic]
- In mm. 17-19, these quarter notes form part of a scale. Can you find other scale figures? [mm. 3, 13, and 15] The descending scale in m. 3 balances the rising notes in mm. 1-2.

TIP: Most Baroque dances are in binary form. The A section shifts to the dominant key, and the B section returns to the tonic key. Does *Gavotte* follow the pattern?

H. Purcell: *Hornpipe in B Flat* (R10, SG14)
Exploring the Score
Circle the melodic notes on the first and third beats of mm. 1-4. The LH part parallels this descending stepwise line. Find the ascending stepwise movement in mm. 9-12.

Practice Suggestions
See the rhythmic exercises in the *Student Guide*. For rhythmic reinforcement, have the student tap the rhythms and create a dance step with stresses on the first and third beats.

F.J. Haydn: *Vivace in D Major, Hob. XVII: Anh.* (R16, SG19)
Exploring the Score
This piece is dominated by a four-note articulation pattern: *staccato–staccato–*two-note slur.
- **TIP:** For a longer musical line, group short, repeated motives into larger units. For example, mm. 1-8 fall into two four-measure phrases.

- Where are the phrases in mm. 9-24? (The dynamic markings provide a clue.)

B. Bartók: *Slovak Peasant's Dance* (R32, SG32)
Practice Suggestions
There is only one *legato* passage in this piece. [LH, mm. 47-54] The rest of the notes are detached. See the *Student Guide* discussion of *staccato, tenuto,* and *portato* articulation. For *portato* practice, play a scale, either with one finger or with a traditional fingering, giving each tone as much of its full length as possible, while playing detached.

A.T. Grechaninov: *Mazurka, Op. 98, No. 13* (R36, SG34)
Exploring the Score
Most mazurkas have dotted rhythms, syncopation, and a stress on the second or third beat. How many of these elements are present in this mazurka?

H. Bertini: *Study No. 4* (S7)
Exploring the Score
- What musical elements unify this piece? [three-note rhythmic motive, accompaniment style]
- How does the B section provide contrast? [melody shifts to LH, key change, position shifts]

C. Czerny: *Study No. 11: Op. 139, No. 24* (S14)
Practice Suggestions
Notice the double notes on the LH downbeats.
1. Divide the LH accompaniment between the hands. Play the first beat with the LH and the second and third beats with the RH.
2. Aim for the same sound with the LH alone. Crush the RH grace notes against the downbeat note.

CREATIVE ACTIVITY
Handel's *Gavotte in G Major* contains a musical question and answer pattern (mm. 1-4 and mm. 5-8). Is the answer parallel or contrasting? [parallel] Improvise other parallel and contrasting answers to Handel's question.

STUDY MODULE 5

Page	List	Composer	Title	Meter and Tempo	Musical and Stylistic Concepts
R6 SG11	A	Christian Petzold, J.S. Bach (attr.)	Minuet in G Minor, BWV Anh. 115	3/4 Tempo di menuetto	✔ two-voice texture ✔ typical Baroque dance articulation ✔ binary form
R20 SG21	B	Wolfgang Amadeus Mozart	Viennese Sonatina No. 4 in B Flat	4/4 Andante grazioso	✔ double 3rds ✔ rounded binary form ✔ *gavotte*-style upbeat pattern
R37 SG35	C	Lajos Papp	Variations	3/4 Allegretto	✔ both variations longer than nine-measure theme ✔ contemporary sound
R38 SG36	C	Samuil Maikapar	Ballad, Op. 28	4/4 Allegretto	✔ Romantic nocturne ✔ Italian terms guide expression
S4		Cornelius Gurlitt	Study No. 1	2/4 Moderato	✔ scale passages in both hands ✔ sequential sixteenth-note passages
S6		Ludwig Schytte	Study No. 3	3/4 Allegro moderato	✔ LH exercise ✔ sixteenth-note figure in sequence
S16		Daniel Gottlob Türk	Study No. 13: Having Fun	2/4 Allegro	✔ RH sixteenth-note scale motion and challenging zig-zag figures ✔ LH constant zig-zag figure (wrist rotation)

Assign first:
Minuet in G Minor, BWV Anh. 115
Viennese Sonatina No. 4 in B Flat . . . .
Ballad, Op. 28 . . . .
Study No. 3 . . . .

Assign next when ready:

Study No. 1
Variations
Study No. 13: Having Fun

The pieces in Study Module 5 emphasize a light, graceful, elegant touch. These pieces provide the opportunity to review and refine musical elements such as balanced phrases, dotted rhythms, wrist rotation, varieties of articulation, and contrapuntal style.

C. Petzold, J.S. Bach (attr.): *Minuet in G Minor, BWV Anh. 115* (R6, SG11)
Exploring the Score
To explore the rhythmic vocabulary of 3/4 meter, have students list all the one-measure patterns of quarters and eighths in this piece:

Use words to reinforce the concept that short notes move the music forward to longer values:

step now you go to here now you go to here

To reveal the descending melodic line, circle the downbeat melody notes in mm. 1-9. Explore different articulation options for the melody. Consult the *Student Guide* and listen to the *Celebration Series* recording for examples. Help students choose an articulation pattern and add markings to their scores.

W.A. Mozart: *Viennese Sonatina No. 4 in B Flat* (R20, SG21)

Exploring the Score

Each two-measure phrase starts with two upbeat quarter notes (compare with the Baroque *gavotte*). Find variations of this basic pattern.

Practice Suggestions

The *Student Guide* provides practice suggestions for *legato* articulation and double 3rds. This sonatina was originally written for wind instruments. Two clarinets could play the double 3rds with a singing *legato* line. It is more difficult for a pianist to play both voices smoothly with one hand. Use the *Celebration Series* recording as a model for a *legato* sound.

Pay careful attention to the accuracy of dotted rhythms, especially in m. 25. On the closed keyboard cover, tap the RH rhythm:
1. by itself;
2. with steady LH quarter notes;
3. with the LH rhythm as written.

L. Papp: *Variations* (R37, SG35)

Exploring the Score

Circle the theme notes in each variation and discuss the different variation techniques.
- Where does the LH take the melodic lead?
- Why did Papp add extra measures to the variations?

S. Maikapar: *Ballad, Op. 28* (R38, SG36)

Exploring the Score

See the *Student Guide* for suggestions on reading music in F sharp major.
- The first two measures are like an introduction. Find two other places where Maikapar uses this musical material. [mm. 16-17 and 22-24]

  TIP: Sequences are often played louder if they are higher than the original phrase, and softer if they are lower. Is this approach to dynamic shaping appropriate here?

In literature, a ballad is a narrative poem about a historical or legendary event. Make up a poem or story to go with Samuil Maikapar's *Ballad*. Use some of the expressive qualities indicated by the Italian terms listed in the *Student Guide*. What dramatic event occurs in mm. 18-21? How is that event resolved in mm. 22-24?

C. Gurlitt: *Study No. 1* (S4)

Exploring the Score

Identify the form (ABA$_1$) and label the sections in the score.
- How does A$_1$ differ from A?
- The expression "what goes up must come down" describes the shape of the A section. How do the ascending and descending figures differ?
- How does Gurlitt provide contrast in the B section (mm. 5-12)?

L. Schytte: *Study No. 3* (S6)

Practice Suggestions

Compare the sixteenth-note figures in this study with those of *Study No. 1*. In this study, each beamed group of four sixteenth notes changes direction. Students will find these figures easier to read and memorize if they focus on groups of notes going in one direction, as shown below.

D.G. Türk: *Study No. 13: Having Fun* (S16)

Practice Suggestions

The motion for zig-zag patterns should come from the forearm. Rotate the forearm back and forth to tip the hand from side to side, as if you were turning a door knob. Practice this movement on the closed keyboard cover. For patterns in this piece, devise practice steps which incorporate forearm rotation.

The RH figures of mm. 7-8 and 14-16 are unpredictable. Divide the sixteenth-note passages into short groups, ending on the thumb. Practice each group several times.

CREATIVE ACTIVITY

Create a new accompaniment for the theme in Papp's *Variations*. Add some variations of your own.

STUDY MODULE 6

Page	List	Composer	Title	Meter and Tempo	Musical and Stylistic Concepts
R11 SG15	A	Johann Krieger	Sarabanda in D Minor	3/4 Andante	✔ consistent rhythm throughout ✔ three-voice texture
R13 SG17	A	Anon., J. S. Bach (attr.)	Musette in D Major, BWV Anh. 126	2/4 Allegretto	✔ position shifts ✔ LH broken octaves ✔ *legato* and *staccato*
R18 SG20	B	Anton Diabelli	Sonatina in G Major, Op. 51, No. 1 (First Movement)	3/4 Andante cantabile	✔ RH melody ✔ *staccato* scales ✔ broken and blocked LH chords ✔ dotted rhythm against triplets
R26 SG26	C	Pyotr Il'yich Tchaikovsky	Morning Prayer, Op. 39, No. 1	3/4 Andante	✔ four-voice chorale style ✔ *legato* fingering, pedal
R28 SG28	C	Béla Bartók	Bagatelle, Op. 6, No. 6	2/2 Lento	✔ expressive melody in both hands ✔ *legato* connections ✔ B major and minor emphasis ✔ unusual harmony
S13		Alexander Gedike	Study No. 10: Op. 32, No. 12	2/4 Moderato quasi andantino	✔ alternating hands on sixteenth notes (graceful effect) ✔ four-voice cadence figure
S17		Hermann Berens	Study No. 14	2/2 Allegro	✔ scales ✔ blocked chords

Assign first:
Musette in D Major, BWV Anh. 126 . . . .
Sonatina in G Major, Op. 51, No. 1
   (First Movement)
Bagatelle, Op. 6, No. 6 . . . .
Study No. 14. . . . .

Assign next when ready:
Sarabanda in D Minor

Morning Prayer, Op. 39, No. 1
Study No. 10: Op. 32, No. 12

Study Module 6 contains some of the most difficult pieces in Level 3. Students will have the opportunity to explore the contrasts between slow, Romantic pieces and faster, more energetic pieces.

Most of the Baroque dances your students have played up to now have had a predominantly two-voice texture. Krieger's *Sarabanda in D Minor* has three, sometimes four voices. Tchaikovsky's *Morning Prayer* presents a similar challenge. Nevertheless, the two-voice *Musette in D Major* is still among the most difficult pieces at this level because of its wide leaps in both hands.

J. Krieger: *Sarabanda in D Minor* (R11, SG15)
Exploring the Score
Compare the *Student Guide* definition of a *saraband* (p. 8) with this piece. Which element is missing? [no emphasis on the second beat]

- This piece has a three-voice texture. Find the four places where the texture expands to four voices.
- To understand the harmonic plan of this piece, name the chords in mm. 4, 8, 12, and 16 and discuss their function. [m. 4: D minor (tonic); m. 8: F major (relative major); m. 12: A major (dominant); m. 16: D minor (tonic)]

Practice Suggestions
Playing two voices in one hand requires special practice, especially when the voices have different rhythms – for example, in mm. 1, 4, and 8. To practice these RH measures:
1. Divide the parts between the hands. Bring out the melody and play the lower voice more softly.
2. Play these passages as written, aiming for the same balance of sound between the voices.

Anon., J. S. Bach (attr.): *Musette in D Major, BWV Anh. 126* (R13, SG17)
Exploring the Score
Musette is one of the most famous pieces in early intermediate repertoire.

- The *musette* incorporates the drone of a bagpipe (see *Student Guide*, p. 8). Which notes represent the bagpipe drone in this piece?
- The A section has a short-short-long phrase structure. How is the phrase structure of the B section different?
- What is the rhythmic surprise in mm. 13-16? [syncopation]

Practice Suggestions

The position shift between mm. 2 and 3 needs special practice. (See "Practicing Jumps" in the *Student Guide*.)
1. Block the D major five-finger positions (mm. 1, 3).
2. Practice shifting from the distant position to the close position.
3. Practice shifting from the distant position to the single F sharps.

A. Diabelli: *Sonatina in G Major, Op. 151, No. 1 (First Movement)* (R18, SG20)
Exploring the Score

Look for short-short-long phrase groups (for example, mm. 1-2, 3-4, and 5-8). **TIP:** In the Classical style, the focus of the phrase is often determined by its length. In a two-measure phrase, the focus is often on the downbeat of the second measure; in a four-measure phrase, the focus is usually on the downbeat of the third measure.
- Use the above guideline to determine the dynamic plan and focus of each phrase of this movement.
- What is the dynamic plan and focus for the RH triplets in mm. 17-24?

P. I. Tchaikovsky: *Morning Prayer, Op. 39, No. 1* (R26, SG26)
Exploring the Score
- How does Tchaikovsky create a reverent atmosphere?
- What tone quality is appropriate for the opening of this piece?
- What is the effect of the *forte* and accent markings in mm. 12 and 16-17?

Practice Suggestions

Playing four notes exactly together is a challenge. Try these practice tips:
- Play each chord with a slight arm push into the bottom of the keys.

- To bring out the top (soprano) voice, first have students play each melody note alone (with a full tone), then play the remaining chord tones together quietly.
- Keep the hand and arm relaxed.

B. Bartók: *Bagatelle, Op. 6, No. 6* (R28, SG28)
Exploring the Score
Dynamic shaping of the phrases and careful balance between melody and accompaniment are important in this lyrical piece.
- Pay attention to places where the melody is in the LH.
- Lift slightly at the ends of phrases.

Bartók uses tritones and half steps to give the melody a poignant quality.
- Circle the tritones and bracket the half-step sighing figures.
- Play these intervals with special expression.

A. Gedike: *Study No. 10: Op. 32, No. 12* (S13)
Practice Suggestions
Help the student approach this study musically as well as technically.
- Listen to the *Celebration Series* recording.
- Give the piece a title which fits its mysterious mood.
- Tap the rhythms hands together, then play the notes.
- Find the sequence in mm. 13-20 and decide on a dynamic plan for that phrase.

H. Berens: *Study No. 14* (S17)
Exploring the Score
- Label the I, IV, and V chords.
- Count the notes in each major scale figure. Plan the dynamics for each figure.

CREATIVE ACTIVITIES

♪ Improvise a melody in the style of Bartók, using the tritones and the half-step sighing motive from *Bagatelle*. Add an accompaniment to your melody.

♪ Play *Study No. 14*. Now compose a piece in C major. Use scale passages and tonic and dominant chords. The chords can be in either the RH or LH. The articulation can be *legato* or *staccato*. If you wish, create a contrasting B section. Give your piece a title.

LEVEL 3 SUMMARY
- Several **Musical Tips** occur throughout Level 3 discussions. How many different ideas did you list on your **Chart of Musical Tips**? Remember these musical concepts and apply them as you begin work in the next album.
- *Repertoire Album 3* includes six sonatina movements. Compare the movements and look for examples of the following: solid- or broken-chord accompaniment, Alberti bass, scale passages, question-and-answer phrases, *coda*, sequence, and waltz bass.
- Many of the pieces from the 19th and 20th centuries are programmatic in nature. Titles often indicate a story, a character, an event, a place, or an animal. How did titles like *A Frightening Story, Turtle*, and *The Haunted Castle* influence your study of the piece?

Level 4

The Publications

Level 4 of the *Celebration Series* includes the following publications:

> *Piano Repertoire Album 4*
> *Piano Studies Album 3 & 4* (level 4 only)
> *Student Guide 4*
> Recording of *Repertoire & Studies 4*

The Repertoire

The *Piano Repertoire Album 4* is divided into three lists:

- List A includes a selection of pieces composed during the Baroque period (*ca* 1600 to *ca* 1750).
- List B includes a selection of pieces composed during the Classical period (*ca* 1750 to *ca* 1820) as well as pieces in the Classical style written during the 19th and 20th centuries.
- List C includes a selection of pieces composed during the Romantic era (*ca* 1820 to *ca* 1910) and the 20th century.

Musical Development

The wide variety of repertoire pieces and technical studies in Level 4 provides the materials through which the intermediate-level student can experience significant musical and technical growth. The three-voice textures require control of balance and projection of melody over accompaniment. Accompaniment styles range from the independent lines of the Baroque repertoire to a variety of figures in the Classical sonatinas.

For the first time in the *Celebration Series*, the sonatina movements present a complete sonata-allegro form with contrasting themes in the exposition and a true development section. The Romantic selections focus on melody, expression, and, of course, the waltz – *the* dance of the 19th century. Challenging rhythmic experiences in this level include constantly changing meters (*Changing Bars* by István Szelényi) and the use of *hemiola* (in David Duke's *Barcarole*).

As in earlier levels, the *Repertoire Album* includes a variety of Baroque dances. Students are encouraged to continue developing their Dance Chart, as suggested in the Level 2 discussion, by listing the title and rhythmic characteristics of each dance they study.

The Range of Difficulty

The range of difficulty in Level 4 is represented by the following pieces:

- *Rigadoon in A Minor* by William Babell is an example of an easier piece from Study Module 1.
- *Sweet Dreams, Op. 39, No. 21* by Pyotr Il'yich Tchaikovsky is an example of a difficult piece from Study Module 6.

The Study Modules

Level 4 is divided into six Study Modules. The discussions of the individual pieces in each Study Module are organized under the following headings:

- *Exploring the Score*
- *Practice Suggestions*
- *Creative Activities*

Exploring the Score is designed as an interactive exercise between teacher and student. These sections include questions you might address to the student during lessons. *Practice Suggestions* are also largely directly to the student. The *Creative Activities* act as reinforcement for your students' understanding of a musical concept and can provide a springboard for their creativity and imagination.

Please refer to the Foreword for an explanation of how to use the suggested order of assignment within each Module.

The chart on the opposite page lists all the repertoire and studies in Level 4. Page numbers for works in the *Piano Repertoire Album 4* and the *Piano Studies Album 4* are found in the first column. Study Module numbers for each composition are found in the fourth column.

	Page	Composer	Title	Study Module
Piano Repertoire Album 4				
List A	R4	Leopold Mozart (attr.)	Bourrée in C Minor	6
	R5	Jeremiah Clarke	Minuet in G Major	5
	R6	Carl Philipp Emanuel Bach	March in D Major, BWV Anh. 122	3
	R7	William Babell	Rigadoon in A Minor	1
	R8	Louis Nicolas Clérambault	Allegro in D Minor	4
	R9	Anon., J.S. Bach (attr.)	Minuet in D Minor, BWV Anh. 132	2
	R10	Henry Purcell	Rigadoon in C Major	1
	R11	George Frideric Handel	Bourrée in G Major	1
	R12	Domenico Scarlatti	Sonata in D Minor, L 423/K 32	2
List B	R13	Muzio Clementi	Sonatina in G Major, Op. 36, No. 2 (Second Movement)	1.
	R14	Jacob Schmitt	Sonatina in C Major, Op. 83	2
	R16	Franz Joseph Haydn	Andantino in E Flat	4
	R18	Anton Diabelli	Sonatina in F Major, Op. 168, No. 1 (First Movement)	5
	R20	Wolfgang Amadeus Mozart (attr.)	Sonatina in C Major (First Movement)	6
	R22	Cornelius Gurlitt	Sonatina in G Major, Op. 188, No. 3	3
	R24	Erkki Melartin	Sonatina	6
	R26	Tobias Haslinger	Sonatina in C Major (First Movement)	3
List C	R28	Felix Mendelssohn	Romance in G Minor	4
	R29	Robert Schumann	The Happy Farmer, Op. 68, No. 10	4
	R30	Susan Alcon	The Wanderer	1
	R31	Carl Maria von Weber	Waltz in G Major	6
	R32	István Szelényi	Changing Bars	5
	R34	Génari Karganov	Little Waltz, Op. 25, No. 3	2
	R36	Pyotr Il'yich Tchaikovsky	Sweet Dreams, Op. 39, No. 21	6
	R38	Howard Hanson	Enchantment	5
	R40	David Duke	Barcarole (for Vivienne)	3
Piano Studies Album 4				
	S18	Samuil Maikapar	Study No. 1	1
	S19	Carl Czerny	Study No. 2: Op. 599, No. 85	5
	S20	Alexander Gedike	Study No. 3: Op. 36, No. 26	6
	S21	Cornelius Gurlitt	Study No. 4: Op. 141, No. 4	2
	S22	Hermann Berens	Study No. 5: Op. 70, No. 50	2
	S23	Jean-Baptiste Duvernoy	Study No. 6: Op. 176, No. 24	4
	S24	Johann Friedrich Burgmüller	Study No. 7: Op. 100, No. 11	3
	S25	Carl Czerny	Study No. 8: Op. 599, No. 83	5
	S26	Carl Czerny	Study No. 9	3
	S27	Johann Friedrich Burgmüller	Study No. 10: Op. 100, No. 18	4
	S28	Stephen Heller	Study No. 11: Op. 45, No. 2	1
	S30	Felix Le Couppey	Study No. 12: Round-About	6
	S31	Carl Czerny	Study No. 13: Op. 599, No. 45	3
	S32	Albert Loeschhorn	Study No. 14: Op. 65, No. 42	2

STUDY MODULE 1

Page	List	Composer	Title	Meter and Tempo	Musical and Stylistic Concepts
R7 SG11	A	William Babell	Rigadoon in A Minor	Alla breve Vivo	✔ A section: two-voice texture with imitation ✔ B section: homophonic texture
R10 SG14	A	Henry Purcell	Rigadoon in C Major	Alla breve Animato	✔ LH plays two independent voices ✔ short trills on strong beats in melody
R11 SG15	A	George Frideric Handel	Bourrée in G Major	4/4 Allegro vivo	✔ syncopation and sequence pattern in melody ✔ LH plays steady quarter notes
R13 SG17	B	Muzio Clementi	Sonatina in G Major, Op. 36, No. 2 (Second Movement)	3/4 Allegretto	✔ ABA form ✔ dotted rhythm throughout ✔ melody changes direction in B section
R30 SG27	C	Susan Alcon	The Wanderer	6/8 Restlessly	✔ constant eighth notes in RH ✔ two-voice texture created by blocked intervals on downbeats
S18		Samuil Maikapar	Study No. 1	2/4 Allegro	✔ *staccato* chords
S28		Stephen Heller	Study No. 11: Op. 45, No. 2	2/4 Allegro vivace	✔ triplets pass between the hands ✔ hand crossings ✔ *legato* chords (some connected with damper pedal)

Assign first:
Rigadoon in A Minor . . . .
Sonatina in G Major, Op. 36, No. 2
   (Second Movement) . . . .
Study No. 1 . . . .
The Wanderer

Assign next when ready:
Rigadoon in C Major

Bourrée in G Major

Study No. 11: Op. 45, No. 2

Many of the pieces in Study Module 1 are dances. Even Clementi's *Sonatina* movement has the character of an elegant minuet with its dance-like dotted figure. Refer to the list of Dance Forms in the *Student Guide* (p. 7) as you discuss each dance with your student. Since each dance has its own characteristic rhythm and tempo, it is interesting to compare them. It is also interesting to examine the differences between two dances in the same form. Here there is an opportunity to compare two rigadoons, both written by English composers – William Babell and Henry Purcell.

There are other opportunities for comparison in this Study Module. For example, compare the consistent dotted rhythm in Clementi's *Sonatina* with the constant eighth-note motion of *The Wanderer* by Susan Alcon.

W. Babell: *Rigadoon in A Minor* (R7, SG11)
H. Purcell: *Rigadoon in C Major* (R10, SG14)
Exploring the Score
- What features do these rigadoons share? [meter]
- How are they different? [texture, upbeat, form]
- Which rigadoon uses imitation?

Practice Suggestion
The *Student Guide* includes a discussion and practice suggestions for playing the two-voice LH accompaniment of Purcell's *Rigadoon*. To help the student hear the two voices, divide the LH part between the hands. Play one hand *forte*, the other *piano*, then reverse the dynamics. Concentrate on note values and emphasize the release of each note at a rest.

G.F. Handel: *Bourrée in G Major* (R11, SG15)
Exploring the Score

Look up the description of a *bourrée* in the *Student Guide*. Does *Bourrée in G Major* match the description? Discuss the structure and key relationships of binary form.

- Find the A and B sections.
- Name the key of the beginning. [G major]
- Name the key at the end of the A section. [D major] What is its relationship to the opening key? [dominant] Highlight the modulation by emphasizing the cadence.
- Name the key at the end of the B section. [G major]

Draw the student's attention to the four-note sequences (for example, mm. 5-6).

M. Clementi: *Sonatina in G Major, Op. 36, No. 2 (Second Movement)* (R13, SG17)
Exploring the Score

Have students draw a line in the air tracing the rise and fall of the melody. The A section has a descending shape. Find the opposite motion in the B section. [mm. 12-14]

Draw students' attention to mm. 24-28. Why did Clementi add this extra phrase? [to emphasize the ending of the movement] Listen for these measures on the *Celebration Series* recording. Keep an even pulse in mm. 7-8, but consider a slight *ritardando* in mm. 27-28.

S. Alcon: *The Wanderer* (R30, SG27)
Exploring the Score

- Alcon unifies this piece with the eighth-note motion. How does she create contrast? [adds third voice, changes melodic shape]
- Which measures do not have a constant eighth-note rhythm?
- Many of the eighth-note figures have an up-down shape. Find measures with a different melodic shape. [mm. 13-15, 19-20]

Practice Suggestions

In mm. 5-7 and 13-15, the RH plays two voices. Students may have difficulty making the *legato* connections over the bar line. Have them practice these measures slowly to determine when each voice (finger) lifts.

S. Maikapar: *Study No. 1* (S18)
Practice Suggestions

The musical goal is to produce a light, joyful sound. The technical goal is to play with relaxation and ease. Have students experiment with one drop-lift motion per measure (rather than one motion for each chord).

1. Practice this motion by playing the RH of m. 4 on the closed keyboard cover.
2. Play m. 1 on the keyboard using the same motion. Say "drop and lift" as you play.
3. Use the same drop-lift motion in the LH.

S. Heller: *Study No. 11: Op. 45, No. 2* (S28)
Exploring the Score

This motive dominates the study:

- Do all the half notes have an accent?

Practice Suggestions

The triplets move forward rhythmically and dynamically to the accented half notes. Emphasize this with a *crescendo* through the triplets.

The chords in mm. 18-20 and 22-24 include both repeated and moving notes.

1. Play the RH melodic notes *legato*, with the fingering **3-4-5**.
2. Play the RH chords, releasing fingers **1** and **2** lightly.
3. Play the RH chords again. Release the lower notes and project the melody.

CREATIVE ACTIVITIES

 Follow these steps to compose your own piece called *Rigadoon*. Use some of the characteristics found in the rigadoons by William Babell and Henry Purcell.
- Create a four-measure melody.
- Add a LH accompaniment.
- Add more phrases until you have a short composition.

Compose a four-measure RH tune using only the dotted rhythm from Clementi's sonatina movement (call this melody "*x*"). Compose a four-measure LH melody the same way (call this melody "*y*"). Add accompaniments to both melodies. Combine these melodies to form a composition with two or three sections – for example "*xy*," "*xyx*," or "*yx*." Give your piece a title.

STUDY MODULE 2

Page	List	Composer	Title	Meter and Tempo	Musical and Stylistic Concepts
R9 SG13	A	Anon., J.S. Bach (attr.)	Minuet in D Minor, BWV Anh. 132	3/4 Moderato	✔ two-voice texture: melody and accompaniment ✔ sequences ✔ varying phrase lengths ✔ contrasting articulation and melodic figuration
R12 SG16	A	Domenico Scarlatti	Sonata in D Minor, L 423/K 32	3/8 Andante	✔ rounded binary form ✔ consistent rhythmic motive ✔ LH chordal accompaniment ✔ expressive *appoggiatura*
R14 SG18	B	Jacob Schmitt	Sonatina in C Major, Op. 83	C Moderato	✔ Classical sonatina: balanced phrases, homophonic style, simple harmony ✔ contrasting LH and RH articulation
R34 SG30	C	Génari Karganov	Little Waltz, Op. 25, No. 3	3/4 Non troppo presto	✔ dynamic shaping and rhythm reinforce *rubato* ✔ LH plays melody in B section
S21		Cornelius Gurlitt	Study No. 4: Op. 141, No. 4	2/4 Allegro	✔ D major, A major, G major, and G minor octave scales starting on different scale degrees ✔ variety of fingerings
S22		Hermann Berens	Study No. 5: Op. 70, No. 50	C Allegro	✔ LH plays F five-finger patterns, C major and F major scales ✔ RH plays blocked, *staccato* 6ths
S32		Albert Loeschhorn	Study No. 14: Op. 65, No. 42	C Andantino	✔ *legato* triplet figures passing between the hands have constantly changing shape and range

Assign first:
Sonata in D Minor, L 423/K 32 . . . .
Sonatina in C Major, Op. 83 . . . .
Study No. 5: Op. 70, No. 50 . . . .
Study No. 14: Op. 65, No. 42

Assign next when ready:
Minuet in D Minor, BWV Anh. 132
Little Waltz, Op. 25, No. 3
Study No. 4: Op. 141, No. 4

Comparison usually leads to insight. Use the following questions to compare the pieces in this Study Module.
- Which pieces are bold and strongly rhythmic?
- Which pieces emphasize elegance of expression?
- Which pieces have a unifying rhythmic motive?
- Which pieces have a unifying technical figure?
- Which piece is the longest? What is its form?
- In which piece(s) does the LH have its own independent line?
- In which piece(s) does the LH provide harmonic support to the RH?

Anon., J. S. Bach (attr.): *Minuet in D Minor, BWV Anh. 132* (R9, SG13)

Exploring the Score

This piece has a variety of melodic figures and rhythms. It may be helpful to find the basic unifying elements. Find all measures using the following "*x*" and "*y*" rhythms:

D. Scarlatti: *Sonata in D Minor, L 423/K 32* (R12, SG16)

Exploring the Score

Read the biography of Domenico Scarlatti in the *Student Guide*. His harpsichord compositions were influenced by the dances and guitar music of Portugal and Spain. The thirty-second-note flourishes are like the strumming of a guitar. This rhythmic figure gives each phrase an energetic "kick-off." Listen to the *Celebration Series* recording for the guitar-like flourishes and the emphasis on non-chord tones (see, for example, the *appoggiatura* C sharp in m. 2).

Practice Suggestions

See the *Student Guide* discussion of the second-beat non-chord tones. Give these notes special emphasis, especially when they are part of a two-note slur, as the performer does in the *Celebration Series* recording.

J. Schmitt: *Sonatina in C Major, Op. 83* (R14, SG18)

Exploring the Score

Look for contrasts in the structure of this sonatina.

- Mark the A and B sections in the score and label the key changes (see the form outline in the *Student Guide*).
- Which of the two A sections is longer? What has been added or extended?
- In the opening theme, notice the contrast between mm. 1-2 and 3-4. Emphasize the light, dance-like quality of mm. 1-2 and the *legato* RH phrasing of mm. 3-4.

Practice Suggestions

Schmitt uses different articulation to contrast the melody and accompaniment. Find the few places where both hands have the same articulation.

Devise exercises that focus on contrasting articulation. Play one hand *staccato* and the other hand *legato*, then reverse the hands.

G. Karganov: *Little Waltz, Op. 25, No. 3* (R34, SG30)

Exploring the Score

Explore the musical variety of *Little Waltz* by finding:
- LH melody
- the loudest section
- the first four-measure phrase [mm. 1-4]
- the first two-measure phrase [mm. 5-6]
- a slight variation of mm. 1-4 [mm. 9-12]

See the discussion of *rubato* in the *Student Guide*. Karganov creates *rubato* with the *poco ritardando* and with rhythm. The eighth notes push toward longer quarter and dotted quarter notes. The high point of a phrase is often on the longest rhythmic value (for example, the dotted quarters of mm. 4 and 6).

C. Gurlitt: *Study No. 4: Op. 141, No. 4* (S21)

Practice Suggestions

Blocking finger groups will help students to play scales accurately. There are a variety of finger groupings in this study. Bracket each group and indicate the number of fingers:

H. Berens: *Study No. 5: Op. 70, No. 50* (S22)
Practice Suggestions
Identify the following musical elements and practice them hands separately:
— *staccato* upbeat figures
— dotted rhythms
— five-finger patterns and scales

A. Loeschhorn: *Study No. 14, Op. 65, No. 42* (S32)
Practice Suggestion
Have students block the triplet figures to learn notes and fingerings.

CREATIVE ACTIVITY
The three studies in Study Module 2 include the following elements:
— one-octave scales
— five-finger patterns
— arpeggios
Compose your own study using one or more of these elements, and give it a title.

STUDY MODULE 3

Page	List	Composer	Title	Meter and Tempo	Musical and Stylistic Concepts
R6 SG10	A	Carl Philipp Emanuel Bach	March in D Major, BWV Anh. 122	Alla breve Allegro	✔ binary form ✔ strict two-voice texture ✔ syncopation ✔ rising melodic sequences create tension
R22 SG22	B	Cornelius Gurlitt	Sonatina in G Major, Op. 188, No. 3	3/8 Allegretto	✔ bold contrasts between themes ✔ voicing of blocked intervals important
R26 SG24	B	Tobias Haslinger	Sonatina in C Major (First Movement)	C Allegro moderato	✔ LH plays variety of accompaniment and melodic figures
R40 SG33	C	David Duke	Barcarole (for Vivienne)	6/8 Slow	✔ colorful harmonies ✔ effective use of the entire keyboard ✔ *hemiola*
S24		Johann Friedrich Burgmüller	Study No. 7: Op. 100, No. 11	2/4 Allegretto	✔ broken triad study, includes all inversions and contrary motion
S26		Carl Czerny	Study No. 9	2/4 Allegretto	✔ five-finger patterns in sixteenth notes ✔ cadences approached with RH swooping scale lines which change direction
S31		Carl Czerny	Study No. 13: Op. 599, No. 45	2/4 Allegretto	✔ sixteenth-note broken-octave chords ✔ scale passages in both hands ✔ short melodic patterns

Assign first:
March in D Major, BWV Anh. 122 . . . .
Sonatina in G Major, Op. 188, No. 3 . . . .
Barcarole (for Vivienne) . . . .
Study No. 7: Op. 100, No. 11

Assign next when ready:
Study No. 9
Sonatina in C Major (First Movement)
Study No. 13: Op. 599, No. 45

Sonatinas of the Classical and Romantic periods focus on a single concept: *contrast*. When students see, hear, discuss, and label elements of contrast in the music, their performance of these works will take on a new sense of musical excitement and effectiveness. The sonatinas by Cornelius Gurlitt and Tobias Haslinger in this Study Module display obvious contrasts of melody, key, articulation, and dynamics.

The three studies highlight technical figures: broken triads (*Study No. 7*), sixteenth-note scales (*Study No. 9*), broken-octave chords and scale patterns (*Study No. 13*). Help students create preparatory drills using these elements. Focus on fingering during practice sessions.

C.P.E. Bach: *March in D Major, BWV Anh. 122*
(R6, SG10)
Practice Suggestions
Independent movement of the hands is important in this piece. For special practice, isolate measures where the hands play similar figures:
- the 4ths in mm. 1-2 and 10-11
- the motive in mm. 4-5
- the 4th, 3rd, and 2nd in m. 7
- the stream of eighth notes at the cadences

Find the passages in which fingering plays a crucial role. Practice these measures hands separately, saying the finger numbers aloud.

C. Gurlitt: *Sonatina in G Major, Op. 188, No. 3*
(R22, SG22)
T. Haslinger: *Sonatina in C Major (First Movement)* (R26, SG24)
Exploring the Score
Contrast plays an important role in the structure of these two sonatinas. See the *Student Guide* for a detailed discussion of their form, and have your student label the sections in the score.
- Which bridge section provides the greater contrast to its surrounding themes?
- Which second theme is twice as long as the corresponding first theme?
- Compare the two development sections with their respective expositions and find the original presentation of each idea used in the development.

Practice Suggestions
Focus the student's attention on the contrasting elements in each sonatina and devise practice plans around these elements:
- contrasting melodic fragments
- contrasting dynamics
- changes in accompaniment style
- varieties of texture
- contrasting articulation

D. Duke: *Barcarole (for Vivienne)* (R40, SG33)
Exploring the Score
Composers use harmony to create expression. Note the colorful chords in Duke's *Barcarole*.
- How many different chords are used in the LH pattern, mm. 1-2? [five]
- Play the pattern and listen to the changing sound quality. Can you label each chord with a color?
- Imagine a picture for mm. 7-8. Play these measures a little slower with a distant sound.

In the *Student Guide*, see the discussion of barcarole rhythm and *hemiola* (under the subtitle "Sonorously").

J.F. Burgmüller: *Study No. 7: Op. 100, No. 11*
(S24)
Practice Suggestions
Practice the broken triads in blocked form.

Pay careful attention to the fingering. Circle the sixteenth notes played by the second finger, or write the fingering in the music.

C. Czerny: *Study No. 9* (S26)
Practice Suggestion
This study highlights sixteenth-note scale patterns. Circle the fingers which cross over the thumb. Block the eighth notes in mm. 3-4.

C. Czerny: *Study No. 13: Op. 599, No. 45* (S31)
Practice Suggestion
Find the notes played by the fourth finger in the broken-octave chords. Pay special attention to the fingering in the LH, m. 24.

CREATIVE ACTIVITY
Choose a chord pattern to play in this barcarole rhythm, such as:

	I	V	V	I
or:	I	IV	V	V
or:	I	vi	vi	I

Write a simple melody above your chords. Give your piece a title.

STUDY MODULE 4

Page	List	Composer	Title	Meter and Tempo	Musical and Stylistic Concepts
R8 SG12	A	Louis Nicolas Clérambault	Allegro in D Minor	6/8 Allegro	✔ two-voice texture until final cadence ✔ sequential writing
R16 SG19	B	Franz Joseph Haydn	Andantino in E Flat	C Andantino, un poco allegretto	✔ rounded binary form (with *coda*) based on one theme ✔ RH plays *legato, portato* double 3rds
R28 SG25	C	Felix Mendelssohn	Romance in G Minor	3/4 Andante	✔ expressive sighing motive ✔ contrast of *portato* with *legato* lines
R29 SG26	C	Robert Schumann	The Happy Farmer, Op. 68, No. 10	C Fresh and lively	✔ balance of melody and accompaniment ✔ frequent position changes ✔ LH plays broken chords
S23		Jean-Baptiste Duvernoy	Study No. 6: Op. 176, No. 24	2/4 Allegretto	✔ *staccato* double 6ths and 3rds ✔ LH plays broken and blocked 5ths
S27		Johann Friedrich Burgmüller	Study No. 10: Op. 100, No. 18	2/4 Allegro agitato	✔ one motive throughout ✔ LH plays *staccato* chords ✔ RH plays varying patterns of sixteenth notes

Assign first:
Allegro in D Minor . . . .
Andantino in E Flat . . . .
Study No. 6: Op. 176, No. 24 . . . .

Assign next when ready:
The Happy Farmer, Op. 68, No. 10
Romance in G Minor
Study No. 10: Op. 100, No. 18

Study Module 4 presents a microcosm of keyboard styles and technical approaches. Clérambault's *Allegro in D Minor* requires precise, facile finger technique. Haydn's *Andantino in E Flat* and Mendelssohn's *Romance in G Minor* employ a variety of subtle expressive touches and require sensitive balance. Schumann's *The Happy Farmer* is a robust, extroverted song with a LH melody. The two studies provide students with new experiences of hand *staccato* and coordination.

L.N. Clérambault: *Allegro in D Minor*
(R8, SG12)

Exploring the Score

Read the *Student Guide* discussion of repetitions and sequences. This piece illustrates ways in which a musical motive can unify a composition. Have the student find:

– repetitions of the opening theme [mm. 3-4 and 9-10; notice LH anticipation of theme in m. 8]
– sequences of the figures in mm. 5, 11, and 13

The sixteenth notes of the opening theme form a tetrachord. There is another tetrachord hidden in the sixteenth-note pattern of m. 5. Also, the LH plays intervals of a 4th – the outline of a tetrachord.

F.J. Haydn: *Andantino in E Flat* (R16, SG19)

Exploring the Score

See the discussion of form and key changes in the *Student Guide*. The theme is an eight-measure question-and-answer pattern. The entire piece is based on this theme, but Haydn employs constant, subtle variations, so that no two phrases are exactly alike.

• Find the repeated melodic phrases.
• Are they all harmonized the same way?
• How does Haydn change the accompaniment?

F. Mendelssohn: *Romance in G Minor*
(R28, SG25)

Exploring the Score

A musical sigh is associated with falling pitches, especially two-note slurs. Mendelssohn intensifies his musical sigh by using a dotted rhythm.

• Find the *outline* of the sigh. [D-A, B flat-F sharp]
• Experiment with the dynamics to find an appropriate dynamic shape for the sigh.
• Look for variations of the sighing figure. [mm. 4, 8, 10, etc.]

Discuss the *appoggiatura* with your student and point out the examples in mm. 12, 16, and 18. Listen to the interpretation of the sighing figures on the *Celebration Series* recording.

R. Schumann: *The Happy Farmer, Op. 68, No. 10* (R29, SG26)

Practice Suggestions

The challenges in this piece include balancing a melody with a chordal accompaniment and fingering the LH broken chords. See the *Student Guide* suggestions for practicing with a metronome and memorizing the LH part. Note the emphasis on melodic projection and a light accompaniment.

Have students practice the melody hands separately and reinforce correct fingerings by saying the finger numbers aloud.

J.-B. Duvernoy: *Study No. 6: Op. 176, No. 24* (S23)

Practice Suggestions

Practice this study first on the closed keyboard cover in these contrasting ways:

1. Play several lines with a hand *staccato* (no up or down movement of the wrist).
2. Play again with a continuous wrist movement for each measure. Say "drop and lift-ing" as you play, to describe the movement of your wrist:

drop   and   lift - ing

Which movement makes this study easier to play?

J.F. Burgmüller: *Study No. 10: Op. 100, No. 18* (S27)

Practice Suggestions

The primary goal of this study is to play perfectly even sixteenth notes. Here are some suggestions:

• Think of the LH chords as the first of a group of four sixteenth notes.
• Count aloud or use words to reinforce an even rhythm (for example, *Mis-sis-sip-pi*).
• Keep your wrist loose and flexible.
• When playing the wider intervals in mm. 13-16, allow your thumb to move off its key as you play the fourth and fifth fingers.

CREATIVE ACTIVITY

 Using Haydn's *Andantino in E Flat* as a guide, compose a question-and-answer melody and notate it on staff paper. Write a simple LH accompaniment for your melody. Now, create variations of your melody by altering rhythms, adding notes, or changing the accompaniment style. Give your piece a title.

STUDY MODULE 5

Page	List	Composer	Title	Meter and Tempo	Musical and Stylistic Concepts
R5 SG9	A	Jeremiah Clarke	Minuet in G Major	3/4 Tranquillo	✔ hands share three-voice texture ✔ challenging fingering ✔ dotted rhythm
R18 SG20	B	Anton Diabelli	Sonatina in F Major, Op. 168, No. 1 (First Movement)	C Moderato cantabile	✔ sonata form ✔ expressive *appoggiaturas* ✔ colorful diminished 7th chord ✔ LH plays Alberti-bass pattern
R32 SG29	C	István Szelényi	Changing Bars	2/8; 3/8; 4/8 Molto allegro	✔ meter changes each measure ✔ RH plays single eighth notes ✔ LH plays blocked 5ths ✔ exclusively on white keys
R38 SG32	C	Howard Hanson	Enchantment	3/4 Allegretto	✔ folk-like melody ✔ chordal accompaniment shared between hands ✔ control of texture and balance is challenging
S19		Carl Czerny	Study No. 2: Op. 599, No. 85	C Allegro	✔ RH plays broken-chord pattern
S25		Carl Czerny	Study No. 8: Op. 599, No. 83	6/8 Allegro	✔ variety of blocked and broken chords ✔ grace notes highlight the melody

Assign first:

Minuet in G Major . . . .

Enchantment . . . .

Study No. 2: Op. 599, No. 85 . . . .

Assign next when ready:

Sonatina in F Major, Op. 168, No. 1 (First Movement)

Changing Bars

Study No. 8: Op. 599, No. 83

Diversity of rhythmic figures is a notable feature of Study Module 5. The dotted rhythms in Clarke's *Minuet in G Major* are a bold contrast to the rhythmic motives in Diabelli's sonatina movement. Both studies have repeated rhythmic figures. Compare them with *Changing Bars*, where Szelényi uses changing time signatures to organize the constant eighth-note motion. For further contrast, examine the long *legato* phrases and colorful harmonies Hanson employs in his expressive *Enchantment*.

J. Clarke: *Minuet in G Major* (R5, SG9)
Practice Suggestions
See the comments on voicing in the *Student Guide*.
1. Practice the RH part paying special attention to fingering. Connect the notes of the *legato* alto line.
2. Play everything except the top melody. Where do you play one voice? Where do you play two voices or three voices? When you play two voices in one hand, bring out the top melody and hold the long notes for their full value.

Other challenges include the fingering and consistency of the dotted-rhythm figures.

A. Diabelli: *Sonatina in F Major, Op. 168, No. 1 (First Movement)* (R18, SG20)
Exploring the Score
Discuss Diabelli's use of the *appoggiatura* in the opening theme. Follow the downbeat *appoggiatura* by a much softer resolution.

Investigate the variety of approaches to the *appoggiaturas* – from below, from above, by step, by leap.
- Because each *appoggiatura* is approached differently, give each one a unique sound. Which one should have the most stress?
- Can you use *rubato* to add expression to an *appoggiatura*?

See the discussion of form in the *Student Guide*.
- Compare the first and second themes. How do they differ? [accompaniment, melody, articulation]
- Which harmony in the development section is most surprising and has the most tension? How will you emphasize this?

I. Szelényi: *Changing Bars* (R32, SG29)
Practice Suggestions
Students will find that the changing meters make more sense when they examine the eighth-note patterns. Try these practice steps:
1. First play the RH alone, counting aloud in eighth notes.
2. Count through the piece, playing only the 4/8 measures.
3. Count through the piece, playing only the 3/8 measures.
4. Count through the piece, playing only the downbeats.

H. Hanson: *Enchantment* (R38, SG32)
Practice Suggestions
The primary musical goal is to project the singing melodic line. The repeated-note motives require careful shaping. No two phrases are alike. Listen for the subtle differences. These practice steps may help your student gain control over the tone and voicing:
1. Play only the RH melody and the lower LH notes. Use the damper pedal and *legato* fingerings.
2. Find the high point of each phrase and pencil in your dynamic shadings.
3. Practice each phrase hands separately with special attention to fingerings.
4. Practice hands together, exaggerating the *crescendo-diminuendo* shape of the phrases.

C. Czerny: *Study No. 2: Op. 599, No. 85* (S19)
Practice Suggestions
1. Block the RH broken intervals on each beat with the correct fingering.
2. Play the repeated RH note of each beat very quickly. Observe the natural motion of the hand.
3. Play the RH part as written. Keep the hand loose and relaxed and use a rotating hand motion.

C. Czerny: *Study No. 8: Op. 599, No. 83* (S25)
Practice Suggestions
1. Play each group of LH eighth notes in one hand movement. Try a drop-lift wrist motion.
2. Crush the RH grace notes against the eighth note and lift off quickly for a light, bright *staccato* sound.

CREATIVE ACTIVITY
Create several short eighth-note motives. Each one should have a different shape: for example, two notes downward, three notes repeated, four notes zig-zag, five notes upward.
- Number each motive and write them on staff paper. Play the motives in random order. You can play them in the same position, or move them around the keyboard.
- For an accompaniment, play a LH blocked 5th at the beginning of each motive.
- Find an order of motives you especially like, write this composition down, and give it a title.
- Compare your piece with Szelényi's *Changing Bars*.

STUDY MODULE 6

Page	List	Composer	Title	Meter and Tempo	Musical and Stylistic Concepts
R4 SG8	A	Leopold Mozart (attr.)	Bourrée in C Minor	C Moderato	✔ rounded binary form ✔ independence of hands in articulation and melodic direction ✔ frequent contraction and expansion of LH position
R20 SG21	B	Wolfgang Amadeus Mozart (attr.)	Sonatina in C Major (First Movement)	C Andante	✔ *legato* double notes require careful fingering and pedaling
R24 SG23	B	Erkki Melartin	Sonatina	3/4 Tempo di menuetto	✔ in style of folk-dance tune ✔ main theme constructed from sequence ✔ use of pedal on cadences
R31 SG28	C	Carl Maria von Weber	Waltz in G Major	3/4 Allegretto	✔ minuet and trio form ✔ main theme derived from chords ✔ challenging *legato* chromatic chord passage
R36 SG31	C	Pyotr Il'yich Tchaikovsky	Sweet Dreams, Op. 39, No. 21	3/4 Moderato	✔ *legato* bass and soprano lines balanced against off-beat chordal accompaniment
S20		Alexander Gedike	Study No. 3: Op. 36, No. 26	2/4 Allegro marziale	✔ sixteenth-note tetrachords ✔ broken chords ✔ blocked *staccato* intervals ✔ combination of double and single notes
S30		Felix Le Couppey	Study No. 12: Round-About	3/4 Allegretto con moto	✔ constant eighth note motion in one hand against *staccato* quarter-note accompaniment ✔ the eighth-note figure whimsically changes direction ✔ correct fingering essential

Assign first:
Bourrée in C Minor
Sonatina in C Major (First Movement) . . . .
Waltz in G Major . . . .
Study No. 3: Op. 36, No. 26 . . . .

Assign next when ready:

Sonatina
Sweet Dreams, Op. 39, No. 21
Study No. 12: Round-About

The pieces in Study Module 6 represent the culmination of technical skill and musical growth in Level 4. The two sonatinas add to the student's understanding of the flexibility of forms, since neither provides a "textbook" example of sonata form. One of the challenges of this Study Module is the control of *legato* tone. The Mozart sonatina movement and Tchaikovsky's *Sweet Dreams* require subtle pedaling to create the necessary *legato*.

L. Mozart (attr.): *Bourrée in C Minor* (R4, SG8)
Practice Suggestions
This dance presents the challenge of hand independence in direction, rhythm, and articulation.

Experience the changes of direction through these practice steps:
1. On the closed keyboard cover, play both hands in a cluster position (finger tips lined up and

touching). Imagine that you are playing each note with the whole hand (or cluster). Practice in two-measure units.
2. On the keyboard, play hands separately, *legato* and *forte*.
3. Play hands together in short practice units, *legato* and *forte*.
4. Add the written articulation and dynamics.

W.A. Mozart (attr.): *Sonatina in C Major (First Movement)* (R20, SG21)
Exploring the Score
Perhaps this movement was inspired by the sound of other instruments. Two woodwind or string players could play the duet in mm. 1-8 with a singing *legato* line. It is more difficult for a pianist to play both voices smoothly with one hand.

The *appoggiatura* was one of Mozart's favorite expressive devices. Find the *appoggiaturas* in this sonatina movement. [mm. 4, 8, etc.] Exaggerate the dynamic shape of these figures.

Practice Suggestion
See the extensive practice suggestions for the RH part in the *Student Guide*.

E. Melartin: *Sonatina* (R24, SG23)
Exploring the Score
The *Student Guide* emphasizes the planning and practice of dynamics. The opening eight-measure phrase is constructed from a two-measure sequence pattern. Decide on a dynamic plan for the two-measure units. Which one will be loudest or most intense? In a musical structure consisting of four units, the best musical shape is often created by a dynamic focus on the third unit – in this case, mm. 6-7. ("Out of four, go for three.")

C.M. von Weber: *Waltz in G Major* (R31, SG28)
Exploring the Score
Focus on the balance and variety of phrase structure. The entire piece is constructed from four-measure units, but Weber uses different combinations and subdivisions to create variety.

For example, mm. 1-4 has a 1+1+2 measure construction, but mm. 17-21 constitute one flowing unit.

Practice Suggestion
The RH fingering of mm. 21-24 deserves attention. Analyze which fingers provide the *legato* connection. Practice RH alone, emphasizing the finger lifts in the non-*legato* voice.

P. I. Tchaikovsky: *Sweet Dreams, Op. 39, No. 21* (R36, SG31)
Practice Suggestions
A successful performance highlights the soprano and bass lines. Try these practice steps:
1. Play the melody and the bass line without pedal. Follow the RH fingering but improvise a *legato* LH fingering.
2. Play these two lines with a pedal change on each beat. (Follow the LH fingering.)
3. Divide the LH part of mm. 1-8 between the hands. Create dynamic contrast between the hands.
4. Divide the RH part of mm. 22-24 between the hands, with distinct dynamic contrast.

A. Gedike: *Study No. 3: Op. 36, No. 26* (S20)
Exploring the Score
Use this study as a summary of several studies in *Album 4*. Have students identify the following technical figures and find those same figures in other studies. Discuss the different hand and wrist motions used for each figure.
- sixteenth-note tetrachords (finger technique for single tones)
- broken chords (rocking motion)
- blocked *staccato* intervals (hand *staccato*)

Use a rotation movement for the combination of double and single notes in mm. 7 and 23.

F. Le Couppey: *Study No. 12: Round-About* (S30)
Practice Suggestions
Use some of the following techniques to practice the eighth-note passages:
- Change the articulation.
- Practice in dotted rhythms.
- Stop on certain notes or beats (for example, the high pitch, the thumb, the downbeat).
- Exaggerate finger lifts.
- Stop on each downbeat and think through the next pattern of notes.

LEVEL 4 SUMMARY
- What are the titles of the Baroque dances in List A? What is the most common form for these dances?
- Several of the pieces in *Repertoire Album 4* have two voices played by the same hand (for example, Clarke, *Minuet in G Major*, Tchaikovsky, *Sweet Dreams, Op. 39, No. 21*). How do you practice two voices in the same hand?
- Seven of the nine List C pieces are in triple meter. Where does the composer try to avoid a downbeat emphasis? Where does the composer emphasize the second beat?

Level 5

The Publications

Level 5 of the *Celebration Series* includes the following publications:

> *Piano Repertoire Album 5*
> *Piano Studies Album 5 & 6* (level 5 only)
> *Student Guide 5*
> Recording of *Repertoire & Studies 5*

The Repertoire

The *Piano Repertoire Album 5* is divided into three lists:

- List A includes a selection of pieces composed during the Baroque period (*ca* 1600 to *ca* 1750).
- List B includes a selection of pieces composed during the Classical period (*ca* 1750 to *ca* 1820) as well as pieces in the Classical style written during the 19th and 20th centuries.
- List C includes a selection of pieces composed during the Romantic era (*ca* 1820 to *ca* 1910) and the 20th century.

The repertoire and studies represent the intermediate level of piano study. The range of composers and mix of well-known teaching pieces with less familiar repertoire make this collection an enjoyable experience for both teacher and student.

In Level 5, students will encounter four new types of pieces: *Allemande* (J.S. Bach), *Prelude* (J.S. Bach), *Postlude* (George Fiala), and *Fugue* (Domenico Zipoli and G.F. Handel). Students are encouraged to add to the Dance Chart begun in Level 2, listing the title and rhythmic characteristics of each dance they study. The dances in Level 5 include an *allemande*, a *gavotte*, a jig, a minuet, a *sarabande* (within the *Gavotte with Two Variations*), and a *valse*.

Sonata and sonatina forms are represented with works by Scarlatti, Clementi, Diabelli, and Kabalevsky, spanning three style periods: Baroque, Classical, and contemporary. A comparison of these works will lead to interesting discussions for both teacher and student.

It may interest the student to know that Domenico Scarlatti, Johann Sebastian Bach, and George Frideric Handel were all born in 1685. All three composers are represented in Level 5.

Musical Development

Challenges in Level 5 include:

- Baroque ornamentation: turns, trills, slides, grace notes, and *appoggiaturas*
- thicker Romantic textures with the melody in octaves between the hands
- more challenging independence of voices in two-voice Baroque textures
- three-voice textures
- LH waltz-bass patterns
- increasingly complicated key signatures including E flat minor and A flat major
- contemporary writing using twelve-tone, *ostinato*, and whole-tone devices

The Range of Difficulty

The range of difficulty in Level 5 is represented by these two pieces:

- *Sonatina in G Major (Third Movement)* by Muzio Clementi is an example of an easier piece from Study Module 1.
- *The Lotus Awakes* by Gordon McLean is an example of a difficult piece from Study Module 6.

The Study Modules

The six Study Module discussions are organized into the following categories:

- *Background Information*
- *Exploring the Score*
- *Practice Suggestions*
- *Creative Activities*

Background Information (present in a few descriptions) provides relevant historical information. *Exploring the Score* is designed as an interactive exercise between teacher and student. These sections include questions you might address to the student during lessons. *Practice Suggestions* are also largely directly to the student. The *Creative Activities* act as reinforcement for your students' understanding of a musical concept and can provide a springboard for their creativity and imagination.

Please refer to the Foreword for an explanation of how to use the suggested order of assignment within each Module.

The chart on the opposite page lists all the repertoire and studies in Level 5. Page numbers for works in the *Piano Repertoire Album 5* and the *Piano Studies Album 5* are found in the first column. Study Module numbers for each composition are found in the fourth column.

Page	Composer	Title	Study Module

Piano Repertoire Album 5

List A
R4	Johann Sebastian Bach	Little Prelude in G Minor, BWV 929	1
R5	George Frideric Handel	Fuga in G Major, HWV 582	6
R6	Johann Pachelbel	Gavotte with Two Variations	1
R8	Gottfried Heinrich Stölzel	Minuet in G Minor	2
R9	Domenico Zipoli	Little Fugue in E Minor	3
R10	Georg Philipp Telemann	Minuet in G Major	4
R12	Johann Sebastian Bach	Allemande in G Minor, BWV 836	3
R13	Georg Philipp Telemann	Canzona d'Imitazione	5
R14	Domenico Scarlatti	Sonata in B Flat, LS 36/K 42 ("Minuetto")	4

List B
R16	Henri Bertini	Andante in A Major	4
R18	Dmitri Kabalevsky	Sonatina in A Minor, Op. 27, No. 18	5
R20	Carl Philipp Emanuel Bach	La Caroline	2
R22	Muzio Clementi	Sonatina in G Major, Op. 36, No. 5 (Third Movement: Rondo)	1
R24	Anton Diabelli	Sonatina in C Major, Op. 168, No. 3 (First Movement)	3

List C
R26	Robert Schumann	A Little Romance, Op. 68, No. 19	3
R27	Edvard Grieg	Arietta, Op. 12, No. 1	3
R28	Henryk Pachulski	Valse mignonne	1
R30	Walter Niemann	Cradle Song (For Dolly Dora)	1
R32	Jean Coulthard	Star Gazing	6
R34	Dmitri Shostakovich	The Mechanical Doll, Op. 69, No. 6	5
R36	Mychael Danna	Sleeping Bells	2
R37	George Fiala	Postlude, Op. 7, No. 6 (à la Shostakovich)	4
R38	Violet Archer	Jig	2
R40	Gordon McLean	The Lotus Awakes	6

Piano Studies Album 5

S4	Carl Czerny	Study No. 1: Op. 139, No. 40	3
S5	Stephen Heller	Study No. 2: A Curious Story, Op. 138, No. 9	5
S8	Antoine Henry Lemoine	Study No. 3: Op. 37, No. 44	1
S10	Alexander Gedike	Study No. 4: Op. 32, No. 16	5
S11	Samuil Maikapar	Study No. 5: Op. 31, No. 6	4
S12	Jean-Philippe Rameau	Study No. 6: La joyeuse	4
S14	Béla Bartók	Study No. 7: Bagatelle, Op. 6, No. 3	1
S16	Johann Friedrich Burgmüller	Study No. 8: The Chase, Op. 100, No. 9	3
S18	Dmitri Kabalevsky	Study No. 9: Scherzo, Op. 27, No. 13	6
S20	Albert Loeschhorn	Study No. 10: Op. 65, No. 40	2
S22	Stephen Heller	Study No. 11: Barcarole, Op. 138, No. 5	6
S23	Pál Kadosa	Study No. 12	2

STUDY MODULE 1

Page	List	Composer	Title	Meter and Tempo	Musical and Stylistic Concepts
R4 SG8	A	Johann Sebastian Bach	Little Prelude in G Minor, BWV 929	3/4 Andante moderato	✔ three independent voices ✔ flowing eighth-note melody ✔ detached quarter-note accompaniment ✔ modulation to relative major
R6 SG10	A	Johann Pachelbel	Gavotte with Two Variations	C; 3/4 Ritmico	✔ LH plays blocked intervals ✔ ornaments in melody ✔ second variation: *sarabande*
R22 SG20	B	Muzio Clementi	Sonatina in G Major, Op. 36, No. 5 (Third Movement: Rondo)	2/4 Allegro	✔ RH plays five-finger slurred sixteenth-note groups ✔ LH *staccato* double-notes ✔ rondo form
R28 SG24	C	Henryk Pachulski	Valse mignonne	3/4 Moderato	✔ four-measure phrases ✔ lyrical melody and waltz bass ✔ ABAB$_1$A ✔ requires careful pedaling
R30 SG25	C	Walter Niemann	Cradle Song (For Dolly Dora)	6/8 Drowsily	✔ LH plays quasi-*ostinato* figure ✔ requires careful balance between tune and accompaniment ✔ AA$_1$BA$_1$
S8		Antoine Henry Lemoine	Study No. 3: Op. 37, No. 44	C Andantino	✔ melodic motive divided between crossing hands ✔ broken chord texture ✔ consistent rhythm ✔ LH uses treble and bass clefs
S14		Béla Bartók	Study No. 7: Bagatelle, Op. 6, No. 3	3/4 Andante	✔ RH plays quintuplet chromatic *ostinato* ✔ singing LH melody ✔ both hands in treble clef

Assign first:
Little Prelude in G Minor, BWV 929 . . . .
Study No. 3: Op. 37, No. 44 . . . .
Valse mignonne . . . .

Study No. 7: Bagatelle, Op. 6, No. 3

Assign next when ready:
Gavotte with Two Variations
Cradle Song (For Dolly Dora)
Sonatina in G Major, Op. 36, No. 5
    (Third Movement: Rondo)

Study Module 1 includes pieces from the four major style periods. There is a variety of textures. *Little Prelude in G Minor* has three independent voices. The Clementi sonatina movement provides an example of typical Classical melody and accompaniment textures. *Valse mignonne* illustrates a waltz-bass accompaniment. *Study No. 7: Bagatelle* by Béla Bartók is built upon a chromatic *ostinato*.

J.S. Bach: *Little Prelude in G Minor, BWV 929*
(R4, SG8)

Background Information
Bach uses a wide variety of styles and forms in his preludes. Some of his preludes are improvisations on harmonic patterns. Others are contrapuntal inventions or dance movements. *Little Prelude in G Minor* could be subtitled "Minuet" because of its stately triple meter.

Exploring the Score
Most Baroque dances are in binary form. The A section modulates to the dominant or the relative major. The B section returns to the tonic.
- What is the key at the double bar in m. 8? [B flat major]
- What relationship is this to the original key of G minor? [relative major]

Practice Suggestions
Baroque composers rarely added slurs or *staccato* marks to their scores, because performers of the day knew to add the appropriate articulation. The footnote in the score suggests playing the LH quarter notes slightly detached.
- Practice combinations of voices: soprano and alto, soprano and bass, alto and bass.
- The suggested articulation for two-note slurs in mm. 5-6 in the *Student Guide* will help to move the musical line forward. Add similar two-note slurs on the eighth notes in m. 7. Follow the fingering suggestion to connect the held notes (voices) smoothly.

J. Pachelbel: *Gavotte with Two Variations*
(R6, SG10)

Background Information
Read the descriptions of *sarabande* and *gavotte* in the *Student Guide* (p. 7). Pachelbel's rhythm sounds like a *gavotte* but the "upbeat" quarter notes are actually on the downbeat.

Exploring the Score
Students can use their musical sleuthing skills to trace the elements of the theme through the two variations:
- Name the beginning and ending harmonies of each four-measure phrase. [mm. 1-4: A minor, C major; mm. 5-8: E major, A minor, etc.]
- Does each variation follow this harmonic scheme? [yes, but the piece ends in A major]

- The melody of the theme has an up-down shape (mm. 1-2 and 5-6). Do the variations have that same melodic shape? [Variation 1 more than Variation 2]
- There is a rising 4th in mm. 5-6. Can you find this interval in the second phrase of the variations?
- Find the bass notes of m. 1 (A-G sharp-A) in the opening of both variations. Find other places where Pachelbel uses half-step movement.

M. Clementi: *Sonatina in G Major, Op. 36, No. 5 (Third Movement: Rondo)* (R22, SG20)

Exploring the Score
The most common rondo forms are ABACA or ABACABA. Study the form outline for this rondo in the *Student Guide*, and mark the sections in the score. This piece is an abridged version. If possible, show your students a score of Clementi's original rondo. Compare the form and find what changes were made to produce the abridged version.

Practice Suggestions
The primary goal is to play the sixteenth notes clearly and evenly. Devise five-finger drills based on mm. 1-4, and see the practice suggestions in the *Student Guide*. Most students will have more difficulty with figures that change direction. Use a rocking hand motion for the zig-zag patterns in mm. 24-25.

Mark the four-measure phrases in the score. Have students play only downbeat notes in mm. 1-16. Shape the sequence of downbeats so that each third measure is the loudest and each fourth measure is the quietest.

H. Pachulski: *Valse mignonne* (R28, SG24)

Exploring the Score
This charming waltz is a carefully crafted composition. Mark the sections in the music (see *Student Guide*).

The melody moves primarily by step. The stepwise motion is quite obvious in the B section.
- Circle the downward steps in mm. 17-24.
- In mm. 41-46, both hands move by step.

The stepwise motion is not readily apparent in the A section:
- Circle the downward steps in mm. 1-8.

"What goes up must come down." "What goes down must come up." Which rule applies in this piece?

Practice Suggestions

See the practice suggestions in the *Student Guide*. Draw students' attention to the dynamic shape of the four-measure phrases. Make a slight *crescendo* to the third measure, then release with a *diminuendo* in the fourth measure.

W. Niemann: *Cradle Song (For Dolly Dora)*
(R30, SG25)
Exploring the Score

Ask students what dynamic level, tempo, meter, and rhythm they would expect to find in a lullaby. The music might suggest:

- that the melody is the mother's song
- that the baby falls asleep
- that the mother tip-toes out of the room

Compare the student's suggestions with Walter Niemann's piece.

Practice Suggestions

The hands have different patterns of drop-lift motions.

- Drop the LH on the downbeat and lift on the fourth beat.
- Drop the RH on the first and fourth beats and lift on the third and sixth beats.
- Practice the coordination of these movements on the closed keyboard cover.

A.H. Lemoine: *Study No. 3: Op. 37, No. 44* (S8)
Practice Suggestions

With the ringing sound of the three accented quarter notes in each measure, this study could be subtitled "The Bells." The quarter notes outline the structure.

- Play only the quarter notes. Use pedal as indicated in the score.
- Practice two- and four-measure segments playing the LH as written and blocking the RH chords.

B. Bartók: *Study No. 7: Bagatelle, Op. 6, No. 3*
(S14)
Practice Suggestions

The RH *ostinato* pattern has a chromatic position.

- Practice the RH separately. Use variations such as a *staccato* touch or dotted rhythms.
- Play the RH as written, and listen for an even sound.

Decide on a dynamic plan for the LH phrases. Exaggerate the dynamics during practice.

CREATIVE ACTIVITIES

Write a new LH accompaniment for the question-and-answer melody (mm. 1-8) in Clementi's *Sonatina in G Major*. Transpose the melody to a minor key and write another accompaniment. Compose your own question-and-answer melody in the style of Clementi.

Make up words for part of the melody of Niemann's *Cradle Song* (for example, mm. 1-2: "Sleep, oh ba-by, go to sleep.").

Create your own lullaby by writing a simple LH rocking motive (for example, C-G-C-G) and adding a melody on top.

Improvise a new LH melody for Bartók's RH chromatic *ostinato* from *Study No. 7*.

STUDY MODULE 2

Page	List	Composer	Title	Meter and Tempo	Musical and Stylistic Concepts
R8 SG11	A	Gottfried Heinrich Stölzel	Minuet in G Minor	3/4 Con deciso	✔ homophonic texture ✔ detailed RH articulation ✔ accompaniment mainly single notes
R20 SG19	B	Carl Philipp Emanuel Bach	La Caroline	2/4 Allegro ma con tenerezza	✔ RH *legato* 3rds and 6ths ✔ LH repeated single notes ✔ rounded binary form
R36 SG28	C	Mychael Danna	Sleeping Bells	6/8 Largo	✔ chordal texture ✔ RH plays double notes ✔ pedal used for chime effect
R38 SG30	C	Violet Archer	Jig	6/8 Lively	✔ LH open 5ths support RH melody ✔ lively dance ✔ prominent articulation and accents
S20		Albert Loeschhorn	Study No. 10: Op. 65, No. 40	2/4 Allegro	✔ irregular division of four-measure phrases ✔ sixteenth-note passages in both hands ✔ LH blocked triads in all positions
S23		Pál Kadosa	Study No. 12	3/8 and 2/4 Vivo	✔ additive meter ✔ LH repeats blocked and broken 5ths ✔ both hands *staccato* throughout ✔ AA₁ *coda*

Assign first:
Minuet in G Minor . . . .
Study No. 10: Op. 65, No. 40 . . . .
Sleeping Bells . . . .

Assign next when ready:
Study No. 12
La Caroline
Jig

Study Module 2 can be subtitled the "Chord Module" because of the consistent use of chords and blocked intervals. Violet Archer's *Jig* and Pál Kadosa's *Study No. 12* both have blocked 5ths in the LH accompaniments. The decisive chords in Stölzel's *Minuet in G Minor* stand in contrast to the largely two-voice texture. The richness of the chordal textures in Mychael Danna's *Sleeping Bells* is enhanced by the use of the damper pedal.

G.F. Stölzel: *Minuet in G Minor* (R8, SG11)
Exploring the Score

Performers in Stölzel's day understood how to combine *legato* and *staccato* touches in an elegant minuet. See the discussion of articulation in the *Student Guide*. Listen for the variety of articulation in the *Celebration Series* recording.

- The *Celebration Series* editing of this Baroque minuet includes four different touches: *legato*, *tenuto*, *staccato*, and *portato*.
- How does Stölzel add emphasis to the downbeats? [chords, slurs, *tenuto* marks]
- Notice the eighth-note figure beginning with a downbeat slur. Play the unmarked eighth notes with a lightly detached touch.

Practice Suggestion

Devise articulation exercises (based on a Hanon study or a five-finger pattern) to explore different articulations such as all *staccato*, or two-note slurs, or a combination:

C.P.E. Bach: *La Caroline* (R20, SG19)
Exploring the Score

This piece is marked *Allegro ma con tenerezza*. The key word is *tenerezza* – delicately, tenderly, softly.

- How does C.P.E. Bach achieve sensitive, tender musical expression? [dynamics, detailed slurs, *legato* touch, two-note sighing motive]
- How can you add expression to the LH repeated-note figures? [try a subtle *diminuendo*]

M. Danna: *Sleeping Bells* (R36, SG28)
Exploring the Score

- Find the measures of chiming bells. [mm. 9-10, 13-14, 27-28]
- Play these measures with pedal as indicated.
- How many different ways does Danna divide the dotted-quarter-note beat? [see mm. 1-2 and m. 12]

The remainder of the piece is tuneful. Make up words to fit the melody (for example, mm. 1-2: "Where are the bells that used to be ring-ing?").

Practice Suggestions

1. Play the melody (top RH notes). Listen for a *legato* tone.
2. Divide the RH voices between the hands. Bring out the melody.
3. Play the RH part as written. Listen for the melody.
4. Play the LH. Change the pedal on each beat.
5. Play hands together with pedal.

V. Archer: *Jig* (R38, SG30)
Exploring the Score

This piece was inspired by traditional French-Canadian fiddle music. Fiddlers often tap their feet as they play. In *Jig*, the RH plays the fiddle tune and the LH imitates foot-tapping.

- How many different LH "foot-tapping 5ths" (rhythms and articulations) can you find? [dotted half note, dotted quarter note, *staccato* eighth note, etc.]
- A jig often repeats rhythms and melody. How does Violet Archer create contrast in this piece? [alternating hands, mm. 9-10 and 13-14; blocked chords, mm. 25 and 29]
- Find repetitions of the LH 5ths in mm. 1-4.

A. Loeschhorn: *Study No. 10: Op. 65, No. 40* (S20)
Exploring the Score

Most four-measure phrases are made up of two equal parts, but the opening four-measure phrase of this study seems unbalanced. It is divided into two slurred groups.

- Count the number of beats in each slurred group. [three and five beats]
- Is the second phrase divided the same way? [three and four beats]
- Find places where material is repeated in a different octave (for example, mm. 1-4 and 5-8). Did you include the LH of mm. 26-27 and 30-31?

P. Kadosa: *Study No. 12* (S23)
Background Information

Pál Kadosa and his teacher Béla Bartók were devoted to the folk music of their native Hungary. Mixed meters are a prominent characteristic of Eastern European folk music.

Exploring the Score

This study has two time signatures: 3/8 and 2/4. Look for patterns of 3/8 and 2/4 measures.

- Are there different patterns? [yes]
- What is the most frequent pattern? [3/8 + 2/4 + 3/8] Bracket the groups of measures that do not follow this pattern.

Point out the relationship between the LH notes and the melodic phrasing. Each LH change of pitch signals the beginning of a new RH phrase. How long are the phrases? [3 measures] In performance, emphasize the changing bass notes.

CREATIVE ACTIVITITY

Create your own jig by improvising a melody over the LH 5ths in mm. 1-4 of Archer's *Jig*.

STUDY MODULE 3

Page	List	Composer	Title	Meter and Tempo	Musical and Stylistic Concepts
R9 SG12	A	Domenico Zipoli	Little Fugue in E Minor	3/8 Energico	✔ imitative two- and three-voice texture ✔ good piece for small hands
R12 SG14	A	Johann Sebastian Bach	Allemande in G Minor, BWV 836	C	✔ variety of sixteenth- and eighth-note combinations ✔ RH single voice ✔ LH plays two voices ✔ upbeat pattern
R24 SG21	B	Anton Diabelli	Sonatina in C Major, Op. 168, No. 3 (First Movement)	C Allegro moderato	✔ sonatina style ✔ varying accompaniment styles ✔ requires careful RH phrasing
R26 SG22	C	Robert Schumann	A Little Romance, Op. 68, No. 19	C Nicht schnell	✔ hands play unison melody and share accompaniment ✔ chordal texture ✔ requires careful voicing
R27 SG23	C	Edvard Grieg	Arietta, Op. 12, No. 1	2/4 Poco andante e sostenuto	✔ typical 19th-century texture: melody, bass, and inner harmony ✔ sensitive dynamic shaping
S4		Carl Czerny	Study No. 1: Op. 139, No. 40	2/4 Moderato	✔ grace notes on each beat of opening theme ✔ *staccato* texture
S16		Johann Friedrich Burgmüller	Study No. 8: The Chase, Op. 100, No. 9	6/8 Allegro vivace	✔ introductory horn call motive ✔ LH melody in double notes ✔ RH motive: broken octave with repeated note ✔ rondo form with distinct B and C sections

Assign first:

Little Fugue in E Minor . . . .

Sonatina in C Major, Op. 168, No. 3
  (First Movement)

Study No. 1: Op. 139, No. 40 . . . .

A Little Romance, Op. 68, No. 19 . . . .

Assign next when ready:

Allemande in G Minor, BWV 836

Study No. 8: The Chase, Op. 100, No. 9

Arietta, Op. 12, No. 1

The focus of Study Module 3 is melody. The melody of *Little Fugue in E Minor* is presented in three contrapuntal voices. In *The Chase*, the LH melody imitates hunting horns. In Robert Schumann's *A Little Romance*, the hands play a unison melody and accompaniment. Edvard Grieg's *Arietta* has a hauntingly expressive melody. The Baroque period is represented by two new genres – an *allemande* and a fugue.

D. Zipoli: *Little Fugue in E Minor* (R9, SG12)
Background Information
Domenico Zipoli was a dedicated church musician. Like most of his keyboard works, this fugue was written for organ and intended for church use.

Practice Suggestions
Here is a set of practice steps for a fugue:
1. Find the subject (theme). Bracket each statement.
2. Determine the mood or character of the subject (for example, playful, serious, energetic), and decide on an appropriate articulation. The articulation should highlight important intervals and clarify the rhythm and meter.
3. Practice hands separately or play individual voices. Pay special attention to the fingering.
4. Practice hands together, slowly, in short sections.

J.S. Bach: *Allemande in G Minor, BWV 836* (R12, SG14)
Background Information
In Bach's time, printed music was expensive and difficult to obtain. Bach's students often studied pieces and exercises which he wrote out by hand. Read the two biographical notes about J.S. Bach in the *Student Guide* (pp. 8 and 14) and introduce your students to Bach's two instructional notebooks: the *Anna Magdalena Notebook* and the *Wilhelm Friedemann Bach Notebook.* (Students first encountered the *Anna Magdalena Notebook* in Level 3 with *Musette in D Major, BWV Anh. 126.*)

Exploring the Score
Have students make a list of the characteristics of this piece and compare the list with the description of an *allemande* on p. 7 of the *Student Guide.*

- Most *allemandes* have an eighth-note upbeat. In this piece, the upbeat introduces a two-beat rhythmic motive:

- This upbeat rhythm unifies the dance. Which rhythms provide contrast? [m. 5, mm. 8-13]

See the outline of the form in the *Student Guide.* The length of the A section – five measures – is unusual.
- Play the A section, ending in m. 4.
- How does Bach use the extra measure? [cadential reinforcement: m. 5 repeats m. 4 an octave lower]

A. Diabelli: *Sonatina in C Major, Op. 168, No. 3 (First Movement)* (R24, SG21)
Exploring the Score
See the form outline in the *Student Guide.*

This rhythm dominates the first theme and the development section:

- How does Diabelli vary the first theme in the exposition? [melody presented an octave higher, change of accompaniment]
- How does Diabelli vary the first theme in the development section? [new harmonization, dotted figure stated chromatically, theme in minor mode, dotted half note subdivided in smaller units]
- How many different LH accompaniment figures can you find?

R. Schumann: *A Little Romance, Op. 68, No. 19* (R26, SG22)
Exploring the Score
How is the title reflected in the music? Perhaps the unison melody suggests a musical duet or romance between the hands. Both hands play both melody and accompaniment – an unusual arrangement.
- Where are the quietest moments?
- Which phrases have the greatest dynamic contrast?

Listen to the *Celebration Series* recording and discuss the balance of sound between melody and accompaniment. As an experiment, play the piece leaving out the LH melody notes.

Practice Suggestions
- Make sure the melody notes sound exactly together.
- Project the melody over the accompaniment.

E. Grieg: *Arietta, Op. 12, No. 1* (R27, SG23)
Practice Suggestions
Dynamics are the clues to the interpretation of this piece. Focus your practice on dynamic control.

1. Play only the melody and bass line. Use pedal. Listen for a *crescendo-diminuendo* pattern in each two-measure phrase. Shape the two-note slurs in mm. 5-8.
2. Play only the inner sixteenth notes, smoothly and quietly.
3. Isolate mm. 9, 11, 19, and 21 for RH practice. Pay attention to the fingering and the *legato* crossing of the third finger.

C. Czerny: *Study No. 1: Op. 139, No. 40* (S4)
Practice Suggestions
This study is organized into eight-measure periods. Use a light *staccato* touch. Play the opening motive with a drop-lift movement of the hand. Keep the thumb notes light. During practice sessions:

- Block and name the chords in the A section.
- Find the RH stepwise motion and circle those notes. [mm. 1-4: F, G, A, C; mm. 5-8: B flat, A, G, F]
- Did you notice the difference between mm. 14-15 and 30-31?

J.F. Burgmüller: *Study No. 8: The Chase, Op. 100, No. 9* (S16)
Background Information
Burgmüller (1806-1874) was a popular pianist who composed hundreds of teaching pieces. *The Chase*, from *Twenty-five Progressive Pieces, Op. 100*, is among the most popular.

Practice Suggestions

- The opening chords are marked with wedges. Give these chords a *staccato* touch.
- Keep your arm and hand loose and flexible for the RH repeated notes in mm. 5-7 and 9-11. Find a hand motion that groups the three eighth notes together. Try these two fingerings: **5-1-2** and **5-1-1**, and choose the one that gives the lightest sound.
- Notice the contrasting articulation in mm. 13-20. The RH plays *legato* double 3rds and the LH plays two-note slurs. Articulate the LH slurs carefully.

CREATIVE ACTIVITY
Play the melody of a familiar tune (for example, *Happy Birthday*). Add accompanying chords to the melody. In the style of the Diabelli *Sonatina in C Major (First Movement)*, use at least three different accompaniment figures.

STUDY MODULE 4

Page	List	Composer	Title	Meter and Tempo	Musical and Stylistic Concepts
R10 SG13	A	Georg Philipp Telemann	Minuet in G Major	3/4 Andantino grazioso	✔ RH arpeggiated figures ✔ LH detached notes ✔ slurred eighth-note figures ✔ rounded binary form
R14 SG16	A	Domenico Scarlatti	Sonata in B Flat, LS 36/K 42 ("Minuetto")	3/4 Andantino grazioso	✔ two-voice texture ✔ ornaments on second and third beats ✔ leaps and skips in each hand ✔ binary form
R16 SG17	B	Henri Bertini	Andante in A Major	C Andante cantabile	✔ contrast between short slurred motives and longer phrases ✔ modulation to parallel minor ✔ LH Alberti bass in B section
R37 SG29	C	George Fiala	Postlude, Op. 7, No. 6 (à la Shostakovich)	2/4 Adagietto	✔ startling harmonic colors ✔ melody with chordal bass ✔ both hands in treble clef
S11		Samuil Maikapar	Study No. 5: Op. 31, No. 6	2/4 Allegretto	✔ study in RH repeated *staccato* 6ths
S12		Jean-Philippe Rameau	Study No. 6: La joyeuse	2/2 Allegro	✔ quasi-imitative eighth-note scale lines between hands at the interval of a 3rd and 10th

Assign first:
Minuet in G Major. . . . .
Andante in A Major . . . .
Study No. 5: Op. 31, No. 6 . . . .

Assign next when ready:
Sonata in B Flat, LS 36/K 42 ("Minuetto")
Postlude, Op. 7, No. 6 (à la Shostakovich)
Study No. 6: La joyeuse

This Study Module includes two Baroque minuets which provide the opportunity to discuss contrasts of rhythm and phrase structure. *Andante in A Major* by Henri Bertini contains both long *legato* phrases and phrases made of short motives. George Fiala's *Postlude* also contains longer phrase groupings and has highly original harmonies. The two studies use different touches and figures: The Maikapar study is dominated by *staccato* blocked intervals. Rameau's *La joyeuse* is made up of imitative scale figures.

G.P. Telemann: *Minuet in G Major* (R10, SG13)
Exploring the Score
Dance rhythms usually emphasize the downbeat. How does Telemann treat the downbeat in *Minuet*? There is a difference in rhythmic emphasis between mm. 1-4 and mm. 5-8.

- In mm. 1-2, the eighth-note figures lead to the following downbeats.
- In mm. 5-8, the eighth-note figures start on the downbeat.
- Find the emphasis and goal for other rhythmic groupings.

Look for accidentals in the score. Each accidental prepares for a modulation.

- Baroque dances usually modulate to the dominant at the end of the A section. What is the key of m. 12? [G major – no modulation]
- Does the B section remain in G major? [no]

Find and label the modulations, then play through these measures to hear how each accidental pulls the music toward the new key.

Review the definition of a sequence.
- A sequence begins in m. 25. How long is the pattern? [4 mm.]

Practice Suggestions

Decide on a dynamic shape for the eighth-note figures. The rise and fall of the melody suggests musical contours. Tap the rhythm, hands together, with the dynamics.

D. Scarlatti: *Sonata in B Flat, LS 36/ K 42* (*"Minuetto"*) (R14, SG16)
Exploring the Score

Realizations for the ornaments are printed below the music. Baroque ornaments start on the beat. Play the first note of the ornament with the note in the opposite hand. (See the discussion of ornaments in the *Student Guide.*)

Scarlatti creates rhythmic interest by placing ornaments on different beats of the measure. Look through the score to find which ornaments emphasize the first beat, the second beat, and the third beat of the measure.

Practice Suggestion

A variety of connected and detached LH notes will give elegance and dance quality to the bass part.

H. Bertini: *Andante in A Major* (R16, SG17)
Exploring the Score

This piece is in ternary form. Within that form, the A sections have two parts. After the B section, the opening material returns as it would in a rounded binary form. The chart in the *Student Guide* outlines the form and gives the keys for each section. Draw your student's attention to the relationships between A major, A minor, and E major.

- The opening melody of the A section is constructed from groups of two, three, and four notes. They form part of a four-measure question. Is the answer also four measures long? [yes, mm. 5-8]
- Does Bertini use this same balance in the B section? [yes]
- Listen for the contrast between the short motives (A section) and the long lines (B section) in the *Celebration Series* recording.

G. Fiala: *Postlude, Op. 7, No. 6 (à la Shostakovich)* (R37, SG29)
Exploring the Score

Have students find the following elements in the score:
- four-measure phrases
- cadences in E flat minor [mm. 4, 15, 23]
- abrupt shifts of harmony [look for accidentals]

Notice the unexpected new color created by the RH 7th in m. 16 where the opening melody returns.

S. Maikapar: *Study No. 5: Op. 31, No. 6* (S11)
Practice Suggestions

The primary goal is to play the *staccato* 6ths with lightness and ease. Think of the sixteenth-note or sixteenth- and eighth-note figures as a single unit. Use a "throw and lift" hand and wrist movement to play these groups in one motion. Drop the hand from a lifted position to play the first note. Play the other notes as you lift your wrist.

J.-P. Rameau: *Study No. 6: La joyeuse* (S12)
Exploring the Score

Point out the *Rondeau* and *Couplet* markings in the score and have your student explore the formal structure. Does this piece have a rondo form? (Refer to the discussion of rondo form in Study Module 1.)

Practice Suggestions

Create a duet by dividing the two-part texture with your student or by sequencing each line on a digital piano track. (With the latter format, you can practice one line while listening to the other line, and vary the speed or tempo.)

- Prepare for this study by practicing D major and A major scales slowly in parallel 3rds and 10ths. This is more challenging than parallel octave scales because of the different relationship of fingerings between the hands.
- Practice each scale fragment in this study with special emphasis on fingering.
- Circle fingerings in the score that represent the crucial crossings.

CREATIVE ACTIVITIES

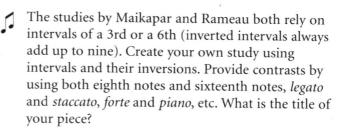

Choreograph the first section of Telemann's *Minuet in G Major*. Let your movements reflect the sound and character of the music.
- Where will the movements be the most active?
- Where does the music move in confined space? [mm. 5, 7]
- What different steps can you use for the measures with only quarter notes?

The studies by Maikapar and Rameau both rely on intervals of a 3rd or a 6th (inverted intervals always add up to nine). Create your own study using intervals and their inversions. Provide contrasts by using both eighth notes and sixteenth notes, *legato* and *staccato*, *forte* and *piano*, etc. What is the title of your piece?

STUDY MODULE 5

Page	List	Composer	Title	Meter and Tempo	Musical and Stylistic Concepts
R13 SG15	A	Georg Philipp Telemann	Canzona d'Imitazione	C Moderato	✔ two-voice imitative texture ✔ cadential ornamentation ✔ hands have independent articulation and phrasing ✔ binary form
R18 SG18	B	Dmitri Kabalevsky	Sonatina in A Minor, Op. 27, No. 18	C Allegretto	✔ energetic dotted and double-dotted rhythms ✔ LH plays blocked chords ✔ exposition and recapitulation; no development section
R34 SG27	C	Dmitri Shostakovich	The Mechanical Doll, Op. 69, No. 6	2/4 Brightly	✔ RH melody based on B minor five-finger pattern ✔ LH plays melody in A_1 section ✔ *legato* sixteenths, *staccato* eighths ✔ ABA_1 form
S5		Stephen Heller	Study No. 2: A Curious Story, Op. 138, No. 9	2/4 Molto vivace	✔ theme combines triplets and dotted rhythms ✔ frequent shifts of position ✔ wide dynamic range
S10		Alexander Gedike	Study No. 4: Op. 32, No. 16	2/4 Allegro moderato	✔ entire piece based on two-sixteenths and eighth motive in both hands ✔ ABA_1C form

Assign first:
Canzona d'Imitazione . . . .
The Mechanical Doll, Op. 69, No. 6 . . . .
Study No. 2: A Curious Story, Op. 138, No. 9

Assign next when ready:
Study No. 4: Op. 32, No. 16
Sonatina in A Minor, Op. 27, No. 18

In Study Module 5, several rhythmic concepts and imitative devices occur in more than one piece, often representing different style periods. There are dotted rhythms in Heller's *A Curious Story* and the more difficult Kabalevsky *Sonatina in A Minor*. Telemann's *Canzona d'Imitazione* and Gedike's *Study No. 4* both use the same rhythmic motive (two sixteenths followed by an eighth). Students can compare the imitative devices used in *Canzona d'Imitazione* and Shostakovich's *The Mechanical Doll* in the context of Baroque and contemporary style periods.

G. P. Telemann: *Canzona d'Imitazione*
(R13, SG15)

Exploring the Score

See the historical account of the term *canzona* in the *Student Guide*. The *Celebration Series* recording provides a fine model of articulation. Discuss this articulation and explore other possibilities. For example, all notes not marked with a slur could be lightly detached.

- Find the points of imitation where the LH imitates the RH.
- Where does the LH anticipate the RH melody? [m. 8]

In Baroque music, the cadence was the goal of a section. Composers often increased harmonic and rhythmic activity to intensify the arrival at a cadence. One method was to use a cadential trill for its effect of dissonance leading to resolution. The cadential trill was so standard that composers often did not write it in the score, knowing that performers of the day would add the ornamentation.

- Find the cadential trills in this piece.
- Look for cadential trills in other Baroque compositions in *Album 5* (for example, Pachelbel's *Gavotte with Two Variations*, R6).

Practice Suggestion

Imitation involves repetition of rhythm, melodic shape, and articulation. Practice each RH phrase, then imitate that sound exactly in the LH.

D. Kabalevsky: *Sonatina in A Minor, Op. 27, No. 18* (R18, SG18)

Exploring the Score

Sonatinas are little sonatas, sometimes with fewer or shorter movements. This sonatina is in modified sonata form. Read the description of the form of this sonatina in the *Student Guide*.

- The two themes are strongly contrasting.
- The return of the first theme in m. 25 is clear.
- There is no development section. (Notice that there is no double bar.)

Practice Suggestions

Precise, accurate rhythm is a top priority in this piece. How can you check the rhythmic accuracy of the dotted motive? There is a tapping exercise in the *Student Guide*. Here are more suggestions:

1. Count sixteenths to check the accuracy of the dotted figure.
2. Tap hands together with a metronome.
3. Tap contrasting rhythmic units (for example: m. 5, mm. 7-8, mm. 17-18, mm. 21-22).
4. Play mm. 1-4, then mm. 13-16. Exaggerate the contrast in dynamics (*mf, p*) and mood.

D. Shostakovich: *The Mechanical Doll, Op. 69, No. 6* (R34, SG27)

Exploring the Score

A wind-up mechanical doll has a limited number of movements (such as walking, moving arms, turning head). Does the rhythm reflect this limitation?

- How many different note values are there?
- How many different combinations of sixteenth notes and eighth notes can you find?
- Tap the rhythm of mm. 1-2. Find any rhythms that are different. Tap those rhythms.

Explore the melody and dynamics.

- How many measures are played *forte*?
- Where does the LH play the opening melody? [m. 30]

Practice Suggestion

Label the rising sixteenth-note five-finger patterns (for example: B minor, A major, F major, etc.). Practice each pattern with its following shift of position.

S. Heller: *Study No. 2: A Curious Story, Op. 138, No. 9* (S5)

Exploring the Score

With your student, label the sections in the score.

- Where is the opening theme repeated? [m. 37]
- What section most resembles mm. 21-28? [falling arpeggios of mm. 85-91]
- Which section has the most relaxed tempo? [mm. 53-60]
- Where is the greatest build-up of tension? [mm. 61-69]

Have your student find and label the diminished 7th chords in mm. 62, 64, and 66.

A. Gedike: *Study No. 4: Op. 32, No. 16* (S10)

Practice Suggestion

This study is built around a single slurred figure. The challenge is to keep this figure clear and precise in a variety of dynamic levels. Help your student decide on a suitable hand and arm movement for the figure. Does the gesture change when the figure is descending rather than ascending?

CREATIVE ACTIVITY

Kabalevsky's *Sonatina in A Minor* is built on two contrasting themes. Invent two contrasting themes of your own: a vigorous theme in a minor key, and a lyrical theme in a major key. Create a suitable accompaniment for each theme, and combine them to build a sonatina! (You can call your piece *First Sonatina* or give it a special name.)

STUDY MODULE 6

Page	List	Composer	Title	Meter and Tempo	Musical and Stylistic Concepts
R5 SG9	A	George Frideric Handel	Fuga in G Major, HWV 582	C Moderato e cantabile	✔ imitative two-voice texture ✔ dotted quarter-note rhythms ✔ moving eighth notes
R32 SG26	C	Jean Coulthard	Star Gazing	4/4 Quite slowly	✔ twelve-tone technique ✔ free tempo, improvisatory ✔ both hands in treble clef
R40 SG31	C	Gordon McLean	The Lotus Awakes	4/4 Quietly	✔ beautiful lyricism, distinctive harmonies, Scriabin-like colors ✔ whole-tone scale ✔ many accidentals
S18		Dmitri Kabalevsky	Study No. 9: Scherzo, Op. 27, No. 13	3/4 Allegro scherzando	✔ running *staccato* eighths between the hands ✔ RH controls both melody and accompaniment ✔ AA₁ coda
S22		Stephen Heller	Study No. 11: Barcarole, Op. 138, No. 5	6/8 Lento, con morbidezza	✔ LH slow waltz-bass pattern ✔ RH motives create rocking effect ✔ highly expressive

Assign first:
Fuga in G Major, HWV 582 . . . .
Star Gazing . . . .
Study No. 11: Barcarole, Op. 138, No. 5

Assign next when ready:
Study No. 9: Scherzo, Op. 27, No. 13
The Lotus Awakes

This final Study Module includes a wide range of styles: a Baroque fugue (*Fuga in G Major* by Handel), a Romantic character piece (*Study No. 11: Barcarole* by Stephen Heller) and an improvisatory twelve-tone experience (*Star Gazing* by Jean Coulthard).

Study Module 6 provides several opportunities to reinforce concepts which have occurred throughout Level 5. Compare the use of imitative devices in Baroque and 20th-century styles. *Star Gazing* and *The Lotus Awakes* provide examples of imitation in a contemporary context.

G.F. Handel: *Fuga in G Major, HWV 582* (R5, SG9)

Exploring the Score
Handel's fugue does not match the textbook definitions of the form, but it is a contrapuntal piece with two distinctly individual voices.

- Find other appearances of the opening RH theme. [look for dotted quarters]
- Find places where a musical idea moves from hand to hand. For example, compare the RH and LH parts of mm. 1-2.
- What is the name of the musical device in mm. 5-8? [sequence]

Consult the *Student Guide* and listen to the *Celebration Series* recording for ideas on articulation. Two generally-accepted rules apply to this piece: detach octave leaps and detach before a syncopated note.

J. Coulthard: *Star Gazing* (R32, SG26)

Exploring the Score
The *Student Guide* is quite indispensable for the study of this piece. It includes a picturesque setting of the scene and an analysis of the twelve-tone technique employed in each of the "star points."

Listen to the *Celebration Series* recording for an example of one way to play the measures marked "freely."

Practice Suggestions
The LH fingerings in mm. 4-6, 9-11, 14-16 and 18-21 promote *legato* playing. Practice first without pedal as follows:

1. Divide the two LH voices between the hands to hear the *legato* connections.
2. Play the LH part as written.
3. Add pedal as indicated to enhance the *legato* line.

G. McLean: *The Lotus Awakes* (R40, SG31)
Exploring the Score

Harmonies created with the notes of a whole-tone scale have a magical, spellbinding sound. Gravity seems suspended and we are removed to a different world. Discuss these qualities with your student in relation to the measures based on the whole-tone scale (mm. 1-4, 15-16).

There is no key signature, but the full flowering of the lotus is associated with B major. Looking backwards from the end, notice the many B major chords. (See the *Student Guide* for a detailed description of the three sections of this piece.)

Practice Suggestions

The sound created with the damper pedal is integral to this piece. Follow the pedal markings carefully.

- How would you describe the tone quality which best suits this piece?
- What touch will you use to achieve that tone? Will you curve your fingers or extend them slightly? Will you use a precise Baroque touch, or an extremely *legato* articulation?

D. Kabalevsky: *Study No. 9: Scherzo, Op. 27, No. 13* (S18)
Exploring the Score

Review the definition of a *scherzo* with your student. This study is truly light-hearted and "joking." Can you hear the *staccato* eighth notes laughing?

Practice Suggestions

Kabalevsky's score is quite detailed. Every note has a mark – *staccato*, *legato*, or *tenuto* – and there is a dynamic indication in most measures. There are two approaches to practicing this piece:

1. Play the piece slowly, making each marking clearly audible.
2. Play the notes firmly, *mezzo forte*, with a *legato* touch. This helps establish correct fingering and technical security.

S. Heller: *Study No. 11: Barcarole, Op. 138, No. 5* (S22)
Exploring the Score

Has your student played other pieces titled *Barcarole*

(for example, the *Barcarole* by Duke in Level 4)? Discuss the origin of the barcarole.

- What is the meaning of *Lento, con morbidezza*?
- Where are the longest groups of slurred notes? [mm. 23-24]
- What are the shortest slurred groups? [two-note slurs]
- Compare the broken 6th figures in mm. 7 and 22. Why would Heller slur the same notes differently?

Short slurs indicate articulation. Emphasize the first note of the group. Longer slurs indicate *legato* groups. However, notice the *staccato* and accent markings within the longer slurs in mm. 9, 14, and 19.

Practice Suggestions

How does the damper pedal contribute to a rocking-boat effect? For a smooth, "seamless" sound, practice the LH alone with pedal.

Where is the dynamic peak of the piece? Listen for each dynamic marking: *piano, pianissimo, mezzo piano, mezzo forte, forte piano,* and *sforzando*. How does the performer on the *Celebration Series* recording interpret these dynamic marks?

CREATIVE ACTIVITIES

 Explore twelve-tone technique:
- Create a twelve-tone row.
- Play Coulthard's *Star Gazing*, substituting your tone row in mm. 2, 7, 12, and 17.
- Vary your tone row by inverting it or playing it backwards.

 There are two possible configurations for a whole-tone scale:

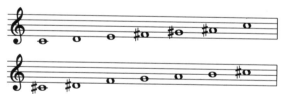

Using *The Lotus Awakes* as a model, compose an ABA piece. In the A sections, use one whole-tone scale configuration. Play only single notes. Base the B section on the other whole-tone scale configuration. Play a combination of single notes and blocked intervals or chords made from that scale.

LEVEL 5 SUMMARY
- In Level 5, which Baroque compositions use ornamentation? What symbols represent the different ornaments? What practice steps did you follow to coordinate the ornaments with the other voice(s)?
- The 19th-century Romantic pieces among the Level 5 repertoire and studies provide a great variety of accompaniment styles. Find examples of: melody in both hands, broken octaves over repeated chords, waltz bass, and melody intertwined with an inner accompaniment over single bass notes.
- Level 5 includes several 20th-century pieces. Find pieces which use *ostinato* figures, additive meter, twelve-tone and whole-tone writing.

Level 6

The Publications

Level 6 of the *Celebration Series* includes the following publications:

Piano Repertoire Album 6
Piano Studies Album 5 & 6 (level 6 only)
Student Guide 6
Recording of *Repertoire & Studies 6*

The Repertoire

The *Piano Repertoire Album 6* is divided into three lists:

- List A includes a selection of pieces composed during the Baroque period (*ca* 1600 to *ca* 1750).
- List B includes a selection of pieces composed during the Classical period (*ca* 1750 to *ca* 1820) as well as pieces in the Classical style written during the 19th century.
- List C includes a selection of pieces composed during the Romantic era (*ca* 1820 to *ca* 1910) and the 20th century.

Musical Development

Level 6 provides a wide variety of late intermediate repertoire and technical studies representing the four major style periods. Students will continue their musical growth as they become acquainted with Baroque dances, Classical sonatinas and sonatas, Romantic character pieces, and contemporary sounds.

Literature from the Baroque period ranges from two- and three-part dances (*gigue, bourrée, allemande*, and *sarabanda*) to J.S. Bach's *Little Prelude in D Minor* from the *Wilhelm Friedemann Bach Notebook* and the four-voice *Aria in A Major* by Telemann.

Six sonata and sonatina movements from the Classical period provide students with an opportunity to explore sonata-allegro form and to compare the approaches of various composers to this form. Topics for student-teacher discussions include the form in general, the number of themes, key relationships and modulations, and how composers create contrast.

The Romantic and early 20th-century repertoire in List C provides opportunities for students to interpret character pieces portraying a specific mood or style, and to explore a larger and more diverse harmonic palette. In this repertoire, students will need more hand and finger independence and will further develop their pedal technique.

The Range of Difficulty

The range of difficulty in Level 6 is represented by these two pieces:

- *Sonatina in G Major* by Matthew Camidge is an example of an easier piece from Study Module 1.
- *Aria in A Major* by Georg Philipp Telemann is an example of a more difficult piece from Study Module 6.

The Study Modules

The six Study Module discussions are organized into the following categories:

- *Background Information*
- *Exploring the Score*
- *Practice Suggestions*
- *Creative Activities*

Background Information (present in a few descriptions) provides relevant historical information. *Exploring the Score* is designed as an interactive exercise between teacher and student. These sections include questions you might address to the student during lessons. *Practice Suggestions* are also largely directly to the student. The *Creative Activities* act as reinforcement for your students' understanding of a musical concept and can provide a springboard for their creativity and imagination.

Please refer to the Foreword for an explanation of how to use the suggested order of assignment within each Module.

The chart on the following page lists all the repertoire and studies in Level 6. Page numbers for works in the *Piano Repertoire Album 6* and the *Piano Studies Album 6* are found in the first column. Study Module numbers for each composition are found in the fourth column.

Page	Composer	Title	Study Module
Piano Repertoire Album 6			
List A R4	Johann Sebastian Bach	Little Prelude in D Minor, BWV 926	5
R6	George Frideric Handel	Allemande in A Minor, HWV 478	3
R8	George Frideric Handel	Gigue in D Minor	1
R9	Domenico Zipoli	Sarabanda in G Minor	4
R10	Johann Sebastian Bach	Bourrée in B Minor	2
R11	Georg Philipp Telemann	Aria in A Major	6
List B R12	Domenico Cimarosa	Sonata No. 6 in G Major	2
R14	Wolfgang Amadeus Mozart	Viennese Sonatina No. 6 in C Major (Finale)	3
R18	Matthew Camidge	Sonatina in G Major (Last Movement)	1
R21	Franz Joseph Haydn	Sonata in G Major Hob. XVI:G1 (First Movement)	5
R24	Jiří Benda	Sonatina No. 3 in A Minor	4
R26	Friedrich Kuhlau	Sonatina in G Major, Op. 88, No. 2 (First Movement)	6
R29	Ludwig van Beethoven	Lustig und Traurig, WoO 54	5
List C R30	Robert Schumann	Waltz in A Minor, Op. 124, No. 4	4
R31	Robert Schumann	From Foreign Lands and People, Op. 15, No. 1	3
R32	Henryk Pachulski	Prelude in C Minor, Op. 8, No. 1	2
R34	Douglas Finch	Cancan	5
R35	Béla Bartók	Dawn	3
R36	Violet Archer	Church Scene	4
R39	Alexander Scriabin	Prelude, Op. 2, No. 2	2
R40	Pyotr Il'yich Tchaikovsky	Waltz in E Flat, Op. 39, No. 8	5
R42	Jean Coulthard	Where the Trade-Winds Blow	6
R44	Karol Szymanowski	Krakowiak	6
R46	Nancy Telfer (arr.)	She's Like the Swallow	1
R48	Luciano Giarbella	Gnomi	1
Piano Studies Album 6			
S24	Stephen Heller	Study No. 1: Op. 119, No. 24	5
S26	Dmitri Kabalevsky	Study No. 2: Toccatina, Op. 27, No. 12	1
S28	Antoine Henry Lemoine	Study No. 3: Op. 37, No. 39	2
S29	Johann Sebastian Bach	Study No. 4: Applicatio, BWV 994	5
S30	Ruth Watson Henderson	Study No. 5: Toccatina	3
S32	Dmitri Shostakovich	Study No. 6: Dance	1
S34	Cornelius Gurlitt	Study No. 7: Op. 132, No. 1	4
S35	Albert Loeschhorn	Study No. 8	2
S36	Ross Lee Finney	Study No. 9: Playing Ball	4
S38	George Frideric Handel	Study No. 10: Entrée in G Minor, HWV 453	3
S40	Stephen Heller	Study No. 11: Abenddämmerung, Op. 138, No. 3	6
S42	Carl Czerny	Study No. 12: Op. 139, No. 91	6
S44	Gerhard Wuensch	Study No. 13: Ping-Pong, Anyone?	6

STUDY MODULE 1

Page	List	Composer	Title	Meter and Tempo	Musical and Stylistic Concepts
R8 SG11	A	George Frideric Handel	Gigue in D Minor	12/16 Allegro	✔ binary dance form ✔ fast driving triplets ✔ consistent harmonic rhythm
R18 SG17	B	Matthew Camidge	Sonatina in G Major (Last Movement)	2/4 Presto	✔ RH sixteenth-note figures ✔ ternary form (ABA) ✔ playful character
R46 SG32	C	Nancy Telfer (arr.)	She's Like the Swallow	3/4 Smoothly flowing	✔ C Dorian mode ✔ arrangement of folk tune ✔ *legato* flowing line
R48 SG33	C	Luciano Giarbella	Gnomi	2/4 Vivace	✔ broken octaves ✔ two-note slurs ✔ blocked 6ths
S26		Dmitri Kabalevsky	Study No. 2: Toccatina, Op. 27, No. 12	2/4 Allegretto marcato	✔ LH melody ✔ RH first-inversion chords parallel LH melody
S32		Dmitri Shostakovich	Study No. 6: Dance	2/4 Allegretto giocoso	✔ LH *staccato* eighth-note accompaniment ✔ RH plays sixteenth-note figures

Assign first:
Gigue in D Minor
Sonatina in G Major (Last Movement)
She's Like the Swallow . . . .
Study No. 2: Toccatina, Op. 27, No. 12. . . . .

Assign next when ready:

Gnomi
Study No. 6: Dance

Study Module 1 contains some of the easiest pieces from each style period in Level 6. Each piece portrays a vivid character and is representative of its style period. Discuss the mood, character, and elements of contrast of each piece with your students. The musical understanding they gain will stimulate insightful performances.

See p. 7 of *Student Guide 6* for definitions and descriptions of dances and other forms.

G.F. Handel: *Gigue in D Minor* (R8, SG11)
Exploring the Score
- What is a *gigue?* Do you picture this dance performed by one person, a couple, or a group? Is it danced indoors or outdoors? Is it a fast or a slow dance?
- What gives *Gigue in D Minor* its energy and intensity? [sixteenth-note triplets, fast tempo, change of harmony on each beat]

Practice Suggestion
The fast-paced harmonic rhythm contributes to the intensity of the piece. Block the chords and listen to each change of harmony.

M. Camidge: *Sonatina in G Major (Last Movement)* (R18, SG17)
Exploring the Score
This is a light, playful piece.
- Where are the main contrasts?
- How does Camidge change the mood or character?

Look at the phrasing. Short-short-long phrase structure (periodic phrasing) is a characteristic of music from the Classical period.
- Label the phrases in the first eight measures: short [mm. 1-2], short [mm. 2-4], long [mm. 5-8].

- Compare mm. 1-8 with mm. 9-16. What is changed? Does that change result in an increase or a decrease of intensity?
- Label the sections of this piece (see the *Student Guide* outline of form). How does Camidge create contrast in the B section? [new key, different sixteenth-note figures, different phrase structure]

N. Telfer (arr.): *She's Like the Swallow* (R46, SG32)
Exploring the Score
Have students sing this Newfoundland folk melody before they begin practicing this arrangement (see text and music in the *Student Guide*).
- How does the melody portray a bird?
- Bracket the phrases which state the folk-song melody. How are Telfer's insertions related to the folk tune?
- What changes can you find in the second verse (mm. 29-51)?

L. Giarbella: *Gnomi* (R48, SG33)
Exploring the Score
This is a musical picture of gnomes in action.
- What are gnomes?
- How would a gnome dance?
- What do they wear? How do they move?
- What sounds would you use for music about gnomes? Compare your impressions with the *Celebration Series* recording of *Gnomi*. (You may find yourself creating a story inspired by this piece.)

Practice Suggestion
To highlight the movements of the gnome's dance, make a special emphasis on the first note of each two-note slur.

D. Kabalevsky: *Study No. 2: Toccatina, Op. 27, No. 12* (S26)
Exploring the Score
- What is a toccatina?
- Which hand has the melody?
- Name the position of the RH chords. [first inversion] Does the position ever change? [see mm. 31-34]
- Which RH notes imitate the LH melody? [top notes of chords]

Toccatina is a study of contrasts and touches. The most obvious contrast is between the LH *legato* and the RH *staccato*.
- What touch will you use for LH melody notes not marked with a slur?

D. Shostakovich: *Study No. 6: Dance* (S32)
Exploring the Score
This dance is a study in mechanical, perpetual motion.
- What kind of puppet is dancing?
- Can you hear tiny bells on the puppet's cap? [grace notes and accents] Perhaps the puppet is hitting a toy tambourine.
- How do you know the puppet doesn't get tired? [constant LH eighth-note motion]
- How should you play the sixteenth notes? [discuss two options: *crescendo* and *diminuendo*, or precise, uninflected sound]

Practice Suggestions
How many different sixteenth-note patterns can you find?
- four notes in step motion
- full octave scales
- zig-zag patterns
- broken chords, etc.

Isolate similar RH patterns and practice them as a group. Then practice two- or four-measure groups, hands together slowly.

CREATIVE ACTIVITIES
♫ Choose blocked chords to accompany the folk tune *She's Like the Swallow*. Your harmonization could be in C minor or C Dorian (see the C Dorian scale in the *Student Guide*, p. 32).

♫ Create a variation by changing the melody, the accompaniment style, or both.

♫ Create your own arrangement of *Toccatina* by playing the melody with the RH and the chords with the LH. (You may wish to select only your favorite phrases.)

STUDY MODULE 2

Page	List	Composer	Title	Meter and Tempo	Musical and Stylistic Concepts
R10 SG13	A	Johann Sebastian Bach	Bourrée in B Minor	2/2	✔ lively contrapuntal dance ✔ two independent voices ✔ variety of figures ✔ melodic sequences
R12 SG15	B	Domenico Cimarosa	Sonata No. 6 in G Major	C Allegro	✔ example of early Italian Classical style ✔ accompaniment provides harmonic background for highly-figured RH melody ✔ ornamental figures written out in thirty-second notes
R32 SG24	C	Henryk Pachulski	Prelude in C Minor, Op. 8, No. 1	2/4 Andante molto	✔ sensitive, expressive Romantic style ✔ *legato, cantabile* melody ✔ LH triplet blocked-chord accompaniment ✔ 7th chords and chromatic harmonies
R39 SG28	C	Alexander Scriabin	Prelude, Op. 2, No. 2	3/4 Andante e rubato	✔ expressive, elusive melody with melodic fragments in both hands ✔ large intervals and octave chords
S28		Antoine Henry Lemoine	Study No. 3: Op. 37, No. 39	2/4 Andantino	✔ graceful RH sixteenth-note passages with scales, trill figures, arpeggio crossings ✔ LH broken-chord accompaniment
S35		Albert Loeschhorn	Study No. 8	3/4 Allegro	✔ RH triplets of broken descending triads ✔ top note of triplet serves as melody

Assign first:
Bourrée in B Minor
Sonata No. 6 in G Major
Prelude in C Minor, Op. 8, No. 1 . . . .
Study No. 3: Op. 37, No. 39 . . . .

Assign next when ready:

Prelude, Op. 2, No. 2
Study No. 8

Concert artists often select recital programs that include a diversity of style and mood. The pieces in Study Module 2 would make a fine recital program if diversity were the goal, because they reflect the changing styles of piano repertoire from the Baroque into the early 20th century. Most piano collections for this level do not include Italian composers of the Classical period. The Cimarosa *Sonata* helps to fill that void in the student's repertoire.

A brief exploration of this Study Module might focus on melodic and accompaniment styles. Compare the instrumental-sounding melody of *Bourrée in B Minor* and *Sonata No. 6 in G Major* with the singing melody of Pachulski's *Prelude in C Minor* and the elusive melody of Scriabin's *Prelude, Op. 2, No. 2*. Compare the highly independent LH in Bach's *Bourrée in B Minor* to the harmonic support provided by the LH in Cimarosa's *Sonata No. 6 in G Major* and Pachulski's *Prelude in C Minor*.

J.S. Bach: *Bourrée in B Minor* (R10, SG13)
Exploring the Score
This lively *bourrée* is typical of its genre. It has a short upbeat, a strong half-note pulse, and a brusque character. See the discussion of rhythmic syncopations in the *Student Guide*.

Practice Suggestions
Pay careful attention to the articulation of both voices. Practice short sections hands separately. (This will establish accurate fingering and articulation, and help students to hear melodic patterns.) Feel the half-note pulse in both hands and use a definite, firm touch.

D. Cimarosa: *Sonata No. 6 in G Major* (R12, SG15)
Exploring the Score
Many piano pieces from the Classical period seem to be inspired by instrumental sounds. With a bit of imagination, you can hear piano pieces played by a full orchestra – a theme in the strings, answered by a flute or clarinet, and the contrast of the brass. Play the *Celebration Series* recording of this piece.
- Label sections which imitate full orchestra.
- Indicate the parts played by solo instruments or small groups. Try to be specific: would the figure sound best played by strings or by woodwinds?
- Can you find a duet? Which two instruments might play this lyrical passage?

H. Pachulski: *Prelude in C Minor, Op. 8, No. 1* (R32, SG24)
Practice Suggestions
- Practice the RH melody alone. Focus on *legato* fingering and dynamic shaping.
- As a rule, stress the first note of triplet accompaniment figures and play the second and third notes more softly. The LH *tenuto* notes highlight the chord changes. Devise a technique for bringing out this expressive countermelody.
- This piece is marked *con pedale*. How will you practice the pedal? What pedal effect would you find unacceptable?

A. Scriabin: *Prelude, Op. 2, No. 2* (R39, SG28)
Exploring the Score
Three of the four phrases of this short piece are defined by the initial motive and their cadences.
- Find the cadences in mm. 5, 9, 13, and 17. Name the final harmony of those cadences. [B, F sharp, E, B] Note their function within the key of B major. [I, V, IV, I]

- How long is each phrase?
- Which two phrases overlap?
- Which phrase is significantly different from the other three?

Practice Suggestions
The tempo marking suggests *rubato*. Linger on the longer values and move ahead on the triplets. Stretch the first note of each phrase (the dotted quarter) and the RH quarter note of mm. 4 and 8.

Listen to the harmonies. Find the unsettled harmonies that require resolution. Play the final harmony of each phrase quietly, with a feeling of repose.

Follow the pedal markings in the score carefully.

A.H. Lemoine: *Study No. 3: Op. 37, No. 39* (S28)
Exploring the Score
Studies are usually based on an aspect of technique. What is the technical basis of this study?

Practice Suggestions
For most students, the difficulty of this study lies in the variety of figures. The consistent use of comfortable, fluid fingering is the secret to success. Encourage students to build a repertoire of practice techniques. Here are some suggestions for fingering practice based on this study:

1. Stop on the thumb notes:

2. Bracket scales in finger groups:

3. Say the fingering aloud as you play.

A. Loeschhorn: *Study No. 8* (S35)
Practice Suggestions
This study is an exercise in projecting the top notes of broken chords. Give the top RH notes (the melody notes) special emphasis and play the other notes quietly, with a relaxed hand.

Be sure students make a natural "rotation" movement as they practice these broken chords. (Some teachers refer to this gesture as a wrist roll.)

Accuracy often improves when students verbalize what they are playing. Have students say the names of the chords aloud as they play this study. Blocking the chords will also be helpful.

CREATIVE ACTIVITY

Follow these steps to write your own study:
1. Make up a simple melody using only quarter notes.

2. Find a chord to harmonize each note of your melody. Play the harmony as broken chords under the melody notes. (See mm. 18-19 of Loeschhorn's *Study No. 8* for an example.)
3. Create a LH bass part to go with your melody.

STUDY MODULE 3

Page	List	Composer	Title	Meter and Tempo	Musical and Stylistic Concepts
R6 SG10	A	George Frideric Handel	Allemande in A Minor, HWV 478	Alla breve	✔ binary form ✔ two independent voices ✔ cadential trills
R14 SG16	B	Wolfgang Amadeus Mozart	Viennese Sonatina No. 6 in C Major (Finale)	3/4 Allegro	✔ sonata form ✔ double 3rds and 6ths ✔ contrasting themes
R31 SG23	C	Robert Schumann	From Foreign Lands and People, Op. 15, No. 1	2/4 Andante con moto	✔ lyrical melody ✔ triplet accompaniment divided between hands
R35 SG26	C	Béla Bartók	Dawn	3/4 Molto Andante	✔ *legato*, expressive touch ✔ calm and quiet ✔ contemporary harmonies
S30		Ruth Watson Henderson	Study No. 5: Toccatina	Alla breve Vivace	✔ lively ✔ two voices ✔ alternating and crossed hands
S38		George Frideric Handel	Study No. 10: Entrée in G Minor, HWV 453	C Andante	✔ two contrapuntal voices ✔ eighths and sixteenths in both hands ✔ sequences

Assign first:
Allemande in A Minor, HWV 478 . . . .
Viennese Sonatina No. 6 in C Major (Finale)
From Foreign Lands and People, Op. 15, No. 1 . .
Dawn

Assign next when ready:
Study No. 10: Entrée in G Minor, HWV 453

Study No. 5: Toccatina

The challenges of Study Module 3 range from independent hands in two compositions by Handel to the subtle melodic shape and tone colors in Schumann's *From Foreign Lands and People* and Bartók's *Dawn*. In the two Handel compositions (*Allemande in A Minor* and *Entrée in G Minor*), the two voices are equal partners, each with its own melodic line, rhythm, and dynamic shape. These pieces require hand independence and planned articulation to bring out each separate voice.

In Mozart's *Viennese Sonatina No. 6 in C Major*, the melody and accompaniment are clearly defined. Compare this style with Schumann's *From Foreign Lands and People* and Henderson's *Toccatina*. Although the Schumann and Henderson compositions differ in mood and style, they share a common feature – the melody and the accompaniment are entwined. In both these pieces, the student must discover the melody and highlight it by means of touch and dynamics. Henderson's *Toccatina* has two voices (melody and accompaniment). The Schumann work actually has three layers of sound: an upper melody, a bass line, and an inner-voice accompaniment.

G.F. Handel: *Allemande in A Minor, HWV 478* (R6, SG10)

Background Information

Read the description of an *allemande* in the *Student Guide* (p. 7). Baroque dances are usually in binary form. The A section modulates to the dominant key (or the relative major) and the B section returns to the tonic key. Most *allemandes* have a short upbeat.

Exploring the Score

Does Handel's *Allemande in A Minor* fit the definition of an *allemande*?

The absence of phrase and articulation markings in the score provides an opportunity for a student-teacher discussion about the functions of articulation:

1. Articulation helps to communicate the mood of a piece. For example, you might play a lively dance with mostly detached notes.
2. Articulation can be used to highlight independence of voices. This is one reason for giving each voice its own distinct articulation.
3. Articulation can be used to highlight important beats. For example, a downbeat might be preceded by a break in sound and slurred to the following note.

Plan an articulation according to these suggestions, and mark the articulation in the score. (The performance on the *Celebration Series* recording illustrates one possible approach to dynamics and articulation.)

W. A. Mozart: *Viennese Sonatina No. 6 in C Major (Finale)* (R14, SG16)

Background Information

The original version of this piece is from the *Divertimento for Two Clarinets and Bassoon or Three Basset Horns, KV 439b, No. 1*, composed in 1783. If possible, have students listen to a recording of the original, so that they can relate the articulation, phrasing, and tone color of this arrangement to the sound of wind instruments.

Exploring the Score

This piece is in sonata form. See the *Student Guide* for a thorough discussion of the form. Make flash cards for each element of a sonata form (exposition, 1st theme, development, etc.) and assemble a diagram of the piece. Use the cards to compare this movement with other pieces in sonata form.

R. Schumann: *From Foreign Lands and People, Op. 15, No. 1* (R31, SG23)

Background Information

Take this opportunity to introduce your student to other pieces in Schumann's *Kinderszenen (Scenes of Childhood), Op. 15.*

- Each of the thirteen pieces in this cycle has a descriptive title. Notice the variety of moods and scenes.
- Do some music research! Most of the pieces in this set include the melodic motive G-F sharp-E-D. Look through a few pieces to spot the motive.

Exploring the Score

The melody, the rolling triplets, the texture, and the range produce a dreamy atmosphere. Read the comments on melodies and countermelodies in the *Student Guide*. The double stems in the bass part of mm. 9-14 indicate the melody. What is the source of this melody? [inversion of the original RH melody] Notice the short-short-long (2+2+4) phrasing.

Practice Suggestions

The texture of this piece is made from three components. Students often find it helpful to assign dynamic priorities to these components:

- melody: loudest
- bass: next loudest
- harmony: quietest

The melody must project above all. Have students practice the accompanying triplets with special care (played quietly). Play different combinations of two components (melody and bass, harmony and bass, melody and harmony), concentrating on dynamic levels.

B. Bartók: *Dawn* (R35, SG26)

Exploring the Score

Dawn is an expressive depiction of a sunrise. What musical elements does Bartók use?

- rhythmic motive of three quarter notes and a half note (the calm sky just before sunrise)
- shifting, blocked intervals (the changing colors of the sky)

The *Celebration Series* recording and the descriptions of musical imagery in the *Student Guide* will help students appreciate the sights and colors of this musical picture. You might think that music about a sunrise would finish with *forte* or *fortissimo* chords. What effect does Bartók create with his quiet ending?

R. W. Henderson: *Study No. 5: Toccatina* (S30)
Practice Suggestions

A toccata or a toccatina is a fast, technical piece. The challenges in this toccatina include alternating, interlocking hands, short melodic fragments, and changes of position.

Follow these practice steps:
1. Circle the first note of each LH position. [mm. 1, 11, 17, 21, etc.] Divide the piece into practice sections according to LH position.
2. Play the RH alone. Are all the RH notes melody notes?
3. Play hands together (without pedal). Experiment with different hand positions. Try keeping the LH above the RH, toward the back of the keys.
4. Practice each section hands together. Keep the RH louder than the LH. Maintain an even rhythm and pay attention to the longer note values. Listen for dynamic rise and fall.
5. Add the pedal.

G.F. Handel: *Study No. 10: Entrée in G Minor, HWV 453* (S38)
Exploring the Score

Begin the study of this piece with a visual analysis.
- Identify the key and meter.
- Find the form and label the sections.
- Circle passages that look difficult.
- Look for repeated patterns and figures. For example, there is a sequence in mm. 11-12. Notice the built-in *crescendo* as the melody rises.
- Look for opportunities to add ornamentation. For example, experiment with trills at the cadences.

Practice Suggestions

Use these questions for a teacher-student discussion on creating a practice strategy for this study:
- Will you begin by tapping the rhythm?
- Will you play hands separately at first? When will you play hands together?
- How will you divide the piece into practice segments? Will you practice the sections in order or group similar passages together?
- When will you deal with the articulation?
- How will you practice the trills?

The sixteenth notes in both hands should be even and smooth. To develop an even touch, practice these passages in dotted rhythms. Pay special attention to the LH in mm. 12-15.

CREATIVE ACTIVITY

 Think of the last sunrise that you saw. Where were you? What were the colors? How did you feel? Improvise a piece which describes your experience. Use some of the elements from *Dawn* by Bartók (for example, dynamics, intervals, rhythm).

STUDY MODULE 4

Page	List	Composer	Title	Meter and Tempo	Musical and Stylistic Concepts
R9 SG12	A	Domenico Zipoli	Sarabanda in G Minor	3/4 Largo	✔ three voices ✔ ornaments ✔ finger independence ✔ binary form
R24 SG19	B	Jiří Benda	Sonatina No. 3 in A Minor	2/4 Allegro	✔ arpeggiated chords ✔ parallel 6ths and 3rds ✔ crossed hands ✔ syncopations ✔ ABA form
R30 SG22	C	Robert Schumann	Waltz in A Minor, Op. 124, No. 4	3/4 Lebhaft	✔ wide range in melody ✔ jumping waltz bass ✔ syncopation ✔ RH parallel octaves ✔ ABA form
R36 SG27	C	Violet Archer	Church Scene	4/4 Very broadly	✔ contemporary sounds depict church scene: bells, chant, four-part chorale
S34		Cornelius Gurlitt	Study No. 7: Op. 132, No. 1	3/4 Con moto	✔ lilting waltz with wide leaps in accompaniment ✔ AABA form ✔ syncopation
S36		Ross Lee Finney	Study No. 9: Playing Ball	2/4 Gaily	✔ root-position chords ✔ LH solo ✔ meter change ✔ contemporary sounds

Assign first:
Sarabanda in G Minor
Sonatina No. 3 in A Minor
Waltz in A Minor, Op. 124, No. 4 . . . .
Church Scene . . . .

Assign next when ready:

Study No. 9: Playing Ball
Study No. 7: Op. 132, No. 1

Study Module 4 provides examples of the variety of moods that can be created outside major tonalities. Four pieces in this Study Module are in minor keys. Violet Archer's *Church Scene* includes modal tonalities, and Finney's *Playing Ball* uses juxtaposed unrelated major chords. The jumping waltz bass in Schumann's *Waltz in A Minor* and Gurlitt's *Study, Op. 132, No. 1,* may be a new technical challenge for the student.

D. Zipoli: *Sarabanda in G Minor* (R9, SG12)
Exploring the Score

Read the *Study Guide* description of a *sarabande* on page 8. What typical *sarabande* characteristics can you find in this piece?

- Most Baroque dances are in binary form. What is the form of this piece? (See form outline in the *Student Guide*.)
- How does Zipoli emphasize the second beat? [LH half notes in mm. 2-4, RH half notes in mm. 6-7, RH eighth notes in mm. 12-15]
- Locate the sequences. Isolate the two-voice LH sequences for special practice.

J. Benda: *Sonatina No. 3 in A Minor* (R24, SG19)
Exploring the Score

Sonatinas are usually based on the contrast of themes and keys. Look for elements of contrast in Benda's *Sonatina:*

- Where does the music look different?
- Where does the rhythm change?
- Where does the register change (LH in treble clef)?
- Can you spot a change of key?
- Can you find syncopation in the RH?

Encourage students to find ways to highlight these contrasts, in order to bring them to the attention of the listener.

Practice Suggestions

In mm. 2 and 4, the RH must move quickly into a new position. Isolate this position shift for special practice:
1. Play m. 1 and the LH downbeat of m. 2.
2. As you play the LH downbeat, quickly shift the RH into position to play the solid eighth-note 6ths.
3. Practice mm. 3-4 the same way.

The sixteenth notes in the B section must be even. This is especially challenging where the hands cross in mm. 17-22 and 33-38. See the suggestions for "A Left-Hand Melody" in the *Student Guide*. Students may find that words or rhythmic chanting help them to keep a steady rhythm (for example, "Mis-sis-sip-pi").

R. Schumann: *Waltz in A Minor, Op. 124, No. 4* (R30, SG22)
Exploring the Score

This waltz has an unusual mood. Listen to the *Celebration Series* recording and ask students for their impressions and reactions. (Read the *Student Guide* discussion of harmony and Schumann's use of the augmented 6th chord.)

- Compare mm. 1, 17, and 21. Each starts with the same pitch but sounds quite different.
- This waltz is in A minor. Find the section in F major. The contrasting section of a piece in a minor key is usually in the relative major key. What are the common tones between A minor and F major triads? [both include A and C]

Practice Suggestions

Notice the LH fingering: whenever possible the fifth finger is reserved for the downbeats. Let the hand move in a graceful arc as it moves from the low downbeat notes to the higher chords.

V. Archer: *Church Scene* (R36, SG27)
Exploring the Score

Students may be unfamiliar with the sound of Gregorian chant. If possible, provide a recorded example. See the *Student Guide* description and interpretation of the different sections.

- Label the sections: Bells, Chant, Hymn.
- What is the time of day? [count the chimes in mm. 8-13]
- Create a text for the chant, for example:

The lord is my shep-herd I shall ne-ver want.

- Find phrases that fit the word "Al-le-lu-ja" in the Hymn (mm. 25-27).

Practice Suggestions

The three different sections require three different sounds and touches.
1. For the bells, play with an accented, ringing sound.
2. For the chant, play with a flowing, *legato* sound.
3. For the hymn, bring out the top notes.

Almost every measure of *Church Scene* has a marking concerned with dynamics, rhythm, articulation, or pedal. The challenge for students is to realize each indication, then put the piece together as a unified whole.

C. Gurlitt: *Study No. 7: Op. 132, No. 1* (S34)
Practice Suggestions
Students will recognize this piece as a waltz. The wide leaps and variety of chord shapes in the LH are a challenge. Here are some tips for the LH:
- Plan your fingering carefully.
- Practice slowly. See and feel the chord on the second beat before you play the first beat.
- Move the hand in a curved arch shape.
- Use the rest on the third beat to move the LH back into position.

The RH plays a variety of figures.
- Use a rocking hand motion (forearm rotation) for the wide intervals in mm. 1-3.
- Circle the finger substitutions (for example, mm. 3 and 6) and practice these measures slowly.
- When the RH plays two voices (for example, mm. 3-4 and 7-8) hold each note for its proper value.

R.L. Finney: *Study No. 9: Playing Ball* (S36)
Exploring the Score
Like J.S. Bach's *Fifteen Two-Part Inventions*, each of Finney's *Twenty-Four Inventions* explores a particular way to combine notes and musical elements. This study uses two elements: LH stepwise motion and RH chords. Analyze the chords:
- Are they all in root position? [yes]
- Are they all major chords? [no, see mm. 11 and 18]
- Are the rhythmic patterns consistent? [no, but there is some repetition, for example, in mm. 1-4 and mm. 13-16)

Practice Suggestion
There are many accidentals in the LH part. What scales are represented? Block the sixteenth-note figures to find finger groupings.

CREATIVE ACTIVITY
Create your own chant, based on the chant section of *Church Scene*, and play it hands together. The phrases should be short enough to sing in one breath. Add blocked 5ths under each note of your chant. Use pedal for a smooth sound. Combine these two elements to form an ABA piece, where the A sections are solo chant and the B section includes the blocked-5th accompaniment.

STUDY MODULE 5

Page	List	Composer	Title	Meter and Tempo	Musical and Stylistic Concepts
R4 SG9	A	Johann Sebastian Bach	Little Prelude in D Minor, BWV 926	3/4 Moderato	✔ two-voice texture ✔ rhythmic ambiguity between 3/4 and 6/8 ✔ eighth-note movement until the sixteenth-note cadenza at the end
R21 SG18	B	Franz Joseph Haydn	Sonata in G Major, Hob. XVI:G1 (First Movement)	2/4 Allegro	✔ sonata form ✔ energetic character ✔ contrasts of rhythm and figure
R29 SG21	B	Ludwig van Beethoven	Lustig und Traurig, WoO 54	3/8 Lustig	✔ a study in musical contrasts between two distinct sections (merry and melancholy)
R34 SG25	C	Douglas Finch	Cancan	4/4 Lively	✔ position shifts ✔ constant eighth-note movement ✔ *sempre staccato* ✔ RH leaps
R40 SG29	C	Pyotr Il'yich Tchaikovsky	Waltz in E Flat, Op. 39, No. 8	3/4 Vivace	✔ LH waltz and drone bass ✔ RH articulation and rhythm avoid downbeat emphasis ✔ ABA form
S24		Stephen Heller	Study No. 1: Op. 119, No. 24	2/4 Allegretto vivo	✔ study in beat subdivisions
S29		Johann Sebastian Bach	Study No. 4: Applicatio, BWV 994	C Andante moderato	✔ ornaments in both hands ✔ three voices

Assign first:
Little Prelude in D Minor, BWV 926 . . . .
Sonata in G Major, Hob. XVI: G1
  (First Movement)
Study No. 1: Op. 119, No. 24 . . . .
Cancan. . . . .

Assign next when ready:
Study No. 4: Applicatio, BWV 994

Lustig und Traurig, WoO 54
Waltz in E Flat, Op. 39, No. 8

The pieces in Study Module 5 represent a middle range of difficulty in the intermediate literature. The two Bach compositions – *Little Prelude in D Minor* and *Applicatio, BWV 994* are both from the *Wilhelm Friedemann Bach Notebook*, written by Bach for the instruction of his son. Both pieces use considerable ornamentation. Haydn's *Sonata in G Major* and Stephen Heller's *Study, Op. 119, No. 24* include a variety of beat subdivisions. There are two dances: *Cancan* by Douglas Finch and *Waltz in E Flat* by Tchaikovsky. Compare the rhythmic variety and use of accents in these two energetic dances. Notice the ways in which Tchaikovsky avoids emphasis on the downbeat.

J.S. Bach: *Little Prelude in D Minor, BWV 926*
(R4, SG9)
Exploring the Score
Most Baroque preludes focus on one theme or motive. This *Little Prelude* is based on a broken-chord pattern. The arrangement of the chord tones in the RH of mm. 1-6 gives emphasis to the low pitch. This creates a feeling of 6/8 rather than 3/4. That ambiguity of meter may be intentional, as it lends tension to this piece. The single bass note in each of these measures propels the music forward, as if there was only one beat to the measure. Help students to be aware of the large pulse patterns of the music. Think in two-measure units and feel the flowing motion of the downbeats.

Practice Suggestions
The *Student Guide* gives examples for blocking and analyzing the harmonic progressions. Play the piece with blocked chords to hear the harmonies. Base the phrasing and dynamic shape on the harmonic structure of the music.

F.J. Haydn: *Sonata in G Major, Hob. XVI:G1 (First Movement)* (R21, SG18)
Exploring the Score
Haydn's early sonatas (called *divertimenti*) were written for harpsichord. The number and form of the movements vary. See the *Student Guide* for an analysis of this sonata movement.
- Label the sections and themes in the score.
- Examine the contour of the themes. Do they descend or ascend? [mostly descend]
- Find the ascending motives. [mm. 9, 18, 22, etc.] Because they are infrequent, give them special emphasis.

In a development section, material from the exposition is varied and reorganized. The music usually travels through several keys, then returns to the tonic.
- Trace material in this development section back to the exposition. What keys are used in the development?

Compare the exposition and recapitulation. What is the key at the end of each section?

Practice Suggestions
This piece requires a firm rhythmic foundation. Give students preparatory exercises such as tapping combinations of eighth, sixteenth, and thirty-second notes and triplets over a steady eighth-note pulse.

L.van Beethoven: *Lustig und Traurig, WoO 54*
(R29, SG21)
Exploring the Score
This piece consists of two highly contrasting sections. Listen to the *Celebration Series* recording with score in hand, and make a list of the contrasts (for example: *"Lustig"* – C major, eighth-note chordal texture; *"Traurig"* – C minor, sixteenth-note arpeggiated texture).

D. Finch: *Cancan* (R34, SG25)
Exploring the Score
This dance is dominated by the energetic perpetual motion of the eighth notes. Discuss the four styles of texture outlined in the *Student Guide*.

Practice Suggestions
Practice slowly in two-measure sections. Devise a practice plan for each of the four eighth-note patterns. For example, block the 2nds in mm. 3-4 and 16-17. These measures descend in stepwise motion. Make a descending scale of the blocked 2nds.

P.I. Tchaikovsky: *Waltz in E Flat, Op. 39, No. 8* (R40, SG29)
Exploring the Score
Composers of waltzes often find ways to vary the familiar strong-weak-weak pattern (3/4 meter) to create rhythmic interest. Look at the melody of this waltz.
- The A section has a typical waltz bass with a clear emphasis on the first beat. However, the RH rhythm is made up of short groups with an accent or a long note on the second beat.
- In the B section, the LH pattern changes. Here the RH two-note slurs give the feeling of a duple meter (rather than a continuous stress on the first of three beats).

Practice Suggestions
To establish the teeter-totter feeling of the LH and RH accents, practice a skeletal version of the A section. Play only the LH downbeats and the RH accented and long notes:

Does the LH use typical waltz-bass fingering? (Compare this piece with Schumann's *Waltz in A Minor* in Study Module 4.)

S. Heller: *Study No. 1: Op. 119, No. 24* (S24)
Practice Suggestions
This study in duple and triple subdivisions of a beat includes a number of different rhythmic patterns. Prepare flash cards of the various rhythms:

Have students practice the following exercises:
1. Tap each rhythm hands together (unison).
2. Tap each rhythm with the RH while tapping a steady eighth-note beat with the LH.
3. Tap each rhythm four times.
4. Tap a series of rhythms one after the other.

J.S. Bach: *Study No. 4: Applicatio, BWV 994* (S29)
Practice Suggestions
The notes and rhythms appear to be relatively easy, but the ornamentation complicates both fingering and rhythm.
1. Practice without the ornaments. Use the given fingering.
2. Practice hands separately with the ornaments. Play each ornament several times, and keep a slow, steady beat.
3. Practice half-measure or one-measure segments hands together.

CREATIVE ACTIVITY

 Beethoven's *Lustig und Traurig* is a study in contrasts. Think of two opposite or contrasting words which might be portrayed in music (for example, dark and light, fast and slow). Improvise or compose a pair of short pieces which illustrate these opposites.

STUDY MODULE 6

Page	List	Composer	Title	Meter and Tempo	Musical and Stylistic Concepts
R11 SG14	A	Georg Philipp Telemann	Aria in A Major	C	✔ four-voice texture ✔ ornaments ✔ independent rhythmic movement of voices
R26 SG20	B	Friedrich Kuhlau	Sonatina in G Major, Op. 88, No. 2 (First Movement)	3/4 Allegro assai	✔ sonata form ✔ broken-chord bass ✔ sequences ✔ triplet scale passages
R42 SG30	C	Jean Coulthard	Where the Trade-Winds Blow	6/4 Moderately	✔ constant eighth-note movement ✔ Aeolian mode ✔ crossed hands
R44 SG21	C	Karol Szymanowski	Krakowiak	2/4 Allegretto grazioso	✔ graceful Polish dance ✔ syncopated rhythms ✔ Lydian mode ✔ frequent tempo and dynamic changes
S40		Stephen Heller	Study No. 11: Abenddämmerung, Op. 138, No. 3	3/4 Lento con espressione	✔ expressive ✔ repeated notes and chords ✔ *legato* melody line ✔ four-note blocked chords
S42		Carl Czerny	Study No. 12: Op. 139, No. 91	6/8 Allegro	✔ fast and playful ✔ sixteenth-note triplets ✔ position shifts ✔ waltz bass
S44		Gerhard Wuensch	Study No. 13: Ping-Pong, Anyone?	4/4 Moderate tempo, mechanically	✔ alternating single notes and pairs ✔ unpredictable changes of pitch, rhythm, and length of groups ✔ contemporary sounds

Assign first:
Aria in A Major . . . .
Sonatina in G Major, Op. 88, No. 2
(First Movement)
Study No. 12: Op. 139, No. 91 . . . .
Krakowiak . . . .

Assign next when ready:
Where the Trade-Winds Blow

Study No. 11: Abenddämmerung, Op. 138, No. 3
Study No. 13: Ping-Pong, Anyone?

The pieces in this final Study Module are among the most difficult pieces in Level 6. Students will call upon their growing knowledge and awareness of form, style, musicality, and technique in order to achieve successful performances.

In Telemann's *Aria in A Major*, students have an opportunity to utilize newly developed abilities in dealing with independent voices, ornamentation, and articulation in a four-voice texture. The Kuhlau *Sonatina in G Major* challenges students to apply their knowledge about standard sonata form and contrasting ideas to discover the unusual aspects of the form of this movement.

Three programmatic pieces – *Where the Trade-Winds Blow*, *Abenddämmerung*, and *Ping-Pong, Anyone?* – challenge students' abilities to develop a specific mood or character. Two dances (Szymanowski's *Krakowiak* and the Czerny study) require a graceful or playful technical approach and a sensitivity to rhythm, tempo, and dynamic changes.

G.P. Telemann: *Aria in A Major* (R11, SG14)
Practice Suggestions

The ornaments and rolled chords add a special flourish to this noble, stately harpsichord piece. See the *Student Guide* for finger independence exercises and suggestions for balancing the sound.

Practice hands separately. Divide the RH part between the hands to check the rhythmic and note accuracy of each voice. Do the same with the LH.

F. Kuhlau: *Sonatina in G Major, Op. 88, No. 2 (First Movement)* (R26, SG20)
Background Information

Kuhlau was a contemporary of Beethoven and was much influenced by Beethoven's sonata writing. Unusual aspects of form in the Kuhlau sonatinas may result from the formal innovations found in Beethoven sonatas.

Exploring the Score

Have students label the exposition, development, recapitulation, and *coda* in the music. Check the measure numbers against the chart in the *Student Guide*, and add labels for the themes. There is something unusual about this sonata form. The rising broken-chord figure in m. 8 starts a new idea.
- Is this the second theme?
- Is this new idea in the dominant key? [no]
- Is it a contrast to the first theme? [yes]

The entire exposition section is in G major, but Kuhlau achieves the feeling of a modulation (each set of two measures ends with a different harmony) and the feeling of a new theme.

Trace the themes in the development.
- What keys are used?
- From which exposition material are the themes derived?

Compare the exposition and the recapitulation. How do they differ?

Practice Suggestions

Circle the notes of the hidden RH melody in mm. 9-15. Play the repeated Bs lightly. (See the *Student Guide* suggestions for dynamic shape.)

In mm. 44-47, the LH accompaniment figure has three-note chords.
1. Practice only the bottom and top notes (first and fifth fingers).
2. Practice different combinations of two chord notes plus the thumb.

J. Coulthard: *Where the Trade-Winds Blow* (R42, SG30)
Exploring the Score

The swells of sound – like the moaning of the wind – create a compelling musical impression of wind and water. Play the *Celebration Series* recording to hear the ebb and flow of the sound. Listen especially for the dynamics, and circle the dynamic markings in the music. This piece is constructed from two elements: a moving eighth-note figure and a pattern of sustained chords. See the discussion of these two ideas in the *Student Guide*.

Alternatively, you might suggest that the eighth notes are "wind music" (or "swoosh") and the longer values are "wind song" (or "moan") Listen for the dynamics of both "swoosh" and "moan."

K. Szymanowski: *Krakowiak* (R44, SG21)
Exploring the Score

Play the *Celebration Series* recording and ask students to make a list of their observations. Discuss these points:
- sectional form
- frequent tempo changes
- melody made of short motives (A section)
- syncopation (mm. 2, 4, 8)
- modal sound

Practice Suggestions

Krakowiak has a characteristic rhythm. Tap the rhythm of the entire piece hands separately, then hands together.

Each section has its own tempo marking. Label the six sections in the music. (See the form outline in the *Student Guide*.) Practice each section following these practice steps:
1. Tap the rhythm hands separately.
2. Tap the rhythm hands together.
3. Practice hands separately. Follow all dynamic and articulation markings.
4. Play hands together on the closed keyboard cover.
5. Play as written.

S. Heller: *Study No. 11: Abenddämmerung,*
Op. 138, No. 3 (S40)
Exploring the Score
With its wide range of harmonic and dynamic
colors, this piece invites a programmatic approach.
There are two main elements: the LH melody in
mm. 2-4, and the repeated-note "come to me"
motive in m. 6:

(come   to me)

- Find all appearances of these two elements.
- How do they change during the piece?
- Explore the tone quality of each section. Decide
  on the balance of sound between the hands, the
  use of pedal, and the articulation (especially for
  the repeated note motive).
- Why would a piece titled *Twilight* have a section
  of *fortissimo* octaves and chords?

C. Czerny: *Study No. 12: Op. 139, No. 91* (S42)
Practice Suggestions
Have students play warm-up drills (scales,
arpeggios, cadence patterns) in B major to
familiarize themselves with the key.

- Which white keys do you play in a B major scale?
- To discover the RH melody, play the first and last
  notes of each four-note motive.
- Play each four-note group as a block. Assume
  that the notes will be on the black keys, but
  watch for the white-key Bs and Es.
- Block the LH chords with the same assumption
  of black keys (except for B and E). Name the
  chords as you play.
- The dotted-quarter bass notes support the
  harmony. Hold each one for its full value. Think
  "heavy-light-light" or "hold-lift-lift" as you play.

G. Wuensch: *Study No. 13: Ping-Pong, Anyone?*
(S44)
Exploring the Score

- How does Wuensch portray the sound of a
  bouncing ping-pong ball? [*staccato* notes, single
  notes, accents, position shifts]
- How do we know that two people are playing the
  game? [back-and-forth motion between hands]
- Circle the meter changes in mm. 18-19.
- Where do mm. 1-4 repeat? [mm. 19-22]

Practice Suggestions
To learn notes and shifts quickly, have students
block the intervals and practice with a *legato* touch.
To guard against learning wrong notes, have
students practice short sections until they become
familiar with the unusual sounds.

CREATIVE ACTIVITY
Create your own ping-pong piece, based on the
programmatic aspects of *Ping-Pong, Anyone?* Use
wide leaps and *staccato* articulations.

LEVEL 6 SUMMARY
- Which Baroque pieces use two voices? three? four? How did you practice to become fluent with the increased
  number of voices?
- Did you listen to the recording of each repertoire piece or study you learned? What aspects of the recorded
  performance did you like? How was your performance similar to or different from the recording?
- Compare the variety of titles among the List C pieces with those from List B. Many of the List C titles suggest
  a mood or scene. How do the composers of sonatinas express moods through the music? Is one mood
  consistent throughout a piece, or does the mood change within a piece?

Level 7

The Publications

Level 7 of the *Celebration Series* includes the following publications:

 Piano Repertoire Album 7
 Piano Studies Album 7 & 8 (level 7 only)
 Student Guide 7
 Recording of *Repertoire & Studies 7*

The Repertoire

The *Piano Repertoire Album 7* is divided into three lists:

- List A includes a selection of pieces composed during the Baroque period (*ca* 1600 to *ca* 1750).
- List B includes a selection of pieces composed during the Classical period (*ca* 1750 to *ca* 1820).
- List C includes a selection of pieces composed during the Romantic era (*ca* 1820 to *ca* 1910) and the 20th century.

Musical Development

Piano Repertoire Album 7 and *Piano Studies Album 7* represent the progression from late intermediate to early advanced materials. The Baroque compositions require independence of hands and skill in the performance of ornaments. The Bach *Two-Part Inventions* are introduced here for the first time in the *Celebration Series*. The sonata movements from the Classical period demand fluency of scale figures and control of accompaniment patterns. For the interpretation of both List B and List C pieces, balance of melody and accompaniment are fundamental considerations. Romantic and contemporary compositions employ an increased use of chromaticism, modality, changing meters, and dynamic extremes. Indeed, this is material to foster musical growth.

The Range of Difficulty

The range of difficulty in Level 7 is represented by these two pieces:

- *Bourrée in F Major* by Georg Philipp Telemann is an example of an easier piece from Study Module 1.
- *Prelude in F Minor* by Dmitri Shostakovich is an example of a difficult piece from Study Module 6.

The Study Modules

The five Study Module discussions are organized into the following categories:

- *Background Information*
- *Exploring the Score*
- *Practice Suggestions*
- *Creative Activities*

Background Information (present in a few descriptions) provides relevant historical information. *Exploring the Score* is designed as an interactive exercise between teacher and student. These sections include questions you might address to the student during lessons. *Practice Suggestions* are also largely directly to the student. The *Creative Activities* act as reinforcement for your students' understanding of a musical concept and can provide a springboard for their creativity and imagination.

Please refer to the Forword for an explanation of how to use the suggested order of assignment within each Module.

The chart on the following page lists all the repertoire and studies in Level 7. Page numbers for works in the *Piano Repertoire Album 7* and the *Piano Studies Album 7* are found in the first column. Study Module numbers for each composition are found in the fourth column.

Page	Composer	Title	Study Module
Piano Repertoire Album 7			
List A R4	Johann Sebastian Bach	Invention No. 1 in C Major, BWV 772	2
R6	François Couperin	Allemande in D Minor	5
R8	Godfrey Keller	Prelude in G Major	1
R10	Johann Sebastian Bach	Minuet in B Flat	3
R12	Johann Sebastian Bach	Little Prelude in C Major, BWV 933	3
R14	Georg Philipp Telemann	Bourrée in F Major	1
R16	Domenico Scarlatti	Sonata in D Minor, L 58/K 64	4
List B R18	Friedrich Kuhlau	Sonatina in C Major, Op. 55, No. 3 (First Movement)	2
R21	Henri-Joseph Riegel	Sonata in D Major (Second Movement)	1
R24	Muzio Clementi	Sonatina in D Major, Op. 36, No. 6 (First Movement)	3
R30	Wolfgang Amadeus Mozart	Sonatina in G Major	2
R34	Ludwig van Beethoven	Sonata in G Major, Op. 79 (Second Movement)	4
R36	Ludwig van Beethoven	Bagatelle in B Flat, Op. 119, No. 11	5
List C R37	Clifford Poole	Ghost Town	3
R38	Viktor Kossenko	Melody, Op. 15, No. 11	4
R40	John Weinzweig	Toccata Dance	5
R42	Frédéric Chopin	Mazurka in A Flat, Op. 24, No. 3	2
R44	Franz Schubert	Waltz in D Flat, Op. 9, No. 14 (D. 365)	3
R45	Franz Schubert	Waltz in A Flat, Op. 9, No. 12 (D. 365)	1
R46	Felix Mendelssohn	Venetian Boat Song, Op. 30, No. 6	5
R48	Vladimir Ivanovich Rebikov	Waltz	4
R50	Gerhard Wuensch	Study in Mixolydian, Op. 41, No. 4	4
R52	Dmitri Shostakovich	Prelude in F Minor	5
Piano Studies Album 7			
S4	Stephen Heller	Study No. 1: Op. 125, No. 19	5
S6	Hugo Reinhold	Study No. 2	2
S8	Samuil Maikapar	Study No. 3: Toccatina, Op. 8, No. 1	3
S10	Edward MacDowell	Study No. 4: Hunting Song, Op. 39, No. 1	5
S12	Gerhard Wuensch	Study No. 5: Study in Rhythm	4
S14	Jenö Takács	Study No. 6: In a Great Hurry, Op. 95, No. 3	3
S16	Johann Sebastian Bach	Study No. 7: Little Prelude in F Major, BWV 927	1
S17	Cornelius Gurlitt	Study No. 8: Op. 132, No. 7	4
S18	Dmitri Kabalevsky	Study No. 9: Op. 27, No. 3	1
S19	Walter Niemann	Study No. 10: The Three Little Chatterboxes, Op. 46, No. 17	2
S20	George Frideric Handel	Study No. 11	5
S22	Stephen Heller	Study No. 12: The Lesson, Op. 125, No. 24	4

STUDY MODULE 1

Page	List	Composer	Title	Meter and Tempo	Musical and Stylistic Concepts
R8 SG11	A	Godfrey Keller	Prelude in G Major	4/4 Allegro	✔ rounded binary form ✔ each section opens with imitation ✔ RH study of hand rotation
R14 SG14	A	Georg Philipp Telemann	Bourrée in F Major	C Allegro	✔ sequences ✔ broken-octave chord patterns ✔ rhythmic independence of hands ✔ rounded binary form
R21 SG17	B	Henri-Joseph Riegel	Sonata in D Major (Second Movement)	3/8 Allemande stirienne	✔ melody in RH ✔ RH often plays two voices ✔ clearly defined contrasting themes
R45 SG26	C	Franz Schubert	Waltz in A Flat, Op. 9, No. 12 (D. 365)	3/4	✔ RH plays three different figures ✔ LH plays waltz bass
S16		Johann Sebastian Bach	Study No. 7: Little Prelude in F Major, BWV 927	C	✔ hand rotation ✔ constant eighth *vs* sixteenth motion
S18		Dmitri Kabalevsky	Study No. 9: Op. 27, No. 3	C Allegro vivace	✔ RH sixteenth-note scale figures have a variety of direction changes

Assign first:
Bourrée in F Major . . . .
Sonata in D Major (Second Movement)
Waltz in A Flat, Op. 9, No. 12 (D. 365) . . . .
Study No. 9: Op. 27, No. 3

Assign next when ready:
Prelude in G Major

Study No. 7: Little Prelude in F Major, BWV 927

The *Repertoire Album* selections in this Study Module are all dance-related. Two pieces – *Bourrée in F Major* and *Waltz in A Flat* – have dance titles. Godfrey Keller's *Prelude in G Major* has many characteristics of a Baroque *allemande*. The sonata movement by Henri-Joseph Riegel is marked *Allemande stirienne*.

Dance music is inextricably linked to rhythm. Differences in meter, tempo, upbeat patterns, and accented beats characterize the various dance forms. Downbeats have special significance in dance music. They are usually emphasized to provide a strong sense of meter.

Although it is important to focus attention on the beat and its subdivisions, a view of larger rhythmic units (macro-rhythms) is also necessary. Composers vary the lengths of rhythmic units to provide interest, variety, and patterns of intensity and relaxation. If your students are aware of these macro-rhythms, they will be able to understand and interpret the composer's organization of the music.

G. Keller: *Prelude in G Major* (R8, SG11)
Exploring the Score
Some figures are organized in macro-rhythmic units of half notes (for example, mm. 6-7). Other figures are organized in quarter-note pulses (for example, mm. 1 and 23). At the cadences (mm. 10 and 30), the macro-rhythmic units are shorter and more intense. Each eighth note is stressed.

Discuss these different rhythmic units with your student.
- Can you find the units by looking at the music?
- Mark (bracket) some of the units in the score.
- Listen for the half-note and quarter-note rhythmic units in the *Celebration Series* recording. As you listen to the recording, conduct the piece with the student (perhaps by tapping at the beginning of each rhythmic unit).

G.P. Telemann: *Bourrée in F Major* (R14, SG14)
Exploring the Score
Read the description of a *bourrée* in the *Student Guide* (p. 8). Help your student analyze the rhythmic figures in Telemann's *Bourrée in F Major* and look for the larger macro-rhythmic units.
- Which phrases start with the characteristic upbeat? [upbeats to mm. 1, 5, 19, 23, etc.]

- Did you notice the three-eighth-note upbeats to mm. 31, 33, and 35?
- Which phrases start on the beat? [mm. 9-12, 16-18, etc.]
- Find a syncopated rhythm. [mm. 2, 20, etc.]

Practice Suggestion
The *Student Guide* suggests a *staccato* articulation for passages based on triads or sequences. Try a *portato* touch or slur the first two of each group of four eighth notes.

H.-J. Riegel: *Sonata in D Major (Second Movement)* (R21, SG17)
Background Information
The marking *Allemande stirienne* suggests that this piece is based on folk music. (Styria is a mountainous region in the southeast of Austria.)

Exploring the Score
Folk dances often repeat melodic ideas.
- Find short melodic units which repeat. [for example, mm. 1-2 and 3-4; mm. 5 and 6]
- Find phrases which repeat. [for example, mm. 1-4 and 9-12; mm. 17-20 and 21-24]
- Find sections which repeat. [mm. 1-16 and 84-99]

Repetitions create unity but they also challenge the performer to make the repetitions interesting to the listener. Listen for slight changes in the repetitions on the *Celebration Series* recording.

F. Schubert: *Waltz in A Flat Op. 9, No. 12 (D. 365)* (R45, SG26)
Exploring the Score
Schubert's placement of accents creates rhythmic groups of one or two measures:

The accent marks help define the one-measure melodic units. Do the two-measure melodic units have a different pattern of accents? Listen for the one- and two-measure units on the *Celebration Series* recording.

Compare the two sections of this binary piece.
- Which section has the more predictable accents? [second]

- Which section has the more predictable harmony? [second]
- Which section has accented non-chord tones? [first section: F in mm. 1 and 4, B flat in m. 5, E in m. 6]

J.S. Bach: *Study No. 7: Little Prelude in F Major, BWV 927* (S16)
Background Information
Bach presented the *Wilhelm Friedemann Bach Notebook* to his son on his tenth birthday, November 22, 1720. This instruction book contains short preludes and inventions as well as several preludes from *The Well-Tempered Clavier*.

Practice Suggestions
1. Play the sixteenth notes as blocked chords. Use accurate fingerings.
2. Practice the sixteenth notes as written with a rocking motion of the hand.
3. In mm. 5-8, practice the LH eighth notes *legato* to learn the fingerings. Say the finger numbers aloud as you play. Then practice with a *staccato* touch.

D. Kabalevsky: *Study No. 9, Op. 27, No. 3* (S18)
Exploring the Score
In this study, the RH scale patterns are accompanied by a two-note slur motive. Analyze the scales. Have the student look for:
- full-octave scales
- scales that are more than an octave by one note
- scales that are more than an octave by several octaves
- scales that fall short of an octave

Practice Suggestions
- Isolate the different lengths of scale lines.
- Practice the LH two-note slurs. Use a drop-lift hand motion and make a break in sound between each slur.

CREATIVE ACTIVITY
Schubert's *Waltz in A Flat* is based on a sequence of chords. Play a cadence pattern (for example, I-IV-V^7-I) or make up a series of chords in the key of A flat. Play these chords with your LH in a waltz-bass pattern. Add a RH melody (made mostly of notes from the chords) on top of the LH accompaniment.

STUDY MODULE 2

Page	List	Composer	Title	Meter and Tempo	Musical and Stylistic Concepts
R4 SG9	A	Johann Sebastian Bach	Invention No. 1 in C Major, BWV 772	C	✔ two-voice contrapuntal texture ✔ eighth- *vs* sixteenth-note rhythms ✔ short trills and mordents
R18 SG16	B	Friedrich Kuhlau	Sonatina in C Major, Op. 55, No. 3 (First Movement)	C Allegro con spirito	✔ sonata form (no restatement of first theme in recapitulation) ✔ clearly contrasting themes ✔ RH scale figures with variety of turn-arounds
R30 SG19	B	Wolfgang Amadeus Mozart	Sonatina in G Major	6/8 Allegretto	✔ rondo form ✔ LH holds bass note while playing sixteenth notes or blocked intervals
R42 SG25	C	Frédéric Chopin	Mazurka in A Flat, Op. 24, No. 3	3/4 Moderato con anima	✔ rounded binary form ✔ *hemiola* in B section ✔ RH arpeggio which ends sections is extended in *coda*
S6		Hugo Reinhold	Study No. 2	3/4 Tempo rubato	✔ A section: RH plays double 3rds and blocked intervals ✔ B section: RH plays arpeggiated figures ✔ LH plays waltz bass
S19		Walter Niemann	Study No. 10: The Three Little Chatterboxes, Op. 46, No. 17	C Lively and cheerful	✔ both hands *staccato* ✔ three-eighth-note motive

Assign first:
Invention No. 1 in C Major, BWV 772
Sonatina in C Major, Op. 55, No. 3
   (First Movement) . . . .
Study No. 2 . . . .
Study No. 10: The Three Little Chatterboxes,
   Op. 24, No. 17

Assign next when ready:

Sonatina in G Major
Mazurka in A Flat, Op. 24, No. 3

In Study Module 2, students can discover the role of changing tonal centers and modulation in determining form, contrasting moods, and colors. Encourage students to compare different pieces they play and to look for common elements. Here are some suggestions:

- Compare the keys of sections in compositions by Kuhlau, Mozart, Chopin, and Reinhold. Look for the contrast between themes in major keys and themes in minor keys. Are the key changes between sections sudden, or are they created through modulation?
- The Reinhold study is quite Chopinesque. Compare this study with the Chopin *Mazurka*, and explore how each composer uses chromaticism.
- Look for common musical elements with different articulation. For example, compare the *legato* double 3rds in *Study No. 2* with the *staccato* 3rds divided between the hands in *Study No. 10*.

J.S. Bach: *Invention in C Major, BWV 772*
(R4, SG9)

Background Information

The *Wilhelm Friedemann Bach Notebook* includes early versions of some of the *Two-Part Inventions* and the *Three-Part Sinfonias*. A revised version of these pieces appears in a manuscript dating from 1723, but they were not published until 1801. The title page of the 1723 manuscript describes these works as examples of how to arrive at original ideas and develop them satisfactorily. Both sets are arranged in ascending key order and make significant use of invertible counterpoint.

Exploring the Score

Baroque composers often added a trill to emphasize a cadence. The cadential trill was so common that performers often added one even if it was not indicated in the score.

- Find two cadential trills and label the keys they help establish. [mm. 6-7, G major; mm. 14-15, A minor]
- How can you make these arrival points especially clear? [slight broadening, *crescendo*]

Read the detailed analysis in the *Student Guide*.

- Review the relationship between the opening motive and the RH and LH parts of m. 3.
- Can you find any figures which do not relate directly to the opening motive?
- Which part of this invention is easiest to play? [mm. 15-18] Do these measures represent musical tension or musical relaxation?

F. Kuhlau: *Sonatina in C Major, Op. 55, No. 3 (First Movement)* (R18, SG16)

Exploring the Score

Friedrich Kuhlau's sonatinas provide excellent examples of variety and contrast in sonata form. The *Student Guide* outlines the form of this sonatina movement.

- Three ideas characterize the two main themes of the exposition: "*x*" (mm. 1-2) of the first theme, and "*y*" (mm. 9-10) and "*z*" (mm. 13-14) of the second theme. Label "*x*," "*y*," and "*z*" throughout the movement.
- Label each theme with a mood or character.
- Name the key of each theme. There is a feeling of arrival in m. 20. What key is confirmed here? [G major]
- Which theme is used (exclusively) in the development? [first theme]
- In mm. 33-35, there is a written-in *ritardando*. What effect does this create? [highlights end of development section, creates anticipation of recapitulation]

- Why do you think Kuhlau avoids the first theme in the recapitulation? [see the *Student Guide*]
- Compare mm. 13-16 with mm. 40-45, and m. 20 with m. 49. How are they alike? How are they different?
- What is the musical purpose of the *coda*? [confirmation of C major tonality]
- Have you played other sonatina movements in which the beginning of the recapitulation was not clear?

W.A. Mozart: *Sonatina in G Major* (R30, SG19)

Exploring the Score

This piece is in rondo form. The *Student Guide* outlines the form and suggests a dynamic plan for the A theme. Label the sections and name the key of each one.

- How do the sections contrast?
- Mozart uses three different accompaniment patterns for the A theme. How do the changes in accompaniment affect the mood?
- Where can you hear a modulation? [mm. 17, 53-56]
- Mozart often substitutes a supertonic (ii) chord for a subdominant (IV) chord at cadences. Analyze the harmony of mm. 9-12.

Practice Suggestion

This rondo falls into four-measure phrases. Find the focus of each phrase. (Frequently, the focus of a four-measure phrase comes in the third measure. Think of the rule: Out of four, go for three.) Make a slight *crescendo* to the third measure of each phrase.

F. Chopin: *Mazurka in A Flat, Op. 24, No. 3* (R42, SG25)

Exploring the Score

See the description of a mazurka in the *Student Guide* (p. 8). How does Chopin emphasize the second beat?

- m. 2: wide leap, grace note, long note
- m. 6: wide leap, *sforzando*, rolled chord, *fermata*
- m. 8: accent on long note

Practice Suggestions

The rhythm in mm. 25-31 does not have a strong 3/4 pulse. In the RH, each eighth-note pair starts a new rhythmic unit. In the LH, the beat groupings fall into a 2+2+4 pattern. Practice hands separately, counting aloud as shown below:

H. Reinhold: *Study No. 2* (S6)
Background Information

Hugo Reinhold was an Austrian composer. He studied with Anton Bruckner and graduated from the Vienna Conservatory in 1874. He taught at the Akademie der Tonkunst until 1925.

Practice Suggestions

Students will find this piece easier to learn if they concentrate first on the fingering.

1. Practice the LH. Follow the given fingering. As a general rule, in a LH waltz bass, play the downbeats with the fifth finger and avoid using the fifth finger on the second and third beats.
2. Practice the RH double 3rds with *legato* connections. Connect both voices whenever possible. When one finger must lift to play successive notes, connect the other voice.
3. Devise a practice method for learning the eighth-note fingerings in mm. 17-31. For example, divide these measures into short units which end with the thumb. Practice each unit until the fingering is secure.

W. Niemann: *Study No. 10: The Three Little Chatterboxes, Op. 46, No. 17* (S19)
Practice Suggestions

- Practice the triplet eighth notes hands separately. Observe the accent marks. (Do you hear the word "chatterbox"?)
- For a clearer *staccato*, experiment with a change of finger on the repeated notes.
- Practice the chromatic line of m. 11 with a *legato* touch to learn the fingering.
- Practice hands together in one-measure units.

CREATIVE ACTIVITY

Write your own *Mazurka*. Create a melody in 3/4 meter with emphasis on the second beat, then add an appropriate LH accompaniment.

STUDY MODULE 3

Page	List	Composer	Title	Meter and Tempo	Musical and Stylistic Concepts
R10 SG12	A	Johann Sebastian Bach	Minuet in B Flat	3/4	✔ RH eighths in zig-zag patterns ✔ LH quarter notes
R12 SG13	A	Johann Sebastian Bach	Little Prelude in C Major, BWV 933	4/4 Moderato	✔ RH chords frequently ornamented ✔ chordal theme contrasted with sixteenth-note broken-chord and scale figures
R24 SG18	B	Muzio Clementi	Sonatina in D Major, Op. 36, No. 6 (First Movement)	C Allegro con spirito	✔ sonata form with clearly defined sections ✔ LH plays variety of accompaniment figures and textures ✔ RH always has melodic lead ✔ challenging scale figures
R37 SG22	C	Clifford Poole	Ghost Town	4/4 Andante espressivo	✔ AA_1BA_2 with introduction and *coda* ✔ variety of dynamics and tempos ✔ LH shifts of two and three octaves
R44 SG26	C	Franz Schubert	Waltz in D Flat, Op. 9, No. 14 (D. 365)	3/4	✔ LH waltz bass ✔ RH has constant eighth-note motion, melody in double-stemmed notes
S8		Samuil Maikapar	Study No. 3: Toccatina, Op. 8, No. 1	4/4 Allegro vivace	✔ rounded binary form with *coda* ✔ A section: variety of sixteenth-note figures within a tetrachord ✔ B section: alternating single notes between hands
S14		Jenö Takács	Study No. 6: In a Great Hurry, Op. 95, No. 3	2/4, 3/4, 4/4 Presto, scherzando	✔ no distinct tonal center ✔ ABA form ✔ *staccato* study ✔ parallel chromatic scale figures with hands a whole tone apart

Assign first:
Minuet in B Flat . . . .
Sonatina in D Major, Op. 36, No. 6
   (First Movement)
Waltz in D Flat, Op. 9, No. 14 (D. 365) . . . .
Study No. 6: In a Great Hurry, Op. 95, No. 3 . . .

Assign next when ready:
Little Prelude in C Major, BWV 933

Study No. 3: Toccatina, Op. 8, No. 1
Ghost Town

Study Module 3 provides examples of typical stylistic characteristics of the four major style periods: Baroque, Classical, Romantic, and contemporary. Have students make a list of the style characteristics for each period. Some ideas are given in the discussions of the individual pieces. Students can use this list to compare pieces within a period and pieces from two different periods. For example, examine the contrasting textures in the two Bach pieces. Compare the use of rounded binary form by Bach in *Minuet in B Flat* with that of Maikapar in *Study No. 3*. Compare the ABA form in Poole's *Ghost Town* and Takács's *Study No. 6*.

J.S. Bach: *Minuet in B Flat* (R10, SG12)
Background Information
Bach's voluminous keyboard works include a number of dance suites. Dances and national styles that were popular in the Baroque era are represented in each suite. The best known are the *English Suites*, the *French Suites*, and the *Six Partitas*. In the late Baroque period, keyboard suites were sometimes titled *partitas*. *Partita No. 1 in B Flat* has seven movements: *Praeludium, Allemande, Corrente, Sarabande, Menuet I* (this piece), *Menuet II*, and *Giga*. Encourage your students to listen to a recording of the complete work.

Exploring the Score
This minuet has a constant eighth-note rhythm. The only sixteenth notes come after cadences.
- Find these cadences and label the keys. [F major (dominant), G minor (relative minor), B flat major (tonic)]
- Compare this key plan with that of Bach's *Invention in C Major* (R4). [see form outline in the *Student Guide*]

This piece is based on a three-note stepwise motive.
- Look for this motive in the RH beat notes (for example, m. 2, D-E flat-F) and circle examples of stepwise motion in the score.
- Listen to the *Celebration Series* recording to hear the melodic importance of this motive.

Much of the RH implies a soprano and an alto voice.
- Find measures where one voice repeats a note and the other moves away. [mm. 2, 4, 14, etc.]
- Find measures where the voices move in contrary motion. [mm. 5, 6, 13, etc.]

J.S. Bach: *Little Prelude in C Major, BWV 933* (R12, SG13)
Background Information
Baroque composers often imitated other instruments and ensembles in their keyboard works. For example, thick textures with full chords imitate an orchestra; single lines may represent a solo instrument. Sixteenth-note melodic figures often resemble motives used in violin music. The LH accompaniments of keyboard dances often imitate a cello or bassoon.

Exploring the Score
Contrast of texture is prominent in this prelude.
- Which measures imitate full orchestra?
- Which measures imitate a solo instrument with light accompaniment?

M. Clementi: *Sonatina in D Major, Op. 36, No. 6 (First Movement)* (R24, SG18)
Background Information
Contrast is the chief goal of the composer writing a sonatina. Making that contrast evident to the listener must be the goal of the performer. Contrast can exist between sections and within sections.

Exploring the Score
Read the form outline in the *Student Guide*. The musical ideas making up the first theme (mm. 1-12) vary in length from two beats to several measures.
- Identify each distinct musical idea in the first theme.
- Find the second theme. What new, contrasting features does Clementi introduce in this theme? [new key, smaller melodic range, simpler rhythm, change of accompaniment, different dynamics, *appoggiaturas*]

Composers rarely introduce new material in the development section. Is this sonatina movement an exception to the rule? How is this development section related to the exposition? [sixteenth-note motive]

Practice Suggestion
When students hear and feel the contrast between sections and themes, they will be much more aware of this important characteristic of the Classical style. Have students practice contrasting themes one after the other.

C. Poole: *Ghost Town* (R37, SG22)
Exploring the Score
Baroque composers rarely included dynamic markings in their music (although these details are often added by modern editors). By contrast, every measure of *Ghost Town* has an indication of some kind. These markings, written by the composer, are an integral part of the composition. The challenge is to realize every indication — accents, *tenutos*, slurs, dynamics, tempo markings, and pedaling. An expressive performance will be the reward. The *Student Guide* gives a number of practice suggestions.

F. Schubert: *Waltz in D Flat, Op. 9, No. 14 (D. 365)* (R44, SG26)

Exploring the Score

See the *Student Guide* for an explanation of the modulation in this waltz. Romantic composers often used harmonic progressions with common tones and stepwise movement. For example, notice the relationship between D flat major and A major:

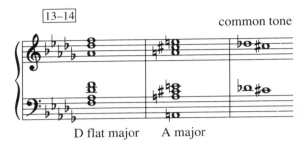

Practice Suggestions

Have the student find the four-measure phrases, and point out the change of harmony in the third measure. Focus the phrase on that harmonic change — "out of four, go for three."

1. Play only the LH downbeats and the RH double-stemmed melody notes. Play the RH with a singing *legato* tone and shape the melody with dynamics.
2. Play the RH melody with the LH accompaniment as written. Play the chords lightly.
3. Practice the RH alone. Exaggerate the dynamic contrast between the melody and the accompanying eighth notes.
4. Play the LH downbeats with the RH as written. Bring out the melody and play the accompanying eighth notes quietly.

S. Maikapar: *Study No. 3: Toccatina, Op. 8, No. 1* (S8)

Practice Suggestions

There are several different patterns of sixteenth notes. Practice each type separately.

- Rotate your hand to play zig-zag patterns.
- Use the articulation shown below for the sixteenth-note groups which begin with a *staccato*:

- Keep your fingers close to the keys for the slurred sixteenth notes, and play the *staccato* notes with a lifted finger.

- Play the scales divided between the hands with a smooth sound. Do not accent the first RH note.
- For alternating notes between the hands, concentrate on an equal *staccato* in both hands.

J. Takács: *Study No. 6: In a Great Hurry, Op. 95, No. 3* (S14)

Exploring the Score

How can a composer create a feeling of agitation in music?

- What are the agitated elements in this study? [fast tempo, short motives (mm. 1-2, 13-14), new figure in m. 3, *crescendi* over two-measure fragments (mm. 9-12)]
- In mm. 33-38, Takács repeats the opening material with a different mood (*Andante tranquillo*). Invent a story that accounts for this change of pace.

CREATIVE ACTIVITIES

♪ What musical elements does Poole use to create a deserted atmosphere in *Ghost Town*? Are the dynamics always quiet? Is there a wide range of pitches? Is the tempo always steady? Use these ideas to explore the relationship of sound and atmosphere. Create your own musical painting about loneliness, deserted places, or times past.

♪ Takács is a wonderfully inventive contemporary composer. In *Study No. 6*, he expresses the agitation of someone in a hurry. Compose your own piece based on agitated, nervous movements. Use *staccato* broken chords, chromatic scale fragments, and a fast tempo. You might title your piece *I Can't Find It!*

STUDY MODULE 4

Page	List	Composer	Title	Meter and Tempo	Musical and Stylistic Concepts
R16 SG15	A	Domenico Scarlatti	Sonata in D Minor, L 58/K 64	2/4 Tempo di gavotta	✔ full LH sound with octave chords and rolled 10ths ✔ RH melody punctuated with short trills ✔ blocked and broken descending 6ths
R34 SG20	B	Ludwig van Beethoven	Sonata in G Major, Op. 79 (Second Movement)	9/8 Andante	✔ tuneful barcarole ✔ A section: RH melody in double 6ths and 3rds ✔ B section: LH arpeggio accompaniment
R38 SG23	C	Viktor Kossenko	Melody, Op. 15, No. 11	3/4 Andantino cantabile	✔ G sharp minor ✔ RH melody often in top note of blocked intervals ✔ active accompaniment
R48 SG28	C	Vladimir Ivanovich Rebikov	Waltz	3/4 Moderato sempre cantabile	✔ F sharp minor ✔ RH melody over blocked intervals and chords ✔ B section: melody alternates between hands
R50 SG29	C	Gerhard Wuensch	Study in Mixolydian, Op. 41, No. 4	4/4	✔ LH has three-note motive ✔ RH off-beat entrances and syncopation ✔ challenging meter and hand coordination
S12		Gerhard Wuensch	Study No. 5: Study in Rhythm	3/4 Allegro	✔ challenge: shifting accents and avoiding strong downbeat
S17		Cornelius Gurlitt	Study No. 8: Op. 132, No. 7	3/4 Moderato cantando	✔ two RH voices require control of balance and finger substitutions ✔ dynamic control essential
S22		Stephen Heller	Study No. 12: The Lesson, Op. 125, No. 24	C Allegro vivace	✔ programmatic piece with contrasting sections ✔ scale figures ✔ five-finger patterns ✔ RH **1-2-1-5** hand rotation patterns

Assign first:
Sonata in D Minor, L 58/K 64 . . . .
Study No. 12: The Lesson, Op. 125, No. 24 . . . . .
Waltz . . . .
Study No. 5: Study in Rhythm . . . .

Assign next when ready:
Melody, Op. 15, No. 11
Sonata in G Major, Op. 79 (Second Movement)
Study No. 8: Op. 132, No. 7
Study in Mixolydian, Op. 41, No. 4

The pieces in Study Module 4 feature an interesting variety of keys. How do composers choose the keys for their pieces? The answers vary from one composer to another, but most composers are highly sensitive to key color. Some keys represent bright, cheerful moods; others are vehicles for dark, menacing musical statements.
- The pieces from *Repertoire Album 7* are in a minor key or are modal. How many of these pieces include a modulation to a major key? How would you describe the resulting change of mood?
- Kossenko uses a natural minor (Aeolian mode) in *Melody*. Compare the sound with the other modal piece, Wuensch's *Study in Mixolydian*.

D. Scarlatti: *Sonata in D Minor, L 58/K 64*
(R16, SG15)
Exploring the Score
This sonata is in D minor, a key used by many composers for vigorous, dark, driving music.
- How does the mood change when the music modulates to F major?
- In mm. 1-4, does the theme move up or down?
- What is the direction of the F major theme in mm. 17-20? [static]

Practice Suggestions
- Initially learn without ornaments.
- Isolate blocked 6ths for spot practice (mm. 36, 43-44).
- Divide the two voices of the RH between the hands (mm. 24, 25-30).
- Practice LH chordal textures alone.
- Isolate parallel eighth-note groups (mm. 21-23).
- Listen carefully for RH slur and *staccato* articulations.

L. van Beethoven: *Sonata in G Major, Op. 79 (Second Movement)* (R34, SG20)
Exploring the Score
The first and last movements of this sonata are in G major. The middle movement of a sonata is usually in a contrasting key.
- What is the key of this second movement? [G minor]
- What is the key of the B section? [E flat major] How does this modulation contribute to the change of mood?
- What is the relationship between the keys of the A and B sections? [E flat is the submediant of G minor]
- Beethoven often uses contrasting keys that are related by a common tone. Which common tones do the tonic chords of G minor and E flat major share? [G and B flat]

V. Kossenko: *Melody, Op. 15, No. 11* (R38, SG23)
V.I. Rebikov: *Waltz* (R48, SG28)
Exploring the Score
These two compositions are similar in mood and color. Both pieces have a 3/4 meter and are in black-key minor tonalities.
- What are the keys of these two pieces? How would the moods change if they were transposed to white-key minors, or to major keys?
- In both pieces, the RH plays the melody – with one exception. Find the LH melody in *Waltz*. [mm. 17-20, 25-28]

Practice Suggestions
See suggestions for practicing voicing and melodic projection in the *Student Guide*. Ask students to list several ways to practice the voicing of the melody. Discuss different techniques for voicing the double notes of *Waltz* and the single line of *Melody*.

Compare the two composers' pedal indications. List a few pedal guidelines for *Melody*. For example, change the pedal:
- with changes of harmony
- to define changes of pitch in the melody
- between phrases
Notice the detailed pedal indications in mm. 17-20 of *Waltz*.

G. Wuensch: *Study in Mixolydian, Op. 41, No. 4* (R50, SG29)
Exploring the Score
How would the mood of this piece change if:
- the LH were *legato*?
- there were no rests in the A section?
- the dynamics stayed the same throughout?

The Mixolydian mode is like a major scale, except that the seventh degree is lowered. To hear the difference, play mm. 1-8 in G major (add F sharps).

G. Wuensch: *Study No. 5: Study in Rhythm* (S12)
Exploring the Score
This study highlights not only rhythm but also contrasts in mood and color. Explore the score with this in mind.
- Look at the dynamics. Where are the sudden dynamic contrasts? Where are the loudest and softest measures?
- Look for changes of register. Where do both hands play in the treble or bass clef?
- The sixteenth-note figures are usually scale fragments. Which scales does Wuensch use? Does the scale key match the accompanying chords?
- Wuensch creates intensity by using chords from two different keys simultaneously. Name the chords in mm. 23-27.

Practice Suggestions
There are several ways to practice rhythm and hand coordination. Here are some suggestions:
- Practice the LH of mm. 1-11 separately.
- Tap the LH rhythm, counting aloud.
- Play the LH as written. Count aloud and accent the beat notes.
- Find the RH sixteenth-note groups which start on a beat. Play those groups, counting aloud.
- Tap mm. 13-14 and 23-27 hands together.

The RH is especially active and has many position changes. To learn the position changes, practice moving quickly from the blocked notes of one position (for example, the first RH slurred group), to the blocked notes of the next position (for example, the second RH slurred group).

C. Gurlitt: *Study No. 8: Op. 132, No. 7* (S17)
Exploring the Score
With its rich harmonic color and flowing rhythm, this piece could be subtitled *Valse élégante*. Find and label the following chord progression in mm. 1-8:

Find pairs of chords that have a dominant-tonic relationship. (The F sharp minor and A major chords are secondary dominants within the key of G major.)

Practice Suggestions
In mm. 1-8 there is one harmony per measure. In mm. 17-18 and 21-22 there are two harmonies per measure. How will this harmonic rhythm affect the pedaling?

Give each RH voice its own dynamic level. As you practice, listen for the louder soprano voice and the softer alto voice.

The LH downbeat notes create a bass line. Give each of these low notes a slight emphasis.

S. Heller: *Study No. 12: The Lesson, Op. 125, No. 24* (S22)
Exploring the Score
This piece tells a story about a piano lesson. As you learn this piece, refine your story:
- Which parts represent the teacher?
- Which parts represent the student?
- What is the student's attitude?
- Does the student improve during the lesson? Why (or why not)?
- What is the mood of the ending?

CREATIVE ACTIVITIES
♫ Wuensch's *Study in Mixolydian* is based on a modal scale (see the *Student Guide*, p. 29). Play a familiar melody or folk song in a major tonality. Locate the leading tones (seventh scale degree). Lower these notes to shift the melody into a Mixolydian mode. Harmonize the melody. (Use the lowered seventh degree in your harmonization as well.)

♫ Follow Heller's example in *Study No. 12* by making up a piece about your own piano lessons! Give a title to your piece.

STUDY MODULE 5

Page	List	Composer	Title	Meter and Tempo	Musical and Stylistic Concepts
R6 SG10	A	François Couperin	Allemande in D Minor	C Lightly	✔ two-voice texture ✔ short trills in both hands ✔ some use of sequence ✔ constant variation of figures
R36 SG21	B	Ludwig van Beethoven	Bagatelle in B Flat, Op. 119, No. 11	C Andante, ma non troppo	✔ binary form with *coda* ✔ *cantabile legato* requires control and expression ✔ challenging RH part balances two and three voices
R40 SG24	C	John Weinzweig	Toccata Dance	mixed meters; Presto, marcatissimo	✔ no tonal center ✔ mainly 4/4 with changing meter and off-beat accents ✔ repeated motives have motoric sound ✔ challenge: coordination between the hands
R46 SG27	C	Felix Mendelssohn	Venetian Boat Song, Op. 30, No. 6	6/8 Allegretto tranquillo	✔ rounded binary form with *coda* ✔ *legato* LH includes extended positions and double 3rds
R52 SG30	C	Dmitri Shostakovich	Prelude in F Minor	6/8 Andantino	✔ complex four-voice texture ✔ each voice states theme three times ✔ two 9/8 measures
S4		Stephen Heller	Study No. 1: Op. 125, No. 19	C Allegro risoluto	✔ A section (C sharp minor): scale patterns hands together and divided between hands ✔ B section (D flat major): RH melody with trills, LH countermelody in double-stemmed notes ✔ LH triplet against RH duple rhythm
S10		Edward MacDowell	Study No. 4: Hunting Song, Op. 39, No. 1	2/4 Allegretto	✔ quick shifts, often from single notes to chords ✔ constant mixture of triplets, duple eighths, and dotted figures
S20		George Frideric Handel	Study No. 11	3/8 Allegro	✔ RH constant sixteenth-note motion with constant change of the figure ✔ little imitation and absence of sequence

Assign first: **Assign next when ready:**
Study No. 11 . . . . *Allemande in D Minor*
Bagatelle in B Flat, Op. 119, No. 11 . . . . *Prelude in F Minor*
Study No. 4: Hunting Song, Op. 39, No. 1 . . . . . . *Study No. 1: Op. 125, No. 19*
Venetian Boat Song, Op. 30, No. 6 . . . . *Toccata Dance*

Study Module 5 includes some of the most difficult pieces in Level 7. Each piece requires careful, attentive practice. The comments on interpretation and practice in the *Student Guide* and the sound model provided by the *Celebration Series* recording will be of special importance for this Study Module: the pieces by Beethoven, Shostakovich, and Weinzweig are particularly challenging in interpretation.

F. Couperin: *Allemande in D Minor* (R6, SG10)
Exploring the Score

Discuss the form and harmonic structure as outlined in the *Student Guide*. Stress the importance of building to the cadences in mm. 7 and 14, and to the climax of the piece on the downbeat of m. 13. (In harpsichord music, the climax of a piece often occurs when the hands are farthest apart. Notice the distance between the hands on the downbeat of m. 13.)

Look for figures which are repeated, for example:
- ornaments followed by a descending 3rd
- four-beat phrases (RH, mm. 1-3)
- imitation between the hands
- broken 3rds (mm. 9-11)

Practice Suggestions

Students may find this piece difficult to learn because there is little repetition. The following practice suggestions should be helpful.
- Practice the sixteenth-note figures in four-beat units, hands separately.
- Study each figure carefully. Note the shape and melodic movement:
  - mostly stepwise
  - mostly zig-zag
  - wide variety of intervals
- Practice each figure at least five times.
- Challenge yourself to memorize the figure.
- Circle stepwise motion in the melodic skeleton. Focus on these circles as visual and musical goals:

Have students practice first without the ornaments, then read the paragraph on ornamentation in the *Student Guide*. Practice the ornaments separately, and experiment with different fingerings. Then practice slowly with the ornaments.

L. van Beethoven: *Bagatelle in B Flat, Op. 119, No. 11* (R36, SG21)
Exploring the Score

The melody of the A section is dominated by the interval of the 3rd:

Similarly, the melody of the second part of the B section (mm. 11-18) is based on two RH notes: E flat-D. Look for E flat-D in the LH as well.

Practice Suggestions
- The harmonies change on each beat and occasionally on half beats (for example, mm. 13 and 17). Change the pedal with each new harmony.
- Project the flowing *legato* soprano melody over the other voices. Play the alto with relaxed fingers, and detach the notes slightly.
- Play the melody of mm. 1-7 with *legato* fingerings and move the music forward by making a slight *crescendo* on the eighth notes. Think of mm. 1 and 3 flowing to the downbeats of mm. 2 and 4 respectively.

J. Weinzweig: *Toccata Dance* (R40, SG24)
Practice Suggestions

The contrasting sections of this piece are clear to the eye and ear. Find sections that look alike, and practice them together. For example:
- mm. 3-4, 27-28, and 33-35
- mm. 13-15 and 29-31
- unison passage: mm. 16-25
- offbeat LH pattern in mm. 10-11 and 35-36 (tap, then play)
- LH pattern on the beat, mm. 12-13 and 39-40 (tap, then play)

Pay special attention to dynamic markings and accents. Exaggerate them in slow practice.

F. Mendelssohn: *Venetian Boat Song, Op. 30, No. 6* (R46, SG27)
Practice Suggestions

Extended melodic lines are one characteristic of 19th-century piano music. In this piece, the combination of eight-measure phrases with the constant, hypnotic, rocking accompaniment paint a most effective musical scene of a Venetian canal.
- Can you find melodic fragments in the LH?
- What practice techniques will you use to bring out these top notes?
- For a convincing rocking motion, stress some LH notes more than others. Which beats should be most prominent?

D. Shostakovich: *Prelude in F Minor* (R52, SG30)
Exploring the Score

Although titled *Prelude*, this piece employs voicing techniques often associated with a fugue. Read the paragraphs on counterpoint and *stretto* in the *Student Guide*. The theme (mm. 1-4) is presented in all voices, and is highlighted with *tenuto* marks. Make sure the entrance of each voice can be heard clearly.

Practice Suggestions

- Locate all entrances of the melody. Follow the *tenuto* markings.
- Practice the *stretto* measures (for example, mm. 9-10, 11-13, and 16-18) playing only the notes marked *tenuto*. Play one voice in each hand.
- Find this motive in mm. 2-3:

Listen for it as you play mm. 10, 12-13, and 18-19.
- Listen to the final sound of the piece. Play the low F in m. 21 with enough tone so that the sound will last through to the final measure.

Read the outline of the form in the *Student Guide*. A successful performance of this piece depends on smoothly flowing phrases. Move the melody gently forward and make a slight *ritardando* at the end of the phrase to define the section.

S. Heller: *Study No. 1: Op. 125, No. 19* (S4)
Exploring the Score

With your student, identify the form [ABA] and label the sections.

- Name the keys of the sections. [C sharp minor, D flat major]
- What technical figures does Heller use in the A section? [full octave scales hands together, sixteenth-note groups, chords]

Practice Suggestions

In mm. 19-28, some LH notes have double stems. Sustain these low tones.

Find examples of duple *vs* triplet eighth notes. [mm. 20, 24, 27] Use the following exercise to practice two-against-three rhythms.

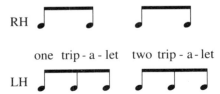

Alternatively you can say, "Together, left, right, left; together, left, right, left."

E. MacDowell: *Study No. 4: Hunting Song, Op. 39, No. 1* (S10)
Background Information

Edward MacDowell, like many other American composers of his time, received his musical training in Germany. He was highly influenced by the German Romantic style. His piano compositions are often virtuosic and reflect a love of nature.

Practice Suggestions

Melody is all-important in this joyful, expressive piece. Accuracy of beat subdivisions is also crucial to the spirit of the composition. The quarter-note beat is divided into:

- two equal parts (eighth notes)
- three equal parts (triplet eighth notes)
- four equal parts (sixteenth notes and dotted rhythms)

Devise tapping and playing exercises with your student. For example, tap a steady quarter-note beat with one hand. With the other hand tap a series of subdivisions: eighth notes, triplet eighths, sixteenth notes, dotted figures.
1. Tap each subdivision three times.
2. Tap each subdivision twice.
3. Play a scale using the subdivisions in succession.

G.F. Handel: *Study No. 11* (S20)
Exploring the Score

Have students imagine the RH part played on a flute.
- Where would the flutist take deep breaths and smaller "catch breaths"? Use these breathing places as a guide for phrasing.
- Shape the rising and falling contours of the RH line with slight *crescendi* and *diminuendi*.
- Experiment with articulation. Use a clear *legato* touch for the stepwise sixteenth notes and detach the notes moving in wider intervals.

Practice Suggestions

Independence of the hands is the challenge in this two-voice piece. To learn this piece efficiently, give special attention to fingering in the beginning days of practice.
- To learn the fingerings quickly, practice with a *legato* touch.
- For reinforcement, say the fingerings aloud as you play (hands separately).
- Practice hands together in one- or two-measure units. Play slowly for accuracy, and repeat each unit several times.

CREATIVE ACTIVITY

 Using the LH rocking motion of Mendelssohn's *Venetian Boat Song* as a guide, write your own *Boat Song*. Use a 6/8 time signature and simple harmonies (perhaps limited to tonic and dominant chords). Imagine an Italian gondolier singing your melody!

LEVEL 7 SUMMARY

- Compare pieces with the same name: prelude, sonatina, toccata, waltz. What similarities or differences can you find?
- In addition to opus numbers, you will notice that composers' works are often categorized by abbreviations such as BWV, K, L, and D. What do these letters mean? With which composers are these letters associated?
- Music is often called the universal language. How many different countries are represented by the composers in Level 7?

Level 8

The Publications

Level 8 of the *Celebration Series* includes the following publications:

Piano Repertoire Album 8
Piano Studies Album 7 & 8 (level 8 only)
Student Guide 8
Recording of *Repertoire & Studies 8*

The Repertoire

The *Piano Repertoire Album 8* is divided into four lists:

- List A includes a selection of pieces composed during the Baroque period (*ca* 1600 to *ca* 1750).
- List B includes a selection of pieces composed during the Classical period (*ca* 1750 to *ca* 1820) as well as pieces in the Classical style written during the 19th century.
- List C includes a selection of pieces from the Romantic era (*ca* 1820 to *ca* 1910).
- List D includes a selection of pieces composed during the late 19th century and the 20th century.

Musical Development

The Level 8 repertoire and studies represent an early advanced level. This Level plays a pivotal role in preparing students for the advanced Levels 9 and 10 of the *Celebration Series*. Students working at this level will most likely be studying three or four different stylistic periods simultaneously. For the first time, students are presented with larger Classical sonata first movements: *Sonata in C Major, KV 545* by Mozart and *Sonata in G Major, Op. 49, No. 2* by Beethoven. This level also includes significant works from the Baroque era as well as a mazurka and nocturne from the Romantic era and preludes from the 20th century.

The Level 8 studies are more than pure technical exercises. They can hold their own as meaningful repertoire and should be prepared with the same musicianship and attention to detail as the repertoire. They also provide excellent preparation for pieces in the *Repertoire Album* because of their emphasis on particular musical or technical features.

The organization of practice time becomes an increasingly important consideration as you progress into more advanced levels. Here are some suggestions for daily practice:

- Organize your practice session(s) by deciding on areas of focus. Articulate your practice goals.
- Evaluate your own playing by listening to taped practice performances.
- Practice all parts of the assignment daily. If you cannot practice a segment of the assignment one day, begin the next day's practice with that task.
- Practice at times when you are fresh and alert. When possible, schedule more than one practice session each day.

The Range of Difficulty

The range of difficulty in Level 8 is represented by these two pieces:

- *Les chérubins* by François Couperin is an example of an easier piece from Study Module 1.
- *Toccatina* by Robert Fleming is one of the most technically challenging pieces from Study Module 6.

The Study Modules

In earlier Levels, the Study Modules have often been arranged around a conscious thread or theme. In Level 8, each Study Module presents an interesting combination of styles and an increased level of difficulty. The six Study Module discussions are organized into the following categories:

- *Background Information*
- *Exploring the Score*
- *Practice Suggestions*
- *Creative Activities*

Background Information (present in a few descriptions) provides relevant historical information. *Exploring the Score* is designed as an interactive exercise between teacher and student. These sections include questions you might address to the student during lessons. *Practice Suggestions* are also largely directly to the student. The *Creative Activities* act as reinforcement for your students' understanding of a musical concept and can provide a springboard for their creativity and imagination.

Please refer to the Forword for an explanation of how to use the suggested order of assignment within each Module.

The chart on the following page lists all the repertoire and studies in Level 8. Page numbers for works in the *Piano Repertoire Album 8* and the *Piano Studies Album 8* are found in the first column. Study Module numbers for each composition are found in the fourth column.

STUDY MODULE 1

Page	List	Composer	Title	Meter and Tempo	Musical and Stylistic Concepts
R4 SG9	A	François Couperin	Les chérubins	2/4 Lightly	✔ imitative texture ✔ melody embellished in second part ✔ RH cadential ornamentation ✔ rounded binary form with variation
R12 SG12	A	Giovanni Battista Pescetti	Presto	2/4 Presto	✔ clearly defined contrasting themes ✔ RH flowing eighth triplets ✔ LH detached quarter- and half-notes
R26 SG17	B	Muzio Clementi	Sonatina in D Major, Op. 37, No. 2 (First Movement)	Alla breve Allegro assai	✔ recapitulation begins with second theme ✔ RH *tremolo* figure ✔ broken-octave and arpeggio patterns ✔ cadential trills
R40 SG21	C	Bedřich Smetana	Chanson, Op. 2, No. 2	2/4 Moderato	✔ lyrical melody ✔ triplet sixteenth accompaniment between hands ✔ requires voicing of melody, interior triplets, and bass line
R52 SG26	D	Béla Bartók	Evening at the Village	4/4 and 3/4 Lento, rubato; Vivo, non rubato	✔ alternating *lento* and *vivo* themes ✔ LH blocked triads ✔ syncopated RH melodies ✔ requires control of *pp* and *ppp*
S38		Edward MacDowell	Study No. 6: Alla Tarantella, Op. 39, No. 2	6/8 Prestissimo	✔ RH plays eighth-note figures ✔ LH plays detached chords ✔ clef changes in both hands ✔ ABA$_1$ form ✔ B section: hands cross, RH has four-octave chromatic scale

Assign first:
Presto . . . .
Sonatina in D Major, Op. 37, No. 2 . . . .
   (First Movement)
Evening at the Village. . . . .

Assign next when ready:
Study No. 6: Alla Tarantella, Op. 39, No. 2
Les chérubins

Chanson, Op. 2, No. 2

Perhaps the single most significant form of the Romantic period is the character piece. Character pieces usually have an ABA or ABA$_1$ structure and an emphasis on mood or atmosphere. The repertoire and studies in Level 8 include a number of character pieces from the 19th and 20th centuries. Encourage students to keep a list of the character pieces they learn in each Study Module. Start the list with *Chanson, Evening at the Village,* and *Study No. 6: Alla Tarantella* from this Study Module.

F. Couperin: *Les chérubins* (R4, SG9)
Exploring the Score
Read the *Student Guide* discussion of keys and accidentals.

- What is the relationship between the keys of the first Part [G minor] and second Part [G major] of this piece? [parallel keys]
- How does Couperin create contrast in the Second Part? [change of key, sixteenth-note activity]

Discuss the performance on the *Celebration Series* recording with your student.

- How does the pianist imitate the clear, crisp sound of the harpsichord?
- Did you notice the small amount of damper pedal at each cadence?
- How does the performer vary the degree of detachment in the LH part?
- Notice the use of dynamic shaping to outline the rise and fall of the melody (for example, in mm. 20-24).

Practice Suggestion
In mm. 36-41 and 58-63, the RH and LH beat notes are a 10th apart. Play only the beat notes (with the correct fingering), then add the RH sixteenth notes.

G.B. Pescetti: *Presto* (R12, SG12)
E. MacDowell: *Study No. 6: Alla Tarantella, Op. 39, No. 2* (S38)
Background Information
Edward MacDowell (1860-1908) was an American composer, pianist, and teacher. Though he is known as the most significant American composer of his time, he pursued most of his musical studies in Europe (1876 to 1888) and his style is firmly rooted in the Romantic tradition. His collection of *Twelve Studies, Op. 39* was written in 1890.

Exploring the Score
Compare *Alla Tarantella* and *Presto*:
- Could both pieces be written either in 2/4 or 6/8? Why (or why not)?
- *Alla Tarantella* is in 6/8 time, and the RH of *Presto* has a triplet figure. How do the LH accompaniments differ? [MacDowell separates notes with rests; Pescetti uses steady quarter notes]
- What is the formal structure of *Tarantella*? [ABA_1] In what key does the B section end? [m. 52, A flat major]
- MacDowell uses chromaticism to return to C minor. Block the chords of mm. 53-61 to hear the chromatic modulation more easily.

Practice Suggestions
The RH of *Presto* contains a mixture of chord shapes, scale patterns, and melodic sequences. Block the broken chords (for example, mm. 9-13) and the scale finger groupings (for example, mm. 14-15 and 19-20).

Divide *Tarantella* into short practice segments.
- Practice the RH bass melody beginning in m. 29.
- Practice the LH chromatic chords, mm. 53-61.
- Block the finger groups of the RH chromatic scale in mm. 61-68. (Students often play the thumb too low in chromatic scales and thus have little facility. Have students play the thumb on the corner of the nail.)

M. Clementi: *Sonatina in D Major, Op. 37, No. 2 (First Movement)* (R26, SG17)
Exploring the Score
Have students read the form outline in the *Student Guide*. In a sonata form, if composers rely heavily on material from one theme in the development, they may omit that theme from the recapitulation. Is this the case here? Has your student played other sonatina movements with the same arrangement of themes? [Friedrich Kuhlau, *Sonatina in C Major, Op. 55, No. 3 (First Movement)* in *Repertoire Album 7*]

Practice Suggestions
Practice the LH melody of mm. 55-58 while blocking the RH chords. You can also block broken octave passages (for example, mm. 62-63). Help your student identify similar sections which are appropriate for blocking.

B. Smetana: *Chanson, Op. 2, No. 2* (R40, SG21)
Practice Suggestions
A sensitive balance of sound between melody and accompaniment is especially important in Romantic character pieces. Read the *Student Guide* discussion of melody, bass line, and balance. Review the concept of directing weight to the outside of the hand in order to project the melody notes.

To help students listen for the balance between melody, bass line, and interior accompaniment, play this piece as a duet. If you have two pianos, have the student play the melody and bass line at one piano (using damper pedal) while you play the sixteenth-note accompaniment at a second piano. Then, reverse the parts.

The return of the A section (m. 25) is marked *con tristezza* (with sadness).

- How is this section different from the opening? [soprano-alto duet]
- How does the performer on the *Celebration Series* recording interpret this indication?

Although the *una corda* pedal is not specifically indicated, consider using it in mm. 31-32 to achieve the softest possible dynamic level.

B. Bartók: *Evening at the Village* (R52, SG26)
Exploring the Score

See the form outline in the *Student Guide*.

- Compare the melody in the three A sections. Does it change? [mm. 1-9 are the same as mm. 21-29; mm. 42-55 differ slightly]
- How does Bartók create variety in the A sections? [varying LH harmony and dynamics]
- Compare the B sections for variation in melodic patterns and accompaniment.

CREATIVE ACTIVITY

Evening at the Village is an excellent example of Bartók's particular attention to details of dynamics, articulation, tempo, and pedaling. This piece can be used effectively in a group lesson or master class. Have one student perform the piece, and assign specific listening activities to the other students. For example, one student might listen for dynamic levels, another for tempo changes, and a third for *staccato* articulations and *legato* phrasing. Directed listening heightens an awareness of details in the score.

STUDY MODULE 2

Page	List	Composer	Title	Meter and Tempo	Musical and Stylistic Concepts
R14 SG13	A	Johann Sebastian Bach	Invention No. 14 in B Flat, BWV 785	C	✔ subject based on thirty-second-note figure and B flat arpeggio ✔ canonic imitation between voices ✔ unison rhythms in middle section
R18 SG15	B	Domenico Cimarosa	Sonata No. 18 in A Major	C Allegro	✔ RH broken-chord figures ✔ sudden dynamic contrasts ✔ LH sixteenth repeated-note figure ✔ two-octave RH double-3rd scale
R42 SG22	C	Edvard Grieg	Puck, Op. 71, No. 3	Alla breve Allegro molto	✔ LH *ostinato* figure ✔ *staccato* touch throughout ✔ RH eighth-note sequences ✔ key of E flat minor ✔ chromaticism in B section: double flats, diminished chords
R60 SG30	D	Andersen Street	Tantrum Tarantelle	6/8 Con fuoco	✔ shifts between major and minor ✔ RH plays two voices at quick tempo
S28		Johann Friedrich Burgmüller	Study No. 2: Morning Bell, Op. 109, No. 9	3/4 Andante sostenuto	✔ lyrical melody ✔ repeating eighth-note figure in alto voice ✔ B section ends with RH cadenza ✔ ABA₁ form ✔ bell effect created by LH crossing
S54		Jenö Takács	Study No. 12: Toccatina, Op. 95, No. 12	2/2 Molto vivace	✔ sixteenth-note study on black and white keys ✔ fast alternating hands in A section ✔ tetrachord patterns in B section

Assign first:
Invention No. 14 in B Flat, BWV 785
Sonata No. 18 in A Major
Study No. 2: Morning Bell, Op. 109, No. 9 . . . . . .
Tantrum Tarantelle . . . .

Assign next when ready:

Puck, Op. 71, No. 3
Study No. 12: Toccatina, Op. 95, No. 12

Study Module 2 includes a number of interesting two-part textures. For example, compare the full sound created by the rapid rhythmic activity in *Invention No. 14 in B Flat* with the more open sound of Cimarosa's *Sonata No. 18 in A Major*. Students can also compare the Bach *Invention* with *Study No. 12*. The two-voice structure of Takács's *Toccatina*, while not imitative, has much rhythmic activity and a quick tempo. Burgmüller's *Study No. 2: Morning Bell* has a duet-like melody over accompanying chords.

Which pieces from Study Module 2 can be added to the list of character pieces?

J.S. Bach: *Invention No. 14 in B Flat, BWV 785* (R14, SG13)

Background Information

Read the *Student Guide* discussions of Baroque keyboard instruments on p. 7 ("Harpsichord Music on a Piano") and p. 13 ("Baroque Keyboard Dynamics"). We usually think of Bach's keyboard music as intended for the harpsichord. However, Bach also played the clavichord. It is possible that the *Inventions* and other teaching pieces were written with the sound of this more intimate instrument in mind. Since the strings of the clavichord are struck (rather than plucked), the performer can shape small *diminuendi* and *crescendi*.

Exploring the Score

Use the following questions to help your student analyze this invention:

- What keys are established in mm. 5 (beat four), 12, and 16 (beat three)?
- When does the full theme first appear in the LH?
- Where does Bach use only the thirty-second-note motive of the theme?
- Find canonic imitation between the hands. [mm. 12-13; 16-18]

Practice Suggestions

In his preface to the *Inventions*, Bach indicated that these pieces were written to develop a *cantabile* touch. As you practice this invention, play with a singing, *legato* tone.

Determine the articulation for the subject. Bracket each presentation and use the same articulation each time. To help students hear two independent voices, play *Invention No. 14* as a teacher-student duet. Practice hands separately, listening to the shape of phrases and the breath between each one.

When practicing hands together:

- Play passages where the hands are alike (for example, mm. 14-16). Lift the hands exactly together.
- Find sections where one hand accompanies the other (for example, mm. 1-4 and 6-11). Review the articulation for each hand.
- Find sections where the hands imitate one another (for example, mm. 12-13 and mm. 16-19). Mark the phrase-end breaths in the score, and exaggerate these lifts.

D. Cimarosa: *Sonata No. 18 in A Major* (R18, SG15)

Exploring the Score

Look for contrast of themes and keys in this sonata. See the form outline in the *Student Guide*. Mark the "*a*" and "*b*" themes in the score and label the main key of each theme. Discuss the differences in mood created by the contrasting figures.

Assume that all the dynamic indications are written by the composer. Did Cimarosa write this piece for the harpsichord or for the piano? Make the dynamic changes clear, but subtle.

Practice Suggestions

The three distinct figures require different technical approaches and separate practice:

- Use forearm rotation for the broken-chord zig-zag patterns (mm. 1-10).
- Play the repeated LH notes (for example, mm. 13-14 and 16-17) with changing fingers and a slight emphasis on the beat.
- Practice the double 3rds (mm. 31-33) in blocked hand positions as suggested in the *Student Guide*.
- Play each 3rd with a slight arm impulse. Keep the fingers close to the keys.

E. Grieg: *Puck, Op. 71, No. 3* (R42, SG22)

Background Information

The increased use of chromaticism, thicker textures, remote keys, and colorful pedaling that characterize Romantic keyboard music were possible, in part, because of 19th-century developments in piano construction. The greater string tension made possible by these innovations gave the piano a more brilliant sound. The range of the keyboard was also extended.

Exploring the Score

Puck is one of the most popular of Grieg's *Lyric Pieces*. Its use of E flat minor and distant keys is exceptional. For example, in mm. 37-44, Grieg presents the main theme in the key of C major. The form outline in the *Student Guide* discusses modulation.

Chromatic movement tends to blur the sense of a tonal center. In the B section, Grieg colors the sound with an abundance of diminished chords whose top notes move chromatically. Notice also the chromatic half-step, B to B flat, in mm. 48-53 and the half-step key relationship between the end of the B section (E major) and the return of the A section (E flat minor).

Practice Suggestions

Block the RH broken triads in mm. 3-14. Notice the relationship between eighth-note figures:

- E flat minor (m. 3) to A flat minor (m. 7): up a 4th
- G flat major (m. 11) to D flat major (m. 12): down a 4th
- C flat major (m.13) to G flat major (m. 14): down a 4th

To learn the chromatic movement of notes in the B section RH chords, tie the repeated notes. Play as *legato* as possible.

A. Street: *Tantrum Tarantelle* (R60, SG30)
Exploring the Score
Read the *Student Guide* description of the form.

- Find measures which repeat. [mm. 26-29 and 30-33]
- Find measures which repeat an octave lower. [mm. 10-11 and 14-15]
- Find measures which repeat an octave higher. [mm. 2-5 and 34-37, RH of mm. 18-20 and 38-40]
- Notice the "circle of 5th" harmonies in mm. 18-21 and 38-40: E-A⁷-D⁷-G⁷-C⁷-F.

Practice Suggestions

The RH plays two voices. This, combined with the quick tempo, makes *Tantrum Tarantelle* a challenging piece. To practice the RH figures (for example, mm. 2-4), play the eighth notes *legato* and release the thumb before each new pitch.

J.F. Burgmüller: *Study No. 2: Morning Bell, Op. 109, No. 9* (S28)
Exploring the Score
Morning Bell and Grieg's *Puck* are both Romantic character pieces. Have students compare them.

- What is their form?
- How do the two composers create contrast in the B section?
- Compare the two transitions from the B section back to the A section (Burgmüller, mm. 21-24; Grieg, mm. 53-61).

Practice Suggestions

1. Play the melody alone, *legato*. Direct arm weight to the outside of the hand.
2. Add the alto accompaniment with your LH. Use the damper pedal.
3. Play the RH melody with the LH as written. Use the damper pedal. Omit the alto voice.
4. Play the entire A section as written. Use the damper pedal.
5. Practice the RH duet in mm. 9-15. Sustain each half note for its full value.

J. Takács: *Study No. 12: Toccatina, Op. 95, No. 12* (S54)
Exploring the Score
Jenö Takács is an Austrian composer who served on the University of Cincinnati music faculty from 1952 to 1970. This dazzling study, one of fifteen pieces from Op. 95, written in 1973, illustrates contemporary compositional techniques.

- The RH and LH have different key signatures. What effect does this create? [a chromatic swirl? polytonality?]
- Notice the precise pedal markings. How does the pedal contribute to the sound?

CREATIVE ACTIVITIES

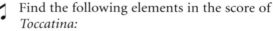 Find the following elements in the score of *Toccatina:*

- LH pentatonic fragments
- tetrachord patterns
- diminished chords

Create a short composition using these elements. You may also want to adopt some of Takács's rhythmic figures.

Like many Classical sonatas, Cimarosa's *Sonata No. 18 in A Major* possesses strong orchestral colors. For example, there is a typical string figure in mm. 13-14. If a digital synthesizer is available, students can sequence different themes with instrumental colors to match sections of the orchestra.

STUDY MODULE 3

Page	List	Composer	Title	Meter and Tempo	Musical and Stylistic Concepts
R7 SG10	A	Georg Philipp Telemann	Fantasia in D Minor, TWV 33:2	Alla breve Presto; 3/2 Adagio	✔ contrapuntal texture in A section ✔ rolled chords in *Adagio* section
R34 SG19	B	Wolfgang Amadeus Mozart	Sonata in C Major, KV 545 (First Movement)	C Allegro	✔ Classical homophonic texture ✔ flowing sixteenth-note scale passages in both hands ✔ recapitulation begins in subdominant
R38 SG20	C	Frédéric Chopin	Mazurka, Op. 24, No. 1	3/4 Lento	✔ large LH chords, some rolled ✔ inner LH chromatic lines ✔ double 3rds in B section ✔ requires careful pedaling
R51 SG25	D	Alexander Scriabin	Prelude, Op. 11, No. 15	C Lento	✔ singing melody ✔ double eighth-note accompaniment ✔ expressive character
S32		Wolfgang Amadeus Mozart	Study No. 4: Allegro in C Major, KV 9a (5a)	C	✔ LH Alberti figure ✔ sonatina-like style
S35		Stephen Heller	Study No. 5: Op. 46, No. 16	6/8 Allegretto	✔ dotted rhythms ✔ ABA form ✔ RH double 3rds over single repeated notes in B section

Assign first:
Fantasia in D Minor, TWV 33:2 . . . .
Study No. 4: Allegro in C Major, KV 9a (5a) . . .
Study No. 5: Op. 46, No. 16 . . . .

Assign next when ready:
Prelude, Op. 11, No. 15
Sonata in C Major, KV 545 (First Movement)
Mazurka, Op. 24, No. 1

Study Module 3 presents a well balanced group of compositions. Each of the four major style periods (Lists A through D) is represented by one of its characteristic forms. There is a contrapuntal *Fantasia*, a well-known Classical sonata movement, a Romantic dance form, and an expressive (almost Romantic-sounding) work from the 20th century. Also, although Heller's *Study No. 5: Op. 46, No. 16* has no title, it can be considered a character piece. Encourage students to give this work a title and add it to their list of character pieces.

G. P. Telemann: *Fantasia in D Minor, TWV 33:2* (R7, SG10)

Exploring the Score

The Baroque fantasia (or *fantaisie*) is usually a continuous piece, built on a single idea. In *Fantasia in D Minor*, Telemann uses the interval of an octave as a unifying idea. In mm. 1-2, both hands travel through an octave. There are different octave patterns in mm. 18-19 (LH), 58-59 (LH then RH), and 91-93 (RH). Look for repetitions of these patterns throughout the piece.

Practice Suggestions

Although this piece is organized around one idea, it is full of contrast. Have students orchestrate the piece as they play, assigning different motives to the full orchestra or to solo instruments.

- The opening motive (mm. 1-3), marked *forte*, might represent the full orchestra. Play with a full tone. Use this same full sound for other statements of this descending broken-chord motive.
- The ascending broken chord in mm. 4-7, marked *piano*, could be imitative of a solo instrument.

Telemann's keyboard *Fantaisies* have a slow B section; in this fantasia it is the contrasting *Adagio*. Explore ways to add interest to the repeated motives and chords by subtle variations in dynamics.

W.A. Mozart: *Sonata in C Major, KV 545 (First Movement)* (R34, SG19)
W.A. Mozart: *Study No. 4: Allegro in C Major, KV 9a (5a)* (S32)

Background Information

Sonata form, the most significant musical form in the Classical era, is based on a balance between unity and contrast. Unity is achieved through the repetition of themes in the exposition and the recapitulation. Contrast is created through contrasting themes and keys.

Exploring the Score

Compare these two pieces by Mozart.

- What textural and thematic similarities can you find?
- How does Mozart create contrast within each piece?

The *Student Guide* outlines the form of the *Sonata in C Major (First Movement)*. Discuss this form with your students, and help them analyze the *Allegro*. Neither piece follows a textbook description of sonata form. The recapitulation of the first movement of *Sonata in C Major* begins in F major (rather than C major). The *Allegro in C Major* has no development section.

Practice Suggestions

- Keep a steady pulse in both pieces. Practice each theme and section with the metronome.
- Avoid playing the opening theme of the sonata too quickly. To find a tempo, play mm. 5-7 at a comfortable speed. Before you begin to play, hear the speed of these measures in your musical ear to establish a tempo.

The quarter-note line in mm. 18-21 and 63-66 is often overlooked.

Play only the quarter notes. Hold them for their full value and listen for an accurate release on the following beat.

F. Chopin: *Mazurka, Op. 24, No. 1* (R38, SG20)

Exploring the Score

The *Celebration Series* recording is a particularly valuable aid for studying this piece. Discuss the meaning of *rubato*, and the performer's interpretation of *rubato* on the recording. Have students conduct the 3/4 meter as they listen to the recording and watch the score.

- Where does Chopin accent the second and third beats?
- On what beat do the dotted rhythms usually appear?
- Using this piece as an example, describe differences between a mazurka and a waltz.

A. Scriabin: *Prelude, Op. 11, No. 15* (R51, SG25)
Practice Suggestions
Scriabin's compositional style was strongly influenced by Chopin. This prelude contains beautiful harmonies requiring an exquisite delicacy of touch, *legato* control of double notes, and careful use of the damper pedal.

Before practicing, have your students listen to the *Celebration Series* recording of this prelude. Draw their attention to tone quality, balance of sound, and dynamic shaping.
- Find the peak of each phrase and plan the dynamic shape of the melody.
- Project the upper voice in the accompaniment, and aim for a *legato* sound. (See the practice suggestions in the *Student Guide*.)

S. Heller: *Study No. 5: Op. 46, No. 16* (S35)
Background Information
Stephen Heller was born in Hungary, but spent most of his life in Paris. His compositional style foreshadowed the music of Saint-Saëns, Chabrier, and Fauré. This piece is from *Thirty Progressive Studies* written in 1844.

Practice Suggestions
This study is challenging because of the quick dotted rhythms and *staccato* articulations. (It is excellent preparation for the Chopin *Mazurka, Op. 24, No. 1* also included in this Study Module.) For a successful performance, keep the *staccato* chords light. Practice mm. 3-4 and use these measures as a sound model for similar passages.
1. Slightly emphasize the first note of the two-note slurs.
2. Keep the *staccato* chords short and light. Lift your wrist as you play.
3. Accent the last chord as marked.

Remember to plan fingering for the LH repeated notes in mm. 10-15.

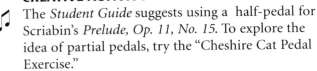

CREATIVE ACTIVITY
The *Student Guide* suggests using a half-pedal for Scriabin's *Prelude, Op. 11, No. 15*. To explore the idea of partial pedals, try the "Cheshire Cat Pedal Exercise."
1. Depress the damper pedal and play a *fortissimo*, *staccato* chord with both hands. (The hands need to be lifted off the keys.)
2. Count the number of times you can half-pedal without completely losing the sound.

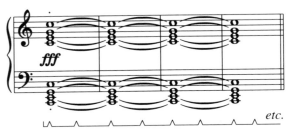

Lift the damper pedal slightly and quickly, without losing the sound.

Try to execute at least six or seven half-pedals before the chord tones completely disappear (much like the Cheshire Cat in *Alice in Wonderland* that gradually disappears except for its smile).

STUDY MODULE 4

Page	List	Composer	Title	Meter and Tempo	Musical and Stylistic Concepts
R16 SG14	A	George Frideric Handel	Allemande in D Minor	C	✔ three-part imitative texture ✔ sequences ✔ subtle melodic shape
R30 SG18	B	Ludwig van Beethoven	Sonata in G Major, Op. 49, No. 2 (First Movement)	Alla breve Allegro ma non troppo	✔ triplet passagework shared between hands ✔ short development begins in minor
R48 SG24	C	John Field	Nocturne in B Flat Major	12/8 Andante cantabile	✔ lyrical melody elaborated in repetition ✔ careful melody-accompaniment balance ✔ wide stretches in LH ✔ repeating chordal texture in B section
R56 SG28	D	Dmitri Shostakovich	Prelude, Op. 34, No. 15	3/4 Allegretto	✔ waltz caricature ✔ LH melody spans more than two octaves ✔ *staccato* touch
S30		Edvard Grieg	Study No. 3: Little Bird, Op. 43, No. 4	6/8 Allegro leggiero	✔ thirty-second note trills depict bird calls ✔ octave shifts ✔ chromatic LH double 3rds
S48		Felix Mendelssohn	Study No. 10: Song without Words, Op. 19, No. 2	3/8 Andante espressivo	✔ flowing eighth-note melody with sixteenth-note accompaniment ✔ two- and three-voice texture
S51		Dmitri Kabalevsky	Study No. 11: Op. 27, No. 24	4/4 Allegro marcato	✔ arpeggio and scale study ✔ unison eighth-note rhythms between hands ✔ homophonic voicing

Assign first:
Allemande in D Minor . . . .
Sonata in G Major, Op. 49, No. 2
  (First Movement)
Study No. 10: Song without Words,
  Op. 19, No. 2 . . . .
Study No. 3: Little Bird, Op. 43, No. 4 . . . .

Assign next when ready:
Study No. 11: Op. 27, No. 24

Nocturne in B Flat Major
Prelude, Op. 34, No. 15

Study Module 4 provides examples of the different ways composers use melody and accompaniment. Mendelssohn creates duet textures with his thematic material. In contrast, Field places a beautiful melody over a moving accompaniment. In Shostakovich's waltz-like *Prelude*, the LH plays the melody and the RH plays a contemporary accompaniment. In Handel's *Allemande in D Minor*, the melody emerges from a two-part texture. Mendelssohn's *Song without Words* has a more straightforward melodic shape. Both Handel and Mendelssohn embed melodies in flowing sixteenth- and eighth-note accompaniment patterns. Beethoven, like Field, uses RH melodies over LH accompaniment figures.

G.F. Handel: *Allemande in D Minor*
(R16, SG14)
Exploring the Score
Read the description of an *allemande* in the *Student Guide* (p. 8). This piece has both two- and three-voice passages. (The three-part texture is excellent preparation for the Bach *sinfonias* in Level 9.) In the three-part measures, the RH plays two voices.

- Compare the figures in the two- and three-part passages. Discuss the differences you find in mm. 1, 3, 5, 6, and 7.
- The descending stepwise motion in mm. 17-18 leads to the tonic in m. 19. Does the same thing happen in mm. 6-8?

Have your student explore Handel's harmonic movement by looking for cadences and naming the relationship of the new keys to the tonic key of D minor. For example, in m. 8, there is a cadence in A major, the dominant key. In m. 14, the ornament announces the momentary F major cadence on the third beat.

Practice Suggestions
- To practice the RH part, divide the two voices between the hands. Hold the longer notes for their full value.
- The melodic shape is especially interesting. Use dynamic shaping and contrasting dynamics to project this melody from within the string of sixteenth notes.

L. van Beethoven: *Sonata in G Major, Op. 49, No. 2 (First Movement)* (R30, SG18)
Exploring the Score
Beethoven uses groups of three notes as a unifying element. Have students look for three-note groups:
- triplet figures (both hands)
- RH eighth-note upbeat (mm. 20, 24, etc.)
- RH quarter-note groups (mm. 2, 4, etc.)
- LH quarter-note groups (mm. 100-101, etc.)

Read the form outline in the *Student Guide*. Notice that the development section is quite short in relation to the exposition and recapitulation. Compare this relationship to the first movement of Mozart's *Sonata in C Major, KV 545* (R34), discussed in Study Module 3.

Practice Suggestions
Divide the movement into short sections. Have students practice details of phrasing, articulation, and ornaments during the lesson. Once they have read through the entire movement, have them practice the piece backwards, section by section. This will ensure that the end of the piece is as well prepared and secure as the beginning.

The two Opus 49 piano sonatas are fairly early works, dating from the mid-1790s. There are relatively few dynamic indications. The movement requires expressive dynamic shaping and an even touch. Have students play passages on the keyboard cover so they can hear, and correct, any unevenness in their touch. Students can also practice the scale passages in different tempos, in dotted rhythms, and with a *staccato* touch.

J. Field: *Nocturne in B Flat Major* (R48, SG24)
Background Information
The biography of John Field in the *Student Guide* includes a brief description of a nocturne. Chopin is the most well-known composer of nocturnes, but other composers, for example, Samuel Barber, have adapted the nocturne style to contemporary writing. If possible, play other nocturnes for your student.

Exploring the Score
Read the form outline in the *Student Guide*.
- Compare mm. 1-4 with 23-26. How does Field vary the RH melody during the restatement of the original theme?
- Can you find other measures where Field elaborates the melody? [compare mm. 6 and 28]
- Does Field ever vary the LH accompaniment? [compare mm. 6-7 and 28-29]

In mm. 21-22, there is a *diminuendo* followed by two *sforzandi*. How does the performer on the *Celebration Series* recording interpret the *sforzandi*?

Practice Suggestions
On a piano, the tone fades after the hammer strikes the string. When you play melodies with long note values, it is important to match the sound of each note with the fading tone of the previous note. Try the following listening exercise with your students.
- Play several long notes, beginning at a *forte* level, without the damper pedal.
- Match the dynamic level of each new note to the fading sound of the previous note.

The following example shows dynamic levels for the RH notes in mm. 1-2:

- Practice each RH phrase without pedal. Listen for a *legato* sound.
- Add the LH and the damper pedal. In each phrase, identify the peak and the softest note.

D. Shostakovich: *Prelude, Op. 34, No. 15*
(R56, SG28)

Exploring the Score

Have students read the *Student Guide* discussion of this piece, then make a list of the ways in which this waltz-like prelude is unlike other waltzes they have studied.

- Which hand plays the accompaniment? Which LH measures look most like a traditional waltz?
- Is the melody smoothly flowing and predictable?

Prelude is a good-natured caricature of a traditional 19th-century waltz. Here are some of the elements Shostakovich uses to create humor:

- LH *staccato* melody
- use of scales in melody
- unpredictable changes of direction in melody
- RH delicate *staccato* accompaniment
- RH accented interruption of LH melody (mm. 28-33)

Discuss these elements with your students and ask them to add to the list.

Practice Suggestions

Encourage students to emphasize the humor and fun in this piece. In mm. 52-59, the longer note values create a written-in *ritardando*. Maintain a steady tempo as suggested in the *Student Guide*.

E. Grieg: *Study No. 3: Little Bird, Op. 43, No. 4* (S30)

Exploring the Score

- What elements does Grieg use to paint a musical picture of a bird?
- How do the measures played in the bass clef fit into that picture?

Listen to the *Celebration Series* recording.

- How does the pedal affect the tone? Did the performer use the *una corda* pedal?
- In which measures would you find it inappropriate to use the damper pedal?

F. Mendelssohn: *Study No. 10: Song without Words, Op. 19, No. 2* (S48)

Background Information

Between 1829 and 1845, Mendelssohn composed eight books of short character pieces which he called *Songs without Words*. Each piece is based on a single technical figure, texture, and mood. The "song" (the main melody) is always clear, whether it is in the top voice or an inner voice.

Exploring the Score

Examine the melody of this piece.

- Is it always in the top voice?
- Can you hear the duet between the melody and the bass line in the opening measures?
- Is there a duet with another voice?
- Notice the wide range between the duet voices in mm. 77-89.

Practice Suggestions

Practice the duet voices separately.

- Do the voices move in similar or contrary motion?
- Which voice should be louder?

Practice in small sections, as written. Keep the harmonic parts softer than the duet voices.

The music is marked *legato e con pedale*. To achieve a clear sound, change the pedal with each changing melodic note. Use the rhythm of the RH melody as a guide for pedal changes.

D. Kabalevsky: *Study No. 11: Op. 27, No. 24* (S51)

Exploring the Score

Locate the following combinations:

- RH and LH in unison
- RH broken-octave chords, LH scale fragments
- LH broken-octave chords, RH scale fragments
- RH descending broken triads, LH stepwise descent

Practice Suggestion

Practice each combination hands separately, then practice hands together. Pay close attention to fingering.

CREATIVE ACTIVITY

Compare Kabalevsky's *Study No. 11: Op. 27, No. 24* to the Bach *Invention No. 14 in B Flat* in Study Module 2. How does each composer use broken-octave chords? Improvise with a broken-octave figure, then create a short composition, imitating the style of Bach or Kabalevsky.

STUDY MODULE 5

Page	List	Composer	Title	Meter and Tempo	Musical and Stylistic Concepts
R10 SG11	A	Johann Sebastian Bach	Invention No. 13 in A Minor, BWV 784	C	✔ imitative texture ✔ detached eighths and phrased sixteenths ✔ requires careful fingering
R54 SG27	D	Aram Khachaturian	Ivan and Natasha	3/4 and C Lento; Poco più mosso	✔ expressive, chromatic ✔ RH double notes in B section ✔ requires careful pedaling
R58 SG29	D	Dmitri Kabalevsky	Prelude, Op. 38, No. 8	4/4 Andante non troppo. Semplice e cantando	✔ jumping LH with challenging RH texture ✔ highly chromatic ✔ requires careful voicing of bass line ✔ LH inner chords and melody
S42		George Frideric Handel	Study No. 7: Capriccio, HWV 483	C Deciso	✔ two-voice imitative texture ✔ sixteenths against eighth notes
S44		Felix Mendelssohn	Study No. 8: Song without Words, Op. 102, No. 2	2/4 (4/8) Adagio	✔ thick chordal texture ✔ flowing sixteenth notes ✔ requires careful voicing and pedaling

Assign first:
Study No. 7: Capriccio, HWV 483 . . . .
Ivan and Natasha. . . . .
Study No. 8: Song without Words, Op. 102, No. 2

Assign next when ready:
Invention No. 13 in A Minor, BWV 784
Prelude, Op. 38, No. 8

Study Module 5 presents students with several technical challenges. The imitative textures in Bach's *Invention* and in Handel's *Capriccio* require meticulous practice and careful attention to fingering and phrasing. The increased chromaticism, accidentals, and thicker textures of the works by Mendelssohn, Khachaturian, and Kabalevsky demand careful reading during the learning stages.

J.S. Bach: *Invention No. 13 in A Minor, BWV 784* (R10, SG11)

Exploring the Score
For more information on Bach's *Two-Part Inventions*, see the Background Information given for *Invention No. 14* in Study Module 2.

Invention No. 13 is a lively contrapuntal piece using imitation, sequences, broken chords, and syncopation.
- Bracket the subject (mm. 1-2).
- Play each hand separately, then bracket each presentation of the subject. Notice that the subject always begins on the second sixteenth of a beat.
- The tied eighth notes in mm. 3-6 and 11-13 create a syncopated rhythm. Stress these notes slightly.

Read the *Student Guide* discussion of modulating

sequences. Label the keys at the cadence points (mm. 6, 13, 18) to discover Bach's harmonic plan. Block the harmonies, as suggested in the *Student Guide*, to clarify the melodic skeleton for your students.

Practice Suggestions
Discuss the *Student Guide* comments on articulation with your student. Have your student determine an articulation pattern for the subject and write it in the score.
- Play the eighth notes detached.
- Practice each hand separately in small sections (for example, mm. 1-2 and 3-6).
- The RH sequence in mm. 14-17 outlines diminished 7th chords. Experiment using the fingering in m. 14 for mm. 15-17.

A. Khachaturian: *Ivan and Natasha* (R54, SG27)
Exploring the Score
Read the discussions on form and harmony in the *Student Guide*. Examine the shape and rhythm of the RH part, mm. 1-4, and play those measures.
- What is the mood of the A section? [sorrowful longing] How does the LH contribute to that mood? [two-note sighing slurs]
- Look at the score. What do you see happening in the B section? [faster tempo, more complex rhythm, rising pitches and *crescendo* followed by soft dynamics and descending pitches]

Listen for these details and the contrast between the A and B sections on the *Celebration Series* recording.

Khachaturian uses unusual harmonies in this piece.
- How does the A₁ section differ from the A section?
- In the B section, where does the opening theme appear in its original key? [mm. 30-33]

Practice Suggestions
The intense emotion of this piece is created by expressive articulation, dynamics, phrasing, and pedaling. Encourage students to exaggerate those markings during practice. Work on selected measures hands separately.
- Let the opening two-note slurs call out *"I-van."* Shape the sound.
- Practice the LH of mm. 1-8. Listen for the sighing two-note slurs and the light, sobbing *staccato* notes in m. 4.
- In the B section, play the accents with special intensity and urgency.
- Where does the melody outline *"Na-ta-sha"*?

D. Kabalevsky: *Prelude, Op. 38, No. 8* (R58, SG29)
Exploring the Score
With score in hand and these questions in mind, listen to the *Celebration Series* recording:
- Does the style of the bass change?
- The RH has two themes – one consisting of eighth notes and quarter notes, the other of sixteenth notes. Spot these two themes in the score as you listen, and assign a character to each one.
- Where does Kabalevsky combine the two themes?
- Where is the moment of greatest intensity?

See the *Student Guide* for a detailed analysis of the form.

Practice Suggestions
- Divide two-voice textures between the hands (mm. 18-19).
- Observe *legato* fingerings in RH double notes (mm. 8-9, 20-21).
- Practice the LH alone with the damper pedal before combining the hands.

G.F. Handel: *Study No. 7: Capriccio, HWV 483* (S42)
Exploring the Score
It is interesting to compare this two-voice contrapuntal piece with Bach's *Invention in A Minor*.
- How long is each subject? Examine presentations of the subject throughout the two pieces. In Handel's *Capriccio*, the subject presentations are consistently three measures long. The figure in m. 4 is not always present. How often does Handel present the subject?
- Do Bach and Handel use similar sixteenth-note figures? Compare m. 18 of *Capriccio* with m. 17 of the A minor *Invention*.

Practice Suggestion
Having established the similarities between Bach's *Invention in A Minor* and Handel's *Capriccio*, help your student decide on practice strategies for learning these two Baroque pieces.

F. Mendelssohn: *Study No. 8: Song without Words, Op. 102, No. 2* (S44)
Exploring the Score
This piece falls into four-measure phrases, each beginning on the half measure.
- How many times is the opening melody (mm. 1-4) repeated? [three times: mm. 4-8, 12-16, 20-24] Mark this theme with an *"x"* in the score.
- Mark the second theme, mm. 8-12, with a *"y."* Where does this theme reappear? [mm. 16-20] Find this theme in G minor. [m. 24-28] Mark each occurrence of *"y"* in the score.

Practice Suggestions
This piece has a challenging texture. The main melody is always the top voice, but other parts have melodic interest, for example:
- tenor in m. 1
- bass in mm. 1-3
- the bass and alto duet in mm. 8-10

- Play the *"x"* melody hands together, in unison. Shape it with a singing *legato* and expressive dynamics. Play the *"y"* melody the same way.
- Practice the bass and soprano lines together, and listen to the duet.
- Practice four-measure units hands separately. Project the most interesting melodic ideas in each hand.
- Practice hands together. Bring out the top melody and listen for an expressive dynamic shape.

CREATIVE ACTIVITY

See the list of modes in the Glossary of the *Student Guide*. Kabalevsky's *Prelude* is based on the F sharp Aeolian mode (natural minor scale). To play modes easily, think of the major scale degree on which the mode begins. (For example, D Dorian begins on the supertonic of the C major scale. The Dorian mode beginning on the note A would have a G major key signature.)

Explore modal scales by finding and playing them. Compose a short melody using notes of the Dorian mode built on A.

STUDY MODULE 6

Page	List	Composer	Title	Meter and Tempo	Musical and Stylistic Concepts
R21 SG16	B	Friedrich Kuhlau	Sonatina in A Major, Op. 59, No. 1 (Third Movement)	2/4 Allegro scherzando	✔ requires facile scale and passagework technique ✔ RH double 3rds and wide leaps
R45 SG23	C	Robert Schumann	The Stranger, Op. 68, No. 29	2/4 Stark und kräftig	✔ LH octaves prominent ✔ large RH chords ✔ dotted rhythms ✔ sudden dynamic contrasts – *sforzando* and *fortissimo* dominate
R62 SG31	D	Harry Freedman	Rent-A-Rag	Alla breve Moderate, not fast	✔ challenging stride bass ✔ RH syncopations ✔ thick texture ✔ many accidentals ✔ LH chromatic figure in B section
S25		Robert Fleming	Study No. 1: Toccatina	4/4 Briskly and rhythmically	✔ variety of touches and rhythms ✔ meter changes ✔ LH *ostinato* with large leaps ✔ crossed hands ✔ harmonic extensions ✔ hints of jazz elements
S46		Johann Friedrich Burgmüller	Study No. 9: The Gypsies, Op. 109, No. 4	C Allegro non troppo	✔ wrist *staccato* for moving quarter-note chords ✔ occasional RH scale lines

---

Assign first:
Sonatina in A Major, Op. 59, No. 1
   (Third Movement)
Study No. 9: The Gypsies, Op. 109, No. 4 . . . .
Rent-A-Rag . . . .

Assign next when ready:

The Stranger, Op. 68, No. 29
Study No. 1: Toccatina

The pieces in Study Module 6 challenge students with a variety of technical demands and thicker textures. The compositions by Kuhlau, Fleming, and Freedman all require considerable finger dexterity and the latter two make use of jazz idioms – ragtime in *Rent-A-Rag* and extended harmonies in *Toccatina*. The compositions by Schumann and Burgmüller allow for a focus on playing octaves and thicker chordal textures.

**F. Kuhlau: *Sonatina in A Major, Op. 59,
No. 1 (Third Movement)*** (R21, SG16)
Exploring the Score

This sonatina movement is marked *Allegro
scherzando*. The joke *(scherzando)* may involve the
contrast between the deceptively simple opening
(delicate *staccato* chords) and the technical outburst
of fast scales, intense sixteenth-note patterns, and
two-octave leaps. A performer who can master these
contrasts can convey delightful surprises to the
listener. Find the following elements:

– loudest dynamic marking
– longest time without dynamic change
– scales played hands together
– longest RH scale line
– sixteenth-note figures other than scales
– widest RH leap
– RH double 3rds
– all LH accompaniment patterns

This movement opens with three chords. Find other
places where Kuhlau groups events in threes. [final
measures, accompaniment of the A minor theme in
mm. 72-75] Notice the variation of the opening idea
in mm. 34-37.

Practice Suggestions

• Isolate the scale passages for metronome practice.
• Devise an exercise for both hands using the broken
  octave chords of mm. 41-43. Try the exercise with
  other major chords.
• Practice the zig-zag pattern of mm. 72-74 in other
  keys. Keep the **4-2-3-1** fingering.
• Practice the turn-around figures of mm. 14-15 and
  76-77 in dotted rhythms.
• Isolate the RH double 3rds (for example, mm. 30-
  31) for spot practice.
• Use a rocking wrist motion to play the LH broken-
  chord accompaniment of mm. 60-70 and
  163-173. Practice these measures one octave lower
  for comfort of position.
• Devise a *staccato* exercise for the wide leaps in the
  RH, mm. 83-84 and 99-101. Here is one suggestion:

R. Schumann: *The Stranger, Op. 68, No. 29*
(R45, SG23)
Exploring the Score

This composition is another example of a Romantic
character piece with an ABA form. Read the
description in the *Student Guide*.

• What is the character of the stranger in the
  A section – strong or weak, happy or sad,
  mysterious or playful? What musical elements does
  Schumann use to paint this portrait? [dynamics,
  thick chords, accents, dotted rhythms]
• Does the stranger's character change in the
  B section? What different musical elements does
  Schumann use here?

Practice Suggestions

See the *Student Guide* discussion of balance and
pedaling. Use dynamics, phrasing, balance, and pedaling
to bring your interpretation of this stranger to life.

Both *The Stranger* and Burgmüller's *The Gypsies* have
extended hand positions, octaves, and chords. The
following practice techniques will help students play
these figures accurately.

• Think of the thumb as the "eye of the hand" when
  playing octaves.
• Isolate mm. 6-12 for special practice. Play only
  the thumb notes.
• "Outside-inside" practice will help students to
  master chordal textures. Play mm. 94-95 as follows:

H. Freedman: *Rent-A-Rag* (R62, SG31)
Practice Suggestions

This delightful rag has three elements: a stride bass, a
syncopated melody, and a chromatic bass accompaniment. Careful practice of each element will result in a
rewarding musical experience. Use the *Celebration
Series* recording as a sound model, and read the
discussion of ragtime style in the *Student Guide*.

Practice the stride bass separately. Naming the harmonies
will help students to play the chords more accurately.

• Determine the fingering. Whenever possible, use the
  LH fifth finger only on the low bass notes. Avoid
  using this finger for the chords.
• Use a light, relaxed touch.

Rhythm is a driving force in this melody. Have students
tap the melody to experience the delightful lilt of the
syncopation.

• Tap with both hands.
• Play the RH while tapping the LH.
• Play the LH while tapping the RH.

R. Fleming: *Study No. 1: Toccatina* (S25)
Exploring the Score
Robert Fleming, a Canadian composer, was perhaps best known for his songs. He incorporated elements of jazz in his writing. The extended (quasi-jazz) chords in *Toccatina* provide colorful harmonies. These complex chords are built by adding 7ths, 9ths, 11ths, and 13ths to the basic triad. Notice how Fleming uses harmonic extensions:

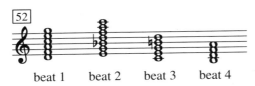

beat 1   beat 2   beat 3   beat 4

- *Toccatina* is a study in hand crossing. Find measures in which the hands do not cross.
- Find the measures in which the meter changes. How many measures are in 3/4?

Practice Suggestions
- Devise exercises for playing with crossed hands. (Since the LH of *Toccatina* is primarily *staccato*, include contrasting touches.)
- Practice in four- or eight-measure sections hands separately and then hands together.
- In mm. 5-20, listen for the RH rhythms, articulation, dynamics, and phrasing. Bring out the contrast between this variety and the steady LH *staccato* eighth notes.

J. F. Burgmüller: *Study No. 9: The Gypsies, Op. 109, No. 4* (S46)
Exploring the Score
Listen to the *Celebration Series* recording and follow the music in the score.
- Identify the sections and name the prominent keys in each one.
- How does the key change alter the character of the music in mm. 22-34?
- Why is this piece titled *The Gypsies?* What details make up Burgmüller's musical picture?

Practice Suggestions
- Bring out the melody. Project the top notes.
- In each measure, identify the loudest beat. (Notice the shifting emphasis between the second and third beats.)

CREATIVE ACTIVITIES
- 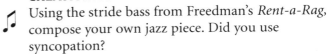 Using the stride bass from Freedman's *Rent-a-Rag*, compose your own jazz piece. Did you use syncopation?

- Compose a toccatina using technical and musical elements from this Module, including:
  - wide leaps (Kuhlau)
  - extended hand positions, octaves, chords (Burgmüller, Schumann)
  - complex harmonies (Fleming)
  - chromatic bass and syncopated melodies (Freedman)

Choose any one element or a combination of elements for your *Toccatina.*

LEVEL 8 SUMMARY
- Look through the Level 8 studies and place each study in a category, such as Finger Dexterity and Facility; Balance of Melody-Accompaniment; Ornamentation; Chord Playing; etc.
- Review the keys used in *Repertoire Album 8.* How many pieces are in minor keys? What is the most unusual key of the entire album?
- "Music either sings or it dances." Can you support that statement as you review *Repertoire Album 8?* Which pieces or sections have a lyrical nature? Which are rhythmic and dance-like?

Level 9

The Publications

Level 9 of the *Celebration Series* includes the following publications:

> *Piano Repertoire Album 9*
> *Piano Studies Album 9 & 10* (level 9 only)
> Recording of *Repertoire & Studies 9*

The Repertoire

The *Piano Repertoire Album 9* is divided into four lists:

- List A includes a selection of pieces composed during the Baroque period (*ca* 1600 to *ca* 1750).
- List B includes a selection of works composed during the late Baroque period and the Classical period (*ca* 1750 to *ca* 1820).
- List C includes a selection of pieces composed during the Romantic era (*ca* 1820 to *ca* 1910).
- List D includes works composed during the late 19th century and the 20th century.

Musical Development

In Level 9, the student's musical horizons are expanded. This Level includes two three-part inventions *(sinfonias)* by J.S. Bach and three-movement sonatas by Haydn and Mozart. Romantic repertoire includes two works by Chopin (a waltz and a prelude) and character pieces by Schumann and Grieg. The 20th century is represented by works of Béla Bartók, Dmitri Kabalevsky, François Morel, Selim Palmgren, Maurice Ravel, R. Murray Schafer, and Leo Weiner.

Even a casual perusal of the Level 9 *Repertoire Album* and *Studies Album* indicates that this is difficult music which represents considerable accomplishment. There are new challenges for the hand (facility and control), the ear (hearing three simultaneous parts, delicate balances, subtle articulations), and the mind (harmonies and form).

Preparation of the Student

The preceding Levels of the *Celebration Series* provide a gradual, thorough preparation for Level 9. Technical preparation has included:

- independence of hands
- balance of melody and accompaniment
- voicing within a hand
- scale and arpeggio figures
- figures with irregular changes of direction

- variety of chord shapes and blocked intervals, leaps, and accompaniment figures
- execution of ornaments

From the earliest Levels of the *Celebration Series*, students have been exposed to repertoire from four centuries, selected and edited to support a growing awareness of style. They have experienced:

- thin textures and independent lines of the Baroque era
- the homophonic style and balanced, shaped phrases of the Classical era
- the wider palette of Romantic harmony and expression
- challenges of stylistic variety, dissonance, and intense expression in 20th-century literature

Organization of Level 9

The preceding Levels have been divided into Study Modules of increasing difficulty, integrating repertoire from the four major style periods with pieces from the *Studies Albums*.

The discussion of Level 9 is not divided into Study Modules, but rather follows the four Lists of the *Repertoire Album* (A, B, C, and D). The pieces are discussed in the order in which they appear in the *Repertoire Album*.

For each list, there is a suggested order of difficulty, a brief general discussion of the stylistic characteristics, and individual discussions of the pieces under the following headings:

- *Background Information:* general stylistic or biographical information
- *Exploring the Score:* suggested material for student-teacher discussions
- *Teaching Suggestions:* addressed to the teacher
- *Practice Suggestions:* addressed to the student

Teachers can determine the order of repertoire assigned, based on the individual student's needs and study program. Teachers are encouraged to formulate units of study, integrating pieces of contrasting style periods from the *Repertoire Album* and the *Studies Album*.

The *Celebration Series* does not include a *Student Guide* for Level 9. It is our hope that the following discussions will facilitate your teaching of this repertoire, provide material for fruitful discussions between you and your students, and increase their musical enjoyment and awareness.

The Studies

The studies are discussed separately at the end of this section. The pieces in the *Studies Album* are similar in purpose to the Chopin *Études*. Although each piece has a specific technical focus, these studies have noteworthy musical value and can be considered as repertoire. The order of the studies in the book is a reasonable order of difficulty. There is a consistent increase of technical demands.

The Recordings

The *Celebration Series* recording of all pieces in this Level is a valuable teaching resource. This professional recording provides a sound model, a pedagogical element which words cannot communicate. Listening to the recording with the student can stimulate discussion on topics such as articulation, balance and dynamics, expressive timing *(rubato)*, pedaling, accentuation, and expressive nuances. You may wish to make listening a regular part of the student's assignment.

The following chart lists the repertoire and studies in Level 9 according to the order of the *Repertoire* and *Studies Albums*. Page numbers for works in the *Piano Repertoire Album 9* and the *Piano Studies Album 9* are found in the first column.

Page	Composer	Title
Piano Repertoire Album 9		
List A – Baroque		
R4	Johann Sebastian Bach	Sinfonia No. 15 in B Minor, BWV 801
R6	Johann Sebastian Bach	Sinfonia No. 3 in D Major, BWV 789
R8	Johann Sebastian Bach	Adagissimo
R10	Louis-Claude Daquin	Le coucou (Rondeau)
R13	Johann Sebastian Bach	Prelude in C Minor, BWV 847
R16	Johann Sebastian Bach	Fugue in C Minor, BWV 847
R18	Johann Sebastian Bach	Prelude in E Minor, BWV 855
R22	Johann Sebastian Bach	Fugue in E Minor, BWV 855
List B – Late Baroque and Classical		
R25	Domenico Scarlatti	Sonata in D Minor, L 413/K 9
R28	Domenico Scarlatti	Sonata in C Major, L 104/K 159
R31	Franz Joseph Haydn	Sonata in D Major, Hob. XVI:37 (First Movement)
R36	Franz Joseph Haydn	Sonata in D Major, Hob. XVI:37 (Second and Third Movements)
R40	Wolfgang Amadeus Mozart	Sonata in G Major, KV 283 (189h) (First Movement)
R45	Wolfgang Amadeus Mozart	Sonata in G Major, KV 283 (189h) (Second and Third Movements)
R55	Ludwig van Beethoven	Six Easy Variations in G Major, WoO 77
List C – Romantic		
R60	Edvard Grieg	Butterfly, Op. 43, No. 1
R64	Felix Mendelssohn	Song without Words, Op. 38, No. 6 (Duetto)
R69	Frédéric Chopin	Prelude in D Flat, Op. 28, No. 15
R72	Frédéric Chopin	Waltz in C Sharp Minor, Op. 64, No. 2
R78	Franz Liszt	En rêve
R80	Robert Schumann	Romance in F Sharp, Op. 28, No. 2
R82	Robert Schumann	Whims, Op. 12, No. 4
List D – Late Romantic and Contemporary		
R87	Selim Palmgren	May Night, Op. 27, No. 4
R90	Maurice Ravel	Menuet
R94	Claude Debussy	Golliwogg's Cake-walk
R99	Alexander Scriabin	Prelude in G Flat, Op. 11, No. 13
R100	Dmitri Kabalevsky	Prelude No. 1, Op. 38, No. 1

Page	Composer	Title
R102	Dmitri Kabalevsky	Prelude No. 2, Op. 38, No. 2
R104	Béla Bartók	Bear Dance
R108	François Morel	Ronde enfantine
R111	Leo Weiner	Fox Dance
R114	R. Murray Schafer	Polytonality

Piano Studies Album 9

S4	Felix Mendelssohn	Study No. 1: Song without Words, Op. 102, No. 3
S6	Moritz Moszkowski	Study No. 2: Op. 91, No. 6
S8	George Frideric Handel	Study No. 3: Lesson, HWV 496
S11	Felix Mendelssohn	Study No. 4: Song without Words, Op. 85, No. 1
S14	Edward MacDowell	Study No. 5: Dance of the Gnomes, Op. 39, No. 6
S18	George Frideric Handel	Study No. 6: Prelude, HWV 428
S20	Stephen Heller	Study No. 7: Op. 47, No. 24
S22	Niels Gade	Study No. 8: Scherzo, Op. 19, No. 2
S24	Edward MacDowell	Study No. 9: Shadow Dance, Op. 39, No. 8
S28	Béla Bartók	Study No. 10: Bagatelle, Op. 6, No. 2
S30	Moritz Moszkowski	Study No. 11: Op. 91, No. 5
S32	Alexander Scriabin	Study No. 12: Prelude for the Left Hand, Op. 9, No. 1
S34	Edward MacDowell	Study No. 13: Arabesque, Op. 39, No. 4
S38	Moritz Moszkowski	Study No. 14: Op. 91, No. 20

LIST A – BAROQUE

Suggested Order of Difficulty

Page	Composer	Title
R10	Louis-Claude Daquin	Le coucou (Rondeau)
R8	Johann Sebastian Bach	Adagissimo
R4	Johann Sebastian Bach	Sinfonia No. 15 in B Minor, BWV 801
R6	Johann Sebastian Bach	Sinfonia No. 3 in D Major, BWV 789
R13	Johann Sebastian Bach	Prelude and Fugue in C Minor, BWV 847
R18	Johann Sebastian Bach	Prelude and Fugue in E Minor, BWV 855

The preceding list assumes that each prelude and fugue in a particular key will be taught as a unit. If the prelude and the fugue are taught separately, then the suggested order of difficulty is:

Page	Composer	Title
R10	Louis-Claude Daquin	Le coucou (Rondeau)
R13	Johann Sebastian Bach	Prelude in C Minor BWV 847
R8	Johann Sebastian Bach	Adagissimo
R4	Johann Sebastian Bach	Sinfonia No. 15 in B Minor, BWV 801
R22	Johann Sebastian Bach	Fugue in E Minor, BWV 855
R16	Johann Sebastian Bach	Fugue in C Minor, BWV 847
R18	Johann Sebastian Bach	Prelude in E Minor, BWV 855
R6	Johann Sebastian Bach	Sinfonia No. 3 in D Major, BWV 789

In Baroque music, clarity and precision are of the greatest importance. (Use the pedal rarely and with great care.) The pieces by Bach and Daquin were written for the harpsichord. They require special attention to touch and articulation. The artists who performed these pieces for the *Celebration Series* recording make effective use of detached and *staccato* articulations. A contrasting mixture of *legato* and detached touches is highly desirable. In general, use detached articulation:
— to articulate skips and leaps
— to imitate bass instruments (for example, a cello)
— before emphasized notes such as syncopations, downbeats, and *appoggiaturas*
— for eighth notes when contrasted against sixteenth notes
— to highlight energetic and joyful moods

The following terminology is important for discussing fugues:
— *subject:* the theme on which the fugue is based
— *countersubject:* accompaniment material which always appears with the subject
— *answer:* the second or fourth statement of the subject, in the dominant key
— *real answer:* a literal transposition of the subject in the dominant key
— *tonal answer:* a transposition with slight adjustments of intervals to accommodate the new key
— *episode:* a group of measures based on a fragment of the subject
— *stretto:* statements of the subject in two or more voices, each entry overlapping the previous one

J.S. Bach (1685-1750): *Sinfonia No. 15 in B Minor, BWV 801* (R4)

Background Information

Bach wrote the *sinfonias* (sometimes called three-part inventions) for the instruction of his son, Wilhelm Friedemann. The *Wilhelm Friedemann Bach Notebook* includes early versions of some of the three-part *sinfonias*. They were first published in the famous *Clavierbüchlein* which also includes the two-part inventions and eleven of the preludes from Book I of *The Well-Tempered Clavier*.

Exploring the Score

The subject is made up of two contrasting ideas. Label them "*x*" and "*y*." Label other material in mm. 1-3 (for example, the stepwise motion in the LH, mm. 1-2) "*z*." Plan contrasting articulations for the sixteenth-note figures in "*x*" and "*z*." Here is a suggestion:

In the score, bracket each full statement of the subject (look for "*x*" and "*y*" in the same voice) and identify the key of each statement. What form does the labeling of these motives reveal?

Teaching Suggestions

In the lesson, play this piece as a student-teacher duet, each person playing one hand. There will be a keyboard traffic jam in m. 28. (Does this suggest that Bach was thinking of a two-manual instrument, such as a harpsichord or an organ?) To avoid the traffic jam, reverse hands on the first group of thirty-second notes.

Practice Suggestions

Isolate the "*x*," "*y*," and "*z*" ideas for special practice.
* Use a consistent articulation for "*x*."
* Pay special attention to the fingering of "*y*."
* Play "*z*" with a *legato* touch. Make a slight break before each downbeat.

J.S. Bach (1685-1750): *Sinfonia No. 3 in D Major, BWV 789* (R6)

Exploring the Score

The joyful subject of this *sinfonia* is characterized by a motive presented in sequence and a stepwise pattern (F sharp-E-D-C sharp-D):

Identify the subject presentations throughout the piece:
* How many different ways does Bach accompany the subject?
* Is there a sequence in the accompaniment figure?

Teaching Suggestions

Help students determine the articulation for the subject and accompaniment. Consistency of articulation is important to the Baroque style. If students follow the articulation pattern suggested in the footnote below the music, they should use this articulation consistently. Hold the quarter notes for their full value.

To help your students develop the ability to hear contrapuntal lines, have them play each voice separately, with special emphasis on articulation and the lengths of notes. Provide your student with a recorded performance of this *sinfonia* at a slow tempo. (Use a tape recorder or a digital keyboard.) The student can play along with the recording, one voice at a time, while listening to the entire texture.

J.S. Bach (1685-1750): *Adagissimo* (R8)

Background Information

Bach's only programmatic keyboard work – *Capriccio on the Departure of a Most Beloved Brother* – is an early work consisting of six short movements. Bach wrote only the melody and figured bass line for *Adagissimo*. In this edition, the harmonies have been tastefully realized by an editor.

Bach wrote this piece as a lament, probably in 1706, on the occasion of the departure of his brother to take up a position in Sweden.

Exploring the Score

This piece is a series of variations over a ground bass, known as a chaconne:

Look for these bass notes in each succeeding four-measure group.

How does the RH melody show consistency? Look at the melodic shape (ascending or descending) and the final note of each phrase.

Practice Suggestions

The RH two-note slurs represent sobbing or sighing. The term *appoggiatura* comes from the Italian verb *appoggiare* (to lean or rest). Play these two-note slurs in a highly expressive manner. Lean on the first note and play the second note more softly.

Use a consistent *legato* touch for the LH part. Look for places where the RH and LH have different articulations. Emphasize these contrasts to give each part a distinct, independent voice.

L.-C. Daquin (1694-1772): *Le coucou (Rondeau)* (R10)
Background Information

With François Couperin and Jean-Philippe Rameau as foremost composers and performers, the late Baroque French harpsichord school achieved a level of refinement and skill highly respected throughout Europe. Many German composers traveled to France to study. German monarchs and nobles employed French composers and performers at their courts.

French harpsichord music was noted for its emphasis on dance and its elaborate ornamentation. A typical French suite consisted of a mixture of dances and programmatic pieces from which performers selected a group of movements for any given performance. The *rondeau* was a favored form. In a *rondeau*, repetitions of the theme or refrain are separated by contrasting sections called *couplets* (A c_1 A c_2 A).

From 1727 until his death, Louis-Claude Daquin was organist at St. Paul. (He won this post in competition with Rameau.) As a composer, he wrote harpsichord and organ music, chamber pieces, and a cantata, *La rose. Le coucou* is a well-known example of harpsichord music of this period. Notice the programmatic imitation of a cuckoo's call (the falling LH 3rds).

Exploring the Score

Find the different sections of this piece and make a diagram of the form. Use these questions to help sort out the order of the sections:

- What measure do you play after the first ending in m. 23 the first time? [m. 24] the second time? [m. 43]
- What measure do you return to after the *Da Capo* in mm. 42 and 69? [m. 1]
- How many times do you play mm. 24-42 and mm. 43-69? [once]
- What is the key of each section?

Practice Suggestions

Determine a precise articulation for the cuckoo motive (*staccato* eighth note, full value quarter note).

Play the RH sixteenth notes precisely and evenly. Practice with a *staccato* touch.

J.S. Bach (1685-1750): *Prelude and Fugue in C Minor, BWV 847* (R13, R16)
Background Information

Up to Bach's time, tuning systems for keyboard instruments used acoustically pure intervals. Because of this, certain keys sounded intolerably out of tune. A tempered scale or tuning system employs intervals that have been slightly modified. New, tempered tuning systems made it possible for Bach to include preludes and fugues in each of the twenty-four major and minor keys in his monumental collection, *The Well-Tempered Clavier*. (For more information on the topic of temperament, see the article in *The New Harvard Dictionary of Music*.)

In general, each prelude or fugue in *The Well-Tempered Clavier* deals with one musical idea. Bach creates contrast by modulating to different keys and varying the texture. In Baroque music, the arrival at a new key or tonal center is an important event. These internal cadences should be stressed because they represent landmarks in the journey through the composition. Most of the preludes are in a free-voiced style, with variations in texture ranging from single lines to a fuller, thicker sound. In contrast, the fugues are in strict contrapuntal style. They are written for a specific number of voices or parts.

Prelude in C Minor (R13)
Exploring the Score
This prelude consists of a rhythmic, motoric section (mm. 1-24) and a free, improvisatory final section (mm. 25-38).

Play or name the first bass note of each measure. Which note is most often repeated? What function does that note play in the key?

Practice Suggestions
- Block the sixteenth-note figures to learn fingerings and position shifts. For example, play just the boxed notes:

etc.

- In mm. 1-24, all measures except one repeat the motive at the half measure. Make special note of m. 18 where the pattern changes at the half measure.
- Between mm. 29 and 33, the patterns shift constantly. Practice slowly in half-measure units to gain security.
- Practice the sixteenth-note figures in different rhythms.
- Introduce a slight *rubato* in the *adagio* measure (m. 34) to heighten the drama.

Fugue in C Minor (R16)
Exploring the Score
This three-voice fugue could be played by three different instruments.
- Find and bracket all appearances of the subject.
- Is the answer in mm. 3-4 tonal or real? [tonal]
- Why do mm. 9-10 not qualify as a presentation of the subject? [full subject not present]
- Find and label the appearances of the countersubject.
- What new keys are established in mm. 13, 17, and 22? How do these keys relate to C minor? [E flat major, mediant; G minor, dominant; C minor, tonic]

Teaching Suggestions
The opening motive of this fugue is distinctive and the presentations of the subject are easy to follow. Articulation is a major factor in establishing independence of the three voices. Because the subject and countersubject appear together, it is

important that they each have a contrasting, independent articulation. Have your student determine articulation patterns for the subject and countersubject and use them consistently. As a general rule, detach the eighth notes of the subject and slur the eighth notes of the countersubject.

Play this fugue as a student-teacher duet. Here are some suggestions:
- student and teacher each play one hand
- (at two keyboards) student plays one voice, teacher plays one or two voices
- (at two keyboards) student plays subject presentations, teacher plays other parts
- (at two keyboards) student plays countersubject, teacher plays other parts

If a digital keyboard and sequencer are available, the student can record each voice on a separate track and practice with the playback of pre-recorded voices at various tempos and in different combinations.

J.S. Bach (1685-1750): *Prelude and Fugue in E Minor, BWV 855* (R18, R22)
Prelude in E Minor (R18)
Background Information
Much of Bach's harpsichord music is reminiscent of instrumental ensembles. Think of this prelude as an *arioso* for soloist and orchestra (for example, a movement from a flute concerto). An *arioso* is an expressive piece. In style, it is midway between a recitative and an *aria*. Notice the *cantabile* marking.

Improvisation was an important, cultivated skill of Baroque performers. The ornaments and elaborations they added to slower movements and repeats of sections were rarely written out.

Exploring the Score
To bring out the improvisatory nature of the sixteenth- and thirty-second-note figures in this prelude, play the RH solo with a spirit of freedom and spontaneity.

The long downbeat notes in the RH form the melodic skeleton. Map out the melodic contour by playing those long notes with the accompanying bass tone.

- This prelude has an improvisatory nature. Can you find any exact repetitions?
- How does Bach unify this highly varied prelude?
- Notice the stepwise descent of the bass in mm. 23-34. How far does the bass descend? What is the goal of that descent? [B, the dominant]
- Notice the slurs in m. 3. Bach rarely wrote slur markings in his manuscripts. How does the performer on the *Celebration Series* recording interpret these slurs?

In the contrasting, faster *Presto* section (mm. 23-41), the RH *arioso* theme disappears and both hands play a constant sixteenth-note pattern. (Only a few preludes in *The Well-Tempered Clavier* include such tempo changes. Another example is the *Prelude in C Minor, BWV 847*, also in Level 9.)

Practice Suggestions

The shorter rhythmic values of the solo part provide energy and move the music forward to the long downbeat tones (rather like the wind-up of the slingshot before the long flight of the stone). Play these improvisatory figures with a slight *crescendo*.

The RH chords support the harmony. Play them lightly. They should not disturb the listener's involvement with the solo line.

Emphasize the LH notes on the first and third beats slightly, especially when they change pitch. To practice this, divide the parts between the hands. Play the bass notes with the LH and the upper moving notes with the RH.

Fugue in E Minor (R22)
Exploring the Score

This is the only two-voice fugue in *The Well-Tempered Clavier*. It is not a very strict fugue because with only two voices, the possibilities of contrapuntal devices are somewhat limited. The chromaticism of the subject suggests a *legato* articulation. Notice the unusual unison writing in mm. 19 and 38, announcing entrances of the subject in A minor (m. 24) and E minor (m. 39).

- Find and bracket the appearances of the subject.
- Find and label the appearances of the counter-subject.
- Is the answer in mm. 3-4 tonal or real?

Practice Suggestions

- Determine the articulation for the subject and countersubject.
- Practice each appearance of the subject and countersubject. Use the correct fingering and keep the articulation patterns consistent.
- Play the subject and countersubject, assigning one part to each hand.

LIST B – LATE BAROQUE AND CLASSICAL

Suggested Order of Difficulty

Page	Composer	Title
R25	Domenico Scarlatti	Sonata in D Minor, L 413/K 9
R28	Domenico Scarlatti	Sonata in C Major, L 104/K 159
R36	Franz Joseph Haydn	Sonata in D Major, Hob. XVI:37 (Second and Third Movements)
R31	Franz Joseph Haydn	Sonata in D Major, Hob. XVI: 37 (First Movement)
R55	Ludwig van Beethoven	Six Easy Variations in G Major, WoO 77
R40	Wolfgang Amadeus Mozart	Sonata in G Major, KV 283 (189h) (First Movement)
R45	Wolfgang Amadeus Mozart	Sonata in G Major, KV 283 (189h) (Second and Third Movements)

In the Classical style, contrast is a principal element. Classical composers used forms with contrasting sections (ternary form, sonata form, rondo) featuring contrasting themes, keys, textures, and accompaniment patterns. The two sonatas by Domenico Scarlatti are placed in List B because they are called "sonatas." However, these works are representative of Baroque binary forms, not Classical sonata forms.

Music of the Classical period has a strong harmonic orientation and a homophonic texture (melody supported by harmonic accompaniment). Some harmonies have a natural tension and receive dynamic stress. Non-chord tones in the melody are a primary means of expression with a dynamic stress on the non-chord tone.

The phrase is the standard unit of construction. Classical music is often described in terms of language: phrases, sentences, punctuation, inflection, accent, and emphasis.

During the Classical period, the harpsichord gradually gave way to the fortepiano, an instrument on which the performer could create a wide variety of dynamic inflections – sudden and grand or refined and sensitive. Haydn's early sonatas were written for the harpsichord. His later sonatas have numerous dynamic markings and were written for the fortepiano. Mozart also demonstrated a strong preference for the fortepiano.

However, in comparison to the modern piano, the early piano had a small sound and limited sustaining power. Beethoven in particular was never satisfied with the contemporary instrument, and piano makers in Vienna strove to make improvements so that the instrument could withstand his forceful playing. Innovations in the first half of the 19th century, such as the use of heavier strings, cross-stringing, and the cast-iron frame, laid the foundation for the modern piano.

Dynamic control is one of the challenges in performing Classical music. The scores of Classical composers include specific dynamic markings (for example, *piano, forte, sforzando, crescendo, diminuendo*) and slurs. The ends of phrases are usually tapered. The balance between melody and accompaniment also requires dynamic control. The performer should determine a dynamic plan for every phrase and for every smaller group of notes within a phrase.

Use these questions to help your student explore the construction of each piece.
1. What is the form of the piece? Does this form have a name (for example, sonata form, minuet and trio, binary form, rondo)?
2. Are there contrasting sections? How does the composer create that contrast (key, melodic style, accompaniment style and texture, rhythm)?
3. Where do the phrases begin and end? Is this phrase part of a larger unit?
4. Where is the focal point in each phrase? How does the composer use rhythm (an important downbeat or a long value), melodic contour (high notes), or harmony (an unusual chord) to create that focal point?

D. Scarlatti (1685-1757): *Sonata in D Minor,*
L 413/K 9 (R25)
Background Information
Domenico Scarlatti was born in Naples. He traveled
widely throughout Italy and held posts in Venice and
Rome. Sometime after 1719, he became maestro of
the chapel at the royal court of Portugal in Lisbon and
gave keyboard lessons to Maria Barbara, daughter of
King John V. When Maria Barbara married the heir to
the Spanish throne in 1729, Scarlatti moved to
Spain with her court. He spent the rest of his life
there, composing, conducting, and teaching.

Scarlatti is most famous for his 555 keyboard
sonatas, many of which were written for the gifted
Maria Barbara. Although these sonatas are all in one
movement with an extended binary form, they have
remarkable variety and color. Ralph Kirkpatrick, the
renowned Scarlatti scholar, suggests that approximately 388 sonatas are grouped in pairs, both with
the same tonal center, and another twelve sonatas
form sets of three. When played on a modern piano,
Scarlatti's sonatas require the same clarity and
precision as the compositions by Daquin and Bach
from List A.

Exploring the Score
In binary form, modulation normally occurs in the
A, or first, section. If the piece is in a minor key, the
modulation is usually to the relative major.
- What is the main key of this piece? [D minor]
- To what key does it modulate? [F major]
- Where is the first appearance of the relative
  major? [m. 16]

In a Scarlatti sonata, the second section starts like a
development. However, much of this section repeats
material from the first section.
- Look for a restatement of material from the
  opening section (mm. 1-26) in the second section
  (mm. 27-60). [compare mm. 39-60 with 5-26]
- How is this rounded binary form different from
  sonata form?

Teaching Suggestions
The articulation, slurs, and dynamics are editorial.
Recommend these to your student and discuss the
degree of detachment of the unmarked eighth and
quarter notes.

The degree of detachment (sharp or slight) will affect
the mood of the piece. Let your ear be your guide.
- Should the LH figure in mm. 16-18 and RH
  eighth notes in m. 23 have the same degree of
  staccato?
- Does the stepwise motion in the RH of mm. 23
  and 27-33 imply *legato?*

The trills provide harmonic dissonance. Begin the
trills on the upper note as shown in the footnote
below the music.

Practice Suggestions
One attractive feature of this piece is the variety of
scale passages.
- Practice the scale passages slowly for accurate
  fingerings, perhaps hands separately.
- Set the metronome for a moderately slow eighth-
  note pulse and practice the scales in rhythm.
  Make careful distinction between eighth notes,
  sixteenth notes, and thirty-second notes.

D. Scarlatti (1685-1757): *Sonata in C Major,*
L 104/K 159 (R28)
Exploring the Score
Scarlatti often imitates other instruments in his
harpsichord sonatas. In some sonatas you can hear
guitars, trumpet fanfares, hunting horns, or
castanets. Scarlatti also used Spanish dances. This
sonata shows the influence of the *jota* (pronounced
ho-tah), a fast dance in triple time, performed to the
accompaniment of castanets. What type of
instruments and dancers can you imagine for the
opening measures of this piece?

Scarlatti does not shy away from dissonance. There
are moments in some sonatas where the performer
plays fistfuls of notes, creating an intense dissonance.
Look for thick textures and dissonant harmonies
(for example, mm. 26-40).

This sonata is in rounded binary form (the A section
is restated at the end of the second section), but dry
definitions cannot fully explain a composer's
creativity.
- Compare mm. 1-25 with mm. 42-62. What has
  been changed? Why do you think Scarlatti made
  those changes?
- The rising eighth notes in mm. 17-19 outline a
  G major triad. In mm. 55-57, the top notes stay
  on C. Scarlatti was unable to complete the
  corresponding C major triad because the top
  notes of the harpsichord only went as far as F.

The editorial dynamics reflect echo phrasing, which
was possible on a two-manual harpsichord.

Practice Suggestions
The opening theme is an imitation of a trumpet
fanfare. That effect is heightened with a sharp
staccato touch.

Scarlatti writes slurs to emphasize the relationship
of dissonance → resolution. The first note of the

slur (beat note) is to be played louder. Eighth notes not marked with slurs can be played *staccato*.

The double 3rds of mm. 13, 16, etc. offer the performer three possibilities for interpretation. Practice the three options and decide which one fits the character of the piece best.

1. Play all double 3rds with a sharp *staccato*.
2. Emphasize the downbeat of each measure by a *legato* connection between the first two eighths:

3. Emphasize each main beat by a *legato* connection between the first two eighths:

Play the quarter-eighth-quarter-eighth LH rhythm which frequently accompanies the RH detached notes.

The footnotes give realizations for the short trills. Practice them with fingers close to the key. Use a "scratching" action of the finger tips.

F.J. Haydn (1732-1809): *Sonata in D Major, Hob. XVI:37* (R31, R36, R37)
Background Information
Haydn was an innovative composer, and his works show great variety. He wrote approximately 62 piano sonatas, some of which have been lost. This sonata dates from Haydn's mature period. It is one of a collection of six sonatas published in 1780. The title of the original edition reads "*Sonate per il Clavicembalo o Forte Piano*," indicating that in the 1780s, publishers were still marketing keyboard compositions for harpsichord or piano.

It is difficult to describe a typical Haydn sonata because of the variety in form, style, and number of movements. Haydn's compositions often include humor. He surprises the listener with a sudden interruption of a theme, an abrupt change of key, an unexpected rest, or a startling new texture or register.

First Movement – Allegro con brio (R31)
Exploring the Score
Label the form in the score:

    exposition mm. 1-40
        1st theme   mm. 1-8
        bridge   mm. 9-16
        2nd theme   mm. 17-35
        closing theme *(codetta)* mm. 35-40

    development mm. 41-60
    recapitulation mm. 61-103

- Name the key of each theme in the exposition.
- Compare the themes. Which themes are based on short motives? Which themes create the greatest contrast?
- Find the themes in the recapitulation.

Paired phrases are typical in Classical style. In mm. 1-8, there are two four-measure phrases. The first phrase (the antecedent or question) ends on the dominant. The second phrase (the consequent or answer) ends on the tonic.

- Haydn rarely repeats a phrase exactly. How does he vary the answer phrase here?
- Notice also the variation in slurs. The slurs in mm. 1 and 5 emphasize the beat. The slurs in mm. 3 and 7 emphasize the off-beat, creating rhythmic humor.

Teaching Suggestions
Learning a movement in sonata form can be a demanding project. To make the learning process more musical and rewarding, begin with an exploration of contrasts in the piece.

- Which themes present the greatest contrast?
- What moods are created by these contrasting themes?
- Where is the greatest dynamic contrast?
- Where are the harmonic surprises?

Base the first week's practice assignment on these issues.

At a later lesson, explore the methods Haydn uses to emphasize specific notes: for example, ornaments, grace notes, and short slurs.

Practice Suggestions
The phrases make good practice units. For each phrase:

- Write in any changes of fingering.
- Drill the fingering.
- Plan the dynamics.
- Practice slowly for accuracy of notes, fingering, and rhythm. Exaggerate the dynamics.

We learn through repetition. How many times must you repeat a phrase until you progress beyond the reading stage? (For most people, the average is five to eight times.)

Second Movement – *Largo e sostenuto* (R36)
Exploring the Score
List ways in which this middle movement provides a contrast to the outer movements of this sonata. [parallel minor key, slow tempo, shorter length, reflective mood]

The thirty-second notes, dotted figures, and grace notes provide variety and give this movement an improvisatory sound.

- As a practice exercise, omit these decorative details. Play only the basic skeleton of the music and listen for the melodic and harmonic structure.
- Which notes will you emphasize in performance – the skeleton or the decorative details? [Exaggerated dynamic contrast creates more intense expression. Give the two-note slurs a loud-soft dynamic shape.]
- In what key does this movement end? [A major, dominant]
- What effect does this create? [unresolved feeling leads directly to the *Finale*]

Teaching Suggestions
This movement is reminiscent of thick-textured Baroque pieces. If Haydn played this movement on his fortepiano, he probably used the pedal sparingly, if at all. To avoid over-pedaling, have students practice first with no pedal. One possibility is to use a surface pedal (slightly lifting the dampers) to increase sonority. Another is to change the pedal after scalewise moving notes. Try both approaches and choose the one you think sounds best.

Third Movement – *Presto ma non troppo* (R37)
Exploring the Score
- What is the form of this movement? [rondo: ABAC transition A]. Find and label the sections.
- What is the key of each section?
- Analyze the harmonies of the A section (mm. 1-20).
- In general, the harmonies change with each measure. Which measures have two harmonies? [mm. 7, 11, 19] What effect does this create? [intensification before the cadence]

Teaching Suggestions
Articulation is the key to an effective performance of this movement. All notes that are not slurred should be played *staccatissimo*. Create practice assignments which focus on articulation.

W.A. Mozart (1756-1792): *Sonata in G Major, KV 283 (189h)* (R40, R45, R48)
Background Information
Mozart's sonatas are more predictable in form than those of Haydn and Beethoven. Mozart's sonatas all have three movements and (with one exception) the first movement is in sonata form. The slow second movements are in a contrasting key. The lively third movements are in either rondo or sonata form. Mozart's themes have strong personality and provide dramatic contrast. They are often compared to characters in his operas.

In this sonata, all three movements are in sonata form. Have students make a chart showing the number of measures in each section of each movement. Compare the proportions of each movement. Look for sections that are especially short or especially long. Which of the three development sections is proportionately the longest?

First Movement – *Allegro* (R40)
Exploring the Score
Identify and label the sections in this sonata form:

exposition mm. 1-53
1st theme	mm. 1-16
bridge	mm. 16-22
2nd theme	mm. 23-53

development mm. 54-71

recapitulation mm. 72-120

- The opening melody is made up of melodic fragments. How do those short ideas convey elegance and grace?
- This movement has several surprises. We expect the first phrase (or period) to end in m. 8, but Mozart extends it to m. 10. Where did these extra measures come from? What is their function?
- Find the rhythmic surprise in mm. 5-10. [syncopation, mm. 8-9]
- In mm. 23-30, there is a good example of Mozart's variation technique. Look for other places where Mozart presents an idea, then repeats it with variations (for example, mm. 45-49).

Teaching Suggestions
As with the Haydn sonata, base an important early assignment on thematic contrast. Students will enjoy assigning characters to the different themes and observing how the plot thickens as the music develops.

Scholars suggest that the drama of these sonatas is closely associated to Mozart's first love, the opera. For example, the abrupt LH *fortes* in mm. 75 and 79 are like the interjections of a gruff baritone.

Mozart marked the articulation in his piano scores with great care. For a proper Mozart interpretation, play slurred notes *legato*. Notes without slurs should be slightly detached. (In Mozart's day, this was referred to as "ordinary touch.")

Practice Suggestions
Keep a steady beat at the beginning of the development section. There may be a tendency to rush the quarter notes starting in m. 54.

Second Movement – Andante (R45)
Exploring the Score
What is the key of this movement? How does this relate to the key of the first movement? Most of Mozart's middle movements are in ABA form. This movement is in sonata form. Find the sections:

exposition mm. 1-14

    1st theme   mm. 1-8

    2nd theme   mm. 9-14

development mm. 15-23

recapitulation mm. 24-39

    1st theme   mm. 24-31

    2nd theme   mm. 32-39

In the development, Mozart passes through G major, D minor, C major, and A minor. (Be on the lookout for the false recapitulation in m. 18 – this is a Haydn trick!)

Mozart often repeats a melodic statement with a slight variation that sounds improvised. Compare the following pairs of measures:
– mm. 9 and 10
– mm. 15 and 16
– mm. 24 and 26
– mm. 32 and 33
Look for other examples of this statement-variation technique.

Teaching Suggestions
Mozart uses two types of *staccato* marks: dots and wedges. For this movement, try these suggested guidelines:
- Give the notes with *staccato* dots half their value. (Anything shorter will reduce the tender quality of the theme to simple joviality.)
- Emphasize the notes with wedges but do not shorten them.

In mm. 1, 3, and 4, the LH accompaniment has two voices. Sometimes the lower voice is indicated with downward stems. In other places, the second voice is implied. Look through the LH part and identify the two-voice structures. Have students practice these measures by playing one voice in each hand.

Performers should follow the composer's articulation markings. Students may find it difficult to realize the slight breaks between slurred groups and between notes that are not slurred. Encourage students to practice first without pedal so that they become aware of these details of articulation. Once these details are refined, the student can determine if and where pedaling is appropriate.

Third Movement – Presto (R48)
Exploring the Score
What is the form of this movement? (The double bar at m. 102 is the first clue.) Label the sections.

exposition mm. 1-102

development mm. 103-171

recapitulation mm. 172-277

Composers often change the lengths of rhythmic units to create interest and contrast.
- Observe the LH rhythm, mm. 1-8. The low G provides special emphasis, and the LH plays a macro-rhythm of four-measure units.
- In mm. 9-12, both hands have a rhythmic unit of one measure.
- In mm. 18-23, the rhythmic units are intensified to a single eighth note.
- Find other changes of rhythmic units. Compare mm. 25-32 (two-measure units) to mm. 33-40 (one-measure units).

This change of rhythmic unit affects the musical intensity of the passage.

The development section is a good example of contrast through harmony.
- Name the harmonies in mm. 103-138.
- What happened to sunny G major and its family? How do these measures differ from the opening in character and mood?

Practice Suggestions
The technical figures of this movement are varied and challenging. The sixteenth-note figures deserve isolated practice. Organize and practice the figures according to gesture. These include:
– rotational gestures:
    LH mm. 33-39
    RH m. 56, LH m. 58
    RH mm. 107-110
    RH mm. 127-130
    RH mm. 264-267

– crossings:
    LH mm. 69-70
    RH mm. 89-90
    RH mm. 132-135

- expansion and contraction:
  LH mm. 25-32
- wrist drop-lift:
  RH mm. 1-2
  RH mm. 9-12

L. van Beethoven (1770-1827): *Six Easy Variations in G Major, WoO 77* (R55)

Background Information

The ability to improvise was an important skill for pianists during the time of Mozart and Beethoven. Improvisation often took the form of variations on popular operatic melodies or folk tunes. Beethoven's ability as an improviser helped establish his reputation as the foremost pianist in Vienna. In addition to his improvisations, Beethoven also composed sets of variations. Many of these are based on familiar melodies, but the theme for this set of variations was composed by Beethoven himself.

Exploring the Score

Themes for most Classical period variations are in binary form. This theme has a rounded binary form:

A   mm. 1-8
B+A₁   mm. 9-16

- Mark the phrases in the score.
- Find an example of paired phrases. (See the reference to paired phrases in the discussion of the first movement of Haydn's *Sonata in D Major*.)
- Do the A and B sections have the same phrase structure?
- Analyze the harmonies of the A section.
- Did you notice the stepwise motion in mm. 9-12?

Now look through the rest of the score. Compare each variation with the theme. Look for the similarities and differences in harmony, bass line, phrase structure, melody, register, rhythm, key or mode, and form. For example:

- The bass register and minor mode of the *Minore* variation (Variation IV) provide a strong contrast.
- Variation VI has a *coda*. What is the relationship of the rhythms, harmonies, and thematic material of these final measures to the theme?

Teaching Suggestions

The detail of Beethoven's notation is noteworthy. The challenge is to help the student realize the notated sound. For example, examine the four articulation markings in mm. 1-4:

1. Use a *portato* touch for the two upbeat eighth notes.
2. Slightly accent the first note of slurred groups.
3. Detach the unslurred eighth notes.
4. Use a *staccato* touch for the notes marked with wedges.

This piece can be played without the damper pedal. However, a few pedal touches in Variation IV and in the final measures will enhance the sonority.

Practice Suggestions

- Circle the thematic notes in each variation before you start to practice that section.
- Beethoven has marked the articulation of the theme, Variation I, and the *coda* with great care. Practice these sections hands separately until your muscles are trained to control the articulation.
- What other sections may require hands-separate practice? [Variation III, LH; Variation V, RH; Variation VI, RH] Hands-separate practice can be inefficient if the practice units are too long. It is better to play multiple repetitions of short units.

LIST C – ROMANTIC

Suggested Order of Difficulty

The 19th century was the century of melody – long, soaring, expressive melody. The variety of melodic construction in the following pieces gives ample testimony to that statement. List C includes piano settings of solo song (the Chopin *Prelude in D Flat* and Liszt's *En rêve*) and duet (Mendelssohn's *Song without Words* and Schumann's *Romance*). The melody of Chopin's *Waltz in C Sharp Minor* is at once nostalgic and flirtatious. Schumann's *Whims* opens with a statement of robust energy followed by a contrasting song of loneliness.

Romantic composers favored the character piece – a concise, intense statement. Expression, mood, and color are at the heart of these short pieces. They were less interested in the extended sonata and variation forms used by their Classical predecessors.

The extended harmonic palette of this music exploits chromaticism, altered chords, dissonance, and modulations to remote keys. (Notice the keys of the List C pieces. Whatever happened to C major?) In addition, composers marked their scores quite precisely, indicating subtle variations in tone quality and dynamic range. The use of contrasts and extremes of tone quality and dynamics adds to the expressive qualities of this music. Tone quality is enhanced and harmonies are blended with the subtle and varied use of pedaling, which was an important aspect of the development of pianism in the 19th century.

The chromaticism, thicker textures, and colorful pedaling that characterize Romantic keyboard music were possible, in part, because of 19th-century developments in piano construction such as cast-iron frames, double escapement action, and cross-stringing. The greater string tension made possible by these innovations gave the piano a more brilliant sound. The range of the keyboard was also extended.

The core of all this expression is melody. If the student can shape and project a beautiful melodic line, the result will be most rewarding. A sensitive balance of sound between melody and accompaniment is especially important in Romantic character pieces.

E. Grieg (1843-1907): *Butterfly, Op. 43, No. 1* (R60)

Background Information

Grieg's ten sets of *Lyric Pieces* represent a significant contribution to the genre of piano character pieces. These sixty-six compositions reveal Grieg's interest in nature and the Norwegian landscape, in Norwegian folk music, and in scenes of daily life. Grieg studied composition in Germany and his work was influenced by the German Romantic style. (Two other *Lyric Pieces* have been included in earlier albums of the *Celebration Series*.)

Exploring the Score

- What are the characteristics of butterfly movement?
- What musical devices would you use in a composition about a butterfly? Listen to the *Celebration Series* recording of this piece, and check the score to see if Grieg used those same musical elements.
- What is the form of *Butterfly*? [ABABA]

This piece is filled with repetition. In m. 1, Grieg uses chromatic movement. In m. 2, he uses a dotted rhythm. Compare the pattern of chromatic movement and dotted rhythms in mm. 1-6 and mm. 17-23. Note how these two elements are used in the remainder of the piece.

To establish a tonal center, composers use strong dominant-tonic cadences. For definition and clarity, they often write the tonic chord in root position. Does Grieg do this in *Butterfly?*
- What is the key of *Butterfly?* [A major]
- Where is the first A major chord in root position? [m. 23]

This lack of a root-position tonic harmony creates a feeling of restlessness (as if the butterfly were searching for a resting place). Other harmonies add to this unresolved, restless atmosphere.
- Notice the downbeat harmonies of mm. 1 and 4. Block these chords, and resolve them to the harmony on the fourth beat of the measure.

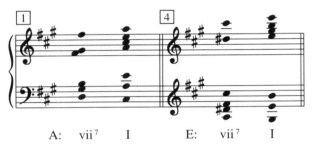

A: vii⁷   I   E: vii⁷   I

- The change of harmonies from m. 6 to m. 7 is unexpected (again, butterflies). Grieg uses a common tone (B) to link the two chords (a typical 19th-century harmonic practice).

E: V⁷   I   f♯: N⁶

The B section (mm. 7-16) is based on a harmonic progression involving the Neapolitan 6th chord (a first inversion major chord usually built on the lowered second degree of the minor scale). Romantic composers frequently used the Neapolitan 6th to add color to the harmony, particularly in minor keys.

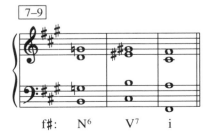

f♯: N⁶   V⁷   i

Teaching Suggestions
The Italian word *rubato* is often used to describe the rhythmic flexibility and nuance associated with Romantic style. *Rubato* seems appropriate for a piece depicting restless, unpredictable movement. During practice, students should play the sixteenth-note passages with precision. However, in final performance, encourage them to add the rhythmic freedom necessary for an effective portrayal of the butterfly. Use the *Celebration Series* recording as an example. The maxim "play similar things differently" is a useful way to describe this rhythmic flexibility to students.

Practice Suggestions
The exact repetition of many measures makes this piece easier to learn. Identify the different figures (for example, chromatic scale, dotted rhythm, zig-zag shape, etc.) and practice groups of similar figures as a unit. Check for changes of fingerings. Concentrate on one of the following aspects with each play-through:
- fingering
- perfect rhythm
- dynamic change
- finger technique (for example, mm. 1, 3, 4)
- rotating wrist (for example, mm. 2, 7, 9, 11)

F. Mendelssohn (1809-1847): *Song without Words, Op. 38, No. 6 (Duetto)* (R64)
Background Information
During the 19th century, the piano became a popular instrument. Middle-class families could afford to purchase a piano and pay for piano lessons for their children. The piano became not only the symbol of culture and good breeding, but also the focus of home entertainment. Families gathered in the evening around the piano. When guests came to the home, music was the entertainment. The piano was used as a solo instrument, in chamber music, and for the accompaniment of singing.

Mendelssohn's *Songs without Words* were an instant success throughout Europe, not only for their musical value but also because they were accessible to the vast public of amateur pianists. These forty-eight short pieces were written between 1829 and 1845, and were published in sets of six. Each piece is based on a single technical figure, texture, and mood, and the main melody is always clear. (For other selections from Mendelssohn's *Songs without Words*, see *Piano Repertoire Album 7* and *Piano Studies Album 9 &10*.)

Exploring the Score

This piece is subtitled *Duetto*. Are the two voices singing of love? How does Mendelssohn use these two voices to provide variety?

- Where does the soprano sing? [mm. 1-5, 10-13, etc.] Where does the tenor sing? [mm. 6-9, 14-17, etc.]
- In mm. 1-32, do they sing the same melody?
- Where do both voices sing together for the first time? [mm. 33-39]
- From the use of accidentals, can you find places where Mendelssohn seems to leave the home key of A flat?

Teaching Suggestions

The main issue in this piece is melodic shaping and projection. This is not a new topic. Your students have been developing this skill for years.

Discuss dynamic shaping with your student. A *crescendo-diminuendo* arch shape will work nicely for most phrases.

Practice Suggestions

- Play the melodic line in unison, hands together (omit the triplets). Concentrate on dynamic shape.
- Divide the melody and the triplet accompaniment between the hands. Exaggerate the difference in the dynamics.
- Play the piece as written, but stop momentarily on each melody note. (This allows the hand muscles to relax so that you can give the following sixteenth notes a controlled, quiet sound.)

F. Chopin (1810-1849): *Prelude in D Flat, Op. 28, No. 15* (R69)

Background Information

Chopin admired the compositions of J.S. Bach, and he both played and taught pieces from *The Well-Tempered Clavier*. Chopin's collection of preludes in each major and minor key was inspired by *The Well-Tempered Clavier*. (Chopin freely admitted that his skills were insufficient to write twenty-four fugues as Bach had done.) Each of Chopin's preludes is a short exploration into a single key color and mood.

Exploring the Score

Surprisingly few of Chopin's preludes are in ABA form. *Prelude in D Flat* is one of the exceptions:

A mm. 1-27
B mm. 28-75
A mm. 76-89

- Notice the difference in length between the A and B sections.
- What is the key of the A sections? [D flat major]

What is the key of the B section? [C sharp minor]

This piece is known as the "Raindrop Prelude" because of the constant repetition of A flat and G sharp.

- What effect does Chopin create with this repetition?
- For most of the piece, these repeated notes are in the background. Is there any point where they should be louder than the melody?
- Notice the phrase marks in the A section. How do the LH eighth notes support the flow of these long phrases?

Teaching Suggestions

Long tones in a melody can create problems for students. The following note may seem accented in comparison with the diminishing sound of the longer note. Matching the dynamic level of these two notes requires sensitive listening. Try the following exercise:

1. Play the first note and listen to the diminishing sound.
2. Play the following quarter note, matching the dynamic level of the fading sound as closely as possible.

Have students play the RH melody alone, listening to the *diminuendo* of the long tones.

The *fortissimo* passages in mm. 40-42 and 56-59 should have a full, ringing sound. Discuss the physical movements necessary to avoid an unpleasant banging quality.

Practice Suggestions

- Practice the RH of the A section separately. Respect Chopin's notation of the long phrases.
- Give special emphasis to the darker atmosphere created by the minor mode in mm. 9-19.
- This piece is marked *con pedale*. Assume that the entire piece is played with the damper pedal. Practice clear pedal changes with each change of harmony and melodic movement. In the B section, change the pedal with each quarter note.
- Decide which LH notes you wish to bring out in mm. 28-35.

F. Chopin (1810-1849): *Waltz in C Sharp Minor, Op. 64, No. 2* (R72)

Background Information

The waltz was a popular dance of Chopin's time. However, Chopin's seventeen waltzes were written as solo piano compositions, not as dance accompaniments. They have clearly-defined sections with contrasting moods which lend variety to the triple meter. The three waltzes in Op. 64 were published in 1847, two years before Chopin's death. (This set also includes the famous *Minute Waltz*.)

Exploring the Score

- Each section of this waltz is thirty-two measures long. Map out the formal plan and label the keys of the sections. Each section has its own distinct mood.
- This waltz is built on a descending stepwise motion – look through the score to find examples. How will this discovery help you memorize the piece?
- Which section emphasizes the third beat of the measure as much as the downbeat?

Teaching Suggestions

The rhythm of mm. 3-4 is a stumbling block for many students. The diversity of subdivisions and the grace notes make these measures difficult to count. As well, students may have heard other performers play these measures with considerable *rubato*. If the student can tap the rhythm precisely, the performance will be more accurate. Try this exercise:

Have students crush the grace note against the main note, and give the grace note a *staccato* release.

Notice the pattern of inverted dynamics in the A section. Some short groups are marked with a *diminuendo* and some with a *crescendo*. Much of the success of the A section is determined by the sighing motive in mm. 1-2. Most students will not play the first downbeat loudly enough, nor the second downbeat quietly enough. Isolate these measures for

special practice. Have students bring out the top note and exaggerate the *diminuendo*.

In the B section (mm. 33-64), play the RH eighth notes with a "small hand" – keep the thumb close to the fingers. Try not to hold the hand stretched over the span of an octave. This will help keep the hand relaxed.

In the C section (mm. 65-96), stress the RH tied notes (for example, mm. 66-67, 70-71, 73-74) to highlight the syncopation.

Students have a tendency to over-pedal these waltzes. Play recordings of several different performances and discuss the varying approaches to pedaling. For example, in the B section, pedaling should be limited to the quarter-note downbeats.

Practice Suggestions

- Plan your fingering for the B section carefully. Notice the finger changes on the repeated notes between mm. 37-39.
- Give special attention to Chopin's precise rhythmic notation of the LH in mm. 67-69 and 72-74. Notice the finger substitutions in the LH. How will you arrange to hold the B flat and the C for five beats?

F. Liszt (1811-1886): *En rêve* (R78)

Background Information

This late composition by Liszt was not published until two years after his death. Liszt's compositions feature an emphasis on chromaticism, augmented and diminished harmonies, and unusual harmonic relationships. Liszt was a great keyboard virtuoso with a unique sense for piano sonority. *En rêve* demonstrates his understanding of the ethereal quality of the upper register of the piano.

Exploring the Score

- What is the key of this piece? [B major with an F sharp pedal point]
- Find a tonic chord in root position (if you can!).
- What is the effect of music without a home tonality in its restful root position? (Remember the title of the piece.)
- Where does the LH move away from F sharp? What effect does this move create?

Teaching Suggestions

This piece looks deceptively simple, but it presents unusual musical and technical challenges. Rarely are students called upon to create the illusion of sound suspended in space, floating and adrift without the security of downbeats and phrase definition. Here is an improvisation exercise to introduce the illusion of suspended gravity:

- Choose a whole-tone position in the treble register.
- Play with both hands and use the damper pedal. Maintain a simple texture and a slow tempo with long note values. (The teacher might provide a slow *ostinato*.)

The *ppp* chords in the final measures are difficult to control. Some students have greatest control when they think of releasing the chord rather than playing down into the key. A slow key descent produces a quieter sound than a fast key descent.

Pedal control is also important. The pedal changes should be imperceptible so as not to disturb the dreamy quality. Have the student practice half-pedaling. A bit of blur may be preferable to clear precision of harmonic changes.

Practice Suggestions

Think of the trills in terms of suspended gravity – a floating sound. A slower, delicate trill is preferable to a fast, uneven trill. To facilitate evenness, try a slight hand rotation. Experiment with different fingerings.

R. Schumann (1810-1856): *Romance in F Sharp, Op. 28, No. 2* (R80)

Background Information

Schumann had a special affinity for tenor register sounds and chose to place some of his most beautiful melodies in the middle register of the piano. Some of Schumann's notational choices were made because of his preference for complex appearance. However, his use of three staves for this piece, although startling to a student's eye, seems purely musical because it clearly separates the melody from the accompaniment.

Exploring the Score

Find and label the sections. [ABACA] Describe the melodic placement (register) and characteristics of each section.

- Which section features descending motion? [B]
- Which section has a duet melody? [A]
- Which section has the melody interweaving between three voices? [C]
- Which section has phrases ending with ascending motion? [A]

Practice Suggestions

The melody of each section requires a distinct technical approach.

The A section (mm. 1-8) has a thumb melody. The goal is a seamless *legato* with no hint of accent.

1. Play a scale using only thumb and damper pedal. Make each note sound exactly alike.
2. Play the scale again, this time with a dynamic plan. Listen carefully.
3. Play only the notes in the thumb duet (thumbs of both hands). Use the damper pedal. Eliminate the attack of the sound as much as possible. Think of sinking into the key slowly, and relax the thumb muscles. Project the RH voice.

In the B section (mm. 9-17), the melody is in the top notes of the RH.

1. Find and play only the RH melody notes.
2. Play the melody note with its accompanying 2nd or 3rd. Make the top melodic tone *forte* and the accompanying tone *pianissimo*.

In the C section (mm. 25-30), the melody is passed between the voices. Practice each phrase separately. Move the music forward to the first eighth note.

R. Schumann (1810-1856): *Whims, Op. 12, No. 4* (R82)

Background Information

Most of Schumann's great piano works are character pieces. He wrote short character pieces, extended character pieces, and extended cycles of character pieces. The Op. 12 *Fantasiestücke* (Fantasy Pieces) is one such cycle. Although we frequently hear individual pieces from this set, Schumann thought of the eight pieces as a single work.

Exploring the Score

Careful examination of the score can result in a more informed, convincing interpretation. What do you expect in a piece titled *Whims?* There are many possible answers, but most students will suggest abrupt change as the most obvious.

Where are the changes in this piece? What does Schumann change? [Look at texture, melody, phrase length, dynamics, and articulation.]

Label the sections and keys:

A	mm. 1-16	B flat minor → D flat major
B	mm. 17-44	F minor → A flat major → F minor
A	mm. 45-60	B flat minor → D flat major
C	mm. 61-96	G flat major → D flat major → G flat major

A	mm. 97-112	B flat minor → D flat major
B	mm. 113-140	B flat minor → D flat major → B flat minor
A	mm. 141-156	B flat minor → D flat major

Schumann's rhythms often create the impression that the bar line has been misplaced. This begins as early in the piece as m. 3:

What is the real meter of mm. 61-68 and mm. 73-80? What beat groupings does your musical ear hear?

Teaching Suggestions

The primary challenge confronting the student may be that of melodic projection. Regardless of the texture, the melody must be stated clearly.

- Have the student identify and compare different textures (for example, mm. 1-4 and 17-24).
- Have the student identify and locate different types of melody:
  - two-note slurs (mm. 25-36)
  - *legato* phrases (mm. 17-24 and 61-66)
  - mixtures of *staccato* and *legato* notes (mm. 1-16)

Discuss practice techniques to project the top note in each texture and melody type.

Successive downward movements in the LH can create a dull, uninflected sound. Chords and extended positions (octaves) are particularly vulnerable (for example, see mm. 2 and 15). Help the student discover large gestures which group several beats of extended position notes. For example, have students feel one large gesture per measure as their hand drops and rebounds on successive chords.

Practice Suggestions

The contrast of sound in this piece is remarkable.

- As you practice, compare the sounds of the different themes and sections. The more contrast you can project, the more whimsical your performance will be. (Notice the marking, *Mit Humor*.)
- Use your sharpest *staccato* for the RH opening chords. Were your fingers off the key or on the key as you started to play? Was your arm movement up or down? Experiment with different hand positions and hand or arm movements to find the most efficient and easiest way to play these chords.

The theme of mm. 25-36 presents special challenges. These practice steps may help:

1. Play the RH melody, hands together in unison octaves. How many pairs of slurred notes create the phrase? [four] Which pair seems to be the focus? [the first]
2. Practice grouping beats two and three of the RH and stopping on beat three. To help feel the rhythmic emphasis, say "go to *here*" or "to the *three*":

Go to **here**   and   go to **here**

Bring out the top melodic tone on beat three.
3. Play the LH accompaniment.
4. Play only the RH melody, with the LH accompaniment as written.
5. Practice the RH separately. Check for accurate fingerings.
6. Practice both hands as written, projecting the top (melodic) notes of the chords. Listen for a clear, singing melody.

LIST D – LATE ROMANTIC AND CONTEMPORARY

Suggested Order of Difficulty

Page	Composer	Title
R104	Béla Bartók	Bear Dance
R102	Dmitri Kabalevsky	Prelude No. 2, Op. 38, No. 2
R87	Selim Palmgren	May Night, Op. 27, No. 4
R94	Claude Debussy	Golliwogg's Cake-walk
R111	Leo Weiner	Fox Dance
R100	Dmitri Kabalevsky	Prelude No. 1, Op. 38, No. 1
R90	Maurice Ravel	Menuet
R114	R. Murray Schafer	Polytonality
R99	Alexander Scriabin	Prelude in G Flat, Op. 11, No. 13
R108	François Morel	Ronde enfantine

Music of the 20th century includes a rich variety of disparate trends, movements, and styles, all of which have provided us with wonderful music. Finding common denominators is difficult.

Several pieces in List D employ aesthetic models from previous centuries: Palmgren's *May Night* and Scriabin's *Prelude in G Flat* are reminiscent of the 19th century, and Ravel's *Menuet* from *Le tombeau de Couperin* uses an early 18th-century form. The syncopated rhythm in Debussy's *Golliwogg's Cake-walk* is rooted in early jazz, and Morel's *Ronde enfantine* has the flavor of an updated children's folk tune. As in all music, characterization and expression are foremost considerations. The crucial question for student-teacher discussion is "What is the composer expressing?"

S. Palmgren (1878-1951): *May Night, Op. 27, No. 4* (R87)

Background Information

Selim Palmgren was a Finnish composer and pianist who taught at the Sibelius Academy in Helsinki. *May Night* is one of his most famous piano compositions. The sonorities evoke an intriguing image of a calm spring evening.

Exploring the Score

- What markings in the score support the calm mood?
- Palmgren's dynamic indications are precise. Notice the groups of measures with no dynamic indication. Does the resulting constant, uninflected dynamic level lend a sense of calm?
- The stepwise eighth-note figure in mm. 2, 14, and 29 marks the beginnings of sections.
- Notice the different chord structures in the accompaniment of each section:
  - A (mm 1-12): 7th chords
  - A₁ (mm. 13-27): octave chords
  - A₂ (mm. 28-32): triads
  - coda (mm. 33-36): octave chords

As you play through the piece, find places where the harmonies resolve to a feeling of tonal center. What feeling is evoked when there is no sense of tonality?

Practice Suggestions

The reading difficulties and technical control of the chords are at odds with the quiet mood of this piece. Identify different types of chords and chord relationships, and make each one a special practice project. For example:

- In mm. 1-8, RH, play the bottom 3rd and then the top 3rd of each four-note chord. Identify the intervals (major or minor), and listen to the sound quality when these intervals are combined.
- In m. 18, LH, notice the movement of the outside voices.
- In m. 20, LH, find the common tone and the chromatic tones.
- In m. 22, RH, play pairs of chords, and note the chromatic top notes and the lower repeated notes.
- In m. 22, LH, practice chord pairs.

After you practice the chords hands separately, put the sections together. Play slowly and accurately.

The control of sound is crucial. In moments where the sounds mix and float, the hands can be quite equally balanced. At other times, certain voices need to be projected. For example, notice the *tenuto* notes in mm. 8-12.

The music is marked *con pedale sempre*. Are there clues in the score regarding pedal changes? How will you decide where to change the pedal?

M. Ravel (1875-1937): *Menuet* (R90)
Background Information
Menuet is a movement from Ravel's last solo piano composition, *Le tombeau de Couperin*, written in 1917. Gone is the lush Impressionism of many of Ravel's other piano works. *Le tombeau de Couperin* is characterized by refined textures, ornamentation, and imitation. The titles of the movements indicate that this suite was Ravel's tribute to the French Baroque harpsichord school: *Prélude, Fugue, Forlane, Rigaudon, Menuet, Toccata.*

Exploring the Score
Ornamentation is an important element of French Baroque keyboard style. Which beats does Ravel favor with his ornaments?

Notice the section marked *Musette*. A *musette* is a small French bagpipe popular in the 17th and 18th centuries. The term also describes an 18th-century dance piece characterized by a drone bass imitating the bagpipe.
- Can you find a drone in this section?
- Compare the *musette* melody in mm. 33-40 with the LH countermelody in mm. 73-80.

Notice the extended tones in the LH – the notes with an open-ended tie – (for example, mm. 9-16, 49-55, and 111-115). This marking indicates that there is no definite time for the release of the sound. Pedal in such a way that these sounds do not end abruptly.

Teaching Suggestions
Ravel has provided meticulous markings indicating articulation, phrasing, ornamentation, dynamics, and pedaling. There are very few notes without an indication of some kind. Ravel's precision and detail must become our teaching and performance mandate.
- Discuss each marking with the student and experiment with the subtleties of sound.
- When the hands have different phrasings, practice hands separately at first.
- The harmonies should be clear. In general, change the pedal with each change of harmony.

Practice Suggestions
Play the ornaments on the beat. Make them quick and precise and with a slight accent on the first note. Play the lower note with the first note of the ornament. Experiment with fingerings. Fast and clear is the goal.

The *musette* theme is played in the RH (mm. 33-40) and then divided between the hands (mm. 41-48). Both versions should have the same sound. How can you perfect the *legato* quality of the chords?

C. Debussy (1862-1918): *Golliwogg's Cake-walk* (R94)
Background Information
Golliwogg's Cake-walk is the last piece of *Children's Corner*, a collection of piano pieces Debussy dedicated to his three-year-old daughter, Chouchou (Claude-Emma). A golliwogg was a black puppet-doll, a popular toy in Debussy's day. The cake-walk is a high-stepping, strutting dance associated with the American minstrel shows which were extremely popular in Europe during the early years of the 20th century. Syncopated, ragtime rhythms were familiar to Debussy because of the popularity of American jazz in Paris.

Exploring the Score
The indication *avec une grande emotion* (with great emotion, m. 61) seems out of place in this light-hearted, high-stepping piece. The melody in this section is a short but well-known quotation from Wagner's opera *Tristan und Isolde*, and expresses Debussy's ridicule of the late German Romantic style. The *staccato* chords in mm. 63-64 and 67-68 sound like scoffing laughter.

Debussy has marked his score carefully. Nothing is left in doubt.
- How many notes are connected in mm. 1 and 3?
- What is the loudest note in mm. 1, 2, and 3?
- Sometimes these precise indications demand musical ingenuity. For example, how will you hold the half-note chord of m. 63 and still play *staccato* eighth notes? [pedal]

Teaching Suggestions
Articulation is a major clue to the success of this dance. Before assigning the piece, devise scale or five-finger pattern exercises using some of the articulation patterns (for example, m. 1).

This bouncy dance requires light but careful pedaling.
- Where would you add pedal for color?
- Where would you add pedal for connection?

- What measures would be impossible to play as notated without use of the pedal?

When there is conflict between an articulation marking and a pedal implication (that is, the length of a note), the "long note wins." For example:
- In m. 71, LH, the half-note D flat can only be held with the pedal. This means the RH top melody notes will not sound clearly articulated.
- In mm. 85-86, the pedal will hold the half notes tied from the previous measure while the RH plays the three-note motive. This means the motive will not sound *staccato*.

Play along with the student at a second piano or in a higher octave. The degree of your accents, dynamic contrasts, and detached quality will be a helpful guide for the student. The *Celebration Series* recording is also a useful sound model.

Practice Suggestions
Practice slowly for absolute accuracy and attention to details of articulation, dynamics, and pedaling.
- In mm. 1-4, most of the notes are *staccato*. Which notes are *legato*? Hold the quarter notes in mm. 2 and 3 for their full value. Release the key exactly on the new downbeat.
- In mm. 10-12, the melody is *mezzo forte* and the accompaniment is *piano*. Exaggerate the dynamics in practice, especially the *piano* accompanying chords. Release the RH syncopated eighth note with the LH eighth-note chord.

Practice the grace notes and chords in mm. 47-59 as follows:
1. Block the grace notes with the 3rds or chords. Release all notes together, *staccato*.
2. Play the grace note and only the top *staccato* note with a slight flick of the hand.
3. Play as written, using a fast hand rotation.

A. Scriabin (1872-1915): *Prelude in G Flat, Op. 11, No. 13* (R99)
Background Information
Scriabin and Rachmaninoff were students together at the Moscow Conservatory, and both composers' styles can be described as late Romantic. Their music is filled with intense expression and colorful harmonies. Scriabin's *Preludes, Op. 11* follow the same key scheme that Chopin used for his *Preludes, Op. 28*. *Prelude in G Flat* is an example of Scriabin's early style, which was strongly influenced by Chopin.

Exploring the Score
Accompaniment figures such as the one in this prelude often include two voices. Find the implied bass line in the lowest bass notes:

This prelude has an AA$_1$BA form and Scriabin uses two rhythmic ideas:
- The rhythm of mm. 1-4 moves the long phrase forward.
- The rhythm of mm. 5-6 is motivic.

Compare the rhythmic structure of the first half of the piece (mm. 1-18) with that of the second half (mm. 19-35). In the second half of the piece, Scriabin reverses the order of the two rhythmic ideas. He uses the motivic rhythm in mm 19-23 and the long phrase in mm. 24-31.

Teaching Suggestions
The LH accompaniment must be carefully shaped.
- Have students identify sub-phrases – places where a singer might catch a quick breath – and shape the sub-phrases to enhance the flexibility and musical function of the eighth-note line.
- In measures where the bass line is obvious (for example, mm. 14-18), practice the LH part divided between the hands.

At first, have students practice the LH alone, without pedal, for *legato* control. To help students develop quick, quiet pedal work, have them change the damper pedal on every beat, depressing the pedal only halfway down. Although they will not pedal the entire piece this way, this practice will help them develop pedal control.

Practice Suggestions
Can you always hear the melody? Where is the peak of the phrase? These two questions are particularly important in this prelude.

The melody requires primary attention.
- In the first weeks of practice, exaggerate the dynamic levels so you can hear a distinctly different dynamic level for the melody, the bass line, and the inner voices.
- Isolate the melody and concentrate on subtle dynamic shaping.
- Listen for the balance of sound between the hands, and the voicing within the RH.

Listen to the *Celebration Series* recording.
- Is the melody approximately twice as loud as the accompaniment?

- How does the performer use *ritardando* to prepare for each new section?
- Listen also for the pedaling technique. The performer uses the pedal to enrich harmonies, extend bass tones, yet clarify the LH stepwise motion.

D. Kabalevsky (1904-1987): *Prelude No. 1, Op. 38, No. 1* (R100)

Background Information

Kabalevsky's compositions are among the most important 20th-century works for piano students. Kabalevsky, like Chopin and Scriabin, wrote preludes in all twenty-four major and minor keys. The first two preludes in Op. 38 illustrate the contrast to be found in Kabalevsky's cycle of preludes.

Exploring the Score

Examine the tempo marking, the dynamics, and the sound of the final measures. What mood do you expect to discover in this prelude?

- Look for textural changes which point to the form:

  Introduction   mm. 1-3

  A   mm. 4-12

  B   mm. 13-19

  A$_1$ mm. 20-27

- The opening is like a solo song. When does the alto assume a more active role? When does the LH shift from blocked harmonies into figuration?
- At m. 19, Kabalevsky might have repeated the C major theme (mm. 4-7). What does he choose instead? Is the C major theme ever restated? [mm. 25-26]

Teaching Suggestions

This is a highly Romantic piece. Approach the balance of sound, harmonic color, and *rubato* at phrase endings, as you would a Chopin prelude.

Pedaling will enhance color and variety of sound in this prelude, and the lack of pedal indications invites experimentation.

- Use the *Celebration Series* recording as a sound model.
- Find the defining low bass notes (there are very few). [mm. 4, 13, 18-19, 22-25, 27] How does the performer on the recording pedal those notes for length and emphasis?

Practice Suggestions

The double 6ths in mm. 16-18 are difficult. Try these practice suggestions:

1. Play the soprano line only, using the given fingering. Keep the thumb close to the hand, loose and relaxed.
2. Play the alto line, using only the thumb.
3. Play the voices together in short groups, stopping on each beat. Aim for a convincing *legato* sound. Practice first without pedal to concentrate on *legato* articulation.

D. Kabalevsky (1907-1987): *Prelude No. 2, Op. 38, No. 2* (R102)

Exploring the Score

Prelude No. 2 is almost entirely in 2/4 meter.

Find the measures which are not in 2/4. Does Kabalevsky use these meter changes consistently?

Find the contrasting material and label the form. [AA$_1$BA] How many presentations of the A material are there? Are they alike?

What is the key relationship between this prelude and Kabalevsky's *Prelude Op. 38, No. 1?* If possible, look at scores of the Chopin *Preludes, Op. 28*, the Scriabin *Preludes, Op. 11*, and J.S. Bach's *The Well-Tempered Clavier*. Do the first two preludes in these cycles have the same key relationship?

Teaching Suggestions

The chords in mm. 1-4 are marked *piano* and *staccato*. The accented chords in m. 5 are marked *forte* and *marcato*. Have the student experiment with and verbalize the different techniques needed to produce these two articulations.

Practice Suggestions

What an enjoyable piece to play and practice! The marking *Scherzando* is appropriate for music which includes a variety of contrasting sounds.

- Practice the *staccato* chords hands separately. How *staccato* do you want these chords to sound? Can you "peck" at the keys with small hand motions?
- In m. 5, lift the hand just before the thirty-second notes.
- Keep the LH sixteenth-note figure in mm. 1-4 and 29-31 even, and shape it with a slight *diminuendo*.
- There is a repeating pattern in the LH sixteenth notes of mm. 11-14. Memorize the notes and fingering, then add the RH.

B. Bartók (1881-1945): *Bear Dance* (R104)
Background Information
Bartók ranks foremost among 20th-century composers who wrote for young pianists. His pieces provide technical and musical development, present folk materials, and acquaint the student with contemporary compositional techniques. *Bear Dance* is the final piece in *Ten Easy Pieces*, one of Bartók's many collections for the developing pianist.

In the early years of the 20th century, Béla Bartók and Zoltán Kodály began research that revealed a treasure of folk music and provided a basis for a re-evaluation of Hungarian folk music. Among the thousands of songs they recorded and transcribed, they distinguished two styles. Tunes from the older style have similarities with musical traditions of Turkey and central Asia as well as with Gregorian chant. The newer style, described by Bartók as fresher and more vigorous, makes use of seven-note modes and regular phrase structures.

Exploring the Score
- Look for repetitions of the opening four measures. This pattern provides a clue to the form. Bartók uses it to separate the three main sections of the piece.
- Look for groups of major chords. Are they always in inversion?
- Look for groups of minor chords. Are they always in inversion?
- Look for chords constructed of 4ths.

Teaching Suggestions
Think of a scene at the circus. The drum roll starts. The bear lumbers into the ring and starts his awkward dance. The ringmaster snaps his whip. Several times the bear almost stops, as if he had forgotten the routine. Then the drum starts again and the dance begins anew, complete with the crack from the ringmaster's whip. At the end of the act, the bear leaves the ring and the lights dim. Have your student relate this story to the different sections of the piece.

Practice Suggestions
The rhythm is straightforward. The basic unit of a half note is divided into four eighth notes to provide the *ostinato*.
- Practice a LH scale, playing each note four times with a **4-3-2-1** fingering.
- Play hands separately, then hands together. Keep the hand relaxed but ready to play the next group of eighth notes.

There are two advantages to changing fingers on repeated notes:
1. It coordinates the hand movement with the half-note beat unit.
2. It makes more efficient use of the piano action.

Here are some suggestions for learning the chords:
- The rolled chords are marked with a wedge. Play them with an accent on the top note.
- Find sets of "look-alike" chords (for example, the descending chords in mm. 7-8, 27-28, 31-32, and 67-68) and practice them together.

Practice chords in two- or four-measure groups (for example, mm. 5-8).
1. Play the rhythm as written, hands together, on the closed keyboard cover.
2. Still on the closed keyboard cover, play the rhythm in the RH and quarter notes in the LH.
3. On the piano, play the melody (the top notes of the chords) with the LH quarter notes.
4. Play the section as written.

F. Morel (1926-): *Ronde enfantine* (R108)
Background Information
Canadian composer François Morel studied composition with Claude Champagne. He was one of the first Quebec musicians to be educated exclusively at the Conservatoire de Musique du Québec à Montreal. (Many of his contemporaries spent a portion of their student years in Paris.) His earlier writing shows influences of Debussy, Ravel, and Bartók. Morel was also strongly influenced by Varèse with whom he had contact in the late 1950s. In later years, Morel has explored both twelve-tone technique and non-serial writing. *Ronde enfantine* is an early work, written in 1949.

Exploring the Score
The title of this piece implies simplicity.
- Label the sections of this piece. What is the form? [rondo]
- How does Morel achieve a simple, childlike quality? [short phrases, repetition, limited melodic range]
- How does Morel introduce variety? [changing sonorities, varying the range] Notice the music-box effect in mm. 9-12 (*délicat et cristalin*) and the frequent clef changes.

Teaching Suggestions
As an introduction, have students learn to play the tunes by ear, and improvise different styles of accompaniment (for example, *ostinato*, traditional harmonies, whole-tone, or pentatonic background).

Look for patterns in Morel's accompaniments.
- Memorize the pattern in 7ths in mm. 1-2.
- Memorize the pattern in 9ths in m. 5.
- Analyze and play the pattern of expanding intervals in mm. 9-10. Can the student memorize the pattern?
- Play the *staccato* quarter-note accompaniment in mm. 26-40. Memorize the final notes of each group (C, F, C, F, etc.).

Practice Suggestions
Since each section of this rondo is different, use a special practice approach for each section. For example:
- In mm. 1-4, block the 7ths. Once you have memorized these, add the falling 3rds.
- Students with small hands may have to break the LH 9ths in mm. 5-8. Play the lowest LH bass tone on the beat, with the RH chord.
- How will you practice the articulation and rhythmic figures in mm. 13-17 and 26-40?

L. Weiner (1885-1960): *Fox Dance* (R111)
Background Information
Leo Weiner's *Fox Dance* and Béla Bartók's *Bear Dance* provide an excellent opportunity to compare two streams of Hungarian folk music. Leo Weiner studied with Bartók. He became a highly respected teacher of composition and chamber music at the Liszt Academy in Budapest. Weiner's music (like that of composers such as Hubay and Dohnányi) has its roots in the German Romantic tradition. *Fox Dance* shows the influence of Brahms, who also had an interest in Hungarian music.

Have students compare *Fox Dance* and *Bear Dance*. If possible, play recordings of other works by Bartók and Weiner and also of the Brahms *Hungarian Dances*. (The *Celebration Series* includes a number of Bartók compositions based on folk tunes.)

Performing folk music from other cultures is a broadening venture. The true rhythmic nuance of folk music is often difficult to notate in a score, yet this rhythmic flexibility is important to the flavor of the musical experience. On the *Celebration Series* recording of this piece, the performer sometimes starts a phrase below tempo and accelerates. Some cadences are stretched, and some accents are especially pronounced. Mark these articulations and tempo variations in the score. This performance can be a short lesson in Hungarian musical style.

Exploring the Score
- Find all the appearances of the opening theme. Are they all exact repeats? What changes does Weiner make?
- Look at the rhythmic design of the other themes. Do any of them stress syncopation? (Syncopation is often found in dance music.)
- How often can you find this rhythm at cadences?

Fox Dance has strong modal implications. The tonal center is D and the music has a minor sound, but there are no B flats until m. 67. The cadences create strong tonal centers. Identify the tonal center at each cadence.

Teaching Suggestions
This piece is an exciting venture into spirited, unrestrained expression. A number of pieces in Level 9 require a large hand span. The fast position changes of the octave chords pose a special challenge.

- Have the student listen to the *Celebration Series* recording while following the score, and mark in performance suggestions.
- On the closed keyboard cover, demonstrate the playing of extended positions (for example, LH mm. 1-4, RH mm. 3-4). Avoid consecutive downward motions.

Practice Suggestions
- Include octave scales in your daily practice routine. Play *staccato* one-octave scales in this rhythm:

- Practice LH octave broken-chord figures (see m. 56).
- When you practice this piece, aim for the shortest possible *staccato*.

R. M. Schafer (1933-): *Polytonality* (R114)
Background Information
Canadian composer and author R. Murray Schafer has a widely varied background. As a student, he was drawn equally to painting and composition. His literary studies include medieval German poetry and the works of Marshall McLuhan and Ezra Pound. As a composer, he has drawn upon the philosophy, literature, mythology, ritual, and symbolism of different times and peoples. Schafer taught at Memorial University in Newfoundland

and Simon Fraser University in British Columbia. While at Simon Fraser, he established the World Soundscape Project, dedicated to the study of the acoustical environment. Schafer's recent works, involving large numbers of musicians in outdoor settings, also reflect this interest. Schafer's work in music education includes not only a variety of compositions for young musicians but also writings on the development of an awareness for sound.

The title *Polytonality* implies a juxtaposition of keys, but this is only part of the story. The relaxed mood and the humor of this piece provide a pleasant and entertaining experience for the listener.

Exploring the Score

The LH churns out its *ostinato*, as if indifferent to the RH activities going on around it.

- What two harmonies comprise this *ostinato*?
- Where does the music become polytonal?
- Have the student label the chords in m. 37. How do the LH and RH chords relate?

Teaching Suggestions

The piece is dominated by repetition. There are only a few dynamic markings and one tempo change (the *poco ritardando* and *a tempo* in mm. 40-41). Look for opportunities to add your own interpretive touches. For example:

- Look for elements of contrast.
- Find other places where you can use a *poco ritenuto* to highlight the end of a section.
- Find places where a change of dynamics would be appropriate. Will the changes be sudden or gradual?
- Notice the articulation. Schafer uses *staccato* articulations sparingly, but they are crucial to the humor of the music.
- What other elements contribute to the humor?

PIANO STUDIES ALBUM 9

The order of the studies in the book is a reasonable order of difficulty, representing a consistent increase in technical demands. This reference list includes correlations with selections from *Repertoire Album 9* as suggestions for study.

Page	Study	Technical Elements	Repertoire Album Correlation
S4	Felix Mendelssohn: Study No. 1: Song without Words, Op. 102, No. 3	✔ *staccato* notes and chords ✔ wrist gestures ✔ groups of three eighth notes	D. Scarlatti: Sonata in C Major L 104/K 159 F.J. Haydn: Sonata in D Major Hob. XVI:37 (First Movement)
S6	Moritz Moszkowski: Study No. 2: Op. 91, No. 6	✔ scales in 3rds and 6ths ✔ direction changes	D. Scarlatti: Sonata in D Minor L 413/K 9; Sonata in C Major L 104/K 159
S8	George Frideric Handel: Study No. 3: Lesson, HWV 496	✔ two independent voices ✔ sixteenth-note groupings ✔ repeated notes	J.S. Bach: Sinfonia No. 3 in D Major, BWV 789; Sinfonia No. 15 in B Minor, BWV 801; Fugue in E Minor, BWV 855
S11	Felix Mendelssohn: Study No. 4: Song without Words, Op. 85, No. 1	✔ melody *vs* accompaniment ✔ entwined melody and accompaniment ✔ two-against-three rhythm ✔ LH plays harp-like triplets	F. Mendelssohn: Song without Words, Op. 38, No. 6 (Duetto)
S14	Edward MacDowell: Study No. 5: Dance of the Gnomes, Op. 39, No. 6	✔ fast tempo ✔ three-note slurs ✔ persistent ✔ repetitious	F.J. Haydn: Sonata in D Major, Hob. XVI:37 (First Movement)

PIANO STUDIES ALBUM 9 (cont'd)

Page	Study	Technical Elements	Repertoire Album Correlation
S18	George Frideric Handel: Study No. 6: Prelude, HWV 428	✔ improvisatory style ✔ scales and arpeggios ✔ *rubato*	J.S. Bach: Prelude in C Minor, BWV 847
S20	Stephen Heller: Study No. 7: Op. 47, No. 24	✔ melodic projection ✔ voicing within the hand ✔ clear pedaling ✔ entwined melody and accompaniment	L. van Beethoven: Six Easy Variations in G Major, WoO 77 R. Schumann: Romance in F Sharp, Op. 28, No. 2 W.A. Mozart: Sonata in G Major, KV 283 (189h) (Second Movement)
S22	Niels Gade: Study No. 8: Scherzo, Op. 19, No. 2	✔ RH ascending scale, descending arpeggio, broken chord pattern, turn figure ✔ three-note figure ✔ LH broken-chord pattern	L. van Beethoven: Six Easy Variations in G Major, WoO 77 W.A. Mozart: Sonata in G Major, KV 283 (189h) (Second and Third Movements)
S24	Edward MacDowell: Study No. 9: Shadow Dance, Op. 39, No. 8	✔ scale with change of direction ✔ *ostinato* accompaniment ✔ two-against-three rhythm ✔ fast tempo, soft dynamics ✔ requires attention to wrist action	L.-C. Daquin: Le coucou (Rondeau) F.J. Haydn: Sonata in D Major, Hob. XVI:37 (First Movement)
S28	Béla Bartók: Study No. 10: Bagatelle, Op. 6, No. 2	✔ coordination of dissimilar figures ✔ *staccato* ✔ leaps and direction changes ✔ wide dynamic contrasts	D. Kabalevsky: Prelude No. 2, Op. 38, No. 2 B. Bartók: Bear Dance
S30	Moritz Moszkowski: Study No. 11: Op. 91, No. 5	✔ LH sixteenth-note passagework ✔ endurance and fingering challenges ✔ RH three- and four-note chords	J.S. Bach: Prelude in E Minor, BWV 855 D. Kabalevsky: Prelude No. 2, Op. 38, No. 2
S32	Alexander Scriabin: Study No. 12: Prelude for the Left Hand, Op. 9, No. 1	✔ melodic projection ✔ pedal ✔ balance between entwined melody and accompaniment	F. Mendelssohn: Song without Words, Op. 38, No. 6 (Duetto) S. Palmgren: May Night, Op. 27, No. 4 R. Schumann: Romance in F Sharp, Op. 28, No. 2 A. Scriabin: Prelude in G Flat, Op. 11, No. 13
S34	Edward MacDowell: Study No. 13: Arabesque, Op. 39, No. 4	✔ fast and light, requires endurance ✔ repeated blocked patterns ✔ octaves ✔ chromatic scale in double 4ths	R. Schumann: Whims, Op. 12, No. 4

Page	Study	Technical Elements	Repertoire Album Correlation
S38	Moritz Moszkowski: Study No. 14: Op. 91, No. 20	✔ *legato* double 3rds and 6ths ✔ balance and voicing ✔ melody *vs* accompaniment	J.S. Bach: Fugue in C Minor, BWV 847 C. Debussy: Golliwogg's Cake-walk D. Kabalevsky: Prelude No. 1, Op. 38, No. 1 A. Scriabin: Prelude in G Flat, Op. 11, No. 13

Students require a variety of technical demands to stimulate technical growth. Fast passagework does not develop control of voicing, finger activity does not develop hand and arm movement. Hand and foot coordination varies with the tempo of the music.

Piano Studies Album 9 provides a wide variety of technical challenges. Two points deserve restatement:
1. These pieces are more than drills. Although they are included in a collection of studies, these selections are piano literature. They deserve the same musical investigation and refined interpretation as the pieces in the *Repertoire Album*. Listening to the *Celebration Series* recording of these pieces reinforces this attitude.
2. Each study affords teachers and students an opportunity to investigate the technical approach. This approach is similar to methods used for teaching repertoire. We find the difficult spots and show students how to practice and solve those problems. The composers of these studies explore one or two technical ideas in each piece. In so doing, they invite us to discover clues to make that technical idea easy, efficient, and interesting.

The following discussions focus briefly on the technical approach of each piece.

F. Mendelssohn (1809-1847): *Study No. 1: Song without Words, Op. 102, No. 3* (S4)
It is important to find a wrist movement for the groups of three eighth notes. Have your student practice the following preparatory exercises hands separately and hands together.

1. While playing a triplet pattern, move the wrist up and down without lifting the fingertips from the keys:

wrist up   wrist down

2. Practice a drop-lift motion using the following patterns:

drop lift-ing   drop lift-ing   drop lift-ing

drop lift-ing drop lift-ing drop lift-ing *etc.*

The first note of the two-note slurs in mm. 9-10 should be slightly louder. To make this easier, lift the wrist on the *staccato* second note.

M. Moszkowski (1854-1925): *Study No. 2: Op. 91, No. 6* (S6)
Playing scales in intervals of a 10th, a 6th, or a 3rd between the hands is an important technique to master. This study includes scales in 3rds (mm. 1-2 and 9-10) and that's the easy part!

The unpredictable changes of direction present a greater challenge. When hands move in parallel motion (for example, in mm. 5-6), the problem can be solved with comfortable fingerings. When parallel and contrary motion are combined (for example, in mm. 3-4), the difficulties increase.

- Look for groups of notes in parallel motion. Stop on the last note of a group, and prepare your hand for the next group:

etc.

- Stop on the first eighth note of each group of three eighth notes.

- Dynamics are crucial to the effective interpretation of this piece. In practice, exaggerate the dynamic changes.

G.F. Handel (1685-1759): *Study No. 3: Lesson, HWV 496* (S8)

The figures and the texture in *Lesson* are typical of an Italian Baroque *concerto grosso* for strings – which complicates matters for the pianist.

The opening section (mm. 1-20) is unproblematic. The detached LH bass line requires only careful reading for changes of direction and fingering. The RH figures fall into five-finger patterns.

The second section (mm. 21-30) is more challenging. Use this preparatory drill to help students develop a hand motion for the repeated sixteenth notes:

and now you lift   and now you lift *etc.*

Although a change of fingers on the repeated notes may be desirable in mm. 21 and 23, finger changes seem impractical for mm. 25-28.

F. Mendelssohn (1809-1847): *Study No. 4: Song without Words, Op. 85, No. 1* (S11)

Who can resist the beauty of this piece? The RH melody is Mendelssohn at his finest. The LH harp-style accompaniment provides consistency and warmth of harmony.

The focus of this study is the independence of melody and accompaniment. The LH accompaniment must not disturb the beauty of the melody.
- Since the RH plays both melody and accompaniment tones, it will be helpful to practice only the accompaniment.
- Keep the LH crossings smooth, with no perceptible up-down motion of the wrist.
- To support the bass line, emphasize the low bass notes and make a slight *diminuendo* through the rest of the sixteenth-note figure.
- In mm. 3, 8, 9, and 11, there is a two-against-three rhythm. The footnote below the music explains Mendelssohn's intention. For rhythmic security, isolate these measures for special practice such as tapping on the closed keyboard cover.

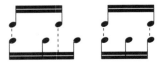

E. MacDowell (1860-1908): *Study No. 5: Dance of the Gnomes, Op. 39, No. 6* (S14)

The main challenge of this study is the three-note inverted mordent figure. As a preparatory drill, have students play scales with a mordent on each note, as quickly as possible. (On the *Celebration Series* recording, the sixteenth notes sound like grace notes.) The musical challenge is to group the mordent figures into four- and eight-measure phrases with appropriate dynamic shaping.

The *legato* octave theme (mm. 49-54, 57-62, 75-80, 83-87, and 91-96) provides technical relief. Make a strong contrast in mood and dynamics.

To play the LH B flat-A natural in mm. 69-70, roll the chord and use the pedal to hold the bass.

G.F. Handel (1685-1759): *Study No. 6: Prelude, HWV 428* (S18)

This Baroque prelude is written in the style of a warm-up improvisation, using the basic harmony of D minor and exploring various keyboard figures. Have the student find and label the scales and arpeggios.

Handel's rhythms are quite detailed. Students must study the rhythmic subdivisions carefully, but a performance of this study should sound like an improvisation. The *Celebration Series* recording illustrates a tasteful use of *rubato* to highlight changing harmonies and figures.

Smooth arm movement is essential for fluent arpeggio technique. Discuss a possible re-distribution of the hands on the arpeggios (for example, in mm. 11-12):

S. Heller (1813-1885): *Study No. 7: Op. 47, No. 24* (S20)

Stephen Heller's Op. 47, *Twenty-Five Studies for the Piano*, is subtitled *For Developing a Sense of Musical Rhythm and Expression*. Melodic projection, voicing within a hand, and clear pedaling are the primary elements in this study.

Slow practice will help students develop control of the voicing in the RH part.

- Play the RH of mm. 1-2, pausing on each melodic tone.
- Using wrist rotation, let the accompanying sixteenth notes push weight and tone into the melody notes (the eighth notes).
- Exaggerate the dynamic difference between melody and accompaniment.

N. Gade (1817-1890): *Study No. 8: Scherzo, Op. 19, No. 2* (S22)

This scherzo has five different technical figures:

- three-note figure (m. 1)
- RH ascending scale and descending arpeggio (mm. 5-6)
- LH broken pattern (mm. 10-13)
- RH turn figure (mm. 14-15)
- RH broken-chord pattern (mm. 27-28)

Isolate each figure for special practice.

The LH figure in mm. 10-13 forms a cross rhythm against the RH. Have the student practice the LH separately to establish the proper rolling motion. When the LH is secure, add the RH.

E. MacDowell (1860-1908): *Study No. 9: Shadow Dance, Op. 39, No. 8* (S24)

Shadow Dance is one of MacDowell's most popular character pieces. Hidden behind its attractive surface is an etude which exploits:

- scale figures (mm. 3-9)
- *ostinato* figures (mm. 11-18, 25-44)
- a two-against-three rhythm (mm. 45-48)

These figures cannot be executed at their ultimate speed and with ease if played only by the fingers. With your student, explore hand, wrist, and arm motions which will facilitate efficiency and ease of movement.

An oval motion of the wrist will make the direction changes in the figures easier to play. This is especially true at the top of RH scale figures and at the bottom of LH accompaniment figures. Try these two preparatory drills:

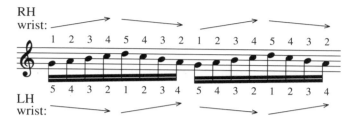

For the RH *ostinato* pattern, practice only the sixteenth notes, stopping on each high C sharp. Lifting the wrist aids the movement to the C sharp.

Here is a drill for the two-against-three rhythm in mm. 45-48.

1. Practice the notes where hands play together. Use the correct fingering.

2. Repeat, but this time, play the RH as written.
3. Repeat step 1. again, this time playing the LH as written.
4. Play both hands as written. Accent the main beats.

Practice the RH figure in mm. 49-52 in short units, starting on the thumb notes.

For the low bass pedal points in mm. 25-44, hold the pedal down for the duration of the tied notes.

B. Bartók (1881-1945): *Study No. 10: Bagatelle, Op. 6, No. 2* (S28)

Coordination of the dissimilar figures is the main challenge in this *Bagatelle*. Concentrate on mm. 3-6, 15-16, and 24-25. Have students practice these passages on the closed keyboard cover.

1. Practice hands separately. Use precise fingering and simulate interval relationships and the locations of black and white keys. Emphasize the tones that play full value.
2. Practice hands together, slowly.

M. Moszkowski (1854-1925): *Study No. 11: Op. 91, No. 5* (S30)

The focus of this study is clear passagework and LH endurance. The opening LH figure is calculated to involve crossings. To practice these figures:

1. Stop on the first sixteenth note of each beat, slightly raise the finger which starts the next group of sixteenth notes, then play to the next beat.
2. Continue this practice method in groups of eight sixteenth notes.
3. Continue in groups of sixteen sixteenth notes.

A. Scriabin (1872-1915): *Study No. 12: Prelude for the Left Hand, Op. 9, No. 1* (S32)

Although this study must be performed with the LH alone, students can play short sections with two hands to establish a sound model. The goal is to project the melody so convincingly that the piece sounds as if two hands were playing.

The LH thumb carries the main responsibility for the melody, and the pedal plays an important role.

- Listen for the length of pedal on low bass notes on the *Celebration Series* recording.
- Have students practice thumb-only scales and simple melodies, connecting the tones with the pedal.

Analyze the thumb movement by discussing the following questions with your student:

- Does the best tone quality result when the thumb plays starting from the key surface or when it is lifted?
- How high should the wrist be for best tone and control of the thumb?
- For best tone, play the thumb notes with a slight hand rotation.

E. MacDowell (1860-1908): *Study No. 13: Arabesque, Op. 39, No. 4* (S34)

In design, the word arabesque is used to describe an intricate, fanciful figure, based on geometrical patterns and using combinations of flowing lines, scrolls, and intertwined leaves. In music, an arabesque is a florid, melodic composition characterized by repeated patterns.

To play the repeated chords quickly with ease and endurance, avoid consecutive downward hand motions. Try this preparatory exercise for the opening figure, first hands separately, then hands together:

- On the closed keyboard cover, place the thumb behind the third finger nail joint. With the third finger, play repeated notes in the rhythm of m. 1, using a throw-and-lift action.

Here is an exercise for the RH figures in mm. 41-44:

- Start with the RH thumb on B double flat. Play quickly to the second beat.

Allow the arm to move the thumb from the white key to the black key as you lift the wrist. Concentrate on the thumb movement rather than on the top line.

M. Moszkowski (1854-1925): *Study No. 14: Op. 91, No. 20* (S38)

The key (G flat major) and the many accidentals make this study difficult to read. The double 3rds and 6ths and the voicing make it technically challenging.

Fingering is the key to a successful performance of this study. Have students practice short groups with a focus on fingering. The short groups can be musical shapes such as the turn and the groups of three or four descending notes.

The *Celebration Series* recording provides a fine example of balance and voicing. Notice especially the projection of the melody in mm. 9-12.

LEVEL 9 CONCLUSION

The greatest gift we give to our students is a life-long enjoyment of playing the piano. In its own way, Level 9 has been that gift. Through Level 9, your student has traversed the musical centuries hand-in-hand with Bach, Handel, Mozart, Haydn, Beethoven, Chopin, Liszt, Grieg, and modern-day Russian, European, and North American composers. Your student has experienced the fascination and thrill of making music.

Our piano lessons provide an opportunity, for teacher and student alike, to explore beyond the printed note, to think more deeply about the music, to gain new insights, and to come closer to each composer's thoughts and musical intentions. Level 9 is also, in many ways, a gift to the teacher. Through investigation and involvement with this literature, we grow musically with our students. Our resources and our fund of information increase, and we enhance the musical richness that we can share with our students.

Level 10

The Publications

Level 10 of the *Celebration Series* includes the following publications:

> *Piano Repertoire Album 10*
> *Piano Studies Album 9 & 10* (level 10 only)
> Recording of *Repertoire and Studies 10*

The Repertoire

The *Piano Repertoire Album 10* is divided into five lists:

- List A includes a selection of pieces composed during the Baroque period (*ca* 1600 to *ca* 1750).
- List B includes a selection of pieces composed during the Classical period (*ca* 1750 to *ca* 1820).
- List C includes a selection of pieces from the Romantic era (*ca* 1820 to *ca* 1910).
- List D includes a selection of works composed during the late 19th and early 20th centuries.
- List E explores more recent 20th-century repertoire.

Musical Development

Piano Repertoire Album 10 and *Piano Studies Album 10* contain the most difficult material in the *Celebration Series*. The teacher can appreciate the years of investment necessary to bring the student to this advanced level. The student's experience, progressing from level to level, is similar to climbing. The higher the climb, the more expansive the musical view. With this final step of the ascent, the musical horizon stretches even wider. The list of composers in the *Piano Repertoire Album 10* and the *Piano Studies Album 10* includes the greatest composers of piano literature.

Organization of Level 10

As in Level 9, the discussion of Level 10 is not divided into Study Modules, but rather follows the five Lists of the *Repertoire Album* (A, B, C, D, and E). The pieces are discussed in the order in which they appear in the *Repertoire Album*.

For each list, there is a suggested order of difficulty, a brief general discussion of the stylistic characteristics, and individual discussions of the pieces under the following headings:

- *Background Information:* general stylistic or biographical information

- *Exploring the Score:* suggested material for student-teacher discussions
- *Teaching Suggestions:* addressed to the teacher
- *Practice Suggestions:* addressed to the student

Teachers can determine the order of repertoire assigned, based on the individual student's needs and study program. Teachers are encouraged to formulate units of study, integrating pieces of contrasting style periods from the *Repertoire Album* and the *Studies Album*.

The *Celebration Series* does not include a *Student Guide* for Level 10. It is our hope that the following discussions will facilitate your teaching of this repertoire, provide material for fruitful discussions between you and your students, and increase their musical enjoyment and awareness.

The Studies

The studies are discussed separately at the end of this section. The pieces in the *Studies Album* are similar in purpose to the Chopin *Études*. Although each piece has a specific technical focus, these studies have noteworthy musical value and can be considered as repertoire. To assist your choice of appropriate works, the authors have provided a suggested order of difficulty and a chart showing the types of technical figures encountered in these studies.

The Recordings

The *Celebration Series* recording of all pieces in this Level is a valuable teaching resource. This professional recording provides a sound model, a pedagogical element which words cannot communicate. Listening to the recording with the student can stimulate discussion on topics such as articulation, balance and dynamics, expressive timing (*rubato*), pedaling, accentuation, and expressive nuances. You may wish to make listening a regular part of the student's assignment.

The following chart lists the repertoire and studies in Level 10 according to the order of the *Repertoire* and *Studies Albums*. Page numbers for works in the *Piano Repertoire Album 10* and the *Piano Studies Album 10* are found in the first column.

Page	Composer	Title
Piano Repertoire Album 10		
List A – Baroque		
R4	Johann Sebastian Bach	Prelude and Fugue in F Major, BWV 856
R8	Johann Sebastian Bach	Prelude and Fugue in F Sharp Major, BWV 858
R12	Johann Sebastian Bach	Prelude and Fugue in C Minor, BWV 871
List B – Classical		
R16	Franz Joseph Haydn	Sonata in D Major, Hob. XVI:51
R25	Wolfgang Amadeus Mozart	Sonata in F Major, KV 280 (189e)
R38	Ludwig van Beethoven	Sonata in C Minor, Op. 10, No. 1
List C – Romantic		
R53	Robert Schumann	The Prophet Bird, Op. 82, No. 7
R56	Franz Schubert	Moment musical, Op. 94, No. 4
R60	Frédéric Chopin	Prélude, Op. 45
R64	Frédéric Chopin	Mazurka, Op. 63, No. 1
R67	Felix Mendelssohn	Song without Words, Op. 67, No. 4 (Spinning Song)
R72	Franz Liszt	Valse oubliée, n° 1
R78	Johannes Brahms	Intermezzo, Op. 116, No. 6
R80	Johannes Brahms	Intermezzo, Op. 76, No. 6
List D – Late Romantic and Impressionist		
R83	Sergei Rachmaninoff	Elegy, Op. 3, No. 1
R88	Alexander Scriabin	Prélude, Op. 11, No. 14
R90	Claude Debussy	Prélude, Book I, No. 1 (Danseuses de Delphes)
R92	Claude Debussy	Prélude, Book II, No. 5 (Bruyères)
R96	Maurice Ravel	Prélude
R101	Manuel de Falla	The Miller's Dance
List E – Contemporary		
R104	Dmitri Kabalevsky	Prelude, Op. 38, No. 15
R106	Dmitri Kabalevsky	Prelude, Op. 38, No. 20
R108	Maurice Dela	Hommage
R114	Béla Bartók	Bagatelle, Op. 6, No. 11
R116	Béla Bartók	Bagatelle, Op. 6, No. 12
R119	Barbara Pentland	Shadows
R122	Pierre Gallant	Six Variations on "Land of the Silver Birch"
R128	François Morel	Étude de sonorité, n° 1
R132	Olivier Messiaen	Prélude, n° 7 (Plainte calme)
R134	Robert Fleming	Sonatina
Piano Studies Album 10		
S39	Felix Mendelssohn	Study No. 1: Song without Words, Op. 30, No. 5
S42	Stephen Heller	Study No. 2: Op. 81, No. 10
S44	Anatoli Lyadov	Study No. 3: A Trifle, Op. 2, No. 12
S46	Albert Loeschhorn	Study No. 4: Op. 67, No. 5
S48	George Frideric Handel	Study No. 5: Passacaglia
S51	Frédéric Chopin	Study No. 6: Trois nouvelles études, n° 3
S54	Edward MacDowell	Study No. 7: Hungarian, Op. 39, No. 12
S58	Felix Mendelssohn	Study No. 8: Song without Words, Op. 102, No. 4
S61	Camille Saint-Saëns	Study No. 9: Prelude for the Left Hand, Op. 135, No. 1
S64	Moritz Moszkowski	Study No. 10: Op. 72, No. 4
S68	Alexander Scriabin	Study No. 11: Op. 2, No. 1
S70	Sergei Rachmaninoff	Study No. 12: Étude-Tableau, Op. 33, No. 8
S74	Camille Saint-Saëns	Study No. 13: Study in Rhythm, Op. 52, No. 4
S78	Béla Bartók	Study No. 14: Bagatelle, Op. 6, No. 5

LIST A – BAROQUE

Suggested Order of Difficulty

Page	Composer	Title
R4	Johann Sebastian Bach	Prelude and Fugue in F Major, BWV 856
R8	Johann Sebastian Bach	Prelude and Fugue in F Sharp Major, BWV 858
R12	Johann Sebastian Bach	Prelude and Fugue in C Minor, BWV 871

The preceding list assumes that each prelude and fugue in a particular key will be taught as a unit. If the prelude and the fugue are taught separately, then the suggested order of difficulty is:

Page	Composer	Title
R12	Johann Sebastian Bach	Prelude in C Minor, BWV 871
R8	Johann Sebastian Bach	Prelude in F Sharp Major, BWV 858
R4	Johann Sebastian Bach	Prelude in F Major, BWV 856
R6	Johann Sebastian Bach	Fugue in F Major, BWV 856
R10	Johann Sebastian Bach	Fugue in F Sharp Major, BWV 858
R14	Johann Sebastian Bach	Fugue in C Minor, BWV 871

When comparing the difficulty of these preludes and fugues, consider the following elements:
- the number of voices (especially for fugues)
- the contrapuntal complexity
- the key (for ease of reading and playing)
- the ornamentation

One characteristic of Baroque music is the unity of character and mood within a composition. Consistency of articulation helps achieve that unity. Fingering and articulation are inseparable musical partners. Careful attention to articulation in the early learning stages lays a firm foundation. Here is a practice strategy for contrapuntal textures:
1. Determine the articulation for the subject.
2. Determine a contrasting articulation for the countersubject or accompanying material.
3. Practice short sections, hands separately, to determine fingering.
4. Practice short sections, hands together. Use a layered approach to build coordination. Begin by practicing one voice and add the others one at a time.

If possible, arrange for your students to play these preludes and fugues on a harpsichord so that they can experience the unique touch and sound of that instrument. A harpsichordist can use subtle timing and articulation (instead of dynamic accent) to create the impression of meter and beat emphasis.

See Level 9 for a list of terms used in the discussion of fugues.

These preludes and fugues are printed in their unedited, original version. Since no tempo, dynamic, or articulation indications are given, you and your student must determine the appropriate tempo and performance style from a study of elements such as figuration, subdivisions of the beat, ornaments, and texture. The *Celebration Series* recording provides a useful model.

J.S. Bach (1685-1750): *Prelude and Fugue in F Major, BWV 856* (R4, R6)
Background Information
Some pairs of preludes and fugues share a common mood and character. Others are highly contrasting. An essential function of an early keyboard prelude is to define the tonality of a following piece (for example, a motet, hymn, mass movement, *ricercar*, set of dances, or fugue). Most preludes are thematically unrelated to the music they preface. Before Bach's time, a number of composers (including Andrea and Giovanni Gabrieli and Girolamo Frescobaldi) wrote collections of preludes in different keys. German organ preludes of the 17th century frequently ended with a short fugal section.

Both parts of Bach's *Prelude and Fugue in F Major* share dance-like characteristics. Articulation and tempo help highlight the mood.

Prelude in F Major (R4)
Exploring the Score
When students understand the direction and shape of the musical contour before playing, it is easier for them to learn the piece. Look at mm. 1 and 2, for example:
- Is the pattern of the sixteenth-note figure consistent? [yes, two-beat sequence]
- Is the pattern of the eighth-note figure consistent? [no]
- How do the directions of the eighth-note and sixteenth-note figures relate to each other? [contrary motion]

Examine the melodic contour of the RH sixteenth notes.
- In mm. 1-2, the pitches fall (F, E flat, D, C, B flat, A). In mm. 3-4, the pitches rise (B, C, C sharp, D).
- Find the highest pitch in the RH. [C in m. 15] How does Bach approach and leave that high note?

In his preludes, Bach establishes a key, modulates to related keys (frequently the dominant, subdominant, and relative major or minor), then returns to the tonic. He uses fluctuations in the speed of harmonic rhythm to provide intensity and contrast.
- How does Bach establish F major at the beginning of this prelude? [I-IV-V-I chord progression]
- Find that same harmonic progression in the relative minor, D minor. [mm. 6-8]
- Notice the intensification of harmonic movement in m. 18.
- Notice the dominant-tonic relations in mm. 3-4, 9-10, 12-13.

Teaching Suggestions
Articulation helps emphasize harmonic changes and rhythmic groupings. Explore different articulation patterns for the LH eighth notes. For example, begin each beat with a slur on the first two of each group of three eighth notes.

Practice Suggestions
The rising notes of the two-beat sixteenth-note figure provide forward motion into the following beat.
- Make a slight *crescendo* on these rising sixteenth notes.
- To hear the larger melodic contour, play the eighth-note figures as written with only the highest pitch of each sixteenth-note group.

There are no dynamics given in the score. Listen for dynamic balance between the trills and the other voice. Do not allow the trill to become too loud or overbearing.

Fugue in F Major (R6)
Exploring the Score
What does *Fuga à 3* mean? [fugue in 3 voices]

The subject of this fugue has an underlying stepwise motion:

- What harmonic progression is implied by the stepwise motion? [IV-I-V⁷-I]
- Locate all subject presentations.
- Notice Bach's use of *stretto* in the bass and alto (upbeat to m. 26-m. 31) and in all three voices (upbeat to m. 37-m. 44 and upbeat to m. 47-m. 53).

Teaching Suggestions
Help the student determine an articulation for the subject. Devise practice methods to check the consistency of the articulation in all voices. Some editors suggest a slur between the second and third eighth notes of the subject. Here are two further suggestions:

- Detach the eighth note before the sixteenth-note groups in mm. 2-3.
- Detach the eighth note before the syncopated quarter note in mm. 13, 14, and 15.

Practice Suggestions
Establish short practice units. Use this checklist as you practice:
- correct fingering
- consistant articulation
- practice each voice separately
- practice two voices
- practice all three voices

J.S. Bach (1685-1750): *Prelude and Fugue in F Sharp Major, BWV 858* (R8)
Background Information
In Bach's time, keyboard instruments were tuned so that intervals on white keys were acoustically pure, or perfect. Certain keys, such as F sharp major, sounded unbearably out of tune. Tempered tuning slightly adjusts all intervals so that they are equal. Bach's *Well-Tempered Clavier* is a practical example of the possibilities afforded by a new, tempered tuning system that made keyboard compositions in all keys possible.

Prelude in F Sharp Major (R8)
Exploring the Score
The melody of this prelude arises from the figuration, and its character from the luminous quality of the key of F sharp major. Notice the rhythmic consistency:
- Find the beats that are not divided into three sixteenth notes.
- What is the purpose of the thirty-second notes? What musical event follows each occurrence? [cadence]

Find and play places where the two voices are in parallel motion.

Find examples of contrary motion or changes of direction.

Bach avoids the subdominant (B) completely, but he pays considerable attention to the dominant, C sharp:
- In mm. 6-7, there is a cadence and thematic statement in C sharp major.
- In mm. 19-20, there is an extended dominant 7th harmony.
- In mm. 26-28, there is a C sharp pedal point.

This prelude also includes cadences in unusual keys:
- D sharp minor (submediant) in m. 12
- A sharp minor (mediant) in m. 15
- G sharp minor (supertonic) in m. 18

Teaching Suggestions
The cadences in this prelude are important landmarks. They are identified by the falling 5ths in the LH: mm. 6, 11-12, 15, 18, and 30. Discuss ways to make these cadences clear to the listener.

Reading a score in F sharp major can be a challenge. Have your students block the broken chords and intervals to help them read the notes correctly and make fingering choices. Circle the E sharps and the B sharp in the LH, m. 13.

Fugue in F Sharp Major (R10)
Exploring the Score
Bach had a remarkable ability to write in a thrifty manner. Here he uses an eighth rest to divide the subject into a head and a tail. Look for Bach's use of the following fragments extracted from the subject:

interval of a 4th   rhythmic motive   interval of a 3rd

- Challenge your student to find material in the fugue which is *not* related to motives presented in the subject and countersubject.
- Have your student prove that the accompanying material deserves the label *countersubject* because of its consistent use.

Teaching Suggestions
Consider the following articulation guidelines:
- Detach upbeats from strong beats.
- Use a *legato* articulation for stepwise motion.
- Detach wider intervals.

For example, in the subject, detach the first note and use a mixture of *legato* and detached articulation for the tail portion.

J.S. Bach (1685-1750): *Prelude and Fugue in C Minor, BWV 871* (R12, R14)

Background Information

Bach finished Book I of *The Well-Tempered Clavier* in 1722. In 1744 he completed Book II, a second collection of preludes and fugues in all twenty-four major and minor keys. The combined two sets are often referred to as the "Great 48." *Prelude and Fugue in C Minor, BWV 871* is the only work in the *Celebration Series* from Book II.

Prelude in C Minor (R12)
Exploring the Score

Discuss the following points with your student:

- Compare the form of this prelude with other binary-form preludes from *The Well-Tempered Clavier*. (A surprising number of preludes in *The Well-Tempered Clavier* are binary.)
- Look for Bach's use of sequence (for example, in mm. 3-7).
- Look for Bach's use of invertible counterpoint. (For example, in m. 1, the RH plays a sixteenth-note figure and the LH plays eighth notes. In m. 2, the hands exchange parts.)
- Notice the emphasis on E flat major (the relative major).
- Notice the chromatic bass line in mm. 17-18.

Teaching Suggestions

This prelude has a consistent sixteenth- and eighth-note texture. A detached articulation for the eighth notes will provide rhythmic energy and contrast.

- Experiment with sharply detached and slightly detached eighth notes, and compare the difference in mood.
- In mm. 1-3, the eighth notes falling on the beat form parallel motion with the sixteenth notes. Emphasize these eighth notes slightly.

Practice Suggestions

- Practice the measures in which the notes on the beat move by step (for example, mm. 1-2, 5-7, and 10-11).
- Practice the measures with sequences (for example, mm. 13-16, 19-20, and 23-24).
- For variety and technical control, practice the entire prelude with varied articulation. For example, play the sixteenth notes *staccato* and the eighth notes *legato*.

Fugue in C Minor (R14)
Exploring the Score

This fugue is the only four-voice fugue in the *Celebration Series*. Discuss the following contrapuntal devices with your student:

- Augmentation: In mm. 14-15 (tenor) and mm. 19-20 (bass), the subject is presented in note values twice the original length.
- Inversion: In mm. 15 and 21, the bass presents the subject upside down (inverted).
- *Stretto:* Notice the overlapping voices in the RH of mm. 16-17. Bach also uses *stretto* starting in m. 23 to add tension to the final measures.

The cadences in mm. 13-14 and 23 are especially prominent. What is the effect of the ensuing change in texture? [defines sections, prepares for augmentation, inversion, and *stretto*]

Practice Suggestions

In a four-voice fugue, each voice must maintain its individuality. This requires careful attention to details. Articulation is of primary importance. Follow these guidelines:

- Play approximately half the notes detached.
- Give each voice its proper articulation.
- Use a *legato* touch for stepwise motion. Use a detached articulation for wider intervals.

To learn a fugue, divide it into short practice units and use the following practice method:

1. Play two voices separately (for example, soprano and alto). Mark the articulation for each voice in the score.
2. Play those two voices together.
3. Add a third voice (tenor). First, play it separately and mark the articulation.
4. Play combinations of two voices (soprano and tenor, alto and tenor).
5. Play all three voices together.
6. Add the fourth voice, following the same procedure.

LIST B – CLASSICAL

Suggested Order of Difficulty

Page	Composer	Title
R16	Franz Joseph Haydn	Sonata in D Major, Hob. XVI:51
R25	Wolfgang Amadeus Mozart	Sonata in F Major, KV 280 (189e)
R38	Ludwig van Beethoven	Sonata in C Minor, Op. 10, No. 1

In Classical style, contrast is a principal element. Classical composers used forms with contrasting sections (ternary form, sonata form, rondo) featuring contrasting themes, keys, textures, and accompaniment patterns.

Music of the Classical period has a strong harmonic orientation and a homophonic texture (melody supported by harmonic accompaniment). Some harmonies have a natural tension and receive dynamic stress. Non-chord tones in the melody are a primary means of expression with a dynamic stress on the non-chord tone.

The phrase is the standard unit of construction. Music is described in terms of language: phrases, sentences, punctuation, inflection, accent, and emphasis.

The sonatas of the three great Classical composers provide the occasion for a comparison of their approaches to sonata form. The following general observations can act as the point of departure for your student to make a more detailed examination of the works of Haydn, Mozart, and Beethoven.
- Haydn is remarkable for the motivic development of his themes. He often chooses to continue a motive from his first theme in the second or closing theme, rather than have distinct thematic groups.
- Mozart is known for his proliferation of beautiful themes, each with a distinct character.
- Beethoven was (for a brief period) Haydn's student, and he carried many of Haydn's ideas to incredible creative lengths. In particular, Beethoven developed the idea of the motive as the core of thematic construction and elaboration. His sonata-form movements are lengthier than those of either Haydn or Mozart, with longer groups of themes and more extensive *codas*.

F.J. Haydn (1732-1809): *Sonata in D Major, Hob. XVI:51* (R16, R22)
Background Information
Haydn wrote approximately sixty-two piano sonatas. This *Sonata in D Major*, written in 1794, was one of the last. Haydn's later sonatas were written for the fortepiano, not for the harpsichord, and dynamic indications in this sonata clearly indicate his preference for the newer instrument.

Haydn's music has a creative, experimental quality. His compositions are filled with surprises and contrasts. The student who approaches this piece with a curiosity for what is different will project a meaningful interpretation. Exaggeration of unusual elements will help communicate Haydn's sense of humor to the listener.

First Movement – Andante (R16)
Exploring the Score
Haydn wrote at least eleven sonatas with only two movements. Look through the Haydn sonatas with your student to find other two-movement works. Haydn exhibits an innovative approach to form in many of his sonatas.
- Some first movements have elements of theme and variations.
- Others mix variation with rondo.
- Key contrast is always present, but some first movements have little thematic differentiation.

You might think of this *Andante* as a "Sonata-Form Shuffle" because Haydn presents the materials of the exposition, development, and recapitulation sections in a somewhat unexpected manner.

The opening fanfare of rolled half-note triads attracts attention. Haydn uses these chords again in mm. 44 and 80 to mark important moments in the

construction of the movement. This fanfare has a motivic relationship to other themes in the movement. Find other motives that include:
- units of three
- stepwise motion
- even rhythm

Examine the exposition (mm. 1-43), taking the following points into consideration:
- Look for musical contrast (for example, rhythm, accompaniment style, melodic direction). Find places where Haydn uses conjunct (stepwise) motion and disjunct (wider intervals) motion.
- Find the passages in D major (tonic) and in A major (dominant).
- Identify the function of mm. 20-25. [modulation to A major]

This is a relatively normal exposition with clear themes and tonal centers.

So far, so good. What happens next? The fanfare in mm. 44-45 introduces a new section, beginning in the home key. Is it a repeat of the exposition, or is it the development section? Haydn combines elements of both. Examine mm. 44-79:
- Trace the thematic material in this development section back to its origin in the exposition. (For example, m. 54 is from m. 26, m. 67 is from m. 20.)
- Can you identify any new material?
- If you were writing a development section for a sonata in D major, would you use sharp keys (which are closely associated with D major) or flat keys? Why?
- Name the tonal centers in mm. 62-69. [F major, B flat major]
- What is the purpose of the chromatic bass movement in mm. 69-73?

The final presentation of the fanfare theme in m. 80 introduces the recapitulation.
- Compare the lengths of the exposition and recapitulation.
- What portions of the exposition are given extended treatment in the recapitulation, and what portions are omitted?

Teaching Suggestions
Students will interpret a sonata movement convincingly when they realize the importance of contrast. Discuss how the composer creates contrast. For example, how does the second theme (mm. 26-41) contrast with the first theme?
- new key (A major)
- new articulation (light *staccato* notes)
- new figure (descending scale)

How does the modulation in mm. 23-25 create tension?
- loss of firm tonal foundation
- intensification of dynamics

Compare Haydn's dynamic and articulation markings in mm. 28, 29, and 35. Measure 29 is a repetition of the scale figure of m. 28, but the *forzato* indications break the scale into groups of three notes. In m. 35, the wedges are nearly superfluous, indicating a sharp release before the next (repeated) pitch.

Second Movement – Finale: Presto (R22)
Exploring the Score
Compare this triple-meter movement with some of Haydn's minuet movements. Notice the placement of the *sforzando* markings. The *sforzandi* do make this movement sound more like a Beethoven *scherzo* than an 18th-century minuet.
- What effect does Haydn achieve by accenting the third beat?
- Where does Haydn use *sforzandi* on the first beat?

Look for the repetitions and label the sections. What is the form of this movement? [rounded binary]

Practice Suggestions
Much of the success of this movement depends on clear execution of all details of articulation. Haydn provides explicit markings.
- Notice the frequent three-note groupings.
- Look for two-note groupings.
- Look for places where Haydn slurs the *sforzando* across the bar line
- Compare the LH of mm. 4-7 with mm. 8-11.

Make an articulation breath between slurred groups (for example, mm. 1-2 and 4-6). Notes not marked with slurs should be slightly detached. In Haydn's day, this slight detachment was referred to as "ordinary touch."

W.A. Mozart (1756-1791): Sonata in F Major KV 280 (189e) (R25, R30, R33)
Background Information
The outpouring of music from the young Mozart is astounding. In 1775, when Mozart wrote this sonata, he was nineteen years old and employed as concertmaster for the Prince Archbishop of Salzburg. However, he was bored with Salzburg and unhappy at court. In 1781, he settled in Vienna where he attempted to make a living as a free-lance composer, performer, and teacher.

The movements of a Classical sonata usually have contrasting forms. However, in this sonata, all three movements are in sonata-allegro form.

First Movement – *Allegro assai* (R25)
Exploring the Score

Music historians and critics frequently compare Mozart's piano sonatas with his operas. The contrasting themes are like contrasting characters in a drama. For example, consider how Mozart uses dynamics and articulation to give each theme an individual character or personality.

Rhythm is one factor that defines character in this movement. Notice how Mozart increases the subdivisions and rhythmic complexity to provide contrast:

mm. 1-2: quarter notes in both hands
mm. 3-4: quarter notes in RH, eighth notes in LH
mm. 7-8: sixteenth notes in both hands
mm. 8-9 and 11-12: syncopation in RH
mm. 13: triplet rhythm identifies a new section

- Are other rhythmic figures used in the movement?
- Analyze the lengths of phrases. Can you find examples of three-measure phrases?

Find places in the exposition where Mozart uses chromatic bass movement. [mm. 18-22 and 35-40] How does this chromaticism create contrast, tension, and color?

Practice Suggestions

Experiment with fingering for the triplet passages. A comfortable fingering for one pianist may not be the best choice for another. Find ways to reinforce your fingering:

- Say the finger numbers aloud as you play.
- Practice passages with a variety of touches, accentuations, and speeds.

Articulation is especially important. Read the score accurately. Mozart marks his music with meticulous care.

- Start short phrase groups with an emphasis (much like stressing the first syllable of a word).
- Make an articulation breath between slurred groups (for example, in mm. 28-29, 36, and 58).

Second Movement – *Adagio* (R30)
Exploring the Score

A mere analysis of themes and form and keys is a disservice to this movement. This music expresses a tender, yearning, pleading quality. Have students listen to the *Celebration Series* recording and also to a recording of the second movement of Mozart's *Piano Concerto in A Major, KV 488*, which uses a similar rhythmic motive.

This movement is in sonata form, with an exposition, a short development, and a recapitulation. The sections are clear to the eye and the ear.

- Examine the way in which Mozart creates his closing theme (mm. 21-24) from rhythmic and melodic elements presented in the earlier themes.
- Notice the false start of the recapitulation in m. 33.

Much of the beauty of this movement lies in the harmony.

- This movement opens in F minor.
- At m. 9, Mozart shifts to A flat major (the relative major).
- Note the special color of the augmented 6th chord in m. 13.
- The development begins in B flat minor (the subdominant minor).
- The return of the theme in m. 33 is a false recapitulation because it is in C minor, not the home key, F minor.

Help your student discover Mozart's use of dissonance. In the opening theme, notice how Mozart uses dynamics to highlight the alternation between consonance and dissonance on successive downbeats. For example, in mm. 16 and 50, Mozart uses a sudden *piano* to emphasize the resolution of the preceding *forte* diminished 7th:

Teaching Suggestions

The short trills (for example, in m. 1) should have a delicate, expressive sound. Explore various options. One possible interpretation is to trill for an eighth note, stopping on the dot.

The slurs in the LH m. 9 are an indication of Mozart's use of finger pedal. Hold the sound of each note under the slur as long as possible with overlapping *legato*. Count the RH rests accurately.

Third Movement – *Presto* (R33)
Exploring the Score

How does Mozart create humor? Look through this movement for unexpected changes of dynamics, sudden change of register, and silences.

Practice Suggestions

A successful performance of this movement will incorporate sharp *staccato* notes (indicated by wedges in the score), precise rests, slurs as indicated by the composer, and clear, even sixteenth notes.

The sixteenth-note passages are the major challenge and will require special practice.

- Categorize the different types of motion you find in the sixteenth notes (for example, scale lines, broken chords, broken octaves, and irregular changes of direction).
- Find all the passages which belong to a given category and practice them as a unit. Find a hand gesture or finger movement that facilitates each passage.
- Practice the sixteenth notes in the following ways:
  – with a *staccato* touch, *forte* then *piano*
  – with a *legato* touch, *forte* then *piano*
  – in dotted rhythms
  – playing each note twice
- For the LH, mm. 42-45, hold the G silently and play the beat tones *staccato* with a rotating hand. Then practice the LH in a dotted rhythm (short-long, short-long), again using a rotating hand motion.
- Use the same dotted-rhythm practice for the broken octaves in mm. 82-84 and 90-97. Play the bottom notes with the finger starting off the key, and the top notes with the finger starting on the key.
- Play the *staccato* double notes (for example, mm. 18-19 and 23) with a quick upward release of the key.

L. van Beethoven: *Sonata in C Minor, Op. 10, No. 1* (R38, R44, R48)
Background Information

In 1792, Beethoven moved from Bonn to Vienna. The Opus 10 sonatas were written between 1796 and 1798, when he was establishing himself as one of the foremost pianists in Vienna. *Sonata in C Minor* is filled with powerful contrast, the evidence of Beethoven's strong personality. The tempo indications in this sonata present the fastest and slowest markings. Great intensity of expression is required for a compelling performance of this work.

First Movement – Allegro molto e con brio (R38)
Exploring the Score

Listen to the *Celebration Series* recording of this movement and follow the score. Map out the sections of the sonata form, then discuss Beethoven's use of contrast.

exposition mm. 1-105
1st theme	mm. 1-30
bridge	mm. 31-55
2nd theme	mm. 56-94
closing theme	mm. 94-105

development mm. 106-168

recapitulation mm. 168-284

- What are the loudest and softest dynamic markings? Where is the moment of greatest dynamic contrast?
- The full chord texture of the first theme contrasts with the two-voice texture of the second theme.
- Examine the melodic figures. Look for contrasts of direction (ascending, descending, zig-zag), motion (broken chords, stepwise, wide leaps), and phrase length (short motives, short phrases, long phrases).
- Where does Beethoven use silence for contrast?
- How many different styles of accompaniment can you find?

Play through the development section.
- Notice how this section begins directly in C major (m. 106) without modulation.
- How does Beethoven vary the second theme?
- Which themes in the development represent new material?

Play through the recapitulation (mm. 168-284) and compare this section with the exposition.
- Notice that the second theme is presented in the subdominant key (F major).
- In m. 229, Beethoven uses an F minor chord to pivot to C minor.

Teaching Suggestions

In mm. 1-30, have students play the *forte*, dotted-rhythm passages (ascending motion), and the *piano* stepwise passages (descending motion), and ask them to describe the nature of the dialogue between these two parts or characters (for example, an angry outburst contrasted with quiet pleading).

In mm. 13-16, the LH provides a *legato*, chordal support for the melody. In mm. 32-55 and 94-105, the LH support is almost contrapuntal. Isolate these measures for special practice of the *legato* line. Notice also the implied bass line in the accompaniment pattern of the second theme.

Practice Suggestions
- The opening measures include four dynamic markings: *piano, forte, pianissimo,* and *fortissimo*. Establish a dynamic framework by playing mm. 1-30. Find other occurrences of *fortissimo*

and *pianissimo* in the movement. As you practice, listen for precise dynamic levels.

- Practice similar figures together (for example, the dotted broken chord in mm. 1-2, 5-6, 22-27, and 86-89).
- Play the octave theme in mm. 118-133 *legato*. Avoid downward motions. Move the hand laterally across the keys.

Second Movement – Adagio molto (R44)
Teaching Suggestions

Students learning this *Adagio* movement can become bogged down in details such as complex beat subdivisions, rhythm and timing of ornaments, and practice strategies for the sixty-fourth-note roulades. These details are important, but the higher priority is to help the student grasp the overall shape of lines, the direction of phrases, the harmonic flow, and the remarkable ways in which Beethoven varies thematic material.

This movement has an ABA$_1$B *coda* form. The *coda* (mm. 91-112) is based on the A theme. Compare the A sections and the *coda* to find the variations Beethoven writes in the LH.

Have students reduce the music to its basic, skeletal framework. For example, the opening measures can be reduced to these chords:

As students work through this process of reduction, they will become aware of Beethoven's variation structure:
- mm. 9-16 are a variation of mm. 1-8
- mm. 28-31 are a variation of mm. 24-27
- mm. 36-39 are a variation of mm. 31-34
- mm. 40-41 are an expanded version of the harmonies of m. 35

When students can hear and play these melodic and harmonic outlines, they can put details such as ornamentation in a proper perspective. The ornamentation is filler, and can be played lightly.

However, it is essential to maintain a steady eighth-note pulse throughout.

Practice Suggestions

- Focus your practice of this movement on tone quality. The opening theme has a somber, spiritual quality. Project the melody.
- The turns in mm. 1, 3, 9, and 11 lead gently from one melodic pitch to the next. Start each turn softly and make a slight *crescendo*.
- The arpeggios of mm. 17, 19, and 21 may be divided between the hands.
- To practice the sixty-fourth-note figures in mm. 28 and 30, first play the outline of each group of three notes. Use a hand rotation.

- Practice the same notes with quick rotation to the higher tone.

- Then add the middle note and play as written, using wrist rotation for the change of direction.

Third Movement – Finale: Prestissimo (R48)
Exploring the Score

Discuss the form of this movement with your student and label the sections in the score. Compare your analysis with this outline:

exposition mm. 1-45
1st theme	mm. 1-11
bridge	mm. 12-16
2nd theme	mm. 17-27
closing theme	mm. 28-45

development mm. 46-57

recapitulation mm. 58-122
(with extended *coda*)

In what key do you expect this movement to end? What is the ending key?

Teaching Suggestions

The meter *(alla breve)* and the tempo marking *(prestissimo)* indicate an extremely fast tempo. Students will need facile scale and octave *tremolo* technique to study this piece successfully. Speed is often impaired by fingers that are too high off the keys and by tension in the hand. Encourage students to practice the sixteenth-note passages in this movement with a loose arm and hand, and with fingers close to the keys.

Prepare students for the passages of four-against-three (for example, in mm. 34-35) by playing scales in that rhythm.

Practice Suggestions
There are a number of challenging figures in this movement:
- a turn around a note followed by a descending scale (mm. 12-14)
- broken-octave chords (m. 15)
- broken-octave *tremolo* (m. 28)
- *tremolo* plus a scale (mm. 34-35)
- sixteenths against triplets (mm. 34-35)
- chromatic scale (mm. 67-68)

Practice each figure in at least three different ways. Create your own exercises from those figures. Avoid tension and excessive movement.

LIST C – ROMANTIC

Suggested Order of Difficulty

Page	Composer	Title
R56	Franz Schubert	Moment musical, Op. 94, No. 4
R78	Johannes Brahms	Intermezzo, Op. 116, No. 6
R53	Robert Schumann	The Prophet Bird, Op. 82, No. 7
R64	Frédéric Chopin	Mazurka, Op. 63, No. 1
R80	Johannes Brahms	Intermezzo, Op. 76, No. 6
R60	Frédéric Chopin	Prélude, Op. 45
R67	Felix Mendelssohn	Song without Words, Op. 67, No. 4 (Spinning Song)
R72	Franz Liszt	Valse oubliée, n° 1

The 19th century is sometimes referred to as the century of the piano. During those years, the instrument evolved from the early fortepiano to the modern piano we know today. For the first time in music history, traveling piano virtuosos attracted huge crowds at their concerts and became wealthy from their performances and publications. More piano music was written during this century than ever before. The parlors of most middle-class families were arranged around their prized possession – the piano.

Although most of the prominent 19th-century composers who wrote for the piano composed sonatas and variations, the majority of their compositions were shorter pieces with titles such as *intermezzo, ballade,* or *impromptu.* These short compositions, usually in ternary form, are known as character pieces because they focus primarily on a strong expression of character and mood. In an effort to create a larger work, Robert Schumann composed cycles of character pieces. *Scenes from Childhood (Kinderszenen), Op. 15* is one of Schumann's best-known character cycles.

The extended harmonic palette of this music exploits chromaticism, altered chords, dissonance, and modulations to remote keys. In addition, composers marked their scores precisely, indicating subtle variations in tone quality and dynamic range. The use of contrasts and extremes of tone quality and dynamics adds to the expressive qualities of this music. Tone quality is enhanced and harmonies are blended with the subtle and varied use of pedaling, which was an important part of the development of pianism in the 19th century.

R. Schumann (1810-1856): *The Prophet Bird, Op. 82, No. 7* (R53)

Background Information

Most of the works we teach and perform by Schumann are from his early period. *Forest Scenes, Op. 82*, written in 1850, is an exception. *The Prophet Bird* is the seventh in this set of nine character pieces depicting life, nature, and activity in the forest.

Schumann was no stranger to the world of fantasy. It is, indeed, the quality of the fantastic that makes his piano music unusual. For a successful interpretation of *The Prophet Bird*, the student is invited to enter this fantasy world and to create a musical image of a bird which lives in no earthly region – a bird of unusual color and delicacy with a spiritual power.

Exploring the Score

This piece has a ternary form:

A   mm. 1-18   (G minor)
B   mm. 19-24   (G major → E flat major)
A_1 mm. 25-42   (G minor)

The A sections focus on the exotic movements of the bird. The chorale-like B section could represent the awesome moment of prophecy.

Practice Suggestions

To practice the main figure of the piece (mm. 1-8):

1. Play only the notes on the beat (leave out the triplet thirty-second notes), with the LH accompaniment as written. Give dynamic shape to this melodic outline with special delicacy on the final tone of each phrase. Change the pedal on each beat.
2. Play the entire RH figure in an even rhythm (all eighth notes). Avoid stretching the entire octave position.
3. Play the RH figure as written, with the pedal. Play with a loose hand, stroking the surface of the key. Rotate the hand as you play these delicate broken-octave chords.

In the B section (mm. 19-24), use *legato* fingerings for the melody.

F. Schubert (1797-1828): *Moment musical, Op. 94, No. 4* (R56)

Exploring the Score

Compare J.S. Bach's *Prelude in C Minor, BWV 871* (R12) and Schubert's *Moment musical*. What similarities do you find?

The apparent consistency of texture is deceptive. Practice will reveal the complexity of the varied RH sixteenth-note figures.

- Look for the contrasts in mm. 22-30 and mm. 50-58.

- Compare mm. 1-2 with mm. 31-32 and mm. 39-40.

The A section is in C sharp minor, and there is no real modulation in this section. The contrasting B section (mm. 62-101) has a new key signature. The sudden appearance of D flat major (the enharmonic tonic major) is surprising. Notice the change of rhythm and texture.

Practice Suggestions

The variety in the RH part is challenging.

- Consider your choice of fingerings. Be consistent.
- Practice the sixteenth-note patterns with *staccato* and *legato* articulations and with different rhythms.
- Practice "stop and go" groups, pausing before each RH bottom note:

The rhythm of the B section is ambiguous. Schubert has written a syncopated rhythm, but it is easy to feel the accented quarter note as the downbeat. Try counting the rhythm as if there were two downbeats in each measure:

F. Chopin (1810-1849): *Prélude, Op. 45* (R60)

Background Information

Several of Chopin's preludes are among the world's best-loved music. The most well known of Chopin's preludes are from Op. 28, a set which includes a prelude in each of the twenty-four major and minor keys. Each piece has a unique color and mood.

The musical motivation of *Prélude, Op. 45* is somewhat the reverse of the Op. 28 set. Here, Chopin seems to include every key in one prelude. True, some keys are not represented, but the impression is one of constant modulation.

Exploring the Score

Romantic composers often used common-tone modulation to create surprising changes of tonal center. They also used chromatic movement of chord tones. Note, for example:

- the change from A to B flat in mm. 26-27
- the change from F^7 to G flat in mm. 30-31
- the change from the sound of E^7 (enharmonic F flat) to E flat in mm. 38-39

An unusual feature of the main melody is the way in which the accompaniment figure rises through three octaves and becomes part of the melody.

Teaching Suggestions

Prélude, Op. 45 includes remarkable modulations. Have students make a chart showing the twenty-four major and minor keys and notate measure numbers for the keys which serve as temporary tonal centers (for example, C sharp minor in m. 4, B major in m. 9, A major in m. 13).

In the measures cited above, each tonal center is defined by a dominant-tonic progression. However, there are many places where a dominant is not followed by its tonic (for example, mm. 26-27, A^7 to B flat). Devise a dynamic plan for these harmonic surprises and use *rubato* to highlight the resolutions.

The cadenza (m. 80) is an unusual feature of this prelude. The first two eighth-note chords of each beamed group form dominant 7th chords which descend chromatically. The ascending chords are diminished 7ths.

F. Chopin (1810-1849): *Mazurka, Op. 63, No. 1* (R64)

Background Information

The fact that Chopin wrote fifty-eight mazurkas gives ample testimony to his love for this dance from his Polish homeland. Many of Chopin's mazurkas make musical reference to folk instruments through the use of a drone (imitating bagpipes) and modal harmonies. The mazurkas are among Chopin's most subtle and rhythmically diverse compositions. They challenge the performer to an ever-closer scrutiny of the score to discover the intricate variations of rhythm and harmony. (Some students will have encountered Chopin mazurkas in Levels 7 and 8 of the *Celebration Series*.)

Exploring the Score

The form of this piece is:

A	mm. 1-32
B	mm. 33-68
A₁	mm. 69-86
coda	mm. 87-102

- The B section ends with a short bridge or *codetta* (mm. 53-68), and the A₁ section ends with a *coda* (mm. 87-102).
- A glance at the *sforzando* markings in mm. 1-16 reveals Chopin's plan for two-measure phrase units. What is the phrase structure of mm. 33-50 in the B section?

The performer of a mazurka must be aware of subtle changes in the music. Compare mm. 1-8 with mm. 9-16:

- Where are the harmonies different?
- Where is the rhythm slightly changed?
- What beats have the dotted rhythm?
- Why does Chopin shift the location of the dotted rhythms?

Compare mm. 1-16 with the return of the A section in mm. 69-86. Where are the exact repetitions?

Chopin summarizes the composition in the *coda*.
- The dotted figure in mm. 87-90 contrasts with the even eighth notes of mm. 91-94. (Compare this with the contrast between mm. 1-16 and 17-24.)
- Examine the melodic shape of mm. 87-95. The notes D sharp and C sharp occur in each measure.

F. Mendelssohn (1809-1847): *Song without Words, Op. 67, No. 4 (Spinning Song)* (R67)

Background Information

Felix Mendelssohn's *Songs without Words* have been well represented in Levels 7, 8, and 9 of the *Celebration Series*. These short character pieces were among the most popular piano works of their day.

Today, hand spinning is only practiced by a few specialists. In the 19th century, the characteristic sound of a spinning wheel was part of everyday life. Several 19th-century composers wrote pieces imitating the rhythmic whirring of the spinning wheel. A well-known example is the Schubert *Lied*, *Gretchen am Spinnrade*.

Mendelssohn's spinner seems to be in a bright, cheerful mood. The continuous sixteenth-note activity imitates the constantly running wheel, while the eighth-note rhythm (for example, in mm. 2-3) represents the pedaling motion which drives the spinning wheel.

Practice Suggestions

Fast playing is a challenge, especially when the accompaniment and melody are in the same hand. When the figures change frequently, the challenge is intensified.

- Isolate each technical figure, for example:
  - the skipping-rhythm melody with a sixteenth-note filler accompaniment (m. 3)
  - the RH eighth-note melody with a LH zig-zag sixteenth-note accompaniment (mm. 4-5)
  - the melody incorporated into a zig-zag figure (m. 11)
  - the *staccato* 3rds, 4ths, 5ths, and 6ths (mm. 4-6)
- Study the fingerings for each passage and decide what fits your hand best.
- Combine similar figures into a practice unit. Notice which passages are exact repetitions and which passages have slight changes.

- Be aware of hand and wrist positions. Keep a loose hand.
- Always bring out the melody notes.

The end result of practicing should produce the light, gossamer-fine sound that is so characteristic of Mendelssohn's style. Encourage students to listen to other compositions by Mendelssohn, especially the *Octet* and *Incidental Music for A Midsummer Night's Dream*.

F. Liszt (1811-1886): *Valse oubliée, nᵒ 1* (R72)
Background Information
Liszt's compositions utilize the tonal resources of the piano in a way unequaled by any other composer. A successful performance of a piece by Liszt is an experience of thrilling sound, most likely including a wide range of the keyboard and dynamic extremes. Chromatic harmonies, common-tone relationships, and the use of augmented and diminished triads are characteristics of his harmonic vocabulary. These characteristics are found in *Valse oubliée* (Forgotten Waltz). Not all of Liszt's compositions are fast and brilliant (see *En rêve, Piano Repertoire Album 9*), but most are technically demanding.

Teaching Suggestions
Here is one possible approach to this piece:
1. Label the sections:
   > Introduction   mm. 1-16
   >
   > A   mm. 17-48
   >
   > B   mm. 49-88
   >
   > C   mm. 89-106, etc.

2. Look for basic harmonic relationships. In the introduction, every second chord is a diminished 7th.
- Play these diminished 7ths in their descending inversions.
- Find the common tones between the diminished 7th and the preceding chord. If students understand the harmonic pattern, they will find the chords easier to memorize.
- In mm. 17-32, notice the C sharp 7th resolving to F sharp. Have students block the chords so that they can see the harmonic relationships clearly. What inversions are used for those chords? (Root position chords feel stable; chords in inversion sound unstable and require resolution.)
- Analyze the harmonies of mm. 33-48.
- The chords of resolution in the A section are shown below. Notice the use of common tones:

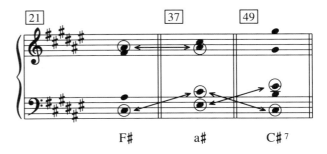

3. Give technical tips. The A section provides opportunities to discuss playing in extended hand positions.
- In the RH, mm. 17-22, let the hand travel to the high dotted-quarter notes so the finger does not need to stretch.
- In the RH, mm. 49-52, do not extend the fifth finger until it is needed to reach its note. Students can practice this repeated-note figure by stopping briefly on the last eighth note before the octave:

- In mm. 53-54, let the wrist move in an oval shape (out and around) as it guides the hand to the notes.

4. Discuss phrases and rhythmic units.
- When analyzing phrase units, it is helpful to count measures instead of beats. The introduction (mm. 1-16) may feel different to the student who can think of this section in long phrases.
- In mm. 49-52, the bass notes help determine the phrasing.

J. Brahms (1833-1897): *Intermezzo, Op. 116, No. 6* (R78)
Background Information
Johannes Brahms was the last of the great German conservative Romanticists. During his lifetime, German composers were writing in a more chromatic style which culminated in the works of Richard Wagner. The *Seven Fantasias, Op. 116* are among Brahms's last piano compositions and are representative of the rich, melodious textures of his mature style.

Exploring the Score
This piece has a ternary form:
> A   mm. 1-24   (E minor)
>
> B   mm. 25-42   (B major)
>
> A₁   mm. 43-64   (E minor)

Teaching Suggestions

Brahms gives a subtle indication of the voicing he wishes to emphasize in the opening dialogue between the two RH voices. The *crescendo* and *diminuendo* through the eighth-note figure in mm. 1-2 is the clue. In the first phrase, the melody is in the lower (alto) voice. In the second phrase, it appears in the higher (soprano) voice. In mm. 5-6, the melody returns to the alto. It is helpful for the student to hear this dialogue without the complexity of the other RH notes.

In mm. 9-14, experiment with the voicing. Emphasize the top line and then the inner voice. Which do you prefer?

In the B section (mm. 25-42), the melody is clearly marked, but the rhythm is ambiguous. Both the melody and the rhythm of the accompanying triplets suggest a duple meter.

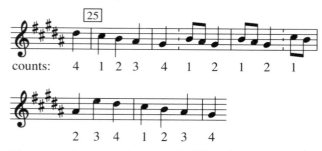

The A sections require extended hand positions. Help your student find ways to relax while playing in these extended positions. For example:

- Allow the hand to assume a smaller, more relaxed position between chords.
- Use the pedal for connection.
- During practice, release the thumb. Let the thumb touch the second finger after each note.

J. Brahms (1833-1897): *Intermezzo, Op. 76, No. 6* (R80)

Exploring the Score

This intermezzo is not a completely typical example of Brahms's piano music writing.

- Most of Brahms's shorter pieces have an ABA form. This intermezzo has a ternary form but the A sections are in rounded binary form:

A	a	mm. 1-8
	b + a$_1$	mm. 9-24
B	b + b$_1$	mm. 25-58
A	a	mm. 59-67
	b + a$_2$	mm. 68-91

- Brahms frequently uses a short-short-long phrase structure in which the two short units together equal the long unit (2 + 2 + 4). Here, Brahms writes phrase structures of 1 + 1 + 1 + 1 + 4 (mm. 1-8) and 1 + 1 + 6 (mm. 9-16).
- Brahms often wrote piano pieces in 3/2 or 6/4 and used *hemiola*. This intermezzo is in 2/4 with a constant two-against-three rhythm. (Find the augmentation of two-against-three in mm. 11-15).

Compare the bass lines of the A and B sections. In the A section, the bass line is constantly moving. Tonality is clarified only at the cadences. In the B section, the bass line is grounded on a repeated note, sometimes for four-measure harmonic units.

LIST D – LATE ROMANTIC AND IMPRESSIONIST

Suggested Order of Difficulty

Page	Composer	Title
R90	Claude Debussy	Prélude, Book I, No. 1 (Danseuses de Delphes)
R92	Claude Debussy	Prélude, Book II, No. 5 (Bruyères)
R101	Manuel de Falla	The Miller's Dance
R88	Alexander Scriabin	Prélude, Op. 11, No. 14
R96	Maurice Ravel	Prélude
R83	Sergei Rachmaninoff	Elegy, Op. 3, No. 1

As 19th-century composers attempted to express themselves personally through their music, they discovered ways to alter the traditional harmonies of the Classical and early Romantic periods.
- They added chromatic notes to help disguise the shift from one harmony to another.
- They related harmonies by common tone or through chromatic relationships rather than the traditional tonic-subdominant-dominant-tonic progressions.
- Impressionist composers employed scale systems other than major and minor by altering pitches or by equalizing the relationship between the notes in the scale – for example, a whole-tone scale. The lack of a clear tonic in whole-tone compositions gives the music a floating sensation, a weightlessness resulting from the loss of tonal gravity pulling toward a center.

S. Rachmaninoff (1873-1943): *Elegy, Op. 3, No. 1* (R83)

Background Information
Rachmaninoff received his musical education first at the St. Petersburg Conservatory and later at the Moscow Conservatory. He established himself in Russia as a composer and a distinguished piano virtuoso. He has been described as one of the greatest pianists since Franz Liszt. In 1918, he left Russia and for the remainder of his career he lived in Switzerland. Rachmaninoff made frequent tours in the United States. His music is close to the German Romantic style, but is flavored with a Russian idiom. Tchaikovsky and Chopin were strong influences.

Elegy is the first piece in *Fantasy Pieces, Op. 3*, written in 1892, shortly after his graduation from the Moscow Conservatory. The other four pieces are the well-known *Prelude in C Sharp Minor*, *Polichinelle*, *Melody*, and *Serenade*.

Exploring the Score
An elegy is a lamentation for the dead. Rachmaninoff uses the key of E flat minor, a descending melody, and the extreme bass register of the piano to create a dark atmosphere.

The arching melodies and sweeping chord motion contribute to the somber mood of the music.

This piece is in ternary form. The opening A and the B sections begin with a relatively open texture which is later thickened with octave chords, often in parallel motion. Notice the extreme chromaticism, for example, in mm. 63-83.

Practice Suggestions
To practice the A section (mm. 1-40):
1. Play the RH top tones along with the *Celebration Series* recording.
2. Mark the long phrase units. Where do the phrases end?
3. Play the melody with both hands. Exaggerate the dynamic shape of the phrases and experiment with expressive dynamic sounds.
4. Play the RH as written. Project the top notes.
5. Choose a LH fingering that allows smooth arm movement.
6. Put the hands together phrase by phrase. Listen for melodic projection.

In the B section (mm. 41-85), notice the different dynamic markings for the melody and the accompaniment.

- Use an in-out arm movement (a "scrub-brush" action) for the double-note passages, mm. 41-53. The lower RH notes are fingered **2 1 2 1 2 1**. Push in to play the thumb and pull out to play the second finger. Practice the double notes with a short-long rhythm. Use the same motion for the similar LH figures in mm. 53-63.

The low bass notes provide important harmonic foundation and color. Follow the pedaling pattern indicated in mm. 1-9.

A. Scriabin (1872-1915): *Prélude, Op. 11, No. 14* (R88)

Background Information

Like Bach and Chopin, Scriabin wrote a set of preludes in all twenty-four major and minor keys. He finished his Op. 11 while on a concert tour in 1896, and some of the preludes are named after concert locations such as Heidelberg, Paris, Vitznau, and Moscow. This one was composed in Dresden.

Exploring the Score

This prelude is in ternary form.

A time signature of 15/8 is unusual. Here the fifteen eighth notes are organized into three groups of five.
- Look for the phrases. Can you find phrase units combining 2 + 2 + 4 measures?
- The opening theme has an arch shape – a six-note ascending scale and a chromatic descent:

Where else does this theme appear? [mm. 3-4, 9-12]

C. Debussy (1862-1918): *Prélude, Book I, No. 1 (Danseuses de Delphes)* (R90)

Background Information

Debussy's twenty-four *Préludes* (published in two books, 1910 and 1913) present a variety of musical scenes. Debussy placed the titles at the end of the pieces, giving primary importance to the music rather than the picture implied by the title.

Delphi was a city at the foot of Mount Parnassus in ancient Greece. The Temple of Apollo, the god of the arts, stood on Mount Parnassus. This prelude evokes an image of a sacred dance.

Exploring the Score

Help students understand and control the layers of sounds.
- Isolate the dotted-rhythm theme. It appears in single notes, in unison octaves, and in full octave chords.
- In those same measures, play the accompanying material. Does the accompaniment move in the same direction as the theme?

What are the functions of the accompanying material?
- In m. 1, it harmonizes the chromatic motion of the theme.
- In m. 8, it has two functions. The bass line provides chromatic movement, and the top RH octaves represent a percussion instrument (such as finger cymbals).
- In m. 11, the LH first establishes a pedal tone, then participates in a two-hand rising chord stream.

Notice the harmonization of the beat notes in mm. 21-24.
- Compare these chords with the chords of mm. 4-5.
- What effect is created when a stream of chords is all major (or all minor, or augmented)?

Practice Suggestions

Make dynamics a high priority in your practice.
- Establish different dynamic levels for the different layers of sounds.
- Plan the voicing of chords. Which chords carry the melody and require projection of the top tone? Which chords emphasize color and sonority and have equal emphasis on all tones?
- Use the damper pedal for *legato* connections.
- Use the *una corda* pedal for soft dynamic levels (*pp*, *più pp*, and *ppp*).

C. Debussy (1862-1918): *Prélude, Book II, No. 5 (Bruyères)* (R92)

Background Information

The preludes in Book II (published in 1913) are considered more difficult than those in Book I. Debussy's three-stave score helps the performer to understand his layered approach to colors, harmonies, and motives. Compare this layering technique with contrapuntal pieces from the Baroque period. Instead of single tones, Debussy uses chord streams, rhythmic motives, and harmonic coloration.

Exploring the Score

Look through the score with your student and identify the various rhythmic groupings:
- predominantly eighth-note movement (mm. 1-7)
- streams of sixteenth notes beginning with a triplet impulse (mm. 8-13)

– short wisps of thirty-second notes (mm. 14-22)
Can you find any other rhythmic ideas?

This music gives an impression of the outdoors. (*Bruyères* is the French word for heather.) Each rhythmic pattern plays a role in the scene. The eighth-note figures seem languid or calm. The sixteenth notes have forward movement, and the thirty-second notes are like fleeting gusts of a breeze. Let the rhythms help guide your interpretation.

Notice the markings *doucement expressif, doux et léger, doux,* and *doucement soutenu.* Delicacy is the basis for the interpretation of this prelude.

Discuss musical motion with your student.
- Which figures indicate movement?
- Is the movement fast or slow? Is it up or down or both? Is it short or extended? Is this motion filled with action or suspended in space?

Teaching Suggestions
Point out the open-ended ties in mm. 29-32. Debussy and other Impressionist composers used this marking to indicate an extended, disappearing sound with no definite release. The quarter rests in m. 30 indicate a release of the harmony from m. 29.

Practice Suggestions
The texture of this prelude is comprised of overlapping and interacting events.
- Identify each overlapping layer of sound.
- As you practice, determine which parts of the texture will be most prominent.

M. Ravel (1875-1937): *Prélude* (R96)
Background Information
Prélude is the first movement of *Le tombeau de Couperin,* Ravel's last solo piano composition. The title suggests a tribute to François Couperin, one of France's greatest Baroque composers. Ravel composed the work in 1914-1917, during World War I, a time of intense patriotism. Each movement honors the memory of a Frenchman killed in the war. (See the discussion of *Menuet,* another movement from *Le tombeau de Couperin,* in List D of Level 9.)

Exploring the Score
Level 10 includes a number of preludes. Your students may find it interesting to compare this prelude, which was written as a tribute to the French Baroque harpsichord school, with any of the Bach preludes in List A. Look for similarities and differences in figuration, texture, and key relationships. (For example, what is the effect of the weakened dominant-tonic relationship in Ravel's *Prélude?*)

Teaching Suggestions
Prélude combines figures reminiscent of the French Baroque harpsichord school with Impressionistic pedal effects and harmonies.
- Finger work must be clear and precise, in imitation of a harpsichord style.
- Ornaments are to be played on the beat.

Practice Suggestions
There are no pedal markings, but use of the damper pedal is assumed. What are Ravel's clues for use of the pedal?
- The open-ended ties (for example, in the LH, mm. 1 and 3) indicate indefinite duration.
- In mm. 1-4, the phrasing and style suggest a pedal change in the middle of each measure.
- Pedal cleanly each change of harmony (for example, mm. 5-6).

M. de Falla (1876-1946): *The Miller's Dance* (R101)
Background Information
Manuel de Falla was born in Paris, where he studied composition with Felipe Pedrell, a nationalist composer. Falla's musical style is deeply embedded in the Spanish tradition, both popular and cultivated. It is his original use of this tradition that gives Falla's music its distinctive stamp. He spent much of his time in France and was strongly influenced by Debussy and Ravel.

The Miller's Dance is a piano arrangement of a dance from *El sombrero de tres picos* (The Three-Cornered Hat), a ballet commissioned by Diaghilev for the Ballet Russe in Paris. Picasso designed the sets for the London premiere in 1919. The orchestral score of the ballet often suggests the transfiguration of a guitar. If possible, have students listen to the orchestral version of *The Miller's Dance* and also to *Pièces Espagnoles* (composed in 1908).

Exploring the Score
- The broken chords imitate guitar strumming.
- The haunting melody of mm. 10-18 and 47-52 has a folk-like quality. Notice the prominence of the notes E and A in this melody and in the bass (mm. 44-76).

Teaching Suggestions
Some chords require a hand span of a 9th, and the penultimate chord in the RH (m. 75) requires an especially large and flexible hand. (It is possible to omit one of the notes in that chord.) The LH chords in m. 33 will probably need to be broken.

Falla uses dynamics to create character, drama, and surprise. Follow the dynamic markings carefully. For an effective performance, students must realize the dynamics, articulation, and final *accelerando* accurately.

LIST E – CONTEMPORARY

Suggested Order of Difficulty

Page	Composer	Title
R104	Dmitri Kabalevsky	Prelude, Op. 38, No. 15
R106	Dmitri Kabalevsky	Prelude, Op. 38, No. 20
R114	Béla Bartók	Bagatelle, Op. 6, No. 11
R116	Béla Bartók	Bagatelle, Op. 6, No. 12
R108	Maurice Dela	Hommage
R119	Barbara Pentland	Shadows
R122	Pierre Gallant	Six Variations on "Land of the Silver Birch"
R132	Olivier Messiaen	Prélude, n° 7 (Plainte calme)
R134	Robert Fleming	Sonatina
R128	François Morel	Étude de sonorité, n° 1

As noted in the Introduction to List D, Impressionist composers employed scale systems other than major and minor, destabilizing traditional harmonic relationships through the use of modes and the whole-tone scale. Twentieth-century composers contributed to the breakdown of traditional harmony by often ignoring familiar chordal functions. The use of the twelve-tone system of writing, in which each chromatic step has equal importance, completed the destruction of tonality. Rhythm became more complex through shifting meters and irregular rhythmic patterns.

In reaction to these trends, some composers, such as Béla Bartók and Paul Hindemith, borrowed from established Classical forms, writing in a neoclassical manner with a personal harmonic vocabulary. Some composers integrated jazz and ragtime elements into their compositions. Composers such as John Cage extended the color of the instrument by attaching nuts and bolts to the strings, or playing directly on the strings with the hand or fingernail.

The pieces in List E of *Repertoire Album 10* represent many of these trends and include works by two of the most influntial composers of the 20th century (Bartók and Messiaen). List E includes music written in each decade between 1940 and 1980. In these ten pieces, teachers and students will find examples of quartal harmony, written-out improvisation, twelve-tone and modal writing, a variety of rhythmic figures, and dense chordal structures. Yet we also see forms used in earlier style periods through titles such as *Prelude, Bagatelle, Sonatina,* and *Variations*. With the teacher's assistance, the student will want to explore how these twentieth-century colors and sounds have been integrated into familiar forms.

D. Kabalevsky (1904-1987): *Prelude, Op. 38, No. 15* (R104)

Background Information

Kabalevsky's cycle of twenty-four preludes follows the same key sequence as those of Chopin and Scriabin. The *Preludes, Op. 38* were composed in 1943-1944, during World War II. Several of these pieces reflect the fear and hopelessness of war.

Exploring the Score

This prelude is a good-humored march in the key of D flat major. In mm. 1-4, both hands present the tune in unison. Subsequent statements of the tune feature challenging imitation between the hands. The short homophonic interludes (mm. 9-12, 21-24) use descending chromaticism and end with humorously surprising cadences (C major in m. 12, D major in m. 24). The *coda* (mm. 29-32) is built on a melodic fragment from mm. 3-4.

Practice Suggestions

Kabalevsky's score includes detailed dynamic and articulation markings. Play with spirit and follow these markings carefully.

Kabalevsky (1904-1987): *Prelude, Op. 38, No. 20* (R106)

Exploring the Score

It is tempting to read a program into this prelude, knowing that it was written during the devastation of World War II. The music seems to be filled with darkness and despair – a belabored and fatigued trudging.

Notice the emphasis on the pitches E flat, D, and C:
– in the LH, mm. 1-2 [D, E flat, C]
– in the RH, mm. 4-6 [E flat, D, E flat, C]
– in the LH, mm. 13-14 [D, E flat, C]

These notes are a reference to the beginning of the *Dies irae* (day of wrath), a sequence which became part of the Requiem Mass:

Di - es   il - la   di - es ___ ir ___ ae

Practice Suggestions

Read the LH intervals in mm. 41-51 carefully. It is easy to misread the 9ths and 10ths as octaves.

M. Dela (1919-1978): *Hommage* (R108)

Background Information

Maurice Dela was a Canadian composer and organist who spent most of his career in Montreal. For fourteen years he worked as a composer and arranger for the Canadian Broadcasting Corporation. Then he turned to music teaching. Dela composed pedagogical pieces and works for recorder, organ, and piano, and he also harmonized numerous popular and folk songs. His music often incorporates polytonality, and occasionally he uses elements of serialism.

Hommage has a sense of seriousness and fervent expression. The harmonic vocabulary of altered 7th and 9th chords is associated with popular music.

The formal design is carefully structured:

A	mm. 1-17
B	mm. 18-43
A₁	mm. 44-61

Practice Suggestions

Approach this piece in much the same way as you would a challenging piece from the Romantic repertoire:
1. Listen to the *Celebration Series* recording.
2. Analyze the form. Look for repetitions and variations. Determine lengths of sections.
3. Practice hands separately. Write fingering decisions in the score. (Blocking chords in the B section will make reading easier.)
4. Practice hands together. Project the top notes and listen for the dynamic shape of each phrase.

B. Bartók (1881-1945): *Bagatelle, Op. 6, No. 11* (R114)

Background Information

In addition to his activities as a composer and pianist, Bartók was a distinguished scholar of folk music. During his lifetime he collected thousands of folk songs from Hungary, Romania, Ukraine, Bulgaria, and Turkey. He was one of the first to record and study this music.

Bartók developed a style of composition using rhythmic, melodic, and harmonic patterns from these folk tunes, and the works from his early period, 1907-1917, are clearly tied to these folk materials. The *14 Bagatelles, Op. 6* were composed in 1908, a year after Bartók was appointed professor of piano at the Budapest Academy of Music.

The three bagatelles in Level 10 (numbers 5, 11, and 12) are humorous and colorful. They often have an improvisatory quality and require a freedom of rhythm and creative *rubato*.

Exploring the Score

Bartók, like Kabalevsky, marked his score with great detail. Notice the metronome indications for each tempo change and the careful, detailed articulation markings. (For example, in mm. 32-33, there is a succession of *staccato, portato,* and *tenuto* notes. In m. 34, the *forte tenuto* notes are slurred.) Notice the footnote below the music regarding the length of lifts for the eighth and sixteenth rests.

Exploring the Score

One of Bartók's most important building blocks is the interval of a 4th. His use of quartal harmony (using both perfect and augmented 4ths) is derived from Hungarian folk melodies rich in 4ths. Look for 4ths in the melodic skeleton. For example:
- In m. 1, the melody descends by a 4th.
- In mm. 5-7, the melody moves in 4ths.
- Notice the melodic 4ths in mm. 34-37 and 55-59.

Teaching Suggestions

To gain a sense of rhythmic flexibility, have students conduct a recorded performance of this bagatelle. If possible, listen to more than one recording.

B. Bartók (1881-1945): *Bagatelle, Op. 6, No. 12* (R116)

Background Information

The repeated-note figure of this bagatelle imitates the characteristic sound of a *cimbalom*, a popular Hungarian gypsy dulcimer. The *cimbalom* has metal strings which the player strikes with wooden mallets. You can approximate the sound of this instrument by striking the strings of a grand piano with a mallet of the type used with a marimba. (The larger type of *cimbalom* has a soundbox and is set on legs. This instrument was used in orchestral works by Bartók, Kodály, Liszt, and Stravinsky.)

Exploring the Score

Every aspect of this piece speaks of improvisation. Following Bartók's dynamic markings, tempo changes, and articulation indications will help guide that sense of improvisation.

- Devise a mental picture to suit the change to the chordal texture at the *Lento* (m. 23).
- Discuss with your student the structural importance of the dotted eighth-note motive:

B. Pentland (1912-): *Shadows* (R119)

Background Information

Canadian composer Barbara Pentland studied composition in Montreal, Paris, and later at the Juilliard School. She taught music in Toronto (1943-1949), and later at the University of British Columbia (1949-1963) in Vancouver. Pentland's numerous compositions include teaching materials for piano. The counterpoint and leaner textures of Pentland's compositions from the 1940s and 1950s show a tendency toward neoclassicism. Her mature style demonstrates an interest in economical textures and contrasting timbres, and she has also explored aleatoricism and quarter tones. Her use of serialism, which began in the late 1940s, is marked by a relatively free treatment of the series.

Pentland's piano music is challenging for ears and fingers. *Shadows*, composed in 1964, is a difficult piece. It is a serial piece, characterized by long pedals and subtle sonorities. The challenge lies in presenting the sound in a convincing manner. To achieve this, the performer must impart a sense of direction, however slowly realized. Without this direction, the music will sound aimless and disorganized. When the performer is absorbed in the activity of creating the piece, then the listener will be fascinated by the unfolding of sounds and their relationships.

Practice Suggestions

Shadows is built on a twelve-tone row, but the music is not strictly serial. The most important clues to interpretation are dynamics and pedaling. Follow the markings meticulously.

To hear the disjunct intervals as melodies, transpose the notes into the closest positions. For example:

1. Play the notes of mm. 2-3 (B-F sharp-A-D) in one octave.
2. Sing the melody as you play.
3. Play mm. 2-3 as written and listen for the conjunct melody in the disjunct pitches.

P. Gallant (1950-): *Six Variations on "Land of the Silver Birch"* (R122)

Background Information

Pierre Gallant was born in the Ottawa Valley. In 1970, he moved to Toronto where he studied with Harry Freedman and Samuel Dolin. In 1979, he joined the faculty of The Royal Conservatory of Music. Gallant has written solo, chamber, and orchestral works and music for the theater.

Land of the Silver Birch is a popular Canadian camp song. There is an easy arrangement of this tune by Nancy Telfer in Level 2.

Exploring the Score

- Gallant preserves the harmonic sound of the original song. How does he do this? [simple harmonization of the perfect 5th, not much chromaticism]
- Notice the lowered leading tone. What is the mode of the original melody?
- From the beginning of Variation I, Gallant creates independent rhythms for the RH and LH accompaniment motive. When the melody enters, the performer must control three independent rhythmic streams. Projecting the theme is all-important.
- In Variation II, the theme starts in the LH and passes to the RH in m. 5. With the changing meter, the melody becomes fragmented and the literal rendition of the theme is lost. Short rhythmic motives, articulation, and a dynamic outburst are the important issues.

- The energy from the end of Variation II spills over into the fast-moving Variation III. The scale lines must be clear and vital.
- In Variation IV, rhythm is the key issue. The melody notes provide rhythmic interest. In some phrases (mm. 3-4, 10-11), combinations of half and quarter notes become straight dotted-quarter values. Eighth notes remain the steady subdivision.
- Variation V is in 5/8 time. The LH *ostinato* is heard as 2 + 3 and the RH melodic figures are 3 + 2.
- The *glissandi* add a dashing flair to Variation VI. This finale includes exciting alternating hand playing (the LH is rhythmically displaced by an eighth rest).

F. Morel (1926-   ): *Étude de sonorité, n° 1* (R128)
Background Information
François Morel was one of the first Quebec musicians to be educated exclusively at the Conservatoire de musique du Québec à Montréal. The 1953 premiere of his orchestral work *Antiphonie* at Carnegie Hall under the direction of Leopold Stokowski marked the beginning of his career as a composer.

The *Deux études de sonorité*, written in 1954, reflect Morel's concern for rhythmic drive and a search for a richer sound palette. These two pieces are fascinating both to hear and to study. The dense chord structures are typical of the writing of Messiaen and his students.

Étude de sonorité, n° 1 includes a vast range of textures and dynamics. For the student who has conquered the reading of the notes, this piece is rewarding to perform because it is so expressive.

Teaching Suggestions
Reading the complex sonorities constitutes one of the greatest challenges of this piece. It may be helpful first to isolate measures which are more easily seen. For example:
- The RH of m. 14 has an F sharp major chord moving to an E major chord.
- In m. 15, the RH chords are E flat major and D flat major. In m. 14, only the top tone of the LH changes.
- In m. 15, you can readily see the distribution of white and black keys in the LH.

The chords in m. 4 are the most complicated.
- Have the student play the second LH chord (all white keys) and analyze the relationship of the notes – the bottom four fingers play whole steps and the top finger a half step. Look for this relationship in all the LH chords in the measure.
- Have the student play the first RH chord (all black keys). This pentatonic chord has no half steps. There is a whole step between the first and second fingers and between the third, fourth, and fifth fingers. Play the RH chords in the second half of the measure and discover the same relationship. (The chords on the second beat do not have this pattern, although one of them is all-black-key.)

Morel uses a combination of French and Italian terms in his score. Here are translations for the French words:
- *rêveur, presque lent:* dreamy, almost slow
- *sans rigueur:* without harshness
- *avec plus d'élan et rubato:* with more vigor and rubato
- *delicat:* delicate
- *croisez:* cross
- *lointain:* distant, far away
- *serrez:* press, push ahead

O. Messiaen (1908-1992): *Prélude, n° 7 (Plainte calme)* (R132)
Background Information
Best known for his organ compositions, Olivier Messiaen is clearly one of the premier composers of the twentieth century. He exhibited considerable influence on his many composition students, including Pierre Boulez and Karlheinz Stockhausen. His piano compositions deserve greater attention. Later keyboard works such as the *Visions de l'amen* (1943) for two pianos, four hands, and the monumental solo piano set, *Vingt regards sur l'enfant Jésus* (1944), reflect the strong influence of Catholicism on Messiaen's writing as well as his lifelong experimentation with rhythm, harmony, and notation of birdsong.

Huit préludes pour piano (1929), from which *Plainte calme* (Gentle Sorrow) is selected, represent Messiaen's early style when he still was a student at the Paris Conservatoire.

This prelude, however, foreshadows the complicated chord textures, dense textures, and interest in unusual rhythmic relationships which became hallmarks of his later compositions.

Teaching Suggestions

Students will find this piece easier to learn if they begin by studying the form.

- Look for clues such as repeated sections and varied endings.
- How many cadences are full stops? On what chords do they end?
- Is the melodic idea in mm. 15-16 a new theme? How does it relate to intervals or theme fragments in the A section?

Practice Suggestions

- The expressivity of the two-note sighing motives increases with the amount of *diminuendo* between the notes.
- Notice Messiaen's explicit direction to bring out the inner voice.

R. Fleming (1921-1976): *Sonatina* (R134, R138)
Background Information

Robert Fleming was a Canadian composer, organist, and teacher. For much of his career he was a staff composer and conductor, and later music director, for the National Film Board. During the last years of his life he taught at Carleton University in Ottawa. His style is lyrical, incorporating basic tonality with mild dissonance and an emphasis on melody. Fleming was a prolific composer, and his works include more than 250 film scores and fifty orchestral and band compositions. *Sonatina* was written in 1941-1942.

Exploring the Score

In the first movement, the exposition ends in m. 48 and the recapitulation begins in m. 49. The only hint of a development is the section marked *Resolutely* (mm. 65-76), an extension of the second theme which appears in m. 77. The falling 3rd (E flat – C) in mm. 47-48 is reflected in the repeated G-E flat of mm. 100-103. The dashing quintuplets in mm. 104-105 are an extension of that 3rd.

The *gigue*-like second movement is in ternary form. The A sections have a spirit of perpetual motion. Keep the wrist relaxed and flexible during the many repetitions of the skipping motive. The B section is pleasantly lyrical with a variety of phrasing patterns in the LH accompaniment.

PIANO STUDIES ALBUM 10

Suggested Order of Difficulty

Page	Composer	Title
R48	George Frideric Handel	Study No. 5: Passacaglia
R58	Felix Mendelssohn	Study No. 8: Song without Words, Op. 102, No. 4
R51	Frédéric Chopin	Study No. 6: Trois nouvelles études, n° 3
R42	Stephen Heller	Study No. 2: Op. 81, No. 10
R44	Anatoli Lyadov	Study No. 3: A Trifle, Op. 2, No. 12
R46	Albert Loeschhorn	Study No. 4: Op. 67, No. 5
R39	Felix Mendelssohn	Study No. 1: Song without Words, Op. 30, No. 5
R54	Edward MacDowell	Study No. 7: Hungarian, Op. 39, No. 12
R61	Camille Saint-Saëns	Study No. 9: Prelude for the Left Hand, Op. 135, No. 1
R68	Alexander Scriabin	Study No. 11: Op. 2, No. 1
R74	Camille Saint-Saëns	Study No. 13: Study in Rhythm, Op. 52, No. 4
R78	Béla Bartók	Study No. 14: Bagatelle, Op. 6, No. 5
R64	Moritz Moszkowski	Study No. 10: Op. 72, No. 4
R70	Sergei Rachmaninoff	Study No. 12: Étude-Tableau, Op. 33, No. 8

Chart of Technical Figures

This chart lists the studies according to main technical focus. A study may be listed under more than one category.

Category	Composer	Study No.
scale figures	Stephen Heller	Study No. 2
	George Frideric Handel	Study No. 5
	Edward MacDowell	Study No. 7
	Sergei Rachmaninoff	Study No. 12
broken chord figures	Stephen Heller	Study No. 2
	George Frideric Handel	Study No. 5
	Sergei Rachmaninoff	Study No. 12
octaves	George Frideric Handel	Study No. 5
	Edward MacDowell	Study No. 7
	Moritz Moszkowski	Study No. 10
	Camille Saint-Saëns	Study No. 13
quick chord shifts	Anatoli Lyadov	Study No. 3
	Albert Loeschhorn	Study No. 4
	Frédéric Chopin	Study No. 6
	Edward MacDowell	Study No. 7
	Camille Saint-Saëns	Study No. 13
	Béla Bartók	Study No. 14
accompanying figures	Felix Mendelssohn	Study No. 1
	Felix Mendelssohn	Study No. 8
	Sergei Rachmaninoff	Study No. 12
melody and accompaniment in the same hand	Felix Mendelssohn	Study No. 8
	Camille Saint-Saëns	Study No. 9
melody presented in extended positions: octaves	Felix Mendelssohn	Study No. 1
	Camille Saint-Saëns	Study No. 13
melody presented in extended positions: chords	Felix Mendelssohn	Study No. 1
	Frédéric Chopin	Study No. 6
	Moritz Moszkowski	Study No. 10
	Alexander Scriabin	Study No. 11
	Sergei Rachmaninoff	Study No. 12
alternating hands	Anatoli Lyadov	Study No. 3
	Edward MacDowell	Study No. 7
repeated technical gesture	Moritz Moszkowski	Study No. 10
	Béla Bartók	Study No. 14
three-note mordent figures	Albert Loeschhorn	Study No. 4
	Edward MacDowell	Study No. 7
two against three	Frédéric Chopin	Study No. 6
	Camille Saint-Saëns	Study No. 13
arpeggiated figures	Camille Saint-Saëns	Study No. 9
	Alexander Scriabin	Study No. 11

The following discussions focus briefly on the technical approach of each piece.

F. Mendelssohn (1809-1847): *Study No. 1: Song without Words, Op. 30, No. 5* (S39)

Exploring the Score

Most of the *Songs without Words* are in ABA$_1$ form. The repeat of the first section gives this piece an AABA$_1$ *coda* form. Find these sections.

Practice Suggestions

- Keep the LH accompaniment light. Practice with fingers close to the keys. Keep the hand and wrist loose and free.
- Give dynamic shape to the RH octave melody.
- Use the damper pedal and *legato* fingerings to create a smooth melodic line.
- Isolate the RH double 3rds (mm. 9 and 32-35) for spot practice.

S. Heller (1813-1885): *Study No. 2: Op. 81, No. 10* (S42)

Practice Suggestions

This piece uses unconventional scale fingerings. The thumb often plays on a black key.

- Practice the sixteenth-note figures hands separately, with special attention to fingering.
- Practice the LH broken-chord accompaniment alone. Play the bottom note of weak beats with the fourth finger.
- The extended RH positions in mm. 41-47 present a special challenge. Shift the arm to move the hand into position (rather than stretching the fingers unnecessarily).

A. Lyadov (1855-1914): *Study No. 3: A Trifle, Op. 2, No. 12* (S44)

Background Information

Anatoli Lyadov was a Russian pianist who studied composition with Rimsky-Korsakov. *A Trifle* is one of fourteen pieces from his Op. 2, composed in 1876.

Practice Suggestions

- Block each measure, hands together, to learn chord positions and shifts.
- Practice in segments of three eighth notes, beginning with the last eighth note of each measure. Learn to play these groups quickly.
- Practice in eight-measure phrases.

A. Loeschhorn (1819-1905): *Study No. 4: Op. 67, No. 5* (S46)

Background Information

Albert Loeschhorn was a German piano teacher and composer. His works include a series of studies and a number of attractive piano solos. This piece, from his *Progressive Studies, Op. 67*, is similar in character to Mendelssohn's *Rondo Capriccioso*.

Practice Suggestions

This study is based on a three-note mordent figure.

- Analyze the harmonies. Look for examples of tonic-dominant relationships.
- Practice the mordent figures with a light touch.
- Experiment with fingering, especially in the LH. Choose a fingering which gives you the most precise, clear sound.

G.F. Handel (1685-1759): *Study No. 5: Passacaglia* (S48)

Background Information

A *passacaglia* is a set of variations built on a bass line or a repeating chord pattern. When he wrote the suite which includes *Passacaglia*, Handel was the musical director and conductor of the Royal Academy, an English theater of Italian opera.

Exploring the Score

- Discuss the ways in which Handel accumulates drive and tension. What is the over-all rhythmic organization of the piece? [subdivisions increase from eighth notes to triplets to dotted rhythms to sixteenths]
- Analyze the basic chord progression:

Notice that every downbeat chord is a step lower: G, F, E flat, D.

Practice Suggestions

- The opening dotted rhythm is reminiscent of the French overture style. Play the dotted rhythm crisply, in an over-dotted manner.
- Practice the chord progression as it occurs in each hand. Memorize the progression.
- Determine the touch for each variation. For example, play mm. 9-20 *legato*, play mm. 21-28 with a lighter touch, and play mm. 29-32 crisply.
- Isolate sixteenth-note passages for hands separate practice. For technical security, practice these passages with a variety of touches.

F. Chopin (1810-1849): *Study No. 6: Trois nouvelles études, n° 3* (S51)

Background Information
Chopin composed *Trois nouvelles études* in 1839 for a method book written by Ignaz Moscheles and François-Joseph Fétis.

Exploring the Score
Chopin uses a consistent texture, theme, and rhythmic figure throughout. How can you determine the structure?
- In m. 17, there is a sudden shift from A flat major and the music modulates freely.
- In m. 41, the opening returns.

Teaching Suggestions
The two-against-three cross rhythm is constant. Students should be comfortable with this rhythmic pattern before beginning the piece. Chopin emphasizes his intention for a flowing sound quality by marking the entire piece as one phrase!

Practice Suggestions
- Tap two-against-three with your feet (right foot triplets, left foot duple eighths).
- Play the melody and the bass. Use pedal. Give dynamic shape to your melody.
- Practice the RH alone, projecting the melody line above the remaining notes of the chords. Connect the top notes whenever possible and direct arm weight to the melody tones.
- Find the tied notes. Practice measures with tied notes hands separately.

E. MacDowell (1860-1908): *Study No. 7: Hungarian, Op. 39, No. 12* (S54)

Background Information
MacDowell was an American composer, pianist, and teacher. He pursued most of his musical studies in Europe from 1876 to 1888, and his style remained firmly rooted in the European Romantic tradition.

Exploring the Score
In a technical study, it is helpful to identify repeating figures. Look for:
- single-note sixteenth figures (as in mm. 3-14)
- sixteenths combined with solid intervals (as in mm. 15-16)
- scales (as in mm. 13-14, 25-26)
- blocked chords (as in mm. 34-35)
- two-against-three rhythms (as in mm. 50-53)
- solid octaves (as in mm. 82-93)
- broken octaves (as in mm. 94-97)
- interlocking octaves (as in mm. 98-101)

Practice Suggestions
- Practice each figure at a slow tempo. When the figure is secure, practice it with the metronome for consistent tempo.
- In slow practice, avoid stiffness and tension in the hand and arm. Cultivate the feeling of relaxation and ease at all times.

F. Mendelssohn (1809-1847): *Study No. 8: Song without Words, Op. 102, No. 4* (S58)

Practice Suggestions
The performance goal of this piece is a smoothly flowing quality and an expressive melody. Use the pedal throughout to enhance *legato* and harmonic color. The sixteenth-note accompaniment consistently moves from the LH to the RH beneath the melody.
- Determine which accompanying tones will be played by the RH. Practice the accompaniment alone with pedal.
- Play the melody with both hands, in unison. Listen for an expressive dynamic shape in each phrase.
- Block mm. 27-28 hands together.
- Practice the entire piece as written, hands together, phrase by phrase. Shape and project the melody.

C. Saint-Saëns (1835-1921): *Study No. 9: Prelude for the Left Hand, Op. 135, No. 1* (S61)

Background Information
Camille Saint-Saëns, a French composer, pianist and organist, was a child prodigy. He later studied at the Paris Conservatoire, and established a musical reputation both in France and abroad. (There is also a study for the left hand in Level 9: *Prelude* by Alexander Scriabin).

Practice Suggestions
Prelude for the Left Hand is placed mainly in the middle register of the keyboard. Find a sitting position which enables you to play comfortably with your LH in that location. (For example, you should be able to reach the notes in mm. 18-20 easily.)
- Important melody notes are marked with accents and double stems. Play those notes starting with the finger lifted off the key.
- Practice the thirty-second note arpeggios with a smooth arm movement.
- Most of the piece consists of single tones. The double notes of mm. 33-37 are an exception. To practice mm. 35-36, repeat pairs of sixteenth notes four to six times. Notice that the natural movement is *in* for the thumb, *out* for the second finger.
- Follow the pedal markings carefully.

M. Moszkowski (1854-1925): *Study No. 10: Op. 72, No. 4* (S64)

Practice Suggestions

The repeated intervals and chords in this study require a highly developed technique.

- Throughout your practicing, keep a loose hand and wrist. Practice quietly with a light touch. Do not add the loud dynamic levels in mm. 25-43 until you can play these passages lightly and easily.
- To avoid tension, keep the hand in straight alignment with the forearm. (Tension results when the hand is turned at an angle.)

Create special practice techniques. For example, in mm. 1-2:

1. Play the LH top notes separately.
2. Play the pairs of sixteenths quickly, with a rest after each pair.
3. Practice groups of four sixteenth notes with a rest after each group.
4. Play the moving top LH notes louder than the repeated lower LH notes.

A. Scriabin (1872-1915): *Study No. 11: Op. 2, No. 1* (S68)

Background Information

Scriabin wrote *Three Pieces, Op. 2* during 1887-1889, when he was a student at the Moscow Conservatory. Scriabin's early style is highly chromatic, and often demands wide hand stretches.

Exploring the Score

- Notice the key signature changes. Do they indicate modulations to major or minor tonalities? How are those keys related to the home key of C sharp minor?
- What are the loudest and softest dynamic indications?
- Compare mm. 1-8 with 25-33 and mm. 17-24 with 34-41. Are these repetitions exact? What changes does Scriabin make?

Practice Suggestions

The arpeggiated chords extend beyond an octave. Pedal changes should:

- establish a clear change of harmony
- include the full LH chord
- enhance the *legato* connection of the melody

S. Rachmaninoff (1873-1943): *Study No. 12: Étude-Tableau, Op. 33, No. 8* (S70)

Background Information

The Russian pianist and composer Sergei Rachmaninoff wrote in a Romantic style at a time when other composers were experimenting with atonality and expressionism. The *Études-Tableaux, Op. 33* were written in 1911. Much of the appeal of Rachmaninoff's compositions lies in the sumptuous texture of his music.

Practice Suggestions

- Listen to the *Celebration Series* recording of this *étude* to hear the way the performer brings out melody and balances thick textures.
- Practice in short sections to achieve dynamic control of the melody and parallel chords.

C. Saint-Saëns (1835-1921): *Study No. 13: Study in Rhythm, Op. 52, No. 4* (S74)

Exploring the Score

This piece is a study in two-against-three rhythms. The variety of combinations seems limitless.

- The rhythm in m. 1 contains both two and three.

- In m. 7, the RH plays three and the LH plays two. In m. 9 they trade.
- In m. 11, the hands trade rhythms on the second beat.
- In mm. 62-65, Saint-Saëns changes the meter to 5/8 and puts combinations of two and three next to each other. How is the rhythm of mm. 62-65 slightly different from mm. 58-61?
- In mm. 92-93, the eighth notes are divided into thirty-second notes.
- Notice the imitation between hands in mm. 47-50.

Teaching Suggestions

Tapping and playing on the closed keyboard cover will facilitate control and coordination, even for advanced students.

B. Bartók (1881-1945): *Study No. 14: Bagatelle,*
Op. 5, No. 5 (S78)

Background Information

For background information, see the discussion of
Bartók's *Bagatelle, Op. 6, No. 11* in List E.

Exploring the Score

The melody of *Bagatelle* is based on a Slovak folk
tune. The chordal accompaniment has a pentatonic
character.

- Listen to the folk-like quality of the melody.
- Where does the melody occur in the RH? [m. 28]
- Circle the *sforzando* marks.

Practice Suggestions

The accompaniment consists of repeated chords.

- Keep the wrist relaxed to avoid tension.
- Practice the RH stepwise sequential chord
  clusters slowly for accuracy.
- Notice the written-in *rubato* created by the
  quarter-note triplets in mm. 56, 60, 70, and 75.
  Tap these four-against-three cross rhythms
  before playing.

LEVEL 10 CONCLUSION

In all courses of piano study, some of the students who enter the series will not finish. Student who reach and
complete Level 10 demonstrate an unusual dedication and accomplishment. These students will have
accumulated not only a rich background of music literature, but also an understanding of the harmonic and
formal structure of music, and information about composers and the history of musical styles and periods. This
musical experience becomes an integral part of a student's life. As far as the *Celebration Series* is concerned, the
goal has been achieved. The summit has been reached, and the view is glorious. You, the teacher, know that Level
10 is something like a graduation ceremony. Finishing Level 10 is a commencement into a lifetime of making
music at the piano.

To return to the analogy of the climb, the student's ascent has been made easier through the expert assistance of a
guide – you, the teacher. You have assisted your student at every step, planning the smoothest path for the
journey, avoiding potential pitfalls, and offering constant encouragement. Your gift to the student has been your
affirmation and guidance. Because of your effort, your student will cherish the cultural tradition of classical
music for a lifetime. What a gift you have given!

"Opus" (Op.) is a term used with a number to designate the position of a given work in the chronological sequence of works by the composer. However, these numbers are often an unreliable guide, and may have been assigned by a publisher rather than the composer. Sometimes a single work will have conflicting opus numbers. Certain genres, such as operas and other vocal works, were not always assigned opus numbers.

For these reasons, individual works by a number of composers are identified by numbers assigned in scholarly thematic catalogues. The catalogues referred to in the *Celebration Series* are listed below. (Some catalogue numbers include the prefix "Anh." (for example, BWV Anh. 121). "Anh." is an abbreviation for *Anhang,* a German word meaning appendix or supplement.)

Works by Carl Philipp Emanuel Bach are often identified by "Wq" and/or "H" (Helm) numbers (for example, *Morceaux divers pour clavecin, Wq 117/39, H 98*). Alfred Wotquenne (1867-1939) was a Belgian music bibliographer and author of *Thematisches Verzeichnis der Werke von Carl Philipp Emanuel Bach* (Leipzig, 1905, revised 1964). Eugene Helm is an American musicologist and author of *A New Thematic Catalogue of the Works of C.P.E. Bach* (New Haven: Yale University Press, 1989).

Works by Johann Sebastian Bach are identified by "BWV" numbers (for example, *Allemande in G Minor, BWV 836*). BWV is the abbreviation for *Bach Werke Verzeichnis,* the short title of the *Thematisch-systematisches Verzeichnis der musikalischen Werke von Johann Sebastian Bach* (Leipzig, 1950), a monumental thematic catalogue of Bach's complete works compiled by the German music librarian Wolfgang Schmieder.

Works published during Ludwig van Beethoven's lifetime were given opus numbers. In the thematic catalogue of Beethoven's works, *Das Werk Beethovens* (Munich and Duisburg, 1955, completed by H. Halm), compiled by German musicologist Georg Ludwig Kinsky (1882-1951), works which were published posthumously were designated "WoO". WoO is an abbreviation for *Werk ohne Opuszahl* (work without opus number).

Works by George Frideric Handel are identified by "HWV" numbers (for example, *Gavotte in G Major, HWV 491*). HWV is an abbreviation for *Handel Werke Verzeichnis.* The full title for this thematic catalogue, compiled by Margaret and Walter Eisen, is *Händel-Handbuch, gleichzeitig Suppl. zu Hallische Händel-Ausgabe* (Kassel: Bärenreiter, 1978-1986).

Works by Franz Joseph Haydn are identified by Hoboken numbers (for example, *Sonata in D Major, Hob. XVI:37*). Anthony van Hoboken was a Dutch

musicologist. His thematic catalogue, *Joseph Haydn: Thematisch-bibliographisches Werkverzeichnis* (Mainz: B. Schott, 1957-1971) divides Haydn's works into a number of categories. The piano sonatas are in category XVI.

Works by Wolfgang Amadeus Mozart are identified by "KV" numbers (for example, *Sonata in C Major, KV 545*). KV stands for *Köchel Verzeichnis.* Ludwig Ritter von Köchel (1800-1877) was an Austrian professor of botany who devoted his retirement years to collecting all the known works by Mozart. He created a chronological catalogue in which these works are listed and numbered.

Works by Domenico Scarlatti are usually identified by two numbers, one beginning with "L" and one beginning with "K." The L numbers are from *Opere complete per clavicembalo* (Milan: Ricordi, 1906-1908), compiled by Alessandro Longo. K stands for Ralph Kirkpatrick, an American harpsichordist and scholar who provided a revised and more exact chronology and a new numbering system for the sonatas in his book *Domenico Scarlatti* (Princeton: Princeton University Press, 1953, rev. 1968).

Works by Franz Schubert are identified by "Deutsch" numbers (for example, *Waltz in A Flat, Op. 9, No. 12, D. 365*). These numbers were assigned by Otto Erich Deutsch (1883-1967) in his thematic catalogue of Schubert's works, *Thematisches Verzeichnis seiner Werke in chronologischer Folge* (*Neue Schubert Ausgabe* Serie VIII, Bd. 4, Kassel, 1978).

Works by Georg Philipp Telemann are identified by "TWV" numbers (for example, *Fantasia in D Minor, TWV 33:2*). TWV is an abbreviation for *Telemann Werkverzeichnis.* This thematic catalogue – *Thematischer-Systematisches Verzeichnis seiner Werke: Telemann Werkverzeichnis* (Kassel: Bärenreiter, 1984) – was compiled by Martin Runke.

Appendix 2: Royal Conservatory of Music Examinations

Repertoire and studies from the *Celebration Series, 2nd edition* can be used for Royal Conservatory of Music (RCM) Examinations in the United States. Of course, any teacher can use the entire *Celebration Series* without participating in the RCM examination system.

For examination purposes, compositions in the *Repertoire Albums* are divided into Lists (A, B, C, etc.) according to stylistic period or genre. This classification system provides a useful, quick chronological and style reference.

Each Level in the RCM Examinations Certificate Program is a stepping stone, established as a logical assessment point for a developing musician. Candidates for practical examinations are tested in the performance of repertoire, studies, and technique. Ear training and sight reading requirements help develop and reinforce solid musicianship skills. Theory Examinations, designed to complement practical studies, begin at Level 5.

RCM Examinations serve a purpose similar to the syllabus and performance auditions sponsored throughout the United States by professional groups such as state-affiliated associations of the Music Teachers National Association.

This index lists all the repertoire and studies in the *Celebration Series* by composer. The works by each composer are listed in order of Level. This enables teachers to find compositions by any given composer according to Level, to search for specific compositions, and to examine the total spectrum of a particular composer.

Within each Level, pieces from the Repertoire Albums (identified by "R") precede pieces from the Studies Albums (identified by "S"). The number immediately following "R" or "S" identifies the Level. The number following the dash identifies the page number of the composition in the Album. For example, Susan Alcon's *The Wanderer* "R4-30" can be found on page 30 of *Repertoire Album 4*. Similarly, Leon Aubry's *Woodland Scene* "S1-16" can be found on page 16 of *Studies Album 1*. All the pieces in the *Studies Albums* are numbered. In this index, the study number is given in square brackets, followed by the title and/or opus number (for example, *[Study No. 15] Woodland Scene* or *[Study No. 7] Bagatelle, Op. 6, No. 3).

Anonymous
  [Study No. 8] Ukrainian Folk Song, S1-9
  Anglaise in D Minor, R3-12

Alcon, Susan (1953-   )
  The Wanderer, R4-30

Archer, Violet (1913-   )
  Jig, R5-38
  Church Scene, R6-36

Aubry, Leon (1869-1942)
  [Study No. 15] Woodland Scene, S1-16

Babell, William (1690-1723)
  Rigadoon in A Minor, R4-7

Bach, Carl Philipp Emanuel (1714-1788)
  Minuet in C Major, R1-6
  March in D Major, BWV Anh. 122, R4-6
  La Caroline, R5-20

Bach, Johann Christoph Friedrich (1732-1795)
  Schwäbisch, R1-5

Bach, Johann Sebastian (1685-1750)
  Minuet in G Major, R1-8
  Bourrée in D Minor (attr.), R2-7
  Minuet in G Minor, BWV Anh. 115 (attr.), R3-6
  Musette in D Major, BWV Anh. 126 (attr.), R3-13
  Minuet in D Minor, BWV Anh. 132 (attr.), R4-9
  Little Prelude in G Minor, BWV 929, R5-4
  Allemande in G Minor, BWV 836, R5-12
  Little Prelude in D Minor, BWV 926, R6-4
  Bourrée in B Minor, R6-10
  [Study No. 4] Applicatio, BWV 994, S6-29
  Invention No. 1 in C Major, BWV 772, R7-4
  Minuet in B Flat, R7-10
  Little Prelude in C Major, BWV 933, R7-12
  [Study No. 7] Little Prelude in F Major, BWV 927, S7-16
  Invention No. 13 in A Minor, BWV 784, R8-10

Invention No. 14 in B Flat, BWV 785, R8-14
Sinfonia No. 15 in B Minor, BWV 801, R9-4
Sinfonia No. 3 in D Major, BWV 789, R9-6
Adagissimo, R9-8
Prelude and Fugue in C Minor, BWV 847, R9-13
Prelude and Fugue in E Minor, BWV 855, R9-18
Prelude and Fugue in F Major, BWV 856, R10-4
Prelude and Fugue in F Sharp Major, BWV 858, R10-8
Prelude and Fugue in C Minor, BWV 871, R10-12

Bach, Wilhelm Friedemann (1710-1784)
  Minuet in G Major, R2-5

Bartók, Béla (1881-1945)
  Bagatelle, Op. 6, No. 6, R3-28
  Slovak Peasant's Dance, R3-32
  [Study No. 7] Bagatelle, Op. 6, No. 3, S5-14
  Dawn, R6-35
  Evening at the Village, R8-52
  Bear Dance, R9-104
  [Study No. 10] Bagatelle, Op. 6, No. 2, S9-28
  Bagatelle, Op. 6, No. 11, R10-114
  Bagatelle, Op. 6, No. 12, R10-116
  [Study No. 14] Bagatelle, Op. 6, No. 5, S10-78

Beethoven, Ludwig van (1770-1827)
  German Dance (arr.), R1-11
  German Dance, R2-16
  Little Piece, WoO 61a, R2-37
  Sonatina in G Major, Anh. 5 (Second Movement: Romanze), R3-14
  Lustig und Traurig, WoO 54, R6-29
  Sonata in G Major, Op. 79 (Second Movement), R7-34
  Bagatelle in B Flat, Op. 119, No. 11, R7-36
  Sonata in G Major, Op. 49, No. 2 (First Movement), R8-30
  Six Easy Variations in G Major, WoO 77, R9-55
  Sonata in C Minor, Op. 10, No. 1, R10-38

Benda, Jiří (1722-1795)
Sonatina No. 3 in A Minor, R6-24

Berens, Hermann (1826-1880)
[Study No. 15], S2-31
[Study No. 14], S3-17
[Study No. 5] Op. 70, No. 50, S4-22

Berkovich, Isak (1902-1972)
Mazurka, R2-23
[Study No. 9], S2-25

Berlin, Boris (1907-)
Old MacDonald Had a Farm (arr.), Intro-16
Surprise Symphony (arr. of theme by Haydn),
    Intro-20
Three Fine Ducks (arr.), R1-31
[Study No. 12] Snowflakes, S1-13
The Haunted Castle, R3-31

Bertini, Henri (1798-1876)
[Study No. 6] Op. 166, No. 6, S2-22
[Study No. 4], S3-7
Andante in A Major, R5-16

Bonis, Mélanie (1858-1937)
Prière, Intro-8
The Sewing Machine, R1-20

Brahms, Johannes (1833-1897)
Intermezzo, Op. 116, No. 6, R10-78
Intermezzo, Op. 76, No. 6, R10-80

Burgmüller, Johann Friedrich (1806-1874)
[Study No. 12] L'Arabesque, Op. 100, No. 2, S3-15
[Study No. 7] The Wagtail, Op. 100, No. 11, S4-24
[Study No. 10] Restlessness, Op. 100, No. 18, S4-27
[Study No. 8] The Chase, Op. 100, No. 9, S5-16
[Study No. 2] Morning Bell, Op. 109, No. 9, S8-28
[Study No. 9] The Gypsies, Op. 109, No. 4, S8-46

Buttstedt, Johann Heinrich (1666-1727)
Air in F Major, R1-7

Camidge, Matthew (1764-1844)
Sonatina in G Major (Last Movement), R6-18

Chatman, Stephen (1950-)
Monkey Business, Intro-22
Freak-Out, Intro-32

Chopin, Frédéric (1810-1849)
Mazurka in A Flat, Op. 24, No. 3, R7-42
Mazurka, Op. 24, No. 1, R8-38
Prelude in D Flat, Op. 28, No. 15, R9-69
Waltz in C Sharp Minor, Op. 64, No. 2, R9-72
Prélude, Op. 45, R10-60
Mazurka, Op. 63, No. 1, R10-64
[Study No. 6] Trois nouvelles études, nº 3, S10-51

Cimarosa, Domenico (1749-1801)
Sonata No. 6 in G Major, R6-12
Sonata No. 18 in A Major, R8-18

Clarke, Jeremiah (*ca* 1674-1707)
Minuet in G Major, R4-5

Clementi, Muzio (1752-1832)
Waltz, R2-12
*Sonatina in G Major, Op. 36, No. 2 (Second
    Movement)*, R4-13
*Sonatina in G Major, Op. 36, No. 5 (Third
    Movement: Rondo)*, R5-22
*Sonatina in D Major, Op. 36, No. 6 (First
    Movement)*, R7-24
*Sonatina in D Major, Op. 37, No. 2 (First
    Movement)*, R8-26

Clérambault, Louis Nicolas (1676-1749)
Allegro in D Minor, R4-8

Coulthard, Jean (1908-)
The Jackhammer, Intro-27
The Whale's Sad Story, R2-28
First Little Dance (Lavender's Blue), R2-34
Star Gazing, R5-32
A Little Joke, R3-34
Where the Trade-Winds Blow, R6-42

Couperin, François (1668-1733)
Allemande in D Minor, R7-6
Les chérubins, R8-4

Crone, Brian (1957-)
March of the Robots, Intro-25

Czerny, Carl (1791-1857)
[Study No. 1], S1-4
[Study No. 3] Op. 777, No. 3, S1-5
[Study No. 2] Op. 777, No. 8, S2-18
[Study No. 5] Op. 777, No. 22, S2-21
[Study No. 14], S2-30
[Study No. 2], S3-5
[Study No. 8] Op. 139, No. 7, S3-8
[Study No. 11] Op. 139, No. 24, S3-14
[Study No. 2] Op. 599, No. 85, S4-19
[Study No. 8] Op. 599, No. 83, S4-25
[Study No. 9], S4-26
[Study No. 13] Op. 599, No. 45, S4-31
[Study No. 1] Op. 139, No. 40, S5-4
[Study No. 12] Op. 139, No. 91, S6-42

Dandrieu, Jean-François (1682-1738)
The Fifes (arr.), R1-10

Danna, Mychael (1958-)
Sleeping Bells, R5-36

Daquin, Louis-Claude (1694-1772)
Le coucou (Rondeau), R9-10

Debussy, Claude (1862-1918)
Golliwogg's Cake-walk, R9-94
Prélude, Book I, No. 1 (Danseuses de Delphes), R10-90
Prélude, Book II, No. 5 (Bruyères), R10-92

Dela, Maurice (1919-1978)
Hommage, R10-108

Diabelli, Anton (1781-1858)
Sonatina in G Major, Op. 151, No. 1 (First Movement), R3-18
Sonatina in F Major, Op. 168, No. 1 (First Movement), R4-18
Sonatina in C Major, Op. 168, No. 3 (First Movement), R5-24

Duke, David (1950-   )
Bear Dance (Phrygian Mode), Intro-6
March (Lydian Mode), R1-35
She's Like the Swallow (arr.), R1-36
Barcarole, R4-40

Duvernoy, Jean-Baptiste (1802-1880)
[Study No. 10] Op. 176, No. 17, S2-26
[Study No. 6] Op. 176, No. 24, S4-23

Elliott, Carleton (1928-   )
Canon, R2-39

Falla, Manuel de (1876-1946)
The Miller's Dance, R10-101

Ferrell, Billie
Little Monster, Intro-18

Fiala, George (1922-   )
Postlude, Op. 7, No. 6 (à la Shostakovich), R5-37

Field, John (1782-1837)
Nocturne in B Flat, R8-48

Finch, Douglas (1957-   )
Cancan, R6-34

Finney, Ross Lee (1906-   )
[Study No. 9] Playing Ball, S6-36

Fleming, Robert (1921-1976)
[Study No. 1] Toccatina, S8-25
Sonatina, R10-134

Freedman, Harry (1922-   )
Rent-A-Rag, R8-62

Gade, Niels (1817-1890)
[Study No. 8] Scherzo, Op. 19, No. 2, S9-22

Gallant, Pierre (1950-   )
Sakura (arr.), Intro-24
This Old Man (arr.), R1-23
Sur le pont d'Avignon (arr.), R1-38
Dorian Invention, R1-40
In the Dorian Mode, R2-38
Jazz Invention, R2-39
Six Variations on "Land of the Silver Birch," R10-122

Gedike, Alexander (1877-1957)
A Song, Op. 36, No. 3, Intro-26
Rigaudon, R1-22
A Happy Tale, Op. 36, No. 31, R1-28
Military Trumpets, Op. 36, No. 53, R2-29
The Shepherd's Pipe, Op. 36, No. 55, R2-32
Fugato, Op. 36, No. 40, R2-35
Fugato, Op. 36, No. 46, R2-40
[Study No. 1], S2-17
[Study No. 13], S2-29
Sonatina in C Major, Op. 36, No. 20, R3-21
[Study No. 10] Op. 32, No. 12, S3-13
[Study No. 3] Op. 36, No. 26, S4-20
[Study No. 4] Op. 32, No. 16, S5-10

Giarbella, Luciano (1934-   )
Gnomi, R6-48

Glinka, Mikhail Ivanovich (1804-1857)
Russian Polka, R2-20

Graeff, Johann Friedrich (1711-1789)
Air in A Minor, Op. 7, No. 4, R3-9

Grechaninov, Alexander (1864-1956)
A Frightening Story, Op. 98, No. 11, R3-27
Mazurka, Op. 98, No. 13, R3-36

Grieg, Edvard (1843-1907)
Arietta, Op. 12, No. 1, R5-27
Puck, Op. 71, No. 3, R8-42
[Study No. 3] Little Bird, Op. 43, No. 4, S8-30
Butterfly, Op. 43, No. 1, R9-60

Gurlitt, Cornelius (1820-1901)
Little Waltz, Op. 117, Intro-9
Waltz (duet), Intro-28
The Hunt, R1-18
[Study No. 5], S1-6
Theme and Variation, R2-19
Canon, R2-36
[Study No. 1], S3-4
[Study No. 9], S3-12
Sonatina in G Major, Op. 188, No. 3, R4-22
[Study No. 4] Op. 141, No. 4, S4-21
[Study No. 7] Op. 132, No. 1, S6-34
[Study No. 8] Op. 132, No. 7, S7-17

Handel, George Frideric (1685-1759)
Minuet in F Major, R1-13
Gavotte in G Major, HWV 491, R3-4
Bourrée in G Major, R4-11
Fuga in G Major, HWV 582, R5-5
Allemande in A Minor, HWV 478, R6-6
Gigue in D Minor, R6-8
[Study No. 10] Entrée in G Minor, HWV 453, S6-38
[Study No. 11], S7-20
Allemande in D Minor, R8-16
[Study No. 7] Capriccio, HWV 483, S8-42
[Study No. 3] Lesson, HWV 496, S9-8
[Study No. 6] Prelude, HWV 428, S9-18
[Study No. 5] Passacaglia, S10-48

Hansen, Joan
[Study No. 7] Irish Jig, S2-23

Hanson, Howard (1896-1981)
Enchantment, R4-38

Harris, Eddie
Bulgarian Shepherd's Tune, R2-25

Haslinger, Tobias (1787-1842)
Sonatina in C Major (First Movement), R4-26

Hässler, Johann Wilhelm (1747-1822)
Suite in C Major, R1-14

Haydn, Franz Joseph (1732-1809)
Surprise Symphony (theme, arr. by Boris Berlin), Intro-20
Allegretto in G Major (arr. by Clifford Poole), R1-12
Quadrille, R2-8
Vivace in D Major, Hob. XVII:Anh., R3-16
Andantino in E Flat, R4-16
Sonata in G Major, Hob. XVI:G1 (First Movement), R6-21
Sonata in D Major, Hob. XVI:37, R9-31
Sonata in D Major, Hob. XVI:51, R10-16

Heller, Stephen (1813-1888)
[Study No. 11] Op. 45, No. 2 (L'avalanche), S4-28
[Study No. 5] A Curious Story, Op. 138, No. 9, S5-5
[Study No. 11] Barcarole, Op. 138, No. 5, S5-22
[Study No. 1] Op. 119, No. 24, S6-24
[Study No. 11] Abenddämmerung, Op. 138, No. 3, S6-40
[Study No. 1] Op. 125, No. 19, S7-4
[Study No. 12] The Lesson, Op. 125, No. 24, S7-22
[Study No. 5] Op. 46, No. 16, S8-35
[Study No. 7] Op. 47, No. 24, S9-20
[Study No. 2] Op. 81, No. 10, S10-42

Henderson, Ruth Watson (1932-)
[Study No. 5] Toccatina, S6-30

Hiller, Johann Adam (1728-1804)
Andante in A Major, R3-8

Hummel, Johann Nepomuk (1778-1837)
[Study No. 8], S3-11

Janus, Edward (1943-)
Plaisir d'amour (arr.), Intro-21
Polish Folk Song (duet, arr.), Intro-30

Joachim, Otto (1910-)
Plastic Soldier, R3-40

Kabalevsky, Dmitri (1904-1987)
Song, Op. 39, No. 8, Intro-7
March-Like, Op. 39, No. 3, Intro-7
Battle Song, Op. 89, No. 30, R1-25
[Study No. 2] A Porcupine Dance, Op. 89, No. 8, S1-4
[Study No. 10] Playing, Op. 39, No. 5, S1-11
[Study No. 16] The Little Juggler, Op. 89, No. 21, S2-32
Sonatina in A Minor, Op. 27, No. 18, R5-18
[Study No. 9] Scherzo, Op. 27, No. 13, S5-18
[Study No. 2] Toccatina, Op. 27, No. 12, S6-26
[Study No. 9] Op. 27, No. 3, S7-18
Prelude, Op. 38, No. 8, R8-58
[Study No. 11] Op. 27, No. 24, S8-51
Prelude, Op. 38, No. 1, R9-100
Prelude, Op. 38, No. 2, R9-102
Prelude, Op. 38, No. 15, R10-104
Prelude, Op. 38, No. 20, R10-106

Kadosa, Pál (1903-1983)
[Study No. 11], S2-27
[Study No. 12], S5-23

Karganov, Génari (1858-1890)
Little Waltz, Op. 25, No. 3, R4-34

Kasemets, Udo (1919-)
Polly-Wolly-Doodle (arr.), R1-26

Keller, Godfrey (-1704)
Prelude in G Major, R7-8

Khachaturian, Aram (1903-1978)
An Evening Tale, R2-26
[Study No. 8] Skipping Rope, S2-24
Ivan and Natasha, R8-54

Kirnberger, Johann Philipp (1721-1783)
Lullaby (arr.), R3-5

Kossenko, Viktor (1896-1938)
Melody, Op. 15, No. 11, R7-38

Sonatina in G Major, R7-30
Sonata in C Major, KV 545 (First Movement), R8-34
[Study No. 4] Allegro in C Major, KV 9a (5a), S8-32
Sonata in G Major, KV 283 (189h), R9-40
Sonata in F Major, KV 280 (189e), R10-25

Niamath, Linda (1939-   )
Balloons, Intro-17
Bears, R1-29
[Study No. 4] Sleepy Little Kitten, S1-6
[Study No. 9] On the Trampoline, S1-10
[Study No. 14] Robots, S1-15
Penguins, R2-21
[Study No. 3] Kangaroos, S2-19
[Study No. 12] Butterflies, S2-28
Turtle, R3-30

Niemann, Walter (1876-1953)
Cradle Song (for Dolly Dora), R5-30
*[Study No. 10] The Three Little Chatterboxes,
   Op. 46, No. 17*, S7-19

Noona, Walter (1932-   ) and Carol (1935-   )
The Peacock's Fan, Intro-5

Oesten, Theodor (1813-1870)
[Study No. 7] Hunting Horns, S1-8

Olson, Lynn Freeman (1938-1987)
Lady Moon, Intro-15

Owens, Terry Winter
Israeli Dance, Intro-23

Pachelbel, Johann (1653-1706)
Gavotte with Two Variations, R5-6

Pachulski, Henryk (1859-1921)
Valse mignonne, R5-28
Prelude in C Minor, Op. 8, No. 1, R6-32

Palmgren, Selim (1878-1951)
May Night, Op. 27, No. 4, R9-87

Papp, Lajos (1935-   )
[Study No. 13] Martellato and *Forte-piano*, S1-14
Variations, R3-37

Parsons, Margaret (1914-1991)
Hush-A-Bye (arr.), Intro-10

Pentland, Barbara (1912-   )
Slow Song, R2-31
Shadows, R10-119

Pescetti, Giovanni Battista (1704-1766)
Presto, R8-12

Petzold, Christian (1677-1733)
Minuet in G Minor, BWV Anh. 115, (attr. to
   J.S. Bach), R3-6

Pleyel, Ignaz (1757-1831)
Rondo in G Major, R3-22

Poole, Clifford (1916-   )
Allegretto in G Major (arr. of theme by Haydn), R1-12
[Study No. 6], S1-7
[Study No. 11] Chords on Parade, S1-12
Fleas, R2-22
Ghost Town, R7-37

Purcell, Henry (1659-1695)
Air in D Minor, R1-9
Hornpipe in B Flat, R3-10
Rigadoon in C Major, R4-10

Rachmaninoff, Sergei (1873-1943)
Elegy, Op. 3, No. 1, R10-83
[Study No. 12] Étude-Tableau, Op. 33, No. 8,
   S10-70

Rameau, Jean-Philippe (1683-1764)
[Study No. 6] La joyeuse, S5-12

Ravel, Maurice (1875-1937)
Menuet, R9-90
Prélude, R10-96

Rebikov, Vladimir Ivanovich (1866-1920)
Waltz, R7-48

Reinecke, Carl (1824-1910)
*Sonatina in G Major, Op. 136, No. 2 (First and
   Second Movements)*, R3-24

Reinhold, Hugo (1854-1935)
[Study No. 2], S7-6

Riegel, Henri-Joseph (1741-1799)
Sonata in D Major (Second Movement), R7-21

Saint-Saëns, Camille (1835-1921)
*[Study No. 9] Prelude for the Left Hand,
   Op. 135, No. 1*, S10-61
[Study No. 13] Study in Rhythm, Op. 52, No. 4,
   S10-74

Sartorius, Erasmus (1577-1637)
Canon, R1-38

Scarlatti, Alessandro (1660-1725)
Aria in D Minor, R2-15

Scarlatti, Domenico (1685-1757)
Sonata in D Minor, L 423/K 32, R4-12
Sonata in B Flat, L 36/K 42 (Minuetto), R5-14
Sonata in D Minor, L 58/K 64, R7-16
Sonata in D Minor, L 413/K 9, R9-25
Sonata in C Major, L 104/K 159, R9-28

Schafer, R. Murray (1933-   )
Polytonality, R9-114

Schmitt, Jacob (1803-1853)
Sonatina in C Major, Op. 83, R4-14

Schubert, Franz (1797-1828)
Ländler, R2-11
Écossaise, R2-14
Waltz in D Flat, Op. 9, No. 14 (D. 365), R7-44
Waltz in A Flat, Op. 9, No. 12 (D. 365), R7-45
Moment musical, Op. 94, No. 4, R10-56

Schumann, Robert (1810-1856)
Melody, Op. 68, No. 1, R2-18
The Happy Farmer, Op. 68, No. 10, R4-29
A Little Romance, Op. 68, No. 19, R5-26
Waltz in A Minor, Op. 124, No. 4, R6-30
From Foreign Lands and People, Op. 15, No. 1, R6-31
The Stranger, Op. 68, No. 29, R8-45
Romance in F Sharp, Op. 28, No. 2, R9-80
Whims, Op. 12, No. 4, R9-82
The Prophet Bird, Op. 82, No. 7, R10-53

Schytte, Ludwig (1848-1909)
[Study No. 3], S3-6
[Study No. 7], S3-10

Scriabin, Alexander (1872-1915)
Prelude, Op. 2, No. 2, R6-39
Prelude, Op. 11, No. 15, R8-51
Prelude in G Flat, Op. 11, No. 13, R9-99
[Study No. 12] Prelude for the Left Hand, Op. 9, No. 1, S9-32
Prelude, Op. 11, No. 14, R10-88
[Study No. 11], Op. 2, No. 1, S10-68

Shostakovich, Dmitri (1906-1975)
Soldier's March, R1-32
The Mechanical Doll, Op. 69, No. 6, R5-34
[Study No. 6] Dance, S6-32
Prelude in F Minor, R7-52
Prelude, Op. 34, No. 15, R8-56

Silvester, Frederick (1901-1966)
Early One Morning (arr.), R1-19

Smetana, Bedřich (1824-1884)
Chanson, Op. 2, No. 2, R8-40

Sperontes (pseud.) (1705-1750)
Minuet in D Major, R2-6

Steibelt, Daniel (1765-1823)
Aria in A Minor, R2-10

Stölzel, Gottfried Heinrich (1690-1749)
Minuet in G Minor, R5-8

Stravinsky, Soulima (1910-)
The New Dress, R1-24
[Study No. 4] Cross Hands, S2-20

Street, Andersen (1933-)
Tantrum Tarantelle, R8-60

Szelényi, István (1904-1972)
Faraway Regions, R2-30
Changing Bars, R4-32

Szymanowski, Karol (1882-1937)
Krakowiak, R6-44

Takács, Jenö (1902-)
[Study No. 6] In a Great Hurry, Op. 95, No. 3, S7-14
[Study No. 12] Toccatina, Op. 95, No. 12, S8-54

Tchaikovsky, Pyotr Il'yich (1840-1893)
Morning Prayer, Op. 39, No. 1, R3-26
Sweet Dreams, Op. 39, No. 21, R4-36
Waltz in E Flat, Op. 39, No. 8, R6-40

Telemann, Georg Philipp (1681-1767)
Fantasia in D Major, R2-4
Minuet in G Major, R5-10
Canzona d'Imitazione, R5-13
Aria in A Major, R6-11
Bourrée in F Major, R7-14
Fantasia in D Minor, TWV 33:2, R8-7

Telfer, Nancy (1950-)
Un canadien errant (arr.), Intro-14
Monté sur un éléphant (arr.), R1-34
Land of the Silver Birch (arr.), R2-24
She's Like the Swallow (arr.), R6-46

Türk, Daniel Gottlob (1750-1813)
Sonatina, Intro-12
A Carefree Fellow, Intro-21
[Study No. 13] Having Fun, S3-16

Weber, Carl Maria von (1786-1826)
Waltz in G Major, R4-31

Weiner, Leo (1885-1960)
Fox Dance, R9-111

Weinzweig, John (1913-)
Toccata Dance, R7-40

Wuensch, Gerhard (1925-)
[Study No. 13] Ping-Pong, Anyone?, S6-44
Study in Mixolydian, Op. 41, No. 4, R7-50
[Study No. 5] Study in Rhythm, S7-12

Zipoli, Domenico (1688-1726)
Little Fugue in E Minor, R5-9
Sarabanda in G Minor, R6-9

Zoilo, Annibale (1537-1592)
Bicinium, R1-40

The *Handbook for Teachers* is organized around the compositions included in the *Celebration Series Piano Repertoire* and *Piano Studies Albums,* and therefore, the information presented in the Study Module discussions is specific to these pieces. However, these discussions do contain definitions and historical information. Moreover, some of the concepts, approaches, and practice suggestions are of a general nature and thus can be applied more broadly. This subject index is not an exhaustive listing of all the topics contained in the Study Module discussions, but rather a *selected* listing of these more general topics.

136; open 5th exercise, 59; using short units, 47, 52, 116; for wide leaps, 153. *See also* specific headings (such as fingering, articulation)

prelude: Baroque, 113, 191; binary form, 193; cycles, 171, 177, 178, 200, 205, 207

Rachmaninoff, Sergei, 177, 204, 215

ragtime, 153, 176

Rameau, Jean-Philippe, 160

Ravel, Maurice, 176, 206

Reinhold, Hugo, 125

repeated intervals and chords, 215; exercise, 186

repeated notes: articulation, 63; dynamic plan, 36; exercise, 184; fingering, 179

rhythm: barcarole, 77, 133, 135; in dance music, 64, 120; and dynamics, 17; and forward movement, 29, 66; macro-rhythm, 120, 121; mazurka, 124, 145; rhythmic units, 121, 167; syncopation, 153; two-against-three, 134, 185, 203, 214, 215; vocabulary, 66

rhythm practice: for beat subdivision, 134; for coordination, 34; for dotted rhythm, 27, 97; introductory level, 14; with physical movement, 14, 17; with words, 17, 27, 66

Romantic era, 169, 199; character piece, 138; extended melodic lines, 133; German Romantic tradition, 134, 180; harmony and tonality, 199, 200, 204; role of piano, 142, 169, 170, 199

rondo form, 87, 124

rubato, 75, 105, 145, 170

Saint-Saëns, Camille, 214

scales: blocking finger groups, 54, 75; pentatonic, 23; whole-tone, 23, 54, 99, 204

Scarlatti, Domenico, 75, 164

Schafer, R. Murray, 180-181

Schumann, Robert, 107, 173, 199, 200

Scriabin, Alexander, 146, 177, 205, 215

sequence, 67

soft pedal. *See* pedal, *una corda*

sonata (sonatina) form, 100, 165; dramatic aspects, 166, 196; elements of contrast, 21, 76, 77, 110, 127, 165; unity and contrast, 145; variations of, 124, 139, 145, 148

staccato: hand *staccato,* 59; wedge marks, 93, 167

stretto, 134, 158, 193

stride base, 153

subject (fugal), 158

surprise, musical. *See* humor and surprise, musical

Takács, Jenö, 143

tetrachord, 31, 79

theme and variation, 27, 67, 87, 168

throw and lift, 10, 95, 186

tonality. *See* harmony and tonality

trill, cadential, 124

triplets, 105, 134

tritone, 54, 69

tuning, 160, 192

twelve-tone technique, 59, 98, 207, 209

una corda pedal. *See* pedal, *una corda*

variation. *See* theme and variation

voicing: four-note chords, 69; melody played by thumb, 173, 186; soprano and bass lines, 83; three-part texture, 107, 139; and tone, 81; two-part texture, 68, 72, 149

Wagner, Richard, 176, 202

wedge marks, 93, 167

Weiner, Leo, 180

whole-tone scale, 23, 54, 99, 204

Wilhelm Friedemann Bach Notebook, 92, 112, 122, 124, 159

wrist motion. *See* hand and arm motion